D1452391

HISTORICAL DICTIONARIES OF U.S. DIPLOMACY
Jon Woronoff, Series Editor

Historical Dictionary of United States–Africa Relations

Robert Anthony Waters Jr.

Historical Dictionaries of U.S. Diplomacy, No. 9

The Scarecrow Press, Inc.
Lanham, Maryland • Toronto • Plymouth, UK
2009

SCARECROW PRESS, INC.

Published in the United States of America
by Scarecrow Press, Inc.
A wholly owned subsidiary of
The Rowman & Littlefield Publishing Group, Inc.
4501 Forbes Boulevard, Suite 200, Lanham, Maryland 20706
www.scarecrowpress.com

Estover Road
Plymouth PL6 7PY
United Kingdom

British Library Cataloguing in Publication Information Available

Library of Congress Cataloging-in-Publication Data

Waters, Robert Anthony, 1960–
    Historical dictionary of United States–Africa relations / Robert Anthony
Waters Jr.
        p. cm. — (Historical dictionaries of U.S. diplomacy, no. 9)
    Includes bibliographical references.   7029925
    ISBN-13: 978-0-8108-5063-7 (cloth : alk. paper)
    ISBN-10: 0-8108-5063-X (cloth : alk. paper)
    ISBN-13: 978-0-8108-6291-3 (ebook)
    ISBN-10: 0-8108-6291-3 (ebook)
    1. Africa—Foreign relations—United States—Encyclopedias. 2. United
States—Foreign relations—Africa—Encyclopedias. I. Title.
DT38.W385 2009
327.730603—dc22   2008039649

To Sarah—my love, who makes me better.

To Donald John—our big boy, tougher than a five-year-old
should have to be.

To Robby Kenny—our little nut, who can always make us laugh.

Contents

Editor's Foreword

For too long the United States has shown less interest in the African continent than other parts of the world, although there is a recent trend toward more concern and commitment. Given its size and resources there is inducement for trade and investment, and given the number of countries Africa plays a significant role in international organizations. The continent until relatively recently was regarded as part of the European zone of influence, but that point of view is now out of favor. Much of the American population has African roots, and more and more Africans are migrating to the United States. But African leaders have at worst been brutal dictators and at best well-meaning reformers whose reforms often did not pan out. Thus Africa continues lurching from one crisis to another. This does encourage bilateral relations, but not of the sort that offers any prospects of constructive cooperation or positive outcomes.

All of this increases the importance of the *Historical Dictionary of United States–Africa Relations* since Africa remains a relatively dark continent in terms of foreign relations. Aside from Egypt and occasionally other countries, and most often for the wrong reasons, media coverage and even history books have presented patchy and often inaccurate information. Moreover, Washington's track record is not very good, as they have usually backed the wrong leaders. This reference work, however, presents U.S.–Africa relations over the long term, via a dictionary section, with numerous entries on significant people, events, legislation, organizations and more importantly countries; an introduction that puts the often confusing picture in better focus; and a chronology, which follows the twists and turns over the centuries. The bibliography then directs readers to further sources of information.

This volume was written by Robert Anthony Waters Jr., who is presently a visiting professor of history at Ohio Northern University while on leave from Southern University at New Orleans. He specialized in foreign relations, with two basic focuses: the Caribbean and Africa. His interest in and knowledge of the latter was enhanced by a stay in Botswana and visits to other countries in the region. That he was previously a civil rights lawyer certainly sharpened his perception, since so much of what is at stake in our relationship with Africa is related to civil rights and the broader field of human rights. Although he has dealt more with sub-Saharan Africa, Dr. Waters has also covered northern Africa, not only widening the scope of the book but showing the relationship between different parts of the continent. He has not hesitated to shed light on many acts that were too quickly forgotten and must be remembered in order to achieve an understanding of Africa and how it is affected by the actions—or lack thereof—of the world's sole remaining superpower. This is certainly a welcome contribution to the series of Historical Dictionaries of United States Diplomacy.

Jon Woronoff
Series Editor

Acknowledgments

I have great reason to provide effusive and grateful acknowledgment to many people whose help and friendship made this book possible.

Jon Woronoff has been a wonderful editor; indeed, he has been more than an author can reasonably hope for thanks to his incredible ability to turn around a manuscript in a matter of days and provide excellent and insightful comments. This author in particular must additionally thank him for asking me to write the book and for having the patience to wait out numerous delays brought on by three job changes, five changed residences, family medical problems, a hurricane that destroyed my manuscript and notes, and time-consuming battles with insurance companies. Plus Jon's kind perseverance, despite the general annoyance of working with a writer tackling his first book.

The Earhart Foundation generously provided me with financial assistance to allow me to free my summer for research and writing. After Hurricane Katrina threatened to leave us destitute, Earhart Foundation President Ingrid Gregg recommended that I receive funding to replace lost salary, which Earhart kindly granted.

My research on Rwanda, Congo, and the AFL-CIO was greatly assisted by Magaly Rodríguez García, whose remarkable kindness, networking skills, and hard work put together funding for me to travel to Europe to present a conference paper, research at the International Institute for Social History in Amsterdam, and interview Professors Saskia van Hoyweghen, Stefaan Smis, and Jan Gorus of the Free University of Brussels.

When the hurricane blew my family to Lima, Ohio, my in-laws, John and Carla Smith, took us in until we got back on our feet and have provided valuable baby-sitting. Carla also typed much of my bibliography, setting land speed records on the keyboard. My sister-in-law, Pat Swallow, and my brothers-in-law, Col. John Smith and Rob Smith, also came to our aid. Sarah's friend Anita Cook organized all her friends in a "Help the Waters" campaign of great magnitude, reaching over four states.

My family in California was an incredible help to us as well. My dad, Don O'Mohundro, organized dozens of his friends to raise money for us, and my sister-in-law, Jomjai Waters-O'Mohundro, organized her friends to raise money and clothes. In the end, hundreds of people helped. My mother, Audrey O'Mohundro, brother, Ken Waters-O'Mohundro, and Aunt Yvonne Brown were and are always there for us. My nephews, Alex (Rasha) and Spencer (Narayn) kept our spirits up with their silly political views, raps, and imitations of Jerry Clower.

After arriving in Lima, my wife, Sarah, and I were hired to teach at Sarah's alma mater, Ohio Northern University. President Ken Baker, Vice President Anne Lippert, Dean Rob Manzer, chairs Ellen Wilson and Nils Riess, and Sarah's mentor Rosie Williams, now tragically deceased, saved us from poverty and helped us to keep our sanity. My departmental colleagues have been wonderful and have treated me as one of them instead of some guy blown in off the street.

As we fled New Orleans, our friends Chad and Kristen Hammons and Gordon and Gloria Daniels let us stay with them as we tried to wind our way north.

As far as the actual research on the book, my wife, Sarah, who is a doctor of musical performance, is largely responsible for the Music entry, probably the best in the dictionary. Philip Edwards provided me nuanced guidance and occasional slashing commentary on Kenyan history and the key role played by Theodore Roosevelt and Ernest Hemingway in creating Americans' interest in Africa. He and his wife, Amelia, took us under their wings when we arrived in Botswana for my wife's Fulbright in 1999–2000, helping us to learn the ropes and acting as our constant guides. Keith Wheelock has freely given me his unparalleled knowledge about the Congo Crisis, Richard Cummings provided fascinating information from his experience in Ethiopia, Stanley Meisler answered many questions from his experience covering Africa for the *Los Angeles Times* and other publications, W. Scott Thompson answered my questions about Nkrumah and Ghana, Daniel Byrne gave me invaluable guidance on North African sources, and Arnaud de Borchgrave spent a fascinating hour talking with me about Africa despite suffering the flu.

The late Karl von Vorys was the man who most fired my imagination about U.S. relations with the third world, and I have also been inspired by my African history and politics professors: the late Carl Rosberg, James Cooke, Ernest J. Wilson III, Harvey Glickman, Raymond Kent, and Lee Cassanelli. Whatever writing ability I have is thanks to the painstaking assistance of the late Gunther Barth. I had looked forward to sending Bill Buckley a copy of the book in thanks for all that he has done for me and mourn his recent passing

Bob Engs, my undergraduate adviser, has been a great friend and advocate. My friend Bruce Frohnen deserves special thanks. For 25 years he has been my best supporter and critic. His "Frohnen Thesis Plan" was invaluable in helping me finish my dissertation, and his guidance since has been unerring. He also has a gift for friendship.

Jared Hardesty has been an outstanding research assistant and good friend. I have never met an undergraduate with his analytical ability or love of history. He has been a joy to work with and played a key role in my finishing this book.

My wife, Sarah, is the person to whom I owe the most. The last few years have often been "interesting" in the sense of the Chinese proverb, but we have survived and often thrived. Without her steadfast support and encouragement, this book could never have been finished.

Acronyms and Abbreviations

AAI	African-American Institute
ABAKO	*Alliance des Bakongo*/Bakongo Alliance
ACS	American Colonization Society
AFL	American Federation of Labor
AFL-CIO	American Federation of Labor–Congress of Industrial Organizations
AFRICOM	United States Africa Command
AGOA	African Growth and Opportunity Act
AID	Agency for International Development
AIDS	Acquired Immunodeficiency Syndrome
AMISOM	African Union Mission to Somalia
ANC	African National Congress
ANC	African National Council
AU	African Union
BBC	British Broadcasting Corporation
BEE	Black Economic Empowerment
CAAA	Comprehensive Anti-Apartheid Act
CCP	Committee on Colonial Policy
CDC	Centers for Disease Control and Prevention
CENTCOM	United States Central Command
CIA	Central Intelligence Agency
CIO	Congress of Industrial Organizations
CJTF-HOA	Combined Joint Task Force–Horn of Africa
CONAKAT	*Confédérations des Associations Tribales du Katanga*/National Confederation of Tribal Associations of Katanga
CTF-150	Combined Task Force 150
ECOMOG	Economic Community of West African States Monitoring Group

ECOWAS	Economic Community of West African States
EPLF	Eritrean People's Liberation Front
EPRP	Ethiopian People's Revolutionary Party
EU	European Union
EUCOM	United States European Command
FIS	*Front Islamique du Salut*/Islamic Salvation Front
FLN	*Front de Libération Nationale*/National Liberation Front
FLNC	*Front pour la Libération Nationale du Congo*/Front for the National Liberation of the Congo
FNLA	*Frente Nacional de Libertação de Angola*/National Liberation Front of Angola
FRELIMO	*Frente de Libertação de Moçambique*/Front for the Liberation of Mozambique
G7	Group of 7
G8	Group of 8
GIA	*Groupe Islamique Armé*/Armed Islamic Group
GM	General Motors
GSPC	*Groupe Salafiste pour la Prédication et le Combat*/Salafist Group for Preaching and Combat
GWOT	Global War on Terror
HBCUs	Historically Black Colleges and Universities
HIPCs	Heavily Indebted Poor Countries
HIV	Human Immunodeficiency Virus
IAEA	International Atomic Energy Agency
ICU	Islamic Courts Union
IMF	International Monetary Fund
IRA	Irish Republican Army
JEM	Justice of Equality Movement
JTF Aztec Silence	Joint Task Force Aztec Silence
KANU	Kenya African National Union
KFL	Kenya Federation of Labor
LNA	Libyan National Army
MCC	Millennium Challenge Corporation
MDC	Movement for Democratic Change
MDRI	Multilateral Debt Relief Initiative

MEC	Middle East Command
MEDO	Middle East Defense Organization
MIA	*Mouvement Islamique Armé*/Islamic Armed Movement
MONUC	*Mission de l'Organisation des Nations Unies en République démocratique du Congo*/UN Mission in the Democratic Republic of Congo
MPLA	*Movimento Popular de Libertação de Angola*/Popular Movement for the Liberation of Angola
NAACP	National Association for the Advancement of Colored People
NATO	North Atlantic Treaty Organization
NBA	National Basketball Association
NGOs	Non-Governmental Organizations
NLC	National Liberation Council
NPFL	National Patriotic Front of Liberia
NPT	Nuclear Non-Proliferation Treaty
NSC	National Security Council
NSSM 39	National Security Study Memorandum 39
OAU	Organization of African Unity
OEF-HOA	Operation Enduring Freedom–Horn of Africa
OEF-TS	Operation Enduring Freedom–Trans Sahara
ONUC	*Opération des Nations Unies au Congo*/United Nations Organization in the Congo
OPEC	Organization of the Petroleum Exporting Countries
OSS	Office of Strategic Services
PAC	Pan-Africanist Congress
PACOM	United States Pacific Command
PDD-25	Presidential Decision Document 25
PEPFAR	President's Emergency Plan for AIDS Relief
PF	Patriotic Front
PGA	Professional Golf Association
PLO	Palestine Liberation Organization
RCC	Revolutionary Command Council
RENAMO	*Resistência Nacional Moçambicana*/Mozambican National Resistance
RF	Rhodesian Front

RPF	*Front Patriotique Rwandaise*/Rwandan Patriotic Front
RUF	Revolutionary United Front
SAC	Strategic Air Command
SACP	South African Communist Party
SALT II	Strategic Arms Limitation Talks II
SAP	Structural Adjustment Program
SLM/A	Sudan Liberation Movement/Army
SNCC	Student Nonviolent Coordinating Committee
SPLM	Sudan People's Liberation Movement
SWAPO	South West Africa People's Organization
TSCTI	Trans-Sahara Counterterrorism Initiative
UDI	Unilateral Declaration of Independence
UMHK	*Union Minière du Haut-Katanga*
UN	United Nations
UNAMID	United Nations-African Union Mission in Sudan
UNEF	United Nations Emergency Force
UNESCO	United Nations Educational, Scientific and Cultural Organization
UNIA	Universal Negro Improvement Association
UNITA	*União Nacional para a Independência Total de Angola*/National Union for the Total Liberation of Angola
UNITAF	United Task Force
UNMIL	United Nations Mission in Liberia
UNOMIL	United Nations Observer Mission in Liberia
UNOSOM I	United Nations Operation in Somalia I
UNOSOM II	United Nations Operation in Somalia II
USIA	United States Information Agency
VOA	Voice of America
WHO	World Health Organization
WMD	Weapons of Mass Destruction
ZANU	Zimbabwe African National Union
ZANU-PF	Zimbabwe African National Union–Patriotic Front
ZAPU	Zimbabwe African People's Union
ZCTU	Zimbabwe Congress of Trade Unions

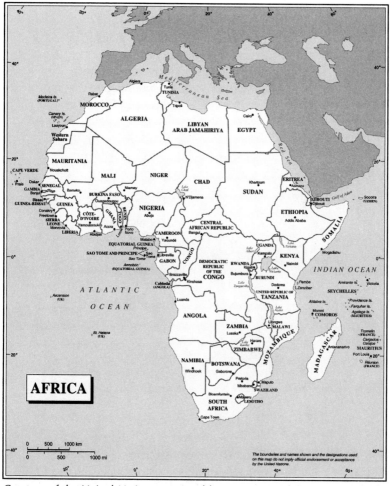

Courtesy of the United Nations, reprinted by permission of the secretary of the United Nations Publication Board.

Chronology

1619 20 August (Virginia): Africans are brought to the Jamestown Settlement (Virginia colony) as indentured servants, the first Africans brought to the British North American colonies.

1641 10 December (Massachusetts): Massachusetts is the first British North American colony to legalize African slavery.

1777 20 December (Morocco): Moroccan Sultan Muhammad III grants protection to U.S. merchant ships, giving *de facto* recognition to the U.S. government.

1787 18 July (Morocco): The U.S. signs a treaty of peace and friendship with Morocco, which remains the longest unbroken treaty by the U.S.

1795 28 November (Algiers/Tunis): To prevent attacks on U.S. ships, the U.S. pays $800,000 and a frigate as tribute to Algiers and Tunis.

1801 14 May (Tripoli): After Jefferson refuses to pay $225,000 in tribute, the pasha of Tripoli declares war on the U.S.

1803 31 October (Tripoli): Tripolitans capture the USS *Philadelphia*, holding its 307 sailors as captive slaves.

1804 16 February (Tripoli): U.S. Navy Lieutenant Stephen Decatur leads a raiding party that destroys the *Philadelphia* in Tripoli harbor, an act praised throughout Europe.

1805 27 April (Tripoli): The U.S. Navy bombs Tripoli. Former U.S. Consul William Eaton leads a successful Marine and mercenary attack on the city of Derna from across the desert. **10 June (Tripoli):** The pasha of Tripoli signs a peace treaty with the U.S. and frees U.S. hostages in exchange for $60,000 in ransom.

1808   1 January (U.S.): The U.S. government outlaws the transatlantic slave trade.

1815   2 March (Algiers): The U.S. declares war on Algiers, beginning the Second Barbary War. **30 June (Algiers):** Commodore Stephen Decatur defeats Algiers and a peace treaty is signed in which Algiers frees hostages and pays an indemnity for past attacks. **5 August (Tripoli):** The U.S. Navy threatens Tripoli, which signs a peace treaty and pays an indemnity. **28 August (Tunis):** The U.S. Navy threatens Tunis, which capitulates, signs a peace treaty, and pays an indemnity, ending the Barbary Wars.

1816   16 December (Liberia): The American Colonization Society is founded.

1821   15 December (Liberia): A local chief is forced to sell land to the American Colonization Society, which will become Liberia.

1822   25 April (Liberia): The first settlers move to Liberia.

1847   26 July (Liberia): Liberian independence is declared.

1884   22 April (Congo): The U.S. is the first nation to recognize Belgian King Léopold II's claim to what would become the Congo Free State. **15 November (Germany):** The Berlin Conference to divide Africa among the colonial powers begins.

1885   5 February (Congo): The Berlin Conference grants the Congo Free State to Léopold II of Belgium as his personal property. **26 February (Germany):** The Berlin Conference ends, having established Africa's colonial boundaries, which almost uniformly became Africa's national boundaries after independence.

1904   18 May (Morocco): Moroccan rebel Ahmad ibn Muhammad Raisuli kidnaps Ion Perdicaris. **22 June (Morocco):** U.S. Secretary of State John Hay cables Morocco with the demand that Perdicaris be returned safely. The U.S. sends seven warships off the Moroccan coast. **25 June (Morocco):** The Moroccan sultan accepts Raisuli's terms and Perdicaris is released.

1908   15 November (Congo): Belgium annexes Congo because of Léopold's murderous rule.

1909   21 April: Former President Theodore Roosevelt arrives in Mombassa, Kenya, to begin his hunting safari sponsored by the Smithsonian Institution and the National Geographic Society. **23 April (Liberia):** Three warships sent by former President Roosevelt arrive in Liberia with delegation sent to assess if the country can be saved from colonization.

1910   15 March (Sudan): Roosevelt ends his safari in Khartoum.

1935   31 August (U.S.): President Franklin Delano Roosevelt signs the Neutrality Act, which makes it illegal for the U.S. to sell weapons to belligerent states. **3 October (Ethiopia):** Italy attacks Ethiopia. **5 October (Ethiopia):** President Roosevelt invokes the Neutrality Act against both Ethiopia and Italy.

1936   7 May (Ethiopia): Italy conquers Ethiopia. **20 June (Ethiopia):** U.S. lifts the arms embargo on Italy. **30 June (Ethiopia):** Haile Selassie pleads for assistance at the League of Nations.

1941   28 November (Ethiopia): British and Ethiopian forces liberate Ethiopia from Italy.

1942   8–10 November (Morocco/Algeria): Allies launch Operation Torch, taking control of Morocco and Algeria from the Axis powers.

1943   22 January (Morocco): President Roosevelt has dinner with Sultan Muhammad V, outraging Free French leader Charles de Gaulle. Muhammad reports that Roosevelt told him he would support postwar independence for Morocco. **26–27 January (Liberia):** President Roosevelt meets with Liberian President Edwin Barclay in Monrovia. **13 May (Tunisia):** Allies win the Tunisian Campaign, defeating the Axis powers in North Africa.

1945   12 April (U.S.): President Roosevelt dies and is succeeded by Vice President Harry S. Truman.

1947   5 December (U.S.): U.S. embargo on arms shipments to the Middle East.

1948   14 May (Egypt): Israel declares independence. **15 May (Egypt):** Armies from five Middle Eastern nations, led by Egypt, invade Israel, starting the Arab–Israeli War of 1948–49.

1949 **20 January (U.S.):** Truman proposes Point Four, the first U.S. foreign aid program directed at the third world. **24 February (Egypt):** Egypt and Israel sign armistice ending the war.

1952 **26 July (Egypt):** Free Officers Corps overthrows King Farouk I. Gamal Abdel Nasser emerges as the key leader. **15 September (Eritrea/Ethiopia):** U.S. pressure leads the United Nations (UN) to assign Eritrea to Ethiopia as an autonomous province.

1953 **20 January (U.S.):** Dwight D. Eisenhower is inaugurated as president. **22 May (Ethiopia/Eritrea):** Ethiopia gives the U.S. communications base at Asmara, Eritrea, in exchange for military and economic aid.

1954 **1 November (Algeria):** The Algerian National Liberation Front (FLN) launches guerilla attacks on French military and civilian targets, known as the *Toussaint Rouge* (Red All Saint's Day) and broadcasts a proclamation of civil war from Egypt.

1955 **24 February (Egypt):** Baghdad Pact signed, infuriating Nasser. **27 September (Egypt):** Nasser buys $200 million worth of weapons from Czechoslovakia in exchange for cotton. **14 December (Egypt):** U.S., Great Britain, and the World Bank announce that they will provide Egypt $270 million to complete the first stage of the Aswan High Dam.

1956 **1 January (Sudan/Egypt):** Sudan declares independence. **22 February (Algeria):** France hijacks an airplane with FLN leaders including Ahmed Ben Bella, and kidnaps them. **19 July (Egypt):** U.S. reneges on promise to fund the Aswan High Dam. **26 July (Egypt):** Nasser illegally nationalizes the Suez Canal. **29 October (Egypt):** Israel invades the Sinai ostensibly to destroy Fedayeen guerilla bases. **31 October (Egypt):** France and Great Britain issue an ultimatum to Israel and Egypt to withdraw 10 miles from the Suez Canal and simultaneously begin bombing Egyptian military targets. **2 November (Egypt):** U.S. proposes a Suez cease-fire resolution in the UN. **5 November (Egypt):** French and British invade the Suez Canal Zone. Soviet Prime Minister Nikolai Bulganin warns the British and French to halt the attack or face Soviet nuclear missiles launched against their cities. U.S. nuclear forces are put on alert. **6 November (Egypt):** Eisenhower wins reelection. British and French stop the Suez invasion. **30 November (Egypt):** Great Britain and France begin to withdraw from Suez. Eisenhower allows oil to be shipped to them.

1957 5 January (Egypt): Eisenhower announces the Eisenhower Doctrine, which is aimed primarily at Egypt. **1 March (Egypt):** Under U.S. pressure, Israel announces it is withdrawing from Egypt. **6 March (Ghana):** Ghana becomes the first black sub-Saharan state to receive its independence. **15 July (U.S.):** Eisenhower sends 5,000 Marines into Lebanon. **5 September (U.S.):** Eisenhower proclaims the Eisenhower Doctrine in a special joint session of Congress.

1958 24 August (Congo–Brazzaville): French President Charles de Gaulle announces in Congo-Brazzaville that French African colonies will be allowed to vote for independence or autonomy under continued French rule. **2 October (Guinea/French Africa):** Guinea is the only French African state to vote for independence, which is promptly granted. **23 October (Egypt):** Soviet Union announces that it lent Egypt money to fund the Aswan Dam. **5–13 December (Ghana):** Ghana holds the All-African People's Conference, which increases nationalist fervor across Africa.

1959 4 January (Congo): Rioting follows speeches by Patrice Lumumba and Joseph Kasavubu, launching the independence movement.

1960 20 January–20 February (Congo): The Belgians hold a Round Table Conference in Brussels with Congolese leaders to discuss independence, which they agree to grant on 30 June following elections. **3 February (Great Britain/South Africa):** Prime Minister Macmillan makes his "Wind of change" speech to the South African parliament in which he declares that independence is coming to Africa. **21 March (South Africa):** Sharpeville Massacre in which police shoot and kill 69 nonviolent protesters against apartheid. **25 June (Congo):** Kasavubu is elected president and Lumumba prime minister. **30 June (Congo):** Belgium grants Congo independence but speeches by Belgian King Baudouin and Lumumba create mutual animosity. **5 July (Congo):** The Congolese army mutinies. Lumumba throws out most Belgian military officers, grants across-the-board pay raises, and allows soldiers to vote for their officers. Rioting Congolese soldiers target whites, especially

Belgians, for rape and mayhem. Whites are evacuated. **9 July (Congo):** Ambassador Timberlake reports to Washington that Belgian intervention would be a disaster. **10 July (Congo):** Belgium sends troops ostensibly to protect Belgian citizens and economic interests; Kasavubu and Lumumba ask the U.S. for help in reorganizing the Congolese military. The State Department concludes that the U.S. should help, but only under the auspices of the UN and under Belgian leadership. **11 July (Congo):** Moïse Tshombe declares Katanga province's independence and appeals to the Belgians for recognition and assistance. **12 July (Congo):** Kasavubu and Lumumba request UN assistance to stop Belgian aggression. The cabinet, meeting without Kasavubu and Lumumba, asks the U.S. for 3,000 troops. Eisenhower orders a U.S. aircraft carrier equipped with nuclear weapons to begin maneuvers near the mouth of the Congo River in case Soviet Premier Nikita Khrushchev sends troops to Léopoldville. U.S. government sources tell journalist Arnold Beichman that if the Soviets were to intervene, the U.S. would follow. **13 July (Congo):** The Soviets call on the UN to stop Belgian aggression. Kasavubu and Lumumba return to Léopoldville and cable the UN that their request for assistance is only against the Belgians and not to restore internal order. **14 July (Congo):** The UN passes resolution agreeing to send troops to Congo. Kasavubu and Lumumba publicly ask Khrushchev to monitor the Congolese situation. Khrushchev replies that the Soviet Union was prepared to take "resolute measures." **15 July (Congo):** UN troops arrive in Congo. **16 July (Congo):** After meeting with Lumumba, UN official Ralph Bunche reports, "Lumumba was crazy and he reacted like a child." **17 July (Congo):** Lumumba threatens to call in Soviet troops to drive out the UN military force if it does not remove all Belgian troops within 72 hours. Kasavubu and Lumumba threaten to call the Soviets for military assistance if the UN does not force the Belgians out by 20 July. **22 July (Congo):** One hundred Soviet trucks arrive in Congo but are not given to UN forces. At a National Security Council (NSC) meeting, CIA Director Allen Dulles tells his colleagues that they could assume Lumumba "has been bought by the Communists." Despite warnings from the U.S. ambassador and key officials from Ghana and Guinea, Lumumba signs a 50-year development agreement worth $2 billion with Louis Edgar Detwiler, a shady U.S. businessman. A large bribe is reportedly involved. The Congolese parliament approves then revokes the deal. **27 July (Congo):** At the UN, Lumumba requests assistance from the UN, U.S., and Soviet Union. Visiting Washington, D.C., Lumumba meets Under Secretary of State Douglas Dillon, who concludes Lumumba is "psychotic" and "impossible to deal with." **1 August (Congo):** Speaking at the UN, Lumumba accuses UN Secretary-General Dag Hammarskjöld of purposely doing Belgium's bidding by refusing to allow UN troops to invade Katanga. Congolese troops respond by attacking small UN military units. **7 August (Congo):** Lumumba visits Ghana and secretly agrees with Kwame Nkrumah to form a future union. **8 August (Congo):** South Kasai declares independence. **15 August (Congo):** Lumumba asks the Soviets for immediate military aid and long-range transport planes to defeat secessionists in South Kasai and Katanga. Behind the scenes, the Eisenhower administration has concluded that Katanga's secession is creating a zone of anti-Communist stability in the copper belt. **16 August (Congo):** The Soviet Union announces that outside troops may be needed to restore order in Congo. Lumumba urges the UN to leave Congo, calling them "United Nations colonialists." **17 August (Congo):** In response to Lumumba's 15 August plea, the Soviets secretly send 10 transport aircraft to Congo painted with Congolese colors. **18 August (Congo):** CIA agent Larry Devlin reports to Washington that Lumumba is launching a "classic" Communist coup; Eisenhower tells the National Security Council that no one can drive the U.S. and the UN out of Congo, which some of those present take as an order to kill Lumumba. The CIA creates Project Wizard, a plan to neutralize Lumumba politically. **21 August (Congo):** Lumumba publicly requests military aid from the Soviets. **26 August (Congo):** Following rejection by UN, Lumumba secretly flies Congolese army units loyal to him to South Kasai on 15 Soviet transport planes and 100 trucks. The troops begin looting and massacring Balubas. Allen Dulles cables Devlin to kill Lumumba. **Late August (Congo):** Soviet military officers arrive in Congo and sources tell the U.S. that Egypt and Guinea have agreed to send arms and vehicles. Lumumba's increasing authoritarianism, reliance on several far Left advisers, and moves toward the Soviets worry Kasavubu. **Early September (Congo):** Khrushchev tells his advisers that "the Congo is slipping through our fingers." Rapid influx of Soviet equipment, military advisers, and, Hammarskjöld alleges, agents, follows. **5 September (Congo):** Kasavubu fires Lumumba as prime minister and Lumumba fires Kasavubu as president. **9 September (Congo):** Lumumba approves payment of $1 million dollars to Léopoldville soldiers. **10 September (Congo):** The UN pays Léopoldville-based Congolese troops but allows army chief Joseph Mobutu to take credit. **14 September (Congo):** Mobutu coup expels Soviet Bloc and Chinese diplomats and advisers. **21 September (Congo):** CIA Director Dulles tells the NSC that Lumumba must be "disposed of." **5 October (Congo):** CIA poison specialist Sidney Gottlieb is sent to Congo to give Devlin poison to kill Lumumba. **10 October (Congo):** The Congolese army's attempt to arrest Lumumba, following a promise of aid by the Belgian government, is foiled by UN soldiers. Thereafter UN soldiers surround Lumumba's official residence, and they are surrounded by Congolese soldiers. **19 November (Congo):** Former Deputy Prime Minister Antoine Gizenga, a Lumumba supporter, rebels against the government from his Stanleyville base, establishing the Free Republic of the Congo. **21 November (Congo):** A non-American is sent to Congo by the CIA to kill Lumumba (he departs Congo in late December). **27 November (Congo):** Lumumba leaves UN protective custody and flees to Stanleyville to take over the rebel Lumumbist government. **1 December (Congo):** Lumumba is arrested and imprisoned at an army base. The CIA may have provided intelligence information that assisted in his capture. **12 December (Congo):** Tshombe declares Katanga independent.

1961 6 January (U.S./Soviet Union): Nikita Khrushchev speech states that wars for national liberation were inevitable and key to "bringing imperialism to its knees." President-elect John F. Kennedy believes Khrushchev is testing him and orders his national security aids to read it. **13 January (Congo):** Lumumba persuades troops holding him prisoner to mutiny; Mobutu, Kasavubu, and other tribal leaders arrive to persuade troops to go back to the barracks, which they do. **17 January (Congo):** Lumumba is handed over to Tshombe, who orders his execution along with two other former ministers. **20 January (U.S.):** John F. Kennedy is inaugurated as president. **9 February (Congo):** Mobutu returns to the barracks. **13 February (Congo):** Lumumba's death is announced. Shortly thereafter, Antoine Gizenga proclaims a Soviet national government in Stanleyville. President Kennedy warns the Soviet

Union not to intervene. **21 February (Congo):** UN declares the Katangan government illegitimate and allows UN forces to use force as a last resort to prevent civil war. **8 March (Ghana):** Kennedy meets with Kwame Nkrumah, the first African leader to visit the president. **20 April (Angola):** Kennedy orders his UN delegation to vote in favor of a resolution calling on Portugal to move Angola toward independence. **1 May (Congo):** The U.S. has carried 20,000 UN troops and advisers from 30 countries and 6,000 tons of equipment to Congo. **28 August (Congo):** UN forces, acting without orders from Hammarskjöld or his assistants, attack Elizabethville, Katanga, and are quickly bogged down. Rusk calls Hammarskjöld and tells him the president is "extremely upset," fearing that the result could be civil war and Soviet intervention. Hammarskjöld accuses him of supporting Katanga. **17 September (Congo):** Hamarskjöld is killed when his airplane crashes in Katanga on a peace mission. **24 November (Congo):** The U.S. votes in the UN to give the secretary-general the power to use force if necessary to apprehend Katangan mercenaries. **5 December (Ghana):** U.S. agrees to fund the Volta River Dam project. **5-19 December (Congo):** Acting Secretary-General U Thant orders UN forces to attack Katangan troops to restore law and order. **21 December (Congo):** Tshombe agrees to renounce Katanga's secession. Shortly thereafter, he reneges.

1962 **14 January (Congo):** Congolese government defeats rebellion in eastern Congo and Gizenga surrenders. **3 July (Algeria):** Algeria wins its independence from France. **22–28 October (U.S.):** Cuban missile crisis. **14 November (Ethiopia/Eritrea):** Bribed and coerced Eritrean legislators vote for annexation by Ethiopia. **28 December (Congo):** After four days of Katangan attacks without retaliation, Thant orders UN troops to attack. President Kennedy, fearing UN withdrawal from Congo, reluctantly agrees.

1963 **14 January (Congo):** Tshombe surrenders and agrees to end Katangan secession. **29 May (Angola):** Kennedy privately informs the Portuguese government that his April 1961 UN vote in favor of Angola independence had been "precipitous." **31 May (Congo):** Mobutu meets with President Kennedy at the White House. **Summer (Congo):** As the UN withdraws, Lumumbist Pierre Mulele launches a Chinese-backed rebellion. **3 August (South Africa):** Five days before it is passed by the

UN, the U.S. imposes a voluntary embargo on the sale of military goods to South Africa. **22 November (U.S.):** Kennedy is assassinated. Vice President Lyndon B. Johnson assumes the presidency.

1964   26 June (Congo): U.S. airplanes and CIA pilots arrive in Congo, creating an "instant air force." **30 June (Congo):** UN military mission withdrawn from Congo. Rebels take control of half of Congo. **6 July (Congo):** Kasavubu appoints Tshombe prime minister. **21 July (Africa):** Cairo Resolution passed by the OAU establishes the inviolability of African borders. **5 August (Congo):** Stanleyville falls to Congolese rebels. Five U.S. embassy staff, including the consul and CIA agents, are captured and held prisoner for 111 days. Rebel forces kidnap over 3,000 foreign nationals. **7 September (Congo):** The People's Republic of the Congo is declared by Antoine Gizenga in Stanleyville. It is recognized by 13 foreign governments. **Early October (Congo):** Eastern and Kwilu Congolese rebellions control two-thirds of the country. Rebel leader Christophe Gbenye issues standing orders for the execution of hostages if attacked. **10 October (Congo):** Kasavubu dismisses Tshombe as prime minister. **24 November (Congo):** After negotiations overseen by Kenya's Jomo Kenyatta and Tanzania's Julius Nyerere fail, Belgium and the U.S. launch a Stanleyville rescue (Operation Red Dragon). Rebels kill approximately 300 missionaries, mostly in the countryside.

1965   24 April (Congo): Che Guevara arrives in eastern Congo with contingent of approximately 120 Cuban troops. **19 June (Algeria):** Algerian Prime Minister Ahmed Ben Bella is overthrown by Defense Minister Houari Boumédienne. Boumédienne cuts off aid to radicals all over Africa, including Congo. **21 November (Congo):** Guevara and his Cubans leave Congo. **11 November (Rhodesia):** Rhodesia unilaterally declares independence. **24 November (Congo):** Mobutu overthrows President Kasavubu. **16 December (Rhodesia):** At British urging, President Johnson agrees to embargo oil to Rhodesia and to airlift oil to Zambia. **17 December (Zambia):** Zambian petroleum airlift begins. **28 December (Rhodesia):** The U.S. announces oil embargo of Rhodesia.

1966   24 February (Ghana): Nkrumah is overthrown. **30 April (Zambia):** Airlift ends after carrying 3,639,028 U.S. gallons of petroleum products at a transportation price of more than $1 per gallon. Assistance continues by ground transport. **16 December (Rhodesia):** U.N. Security Council imposes mandatory trade sanctions against Rhodesia, the first time that it has imposed mandatory sanctions. U.S. and British efforts prevent African attempts to compel the British to use force if necessary to prevent Rhodesia from receiving oil from South Africa and Portuguese Mozambique.

1967 5 February (Tanzania): Julius Nyerere issues the Arusha Declaration, the model for his *Ujamaa* socialism. **13 May (Egypt):** Soviet ambassador to Egypt falsely reports that Israel is massing troops on the Syrian border. **14 May (Egypt):** Egypt begins to mass troops along the Sinai border with Israel. **16 May (Egypt):** Egypt demands that UN peacekeepers leave Egypt. **18 May (Egypt):** Following Nasser's order, UN forces leave the Egyptian–Israeli border. **22 May (Egypt):** Nasser announces that Egypt will close the Strait of Tiran to Israeli shipping the next day, an act of war, regardless of whether or not doing so will lead to war. **29 May (Nigeria):** The Eastern Region secedes, calling itself the nation of Biafra following massacres of Ibo in Nigeria's Northern Region. Civil war follows. **June (Congo):** Mobutu orders mercenary units fazed out, prompting revolt by Katangan gendarmes in support of the exiled Tshombe. The rebellion spreads across eastern Congo. **5 June (Egypt):** Israel launches surprise attack, destroying Egypt's air force on the ground, commencing the Arab–Israeli War of 1967. Israeli forces also attack the Sinai. **6 June (Egypt):** Nasser closes the Suez Canal and breaks relations with the U.S. Iraq and Kuwait cut off oil shipments to the U.S. **10 June (Egypt):** Egypt is defeated. **30 June (Congo):** Tshombe is lured from Spain to meet with prospective supporters. His airplane is hijacked and he is taken to Algeria, where he is imprisoned. **8 July (Congo):** President Johnson sends three U.S. Air Force cargo planes to carry Congolese soldiers to Kisangani (formerly Stanleyville) to prevent a rebel takeover. Congressional reaction is overwhelmingly negative. **4 November (Congo):** Defeated Congolese mercenary rebels flee to Rwanda. **22 November (Egypt):** UN Security Council approves Resolution 242, a broad framework for Middle East peace.

1968 29 May (Rhodesia): The UN imposes comprehensive mandatory sanctions against Rhodesia that require the cessation of all trade. **26**

August (Zambia): U.S. petroleum assistance to Zambia ends with completion and successful test of an oil pipeline from Tanzania.

1969   20 January (U.S.): Richard M. Nixon is inaugurated as president. **30 June (Congo):** Algerian government announces that former prime minister Tshombe has died of a heart attack while under house arrest. **25 July (U.S.):** Nixon proclaims the Nixon Doctrine. **3 August (Egypt):** Israel announces plans to keep the Gaza Strip, most of the Sinai peninsula, and the Golan Heights. **1 September (Libya):** Colonel Muammar Qaddafi overthrows King Idriss I of Libya.

1970   28 September (Egypt): Nasser dies and is succeeded by Vice President Anwar Sadat.

1971   28 May (Egypt): Egypt signs 15-year Treaty of Friendship and Cooperation with the Soviet Union. **27 October (Zaïre):** Mobutu changes Congo's name to the Republic of Zaïre and the Congo River to the Zaïre River, changes his name to Mobutu Sese Seko, and orders other Zaïrians to change their European names to indigenous names. **17 November (Rhodesia):** Nixon signs the Military Procurement Act of 1971, which includes the "Byrd Amendment," which defies the UN by ending the U.S. ban on Rhodesian chrome imports.

1972   18 July (Egypt): Egypt expels Soviet advisers.

1973   11–20 January (Zaïre): Mobutu visits China. U.S. officials believe his increasing radicalization comes from his admiration for the Chinese system. **27 January (U.S.):** U.S. signs the Paris Peace Accords, which officially end hostilities in Vietnam and call for the withdrawal of U.S. forces. **29 March (U.S.):** Last U.S. troops leave Vietnam. **4 October (Zaïre):** Mobutu breaks relations with Israel during a speech at the UN, outraging the U.S. **6 October (Egypt):** Egypt attacks Israel, launching the Arab–Israeli War of 1973. **10 October (Egypt):** Egyptian forces cross the Suez Canal. **15 October (U.S.):** U.S. begins to resupply Israel with arms. **21 October (U.S.):** Arabs impose oil embargo on the U.S. **25 October (U.S.):** Nixon puts U.S. military forces on worldwide alert. **6 November (Tanzania):** Militarily enforced *Ujamaa* villigization begins and continues until late 1977. **7 November (Egypt):** U.S. and Egypt restore diplomatic relations. **30 November (Zaïre):** Mobutu announces the Zaïrianization (nationalization) of over

2,000 foreign-owned properties without compensation, continuing through 1974. The properties are given to Mobutu cronies rather than the state of Zaïre. Most are quickly bankrupted, badly damaging the economy.

1974   17 January (Egypt): Egypt agrees to reopen the Suez Canal and buffer zone between Israeli forces in the Suez region following "shuttle diplomacy" meetings with Secretary of State Henry Kissinger. **13 March (U.S.):** Arab nations end oil embargo against U.S. **25 April (Angola/Mozambique):** Portugal's "Revolution of the Red Carnations," sparked largely by military dissatisfaction with wars in Africa, triggers the fall of Portuguese Prime Minister Marcelo Caetano. Thereafter, 90 percent of Portuguese depart Angola and Mozambique, leaving them bereft of skilled workers and farmers. The Soviet Union orders its ambassadors to "repair" the Popular Movement for the Liberation of Angola (MPLA). **14 June (Egypt):** U.S. and Egypt sign treaty of friendship. **August (Angola):** Chinese military technicians are training National Liberation Front of Angola (FNLA) rebels at a base in Zaïre. The training will continue almost until Angolan independence. **8 August (U.S.):** Nixon resigns the presidency and is succeeded by Vice President Gerald R. Ford. **12 September (Ethiopia):** Emperor Haile Selassie arrested and deposed by military junta called the Derg ("committee").

1975   15 January (Angola): The Alvor Agreement is made between the Portuguese and the MPLA, FNLA, and the National Union for the Total Independence of Angola (UNITA), which calls for elections and power to be handed over on 11 November. **30 January (Angola):** Soviet Union agrees to big shipments of military aid to the MPLA. **March (Angola):** Soviet weapons begin arriving to the MPLA. **23 March (Angola):** FNLA guerillas attack MPLA cadres in Luanda and northern Angola. **19 April (Zambia/Angola):** Zambian President Kenneth Kaunda visits U.S. and tells President Ford that Africans want the U.S. to stop the MPLA from winning with Soviet arms. Kissinger later learned that this was not true. **30 April (Vietnam):** South Vietnam falls to North Vietnam. **May (Angola):** Approximately 250 Cuban military advisers are playing a major role in planning operations and training for the MPLA, acting as a general staff. **June (Angola):** FNLA leader Holden Roberto asks South Africa for help. Mobutu begins pushing the U.S. to intervene in Angola, saying he will send troops. **18 June (Zaïre):** U.S. Ambassador Deane Hinton bluntly tells Mobutu that he must fix his economy. Mobutu expels Hinton, announces that the CIA has tried to overthrow him, and purges his military, executing seven high-ranking officers. **25 June (Mozambique):** Portugal grants Mozambique its independence. **27 June (Angola):** Kissinger tells his advisers that Angola is "important but not vital" to U.S. interests. **14 July (South Africa/Angola):** South Africa launches $14 million covert operation to provide military assistance and training to Angola's FNLA and UNITA. **18 July (Angola):** Ford administration launches Operation IAFEATURE, providing economic assistance and CIA training to the FNLA and UNITA. **21–24 July (Egypt/Libya):** Significant border fighting between Egypt and Libya. **5 August (Angola/South Africa):** First South African military incursion into Angola. **4–11 October (Angola):** Fidel Castro sends 480 troops to Angola in support of the MPLA. **14 October (South Africa/Angola):** South Africa invades Angola in support of UNITA. **23 October (Angola):** Cuban troops see their first action fighting for the MPLA. **27 October (Angola/Zaïre):** Chinese instructors, who had been training the FNLA, leave Zaïre. **3 November (Angola):** Tanzanian President Julius Nyerere tells the Soviet Union that South African intervention in Angola makes necessary Soviet assistance for the MPLA. **4 November (Angola):** Castro decides to send combat troops and 100 heavy-weapons experts to assist the MPLA. Between November and March 1976, 30,000 Cubans arrive in Angola. **10 November (Angola/South Africa):** Newly arrived Cuban troops help the MPLA crush the FNLA at the Battle of Quifangondo Valley. UNITA's Jonas Savimbi arrives in Pretoria for a secret meeting with South African Prime Minister John Vorster. **11 November (Angola):** The Portuguese grant Angola independence. **27 November (Angola):** The CIA director's contingency fund is used up, necessitating going to Congress for more money for the Angolan covert operation. **2–3 December (Angola):** Ford and Kissinger meet with Chinese leader Mao Zedong and Deng Xiaoping and request resumption of assistance in Angola. Mao refuses due to the South African intervention. **5 December (Angola):** At congressional hearings, the CIA admits to a covert operation in Angola. **13 December (Angola):** *The New York Times* reveals the extent of U.S. covert operations in Angola. **Mid-December (Angola):** Cuban and MPLA forces defeat UNITA and the South Africans. **19 December**

(Angola): Congress cuts off all U.S. covert funding for Angola, the first time a president is forced to stop a covert operation against his will.

1976   9 February (Angola): President Ford signs the Tunney Amendment, which formally halts U.S. covert aid in Angola. 11 February (Angola): The MPLA captures Savimbi's capital, Huambo, and Savimbi flees into the bush. The OAU recognizes the MPLA as the government of Angola. 18 February (Angola): Congress passes the Clark Amendment, which bans covert military aid to Angolan rebels. 6 March (U.S.): Kissinger warns Cuba and the Soviet Union against further Cuban "military adventures" in Africa. 14 March (Egypt): Sadat abrogates friendship treaty with the Soviet Union. 27 March (South Africa/Angola): South Africa completes military withdrawal from Angola. Spring (Soviet Union): Soviet leaders conclude that victory in Angola shows the ideological power of communism and their ability to project military power in Africa. They conclude they can advance communism in Africa during détente. 7 April (Rhodesia): Kissinger tells NSC that the U.S. must act to block the Soviets and their proxies from winning in Rhodesia. 12 April (Ethiopia): The Derg announces a detailed political program, "National Democratic Revolution," working with the pro-Soviet Marxist All Ethiopian Socialist Movement (MEISON). 23 April (Rhodesia): Kissinger goes to Africa to negotiate an internal settlement in Rhodesia to prevent another Angola fiasco and a domino effect across southern Africa. He stated that Cuba had to be stopped, even by force. 16 June (South Africa): Soweto riots kill 58 and are followed by riots across South Africa that kill over 575. 19 June (South Africa): UN Security Council condemns South African government's response to Soweto riot. Summer (South Africa): The Soviet Union opens training bases in Angola for African National Congress (ANC) guerillas to accommodate young people fleeing in the wake of the Soweto uprising. The Soviets believe it is a sign of revolution coming to South Africa. 24 June (South Africa/Rhodesia): Kissinger meets with Vorster in West Germany, persuading him to end support for Rhodesia. The meeting outrages Africans and liberals in the U.S. August (Soviet Union): KGB chief Yuri Andropov increases KGB operations in Africa, having concluded that victories in Angola and Mozambique and continued revolutionary acts in Ethiopia mean that Africa is turning to communism. 19 September (Rhodesia): Kissinger meets with Rhodesian Prime Minister Ian Smith and tells him that he must give way to majority rule. Smith agrees conditionally. Guerilla leaders Joshua Nkomo and Robert Mugabe reject the conditions. **8 October (Angola):** In Moscow, President Agostinho Neto signs a Treaty of Friendship and Cooperation giving the Soviets the right to use Angolan airports and Luanda harbor. **28 October (Rhodesia):** Geneva Conference on the future of Rhodesia. **14 December (Ethiopia):** Derg leader Mengistu Haile Mariam secretly goes to Moscow and signs a secret arms deal worth $100 million. **14 December (Rhodesia):** Geneva Conference ends without resolving the Rhodesian situation.

1977   20 January (U.S.): Jimmy Carter is inaugurated as president. His inaugural speech calls for a new foreign policy based on human rights and America's moral example. **3 February (Ethiopia):** Mengistu publicly turns to the Left and begins the "Red Terror" in which he massacres his opposition. **Mid-February (Ethiopia/Somalia):** Reports of 1,500 Somali troops fighting in the Ogaden Desert. **24 February (Ethiopia):** Expressing human rights concerns, the Carter administration announces that it is cutting some forms of aid to Ethiopia. **3 March (Ethiopia):** Mengistu publicly visits the Soviet Union. The U.S. quickly learns that he did well there. **18 March (Rhodesia):** President Carter signs bill repealing the Byrd Amendment. **March (Zaïre):** Former Katangan gendarmes, driven into exile in Angola after the fall of Tshombe, invade Zaïre's Shaba region (formerly Katanga), meeting almost no resistance from the Zaïrian army. **23 March (Ethiopia):** Mengistu orders the U.S. to close its communications base at Asmara and remove most U.S. government personnel within four days. **27 March (Ethiopia):** U.S. personnel close the Asmara base and leave Ethiopia. **4 April (Egypt/Somalia):** During a White House meeting, Egyptian President Sadat personally asks Carter to assist the Somalis against Ethiopia. **7 April (Southwest Africa/South Africa):** U.S. forms the Western Five Contact Group (the U.S., Great Britain, Canada, West Germany, and France) and they meet with South Africa's Vorster to push negotiations toward Namibian independence. **19 April (Ethiopia):** U.S. stops all military aid to Ethiopia. **22 April (Ethiopia):** U.S. announces early withdrawal from Kagnew communications base. **23 April (Ethiopia):** Mengistu orders most Americans to leave Ethiopia in four days. **27 April (Ethiopia):** U.S. complies with Mengistu's order, reducing the U.S. government presence from over 4,000 to 81. **23 May (Somalia):** Carter orders Secretary of State Cyrus Vance and National Security Adviser Zbigniew Brzezinski to do everything they can to make Somalia an ally of the U.S. **27 May (Zaïre):** French, Belgian, and Moroccan troops drive out Zaïrian rebels. The U.S. provides minimal nonlethal assistance, which Mobutu's generals sell on the black market. Vance concludes that the U.S. cannot allow Mobutu to fall due to the danger that Zaïre will fragment and allow possible "radical penetration." **July (Somalia):** Soviets withdraw their 1,000 advisers from Somalia. **1 July (Somalia):** Vance announces that the U.S. is considering aid to Somalia. **13 July (Somalia/Ethiopia):** Thirty-thousand Somali troops invade Ethiopia's Ogaden region. **26 July (Somalia):** State Department announces that it will send arms to Somalia. **28 July (U.S.):** Carter calls on the Soviets to join the U.S. in urging restraint on Ethiopia and Somalia. **August (Ethiopia):** Carter's administration discusses covert action to help remove Mengistu but decides against taking action. **4 August (Tanzania):** Nyerere is the first African head of state to meet with Carter in the White House. **September (Ethiopia):** KGB uses fake documents to worsen U.S.'s relations with Ethiopia, falsely alleging an invasion plot. A desperate Mengistu asks the Soviet Union for additional help. **12 September (South Africa):** Black Consciousness leader Steve Biko is beaten to death by prison guards. **1 November (Somalia):** Somalia announces the abrogation of its Treaty of Friendship and Cooperation with the Soviets and suspends diplomatic relations with Cuba. **4 November (South Africa):** UN Security Council resolution calls for mandatory arms embargo against South Africa. Carter administration broadly defines this to include sales of any goods to the South African army and police. **19 November (Egypt):** Sadat is the first Arab leader to go to Israel. **20 November (Egypt):** Sadat addresses Israeli Knesset (parliament). **25 November (Ethiopia):** Fidel Castro decides to send troops to Ethiopia, but tells Mengistu they cannot be used against rebels in Eritrea. **31 December (Ethiopia/Somalia/Eritrea):** 15,000 Cuban soldiers have been sent to Ethiopia to fight Somalia, which allows Mengistu to concentrate Ethiopian forces against Eritrean rebels.

1978   2 March (U.S.): Brzezinski argues to the president that the Soviets are exploiting local problems, especially in the Horn of Africa, and have bigger plans to imperil Western oil supplies. **3 March**

(Rhodesia): Ian Smith, Bishop Abel Muzorewa, Ndabiningi Sithole, and Chief Jeremiah Chirau sign an internal settlement for majority rule. **8 March (Somalia/Ethiopia):** President Muhammad Siad Barré agrees to withdraw Somali forces from the Ogaden. **10 April (Southwest Africa):** The Western Five Contact Group proposes a "package plan" for Namibian independence, which serves as the foundation for Namibian independence in 1988–1990. **3 May (Zaïre):** Former Katangan gendarmes again attack Zaïre's Shaba region, taking Kolwezi, an important copper mining center, and killing over 1,000 Zaïrians and 200 foreigners during the next two weeks. **4 May (Angola):** South Africa attacks SWAPO training camp in Angola. **13 May (Zaïre):** U.S. government concludes, based on what is later reported by Secretary of State Vance to have been weak evidence, that Cuba was behind the second Shaba invasion. **17 May (Zaïre):** The U.S. uses 18 C-141 transport planes to carry 2,500 Belgian and French paratroopers to Shaba where they drive out the Katangan gendarmes. **29 May (Zimbabwe–Rhodesia):** Muzorewa wins landslide election as Zimbabwe–Rhodesia's first black prime minister. **Summer (Ethiopia):** Famine in Wollo and Tigre provinces. The U.S. provides over in $2 million in food aid. **7 June (U.S.):** In a major policy address, Carter attacks the Soviet Union and Cuba for their African interventions, warning that the future of détente could be at stake. **5–18 September (U.S.):** Egyptian President Anwar Sadat and Israeli Prime Minister Menachem Begin meet at Camp David Summit and sign the Camp David Accords (on the 17th), setting the framework for peace between the two nations. **27 September (Libya):** President Carter's brother Billy makes a business trip to Libya, which later loans him $220,000. Billy is later forced to register as an agent for the Libyan government. **30 October (Uganda/Tanzania):** Ugandan troops invade Tanzania and occupy 90 square miles of territory. **20 November (Ethiopia):** Mengistu signs a Treaty of Friendship and Cooperation with the Soviet Union.

1979   16 January (Iran): The Shah of Iran flees. **1 February (Iran):** The Ayatollah Ruhollah Khomeini returns to Iran. **26 March (Egypt):** Egypt and Israel sign treaty of peace and mutual recognition. **14 April (Liberia):** Riots follow a government-ordered 50 percent increase in the cost of rice, the national food staple, killing over 200. **10 September (Zimbabwe–Rhodesia):** Lancaster House Conference begins. **4 November (Iran):** Students seize the U.S. embassy in Iran. **20 November**

(Libya): Brzezinski asks Billy Carter to intercede with Libya to help recover the U.S. embassy hostages held by Iran. **27 November (Libya):** Brzezinski and Billy Carter meet with a Libyan official to ask for help in securing the release of Iran's U.S. hostages. **15 December (Zimbabwe):** Lancaster House Conference ends, with agreement for new all-party elections under British supervision. **26 December (Soviet Union):** The Soviet Union invades Afghanistan.

1980   23 January (U.S.): Carter announces the Carter Doctrine to Congress as part of his State of the Union message. **12 February (Somalia):** The U.S. announces an agreement to use port facilities in Berbera and Mogadishu in exchange for economic and defensive military aid over the next two years. **12 February (Kenya):** U.S. base deal for use of the Kenyan port at Mombassa is announced. **4 March (Zimbabwe):** Robert Mugabe is elected prime minister. **12 February (Uganda/Tanzania):** Tanzania invades Uganda. **11 April (Uganda/Tanzania):** Idi Amin's government collapses and he flees into exile. **12 April (Liberia):** President William Tolbert, a close U.S. ally, is overthrown and killed. He is succeeded by Sergeant Samuel Doe. **18 April (Zimbabwe):** Zimbabwe is granted independence from Great Britain. **May (Chad/Libya):** Four thousand Libyan troops arrive to help the government of Goukouni Oueddei. **15 June (Chad/Libya):** Chad and Libya sign a mutual defense treaty. **15 December (Chad/Libya):** Goukouni's Chadian forces and Libyan forces drive former Prime Minister Hissene Habré into exile in Sudan. Shortly thereafter, Habré begins to receive military assistance from the CIA.

1981   6 January (Chad/Libya): A national merger between Chad and Libya is announced. **19 January (Algeria):** U.S. and Iran sign Algiers Accord, freeing U.S. embassy hostages. **20 January (U.S.):** Ronald W. Reagan is inaugurated as president. **8 February–18 March (Niger):** During this period, Iraq buys 200 tons of yellowcake from Niger, which can be enriched for use in nuclear bombs. It does not inform the International Atomic Energy Agency (IAEA). Iraq buys another 200 tons in 1982. **6 October (Egypt):** Sadat is assassinated by Islamist terrorists. He is succeeded by Vice President Hosni Mubarak. **29 October (Chad/Libya/France):** Under heavy U.S. pressure, France and many African nations successfully pressure Goukouni to demand that Qaddafi remove Libyan forces from Chad. **16 November (Chad/Libya):** All Libyan troops in Chad withdraw to the Libyan-claimed Aouzou Strip on the Chadian–Libyan border.

1982   10 March (Libya): U.S. bans import of Libyan oil because of Libyan support for terrorism. **7 June (Chad):** Habré defeats Goukouni, who flees to the remote desert mountains of northern Chad. **21 October (Chad):** Habré is sworn in as Chad's president.

1983   10 July (Chad/Libya): Goukouni's Libyan-supported forces retake most of northern Chad. **July (Chad/Libya):** The U.S. agrees to provide Habré with $10 million in military and food aid. The U.S., France, and Zaïre begin an airlift to Habré. U.S. aid continues thereafter. **3 August (Chad/Libya/France):** Under U.S. pressure, France sends in troops to stop Goukouni's invasion at the 16th Parallel. **17 September (Chad/Libya/France):** France and Libya mutually agree to remove their troops.

1984   16 March (Mozambique/South Africa): Nkomati Accord is signed in which South Africa agrees to stop assisting RENAMO rebels and Mozambique agrees to expel the ANC. Both sides renege in small ways. **16 October (South Africa):** Archbishop Desmond Tutu is awarded the Nobel Peace Prize.

1985   10 February (Chad/Libya/France): Goukouni's troops, backed by 5,000 Libyans, attack Habré, but are routed with the assistance of 1,200 French forces. **11 March (Soviet Union):** Mikhail Gorbachev takes power in the Soviet Union. **8 August (Angola):** U.S. repeals the Clark Amendment, which had banned assistance to Angolan rebels.

1986   8 January (Libya): Reagan freezes Libyan assets in the U.S. **30 January (Angola):** Savimbi meets with Reagan in the Oval Office. **March (Angola):** U.S. begins to provide covert military aid to Savimbi through Zaïre. **24 March (Libya):** U.S. forces shoot down Libyan warplanes over the Gulf of Sidra. **5 April (Libya):** Libyan-backed terrorists blow up West German disco that is popular with U.S. troops. **15 April (Libya):** U.S. bombs Libyan targets including Qaddafi's home, reportedly killing his daughter. **2 October (South Africa):** Overriding the veto of President Reagan, Congress passes the Comprehensive Anti-Apartheid Act.

1987 8 December (U.S./Soviet Union): Reagan and Soviet leader Mikhail Gorbachev consider working together on regional conflicts.

1988 1 January (Angola): The number of Cubans peaks at 52,000 soldiers. **1 June (U.S./Soviet Union):** U.S. and Soviet Union agree jointly to 29 September as a target date to finalize Namibia/Angola settlement. **27 June (Southwest Africa):** The South African army is defeated by Cuban forces at the Battle of Calueque in Angola, leaving South Africa's Ruacana Falls hydroelectric project vulnerable to attack. South African public morale falters. **22 August (Southwest Africa):** Treaty of Ruacana signed by Angola, Cuba, and South Africa, which stops the South West African war. **21 December (Libya):** Airliner over Lockerbie, Scotland, is blown up by Libyan intelligence operatives, killing 270. **22 December (Southwest Africa):** New York Accords are signed by South Africa, Angola, and Cuba, laying the groundwork for Namibian elections and independence, withdrawal of South African forces, and withdrawal of Cuban forces from Angola.

1989 4 January (Libya): U.S. airplanes shoot down two Libyan fighters over the Gulf of Sidra. **10 January (Angola):** Cuban troops begin withdrawal. **20 January (U.S.):** George H.W. Bush is inaugurated as president. **4 May (Namibia/South Africa):** U.S. and Soviet Union successfully pressure SWAPO to remove 1,800 guerillas it had infiltrated into South West Africa the previous month. **29 June (Zaïre):** Mobutu is the first African head of state to meet with President Bush at the White House. **22 June (Angola):** Angolan government and Savimbi agree to a cease-fire. **30 June (Sudan):** General Omar Bashir and radical Islamist Hassan Turabi overthrow the democratically elected Sudanese government. **5 July (South Africa):** Nelson Mandela is smuggled out of jail for a secret meeting over tea with President P.W. Botha. **15 August (South Africa):** President Botha resigns and is replaced by F.W. de Klerk, a reformer. **23 August (Soviet Union):** Communist Hungary removes border restrictions with Austria, allowing people to leave the country. The Soviet Union does nothing to stop it. **9 November (Soviet Union):** East Germany opens the Berlin Wall. The Soviet Union does nothing to stop it, signaling the end of the Soviet Empire. **11 November (Namibia):** SWAPO wins 57 percent of the vote in Namibia's elections. **24 December (Liberia):** Charles Taylor launches an invasion of Liberia from the Ivory Coast.

1990   2 February (South Africa): President F.W. de Klerk announces that the ANC and the South African Communist Party are legalized. **11 February (South Africa):** Nelson Mandela is released from jail. **21 March (Namibia):** Namibia is granted independence with Sam Nujoma president. **22–23 March (Namibia):** Meeting during the Namibia independence celebration, James Baker and Eduard Shevardnadze agree to work together to create an Angolan peace settlement. **26 July (Ethiopia):** Cuban troops begin withdrawal from Ethiopia.

1991   June (Sudan): Osama bin Ladin relocates to Sudan. **21 May (Ethiopia):** Mengistu is overthrown and flees to Zimbabwe. Rebel leader Meles Zenawi assumes the presidency. **23 May (Angola):** Last Cuban troops leave Angola. **31 May (Angola):** Angola and Savimbi's UNITA sign the Bicesse Accords, ending the civil war and beginning the transition to democratic elections.

1992   29–30 September (Angola): Savimbi comes in a poor second place in the first round of elections. MPLA forces kill UNITA cadres in urban areas; UNITA forces kill MPLA cadres in rural areas. The civil war resumes. **9 December (Somalia):** U.S.-led Operation Restore Hope begins UN military occupation of Mogadishu to feed famine and war victims. **29 December (U.S./Somalia):** Bin Ladin allegedly launches first terrorist attack, which fails to kill U.S. soldiers headed for Somalia.

1993   20 January (U.S.): Bill Clinton is inaugurated as president. **25 April (Eritrea/Ethiopia):** Eritrea votes for freedom from Ethiopia, which is granted on 24 May. **5 June (Somalia):** Muhammad Farah Aideed's militia ambushes and kills 24 Pakistani UN peacekeepers. **3–4 October (Somalia):** Eighteen U.S. soldiers and as many as 1,000 Somalis are killed in the Battle of Mogadishu.

1994   11 January (Rwanda): A high-ranking Rwandan government official tells UN peacekeeping commander General Roméo Dallaire that the Rwandan government is preparing to commit genocide against its Tutsi population. Dallaire faxes the information to the UN, which orders him to tell the Rwandan president but do nothing else. **6 April (Rwanda):** An airplane carrying the presidents of Rwanda and Burundi is shot down, killing both. The Rwanda genocide immediately begins and 10 Belgian peacekeepers are murdered by the Rwandan army. **9**

April (Rwanda): The U.S. closes its embassy and withdraws all Americans from Rwanda. **10 April (Rwanda):** Dallaire requests that the UN double his forces to 5,000. The UN refuses. **Mid-April (Rwanda):** U.S. officials are ordered not to use the word "genocide" in describing the killings in Rwanda. **15 April (Rwanda):** At the behest of the Belgians, Secretary of State Warren Christopher orders UN Ambassador Madeleine Albright to vote to disband the UN peacekeeping mission. Albright persuades him and the UN to allow 270 troops to remain. Dallaire illegally keeps over 500. **27 April (South Africa):** Nelson Mandela is elected president in the country's first multiracial elections. **29 April (Rwanda):** Kofi Annan orders Dallaire to remain neutral. **3 May (U.S.):** Clinton signs Presidential Decision Directive 25 (PDD-25), formally limiting U.S. participation in peacekeeping operations. **7 May (Rwanda):** Clinton calls for a cease-fire in Rwanda. **10 May (South Africa):** Mandela is inaugurated president of South Africa. **15 June (Rwanda):** President Clinton allows U.S. officials to call the killing in Rwanda "genocide." **31 October (Angola):** Angolan government and UNITA sign the Lusaka Protocol, which calls for an end to the civil war followed by political and military integration and disarmament of UNITA, with the U.S. to help oversee the transition.

1995   15 June (Somalia): Clan leaders elect Aideed president of Somalia. **10 November (Nigeria):** Ten days after their death sentences, environmental activist Ken Saro-wiwa and eight colleagues are executed by the Nigerian government of General Sani Abacha, outraging the Clinton administration.

1996   19 May (Sudan): Sudan expels bin Ladin. **2 August (Somalia):** Aideed dies after being shot in a battle with a rival clan. **22 August (Zaïre):** Mobutu leaves Zaïre for cancer treatment in Switzerland. Rwanda-backed rebels invade eastern Zaïre. **23 August (U.S.):** Bin Ladin issues the first of two *fatwas* calling on Muslims to kill Americans. **24 October (Zaïre):** The Rwanda invasion is joined by Angola and exiled Katangans.

1997   16 May (Zaïre): Mobutu flees into exile on an airplane owned by Angolan rebel leader Savimbi. **17 May (Zaïre):** Rebels enter Kinshasa. **29 May (Congo):** Laurent-Désiré Kabila is sworn in as president and returns the country's name to the Democratic Republic of Congo. He promises elections to be held in April 1998. They are not. **19 July (Liberia):** Charles Taylor elected president of Liberia in a flawed election. **7 September (Congo):** Mobutu dies in hospital in Rabat, Morocco.

1998 22 March–2 April (U.S.): Clinton travels to Africa, the first president to do so since Carter. He praises several African leaders for leading an "African Renaissance." **26 March (Rwanda):** Clinton issues a formal apology for the failure of the U.S. to stop the genocide. **6 May (Eritrea/Ethiopia):** War breaks out between Eritrea and Ethiopia. **27 July (Congo/Rwanda):** Kabila expels 100 Rwandan army officers, who are leading his army, and begins rounding up Tutsis who live in Kinshasa, the capital. **2 August (Congo/Rwanda/Uganda/Burundi/ Namibia/Zimbabwe/Angola/Chad):** Congolese Tutsi (known as Banyamulenge) rebel against government repression, prompting Rwanda, Uganda, and Burundi to invade Congo to overthrow Kabila. Kabila is supported by troops from Namibia, Zimbabwe, Angola, and Chad. **7 August (Kenya/Tanzania):** Al Qaeda blows up U.S. embassies in Kenya and Tanzania. **7 December (Angola):** Government forces bomb UNITA strongholds, resuming the civil war.

1999 8 February (Niger): Wissam Zahawie, formerly Iraq's top negotiator on nuclear weapons issues, heads an Iraqi delegation visiting Niger, allegedly to purchase yellowcake. **5 April (Libya):** Qaddafi turns over for trial two intelligence officers accused of having perpetrated the Lockerbie airliner bombing. **7 July (Sierra Leone):** Special presidential envoy Jesse Jackson oversees the creation of a power-sharing agreement between the government of Sierra Leone and Revolutionary United Front (RUF) rebels. **10 July (Congo):** Congolese belligerents sign a cease-fire in Lusaka, Zambia. **16 August (Congo/Rwanda/Uganda):** The armies of Rwanda and Uganda fight each other in Kisangani, Congo.

2000 24 February (Congo): The UN Security Council authorizes 5,500 soldiers to monitor the Congolese cease-fire. **18 June (Eritrea/ Ethiopia):** Eritrea and Ethiopia agree to comprehensive peace agreement and binding arbitration over disputed borders after combined losses estimated as high as 100,000 soldiers.

2001 16 January (Congo): Kabila's bodyguard kills him. His son, Joseph Kabila, is appointed president. **20 January (U.S.):** George W. Bush is inaugurated as president. **31 January (Libya):** Libyan intelligence operative is found guilty of having perpetrated the December 1988 Lockerbie, Scotland, airliner bombing. **11 September (U.S.):** Al Qaeda attacks at the Twin Towers in New York, the Pentagon in Washington, D.C., and in a field in Pennsylvania.

2002 22 February (Angola): Savimbi is ambushed and killed. **4 April (Angola):** UNITA surrenders. **9 July (Africa):** The OAU is disbanded and replaced by the AU. **30 July (Congo/Rwanda):** Kabila and Rwandan President Paul Kagame sign a peace agreement under which Rwanda will withdraw from Congo and Congo will disarm and arrest Rwandan Hutu extremist exiles. **6 September (Congo):** Kabila and Ugandan President Yoweri Museveni sign a peace agreement.

2003 14 February (Sudan): Generally accepted date for the beginning of the Darfurian genocide as rebels attack Sudanese soldiers in retaliation for repeated assaults by government-backed Janjaweed militias. **March (Libya):** Qaddafi contacts U.S. and British governments about dismantling his weapons of mass destruction (WMD) program. **27 May (U.S.):** Bush signs President's Emergency Plan for AIDS Relief (PEPFAR), a five-year $15 million program to fight AIDS around the world. **27 June (Liberia):** President Bush calls on Liberian President Taylor to resign. **11 August (Liberia):** Taylor steps down as president of Liberia and flees to Nigeria. **15 August (Libya):** Qaddafi agrees to pay Lockerbie survivors $2.7 billion. **12 September (Libya):** UN ends all sanctions against Libya. **19 December (Libya):** Qaddafi announces that Libya will give up its WMD program.

2004 7 April (Sudan): Bush condemns atrocities committed by the Sudanese government in Darfur. **26 May (Sudan):** U.S. brokers peace agreement between Sudanese government and southern Sudanese rebels. **9 September (Sudan):** Secretary of State Colin Powell publicly calls Sudanese oppression in Darfur genocide. Bush publicly agrees. **18–19 November (Sudan):** The Chinese and possibly Russians force the UN Security Council to water down a resolution with a mild threat of sanctions against Sudan for its genocidal policy in Darfur.

2005   **9 January (Sudan):** Peace treaty is signed between the government and southern Sudanese rebels, ending the almost 22-year-old civil war. **30 June (U.S.):** Bush announces five-year, $1.5 billion U.S. initiative to fight malaria in Africa. **19 December (Congo):** The International Court of Justice rules that Uganda must compensate Congo for rights abuses and plundering resources from 1998 to 2003.

2006   **16 January (Liberia):** Ellen Johnson-Sirleaf sworn in as president, the first African woman to be elected president. **Early February (Ethiopia/Eritrea):** U.S. government secretly asks U.N.-appointed boundary commission to award the town of Badme to Ethiopia, reversing its 2002 decision that all disputed border territory belonged to Eritrea. The proposal was rejected. **5 June (Somalia):** Al Qaeda–supported Islamic Courts Union (ICU) takes control of Mogadishu. **22 June (Somalia):** The U.S. informs the ICU that several al Qaeda terrorists are under their protection and requests their extradition. The ICU refuses. **15 November (Congo):** Joseph Kabila is declared the winner of first election since 1960. **27 December (Somalia):** With U.S. aerial reconnaissance assistance, Somali Transitional Federal Government and Ethiopian forces drive the ICU out of Mogadishu. Many ICU leaders flee to Eritrea. The U.S. also launches air strikes on ICU positions that include alleged al Qaeda members.

2007   **30 May (U.S.):** Bush announces a five-year, $30 billion program that will double U.S. funding for fighting global HIV/AIDS. **4 June (Liberia):** Trial of Charles Taylor for violating human rights and committing war crimes begins in The Hague. **31 July (Darfur):** The UN and AU authorize the United Nations–African Union Mission in Darfur (UNAMID) to act as peacekeepers. By mid-2008, UNAMID had few soldiers and was sometimes unable to protect itself from government and rebel forces. **27 December (Kenya):** Presidential election is widely considered stolen by President Mwai Kibaki, resulting in riots and tribal violence across the country that kills over 1,000 and leaves 350,000 people displaced.

2008   **15–21 February (Benin/Tanzania/Rwanda/Ghana/Liberia):** Bush visits five African countries, emphasizing his government's effort to fight HIV/AIDS, malaria, and poverty. **18 February (Kenya):** Secretary of State Condoleezza Rice goes to Kenya and meets with Kibaki, bluntly telling him to agree to "genuine powersharing" with opposition leader Raila Odinga. **29 March (Zimbabwe):** Presidential elections held while Zimbabwe suffers 80 percent unemployment and inflation estimated to be as high as 4 million percent. **2 May (Zimbabwe):** Official results are announced for presidential election. President Mugabe and opposition leader Morgan Tsvangirai are required to have a runoff because neither obtained 50 percent of the vote although observers believe that the election was stolen from Tsvangirai. **17 April (Kenya):** Following a power-sharing agreement with Kibaki, Odinga takes office as prime minister. **28 May (Sudan):** The three major U.S. candidates for president pledge to take immediate action against Sudan if "peace and security" were not restored to Darfur by 20 January 2009. **22 June (Zimbabwe):** Government-backed violence kills over 100 opposition party members. President Mugabe ignores international condemnation. Tsvangirai flees to Dutch embassy. The Bush administration demands that the government "and its thugs" halt the violence. **11 July (Zimbabwe):** China and Russia veto sanctions against Zimbabwe introduced by the U.S. **14 July (Sudan):** Chief prosecutor of the International Criminal Court Luis Moreno-Ocampo asks judges to issue an arrest warrant for President Bashir on charges of crimes against humanity in Darfur. **21 July (Zimbabwe):** Mugabe and opposition leader Tsvangirai meet and agree to preconditions for negotiations to create a government of national unity. **30 July (U.S.):** Bush signs legislation reauthorizing PEPFAR, increasing total monies for combating international HIV/AIDS, malaria, and tuberculosis to $48 million.

Introduction

The image of Africa among Americans at the beginning of the 21st century is tragic; America's image among Africans is of a place that is splendid but arrogant and unfeeling. Both have large elements of truth. Poverty, coups, corruption, pandemic disease, and tribal, racial, and religious violence are all too common in Africa. So too is Americans' lack of concern about the people of a continent that suffers from these tragedies, as well as their government's support for African governments that treat their people as prey instead of citizens.

That this perspective rarely goes beneath these facile observations is due largely to U.S. abundance. With vast internal markets and natural resources, the United States was never dependent on foreign markets and thus had little need for trade or even contact with Africa following the 1 January 1808 cessation of the transatlantic slave trade. Indeed, the primary relationship between the United States and Africa in the 19th and early 20th centuries was with Liberia, the purpose of which was to export people to Africa, not goods, and then periodically to take remedial steps to ensure the country's continued independent survival.

Africa grew in importance for Americans thanks to the cold war as the United States vied with the Soviet Union for support in the UN and sought to protect strategic minerals from Soviet control, especially in Congo and Southern Africa, and to protect sea lanes along the Horn of Africa and around the Cape of Good Hope. The resulting U.S. alliances with corrupt and often brutal anti-Communist dictators and accommodation of racist or colonial governments did much to sully America's image across the continent and particularly among African elites.

Cold war's end saw commensurate U.S. loss of interest in Africa. Paradoxically, much of the U.S. interest that remains comes from Africa's multiple and myriad tragedies. President George W. Bush has made African development and eradication of disease important albeit secondary foreign policy goals, and by the end of his presidency many commentators were calling his Africa policy the most positive aspect of his foreign policy legacy. The Global War on Terror has also increased U.S. interest in Africa, just as the cold war had done, and the United States again finds itself sullied by support for unsavory allied dictators in pursuit of a larger cause.

African Americans are the most important result of the U.S.–Africa relationship. Importing some 600,000 people for cheap labor resulted in acculturation to European ways by Africans and cultural borrowing by white Americans, especially in the South, most famously in music, dance, and food, but also in manner of religious worship, telling of folk tales, and even grammatical structure. African Americans as an interest group with distant historical ties to Africa have shown comparatively little interest in the continent's politics, with exceptions being support for Ethiopia following the Italian invasion in 1935 and opposition to South African apartheid during the 1980s, but increasing numbers of African immigrants since the Immigration Reform and Control Act of 1986 (popularly known by the names of its authors, Simpson and Mazzoli) are creating a stronger African American tie to Africa.

FROM EUROPEAN SETTLEMENT TO COLD WAR

The transatlantic slave trade was the earliest relationship between Africa and Americans. A series of business deals between American or European traders and West African rulers or their agents, it was not a state-to-state relationship involving British American colonial governments or the U.S. government. The U.S. government ended the slave trade by law on 1 January 1808 although slavery itself continued. The question of what to do with freed slaves became a significant issue in U.S. domestic policy that led to a new foreign policy, the creation of the West African nation of Liberia as a home for African Americans. African American calls to go "Back to Africa" would occasionally emerge as passionate but unrealistic and almost uniformly unfulfilled movements in the years following slavery's abolition.

North Africa was of much greater consequence for U.S. foreign policy during the early years of the United States. After independence, the Barbary Pirates preyed on U.S. shipping in the Mediterranean and the

Atlantic Ocean, forcing the U.S. government to pay as much as 10 percent of its national budget in tribute to their rulers and forcing some of the earliest treaties in U.S. history. Tribute, predation, and sometimes effective U.S. retaliation became a cycle that only concluded with U.S. victory in 1815.

Thereafter until World War II, interest in Africa was limited to occasional incidents such as journalist Henry Stanley's search for the Rev. David Livingstone, U.S. government support for the Central African civilizing mission, so-called, of King Léopold II and public disgust and approbation as word of his brutal rule trickled out, and President Theodore Roosevelt's confrontation with Moroccan guerilla leader Mulai Ahmed er Raisuli. Likewise, there was growing American interest in African wildlife thanks to heavy newspaper reporting about Roosevelt's postpresidential safari, the extraordinary African wildlife exhibits created for the American Museum of Natural History in New York City by naturalist Carl Akeley, and the novels and adventures of Ernest Hemingway.

Italian dictator Benito Mussolini's October 1935 invasion and rapid conquest of Ethiopia and Emperor Haile Selassie's dramatic speech asking for assistance from the League of Nations raised American consciousness about Africa, especially among African Americans, but only General Dwight D. Eisenhower's invasion of North Africa truly focused Americans' attention on the continent. President Franklin Delano Roosevelt's anti-colonialism and his calls for freedom and self-determination inspired African elites while worrying the colonial powers. Roosevelt's successor, Harry S. Truman, also supported decolonization but was concerned about its impact on the European powers, which saw their prestige tied to their empires and needed their colonies to provide the natural resources for national postwar recovery. As a result, Truman and Secretary of State Dean Acheson backed away from the push for decolonization that Roosevelt had initiated, occasionally speaking out but applying little effective pressure. Whether Roosevelt also would have been forced to compromise in this way is debated among historians.

THE COLD WAR AND ITS AFTERMATH

With the exception of Egypt, U.S. post–World War II policy toward Africa was an adjunct of the West–East struggle: so much so that even when U.S. presidents and their administrations looked to the global South, they saw the Communist East. Whether providing economic assistance, food, economic and political advice for successful modernization, or police and military assistance to maintain order, the U.S. purpose was at least in part, and usually much more than that, to prevent Communist subversion and conquest. Economic development and modernization would lift people out of the poverty that American political leaders believed was the kindling for the Communist spark. Military aid would be used to keep order and prevent Communist insurgents from taking advantage of the difficult transition from traditional society to modernity. Following the collapse of the Soviet Union and the end of the cold war, Africa was a foreign policy afterthought until the 11 September 2001 attacks by al Qaeda, which made the economic, political, and military development of African states an important part of President George W. Bush's Global War on Terror.

U.S. policy toward Egypt transcended cold war issues, tied as it was and is to protection of Persian Gulf oil supplies and U.S. commitment to the survival of Israel. Only President Dwight D. Eisenhower made the struggle against the Soviet Union into the primary focus of U.S.–Egyptian policy, yet his Egyptian policy also forced the decisive turn toward European decolonization when he stopped the British, French, and Israelis from overthrowing Gamal Abdel Nasser and forced the invaders to withdraw from Egypt.

Dwight D. Eisenhower Administration (1953–1961)

President Eisenhower oversaw one of the most comprehensive foreign policies in U.S. history, combining and coordinating traditional state-to-state diplomacy with public diplomacy, economic assistance, and covert action in a way unseen before or since. Beginning in the late 1970s, with the release of significant quantities of Eisenhower administration papers, political scientists and historians have shown that, *contra* the image that he himself created and the press happily yet ignorantly trumpeted, Eisenhower was in complete control of his administration, especially its foreign policy. Eisenhower, not Secretary of State John Foster Dulles, set the policy and created the bureaucratic procedure by which it was made. Eisenhower's military experience, particularly as commander of the North African invasion, Operation

Torch, and the invasion of Southern and Western Europe, had taught him the vital need for systematic analysis of military and diplomatic policy through a well-defined bureaucratic structure. Eisenhower used the National Security Council (NSC) for this purpose. Prior to NSC meetings, each piece of the upcoming agenda would be thoroughly researched. Eisenhower also believed in setting detailed blueprints for each area of foreign policy. It is notable that there was no sub-Saharan African blueprint until 1957.

Eisenhower's foreign policy focus was the cold war but due to the pressures of decolonization, he could not simply look East. Decolonization offered the United States the opportunity to enter markets previously restricted by colonial powers, and during Eisenhower administration meetings, officials frequently discussed an "Open Door" policy in Africa, but decolonization's dangers were far greater than its opportunities. The first danger was worsening relations with the colonizers. The second was difficult relations with the colonized. Eisenhower believed colonialism's time was past. His instinct was to oppose colonialism. But his position was not so simple. At the end of World War II, the British and especially the French were determined to hold onto their empires as symbols of their national greatness and Great Power status. The Portuguese and Spanish also desperately clung to their colonial possessions as symbols of long-lost international standing and to continue their self-appointed "civilizing missions." The Belgians, ever practical, eschewed national glory, instead working to keep the resources and profits flowing homeward from Central Africa. Of course the colonial powers were happy with their own imperial favored trading status. Making the situation still more difficult for the colonial powers were settler colonies. Several million white British, French, and Portuguese had moved to Africa; indeed, French Algeria was not even a colony. Under the French constitutions dating back to 1840, Algeria was as French as Paris or Tours, and with its coast just 220 miles from France, it is closer to the French mainland than Alaska or Hawaii to the U.S. mainland.

Refusing to push the Europeans toward decolonization posed potentially greater long-term dangers. Eisenhower believed that the Europeans' efforts to hold onto their empires would alienate the third world from the West, driving it into the embrace of the Soviet Union, which would win over their peoples through professions of sympathy and calls to end colonialism and racist government, votes in the United Nations (UN), military assistance for rebellious colonies and those caught in civil wars, and economic assistance for those who received their independence. Both Eisenhower and Dulles believed that this alienation could foster unity and anti-Western solidarity of black Africans, Arabs, Asians, and even an Afro-Asian alliance. The prospective loss of access to strategic resources and general trade would be disastrous for the United States and the West.

So Eisenhower faced the dilemma: calling for immediate or even rapid independence would alienate his North Atlantic Treaty Organization (NATO) allies, even putting the Alliance itself at risk; supporting the colonizers, especially in those colonies where they were often brutally repressing colonial revolutions, risked alienating the third world. At first, Secretary of State Dulles used public diplomacy in an attempt to jujitsu the Soviets with colonialism, proclaiming that while the West was decolonizing, the Soviets had colonized Eastern Europe and the Far East as first steps in their drive to supplant Western Europe and create a worldwide empire. Africans rejected the argument. For them, white-on-white oppression did not resonate as colonialism, and the People's Republic of China seemed to be a new Great Power under the Communists, able to overwhelm American forces upon their entry in the Korean War of 1950–53, and able to hold their own thereafter. African perceptions were worse than that though. Although Eisenhower used his "bully pulpit" to argue that the United States was the leader of the anti-colonial movement—by dint of its historical experience as the first colony to win its independence from Europe, its historic commitment to liberty and equality, and its traditional opposition to colonialism—Africans instead saw the United States as a bulwark of the colonial world, providing the colonizers with economic and military aid. Dismal race relations in the Southern states also seemed to put the lie to Eisenhower's claims. Headlines from the American South showed a mirror image of what was happening in Africa, with black people protesting for their freedom and suffering brutal, sometimes murderous, attacks by whites as police looked on or even participated.

At the same time, Eisenhower and Dulles tried to finesse the issue by using exquisitely gentle public diplomacy combined with often brutally frank behind-the-scenes talks to push the Europeans toward divesting themselves of their empires, in which they told European leaders that they had to accept that colonialism was doomed. The hope was that the Europeans would not be alienated by a softer public approach while the colonized would be encouraged toward deliberate speed rather than a breakneck pace in their demands for independence. The United States advised its allies to follow a measured decolonization with gradual, phased movement to self-government. This would slow down demands from the colonized for immediate independence, which would give the colonizers time to prepare colonial elites to rule while blunting the influence of disruptive and potentially revolutionary pro-Soviet radicals. The Eisenhower administration especially pushed this "go slow but not too slow" approach for Africa, where the president and his advisers believed that few colonies were ready for independence. Most African colonies had minuscule educated elites and middle classes, huge numbers of illiterates, and few sources of income.

Unfortunately, the administration's opinion was based as much on racist notions about Africans as it was on demographic and economic data. Eisenhower and members of his administration were not racial progressives. On more than a few occasions, records of administration discussions about Africa showed that officials, including the president himself, referred to Africans as "barely out of the trees." Vice President Richard Nixon also used such language, and he was considered to be the administration's point man on Africa. Following an African tour centered on attending Ghana's independence celebration, Nixon convinced Eisenhower that the Communist threat was such that the administration needed a comprehensive Africa policy.

Few members of the U.S. Congress cared about Africa, and Eisenhower was able to follow his policy largely without dissent. The key exception was Senator John F. Kennedy of Massachusetts. Kennedy attacked the Eisenhower administration's Algerian policy in 1956 and 1957 speeches, arguing that its support for the French was hopelessly retrograde, and calling on the United States to support the efforts of all colonized peoples to win their freedom. The speech forced Eisenhower to match his administration's strong anti-colonial private diplomacy with a more vigorous but still gentlemanly public call for decolonization. Eisenhower also began to push for greater economic assistance to Africa, but Congress' refusal to fund foreign aid in the amounts that he considered necessary prompted Eisenhower repeatedly to complain that Congress and the American people did not understand foreign policy.

Egypt saw the most striking example of Eisenhower's anti-colonialism, when he used overwhelming economic pressure combined with strident public diplomacy at the UN to force the British, French, and Israelis to abort the Suez invasion. Despite having saved Egyptian strongman Gamal Abdel Nasser, Eisenhower's cold war focus with such policies as the Baghdad Pact and his decision to withdraw funding for Egypt's Aswan High Dam had disastrous consequences as they either alienated Nasser and drove him to the Soviets, or gave him a pretext for making the informal alliance.

John F. Kennedy Administration (1961–1963)

President Kennedy's public support for Algerian independence and his active chairmanship of the Senate Foreign Relations Subcommittee on Africa made him well known and liked among African leaders even before he was elected president. During the 1960 presidential election, in which he defeated Vice President Nixon, Kennedy frequently focused attention on Eisenhower's lack of interest in Africa, arguing that by ignoring Africa, he created cold war opportunities for the Soviet Union to exploit. Kennedy also criticized the president's emphasis on trade instead of economic aid, as well as the late Secretary of State Dulles' publicly expressed moral aversion to neutral nations. Kennedy said that the goal of U.S. policy in Africa should be to show that democracy and development could grow together, but privately he told his staff that democracy would be almost impossible in some developing countries because of tribalism or endemic poverty. Kennedy had been strongly influenced by "modernization" theorists and tried to put into practice their argument that large doses of foreign aid to Africa would help countries overcome poverty and move into sustained economic development.

With foreign aid as a priority, Kennedy immediately antagonized the former colonial powers by quietly reversing the Eisenhower administration's practice of first referring African aid requests to them. Kennedy's administration saw land reform, literacy drives, and central planning not as Communist slogans but as things to be encouraged and even required in order to receive assistance from the United States. Kennedy did not seek to impose the U.S. system to a world where most people "are not white ... are not Christians ... [and] know nothing about free enterprise or due process of law or the Australian ballot." In May 1961, the Kennedy administration successfully proposed the creation of the Agency for International Development (AID), which would consolidate foreign aid programs, and a large foreign aid budget for it to oversee, including money for building schools, low-cost housing, and hospitals in addition to the infrastructure improvement that had been the focus of Eisenhower aid efforts.

African leaders were predisposed to like Kennedy when he took office, and the president solidified this through Oval Office meetings and occasional personal letters for heads of government. Unlike Eisenhower, who treated meetings with African leaders as meet-and-greet visits the purpose of which was to give the visitor a photo with the president and get them out the door, Kennedy made a thorough study of each country's history, economics, and politics before meetings. The Africans were thrilled that the president had a seemingly intimate knowledge of their goals and problems.

At the highest levels of his administration, only Under Secretary of State Chester Bowles shared Kennedy's interest in Africa, but Kennedy forced Bowles out of office in November 1961 because of chaotic management and frequent leaks that he had opposed the Bay of Pigs invasion. Nonetheless, Africa was well represented in the Kennedy administration because the president appointed former Michigan Governor G. Mennen "Soapy" Williams assistant secretary of state for African affairs. Appointing a political figure of Williams' stature to lead a regional bureau is highly unusual because bureaus are normally led by career diplomats. Thus did Kennedy give African affairs a high profile and tremendous clout within his administration.

Soon after his election, Kennedy was deeply affected by a 6 January 1961 speech by Soviet Premier Nikita Khrushchev in which he pledged Soviet support for third-world revolutions. For Kennedy, this validated his focus on Africa policy. Kennedy made wooing Leftist governments out of the Soviet camp a chief goal. The first sub-Saharan African leader he met with was Kwame Nkrumah, Ghana's increasingly pro-Soviet leader, and in October 1962 he had White House meetings with Guinea's Ahmed Sékou Touré and Algeria's Muhammad Ahmed Ben Bella, the latter of whom Kennedy had publicly supported during Algeria's war for independence from France. Kennedy also sought better relations with Egypt's Nasser, but these efforts were derailed by Egypt's intervention in Yemen. The only real benefit from Kennedy's détente with radical African leaders proved to be significant: Touré, Nkrumah, and Ben Bella each refused to allow the Soviets to use their countries to refuel Cuba-bound airplanes during the missile crisis, thus reinforcing the naval blockade of the island, although Ghana's UN ambassador bitterly excoriated the United States in the UN General Assembly.

There was also cost, as Kennedy initiated aid programs to each, including tens of millions of dollars funding Ghana's Volta River Dam project, money he later came to regret having spent as Nkrumah moved further Left. More important, Ben Bella, Nkrumah, and Nasser continued public attacks on the United States, and Ben Bella flew directly from his meeting with Kennedy to Cuba, where he met with Fidel Castro just days before the Cuban missile crisis began. Congress cited this public anti-Americanism as justification for cutting the entire foreign aid program despite administration efforts to increase the appropriation. The resulting reduction was so great that the total was below the amount spent by the Eisenhower administration in its final year in office, a sum that Kennedy had derided as having shown that the Eisenhower administration lacked vision and world leadership.

While moving closer to anti-American states, Kennedy began to edge U.S. policy away from traditional American allies, voting in the UN for Angolan independence from Portugal and cutting military assistance to the Portuguese until the Portuguese threatened to end U.S. military aircraft use of the Azores Islands as a refueling stop. On South Africa, Kennedy declared a unilateral U.S. embargo on arms sales and subsequently voted for such a resolution at the UN.

Lyndon B. Johnson Administration (1963–1969)

President Johnson's interest in Africa, except for Egypt, was minimal, and he was able to keep Egypt from becoming a major issue until the Arab–Israeli War of 1967. Focusing first on domestic affairs, then on Vietnam, Africa only entered his consciousness during crises, and then only to the extent of getting them resolved so that he could go back to ignoring Africa. The key sub-Saharan African crises of his presidency were renewed violence in Congo during 1964 and 1967 and the Nigerian civil war, which began in 1967 and continued through the end of his presidency. Johnson's Congolese intervention, assisting the Belgians in rescuing U.S. and European captives from the Leftist Simba rebels, outraged Africans, whose leaders and press viciously attacked the president. Their reaction, which Johnson and even his UN Ambassador Adlai Stevenson considered wildly disproportionate, killed whatever small interest he had had in African issues and policy. The 1967 Congolese intervention, in which he assisted the government in putting down a white mercenary rebellion, was popular with Africans but infuriated Congress, which he had failed to consult. Unlike in Congo, Johnson decided to keep the United States out of the Nigerian civil war, even embargoing arms sales to both sides, which antagonized the Nigerian government. The Nigerian civil war only rose to the level of presidential concern because of public demands for action sparked by the intense television coverage given to starving babies in the breakaway province that called itself Biafra. In mid-1968, the president allegedly demanded of his advisers that they "get those nigger babies off my TV set." The result was a significant food relief program.

A personal crisis also briefly sparked Johnson's interest in South Africa. In May 1966, Johnson learned that his enemy and possible future electoral opponent Robert F. Kennedy was going to visit South Africa for a speaking tour. Realizing that Kennedy's visit would generate tremendous favorable coverage for the rhetorical attacks he would certainly launch against apartheid, Johnson decided "it was time to look at the area as a whole" in preparation for a new "Johnson Doctrine for Africa" accompanied by a nationally televised speech on Africa, which would preempt publicity for Kennedy's visit. His assistant, Bill Moyers, also suggested that a speech would be an easy and cheap way to win support from African American civil rights leaders. Johnson delivered the speech, which marked the third anniversary of the Organization of African Unity (OAU), to 300 African diplomats assembled at the White House. Thereafter the Johnson Doctrine for Africa disappeared due to a lack of ideas from African Bureau Chief Williams and his bureaucracy, and lack of interest by the president.

Richard M. Nixon Administration (1969–1974)

Vice President Nixon had been Eisenhower's point man on sub-Saharan Africa, and had encouraged Eisenhower to take a more active African role because of the Communist threat. By 1969, he had lost interest in the continent. President Nixon's closest foreign policy adviser, National Security Adviser Henry Kissinger, never had been interested. Nixon famously told Kissinger to leave Africa policy to Secretary of State William Rogers: "Henry, let's leave the niggers to Bill and we'll take care of the rest of the world." With U.S. foreign policy overstretched and the military stuck in Vietnam, Nixon sought to rein in U.S. responsibilities while at the same time preventing Soviet expansionism. The result was the Nixon Doctrine, which called for creation of a system of friendly regional powers such as Mobutu Sese Seko's Zaïre, Haile Selassie's Ethiopia, and possibly Nigeria and South Africa in the sort of role that the United States had heretofore played globally in containing communism. Mobutu was the first African leader to visit Nixon at the White House and that was not until August 1970, a year and a half after Nixon had taken office. In Southern Africa, Nixon oversaw a shift in policy based on his and Kissinger's conclusion that the whites would continue to rule Southern Africa for the foreseeable future and economic pressure and moral blandishment would make them more stubborn and less likely to reform. Instead, the Nixon administration unsuccessfully used economic incentives and relaxation in tensions as a means to work with the white governments and gradually move them toward more equitable treatment of their black populations.

Nixon's and Kissinger's interest in the Middle East was also negligible because Israel seemed to be unassailable after its brilliant six-day victory in the Arab–Israeli War of 1967. Kissinger even reportedly blocked efforts by Secretary of State William Rogers to broker a region-wide peace during December 1969. Kissinger's interest changed with Egypt's surprise attack and early victories against Israel in the Arab–Israeli War of 1973. Nixon was debilitated by the Watergate scandal during key moments in the war, but he backed Kissinger's actions in warning the Soviets not to involve themselves, airlifting Israel materiel, and launching shuttle diplomacy to begin the Middle East peace process.

Gerald R. Ford Administration (1974–1977)

Although it is a cliché that President Ford left foreign policy to Henry Kissinger, whom he appointed secretary of state and national security adviser, it is also true. Kissinger continued to show no interest in Africa until the Vietnam endgame. As South Vietnam collapsed in

April 1975, Zambia's President Kenneth Kaunda, a socialist but anti-Communist who had long assisted guerillas fighting against Southern Africa's racist regimes, pleaded for U.S. intervention in Angola to stop the military wing of the Communist-led and Soviet-supported *Movimento Popular de Libertação de Angola*/Popular Movement for the Liberation of Angola (MPLA) from taking power following independence from Portugal. Kissinger concluded that the United States had to intervene in Angola to stop the worldwide momentum of Soviet advance while demonstrating that Vietnam had not made the United States so dispirited that it could not respond to foreign policy challenges. Kissinger also wanted to stabilize Central and Southern Africa, so he joined the United States with Zambia, Zaïre, and (based on strong circumstantial evidence adduced by historian Piero Gleijeses from declassified U.S. and South African documents) South Africa to defeat the MPLA by covertly supporting opposition guerilla movements. The operation, called IAFEATURE, began in July 1975 and provided paramilitary trainers and $48 million in aid while the South African army entered Angola.

IAFEATURE was defeated by Cuba's Fidel Castro, who sent 12,000 soldiers, and then was ended thanks to U.S. newspapers, which reported about the Central Intelligence Agency (CIA) operation and the South African intervention, leading the U.S. Congress to pass the Tunney and Clark Amendments, banning further U.S. intervention in Angola. Instead of a prestige-restoring triumph, Angola made the United States look like a hamstrung and ineffectual ally of the apartheid regime while the Communist Bloc solidified its post-Vietnam prestige.

Kissinger feared a domino-producing general race war across Southern Africa that could knock over Zaïre and Zambia as well—a cascade the Soviets saw as plausible and desirable, but which Kissinger believed could lead to direct Super Power intervention. To stop it, he spoke out against racism and in support of majority rule in Rhodesia, then began shuttle diplomacy to bring it about. His effort was brought short by including South Africa in the negotiations and treating it as a legitimate state, albeit one whose social system the United States abhorred. For Kissinger, meeting with South African Prime Minister John Vorster was comparable to meeting with the Soviet Union's Leonid Brezhnev or China's Mao Zedong, but black African leaders and liberals in the United States were outraged. When Kissinger either mixed up details of his proposal for majority rule or tried to finesse differences between what he had told the white-ruled government leaders and then the black government and guerilla leaders (he gave both explanations), his diplomatic effort collapsed, but the British adopted the agreements he had brokered and made them the starting point for an all-parties conference on Rhodesia in Geneva late in 1976. Following Ford's defeat by Democrat Jimmy Carter, guerilla leaders Robert Mugabe and Joshua Nkomo concluded they could get a better deal if they continued the civil war, so after the conference adjourned, they did not return.

In the Middle East, Ford allowed Kissinger to continue shuttle diplomacy, which culminated in the September 1975 Sinai II agreement between Egypt and Israel. Both sides agreed to solve their differences peacefully, Israel returned important strategic territory and oil wells, and the United States built and staffed monitoring stations at crucial border positions on Egyptian territory.

Jimmy Carter Administration (1977–1981)

With John Kennedy, Jimmy Carter is the only other U.S. president who had a strong personal interest in sub-Sahara African affairs before taking office. Like Kennedy, he tried but failed to move Africa to a more central place in his foreign policy. Carter's primary African goals were development, human rights, and most important, to bring majority rule to Southern Africa. The cold war was not a priority for his Africa policy. Shortly after taking office, Carter proudly announced in a speech that the United States had freed itself of its "inordinate fear of communism," and Carter sought to remove Africa from the cold war by ignoring African nations' relationship with the Soviets and by tolerating Marxist–Leninist governments.

Carter's schizophrenic foreign policy team was divided among those such as National Security Adviser Zbigniew Brzezinski, a traditional Great Power realist who believed that most developments in Africa were a cold war sideshow at best and a distraction at worst, but also believed that human rights was a good issue for gaining international support against the Soviet Union; Secretary of State Cyrus Vance, whose views had migrated from cold warrior to strict détentist, but whose emphasis was also decidedly on the Great Power relationship, which also led him to see Africa as something of a sideshow; and UN Ambassador

Andrew Young, a regionalist who had adopted many of the foreign policy views of the New Left.

To show the continent's new importance to the United States, Carter sent Young on a 10-day African tour less than two months into his administration. Young's public and private discussions about U.S. policy convinced many previously anti-American leaders that U.S. policy had definitely changed. Carter himself went to Africa in March 1978. These visits were not just symbolic: during the first half of Carter's administration, Young's African views were in the ascendancy, and Carter focused tremendous time and resources to force Rhodesia's white supremacist government to majority rule. The world understood that this was a different kind of U.S. administration when Young called Cuban troops a "stabilizing force" in Angola and publicly described U.S. allies and former U.S. presidents as "racists." The State Department's Human Rights Bureau, created by Congress in 1976 but ignored by President Ford, was also at the center of U.S. policy during these early years. Bureau chief Patricia Derian was a vocal critic of authoritarian governments, but her definition of human rights owed much to the New Left, as it emphasized economic, social, and cultural rights at the expense of political freedom, civil rights, and property rights. Ambassador Young shared this view, repeatedly arguing that African governments should be allowed to "experiment" with various forms of government and economic system.

Carter's new Africa policy was seen in March 1977 when Cuban-trained rebels invaded Zaïre, and the president responded by proclaiming that the United States would not intervene. In April, Ethiopia's revolutionary government moved closer to the Soviet Union and ordered the United States to close down its facilities, including a secret communications base, within 96 hours. Carter complied. In May, Vice President Walter Mondale told South African Prime Minister John Vorster that apartheid was going to cause poor relations between the nations. Andrew Young followed the meeting with a private visit to South Africa in which he expressed solidarity with black South Africans and said that President Carter would force South Africa to give up apartheid since he had dealt with racists like the Afrikaners while growing up in Georgia and had beaten them as governor.

Working with the British, Carter put together a majority-rule plan for Rhodesia and then persuaded Nigerian President Olusegun Obasanjo to give it his strong support. The plan collapsed when Secretary of State Vance, apparently told by Ambassador Young that he had Nigerian assurance that the Rhodesian Marxist rebels, the Patriotic Front, would accept the plan, was publicly rebuffed by the rebels in April 1978. Changes in the international correlation of forces were pushing Carter toward accepting that the United States did indeed have cold war obligations in Africa. In May, rebels whom Carter claimed were Cuban-directed (based on what Vance later called weak evidence) again invaded Zaïre. This time the president loaned military cargo planes to the French and Belgians so that they could fly in troops, and he authorized $20 million in military assistance to the Zaïrean government. In June, Carter delivered an important speech in which he announced that Soviet and Cuban meddling in Africa endangered détente. As Brzezinski's power waxed, Vance's and Young's waned.

In the Middle East, soon after he took office, Carter proposed a Geneva peace conference that would include the Soviet Union. Fear of Soviet return to the center of the region's politics prompted Egyptian President Anwar al-Sadat to fly to Israel in November to try to make peace himself. When this effort bogged down, Carter invited Sadat and Israeli Prime Minister Menachem Begin to Camp David, where he hammered out the September 1978 Camp David Accords, and back to Camp David in early 1979 to win a peace treaty. Carter's efforts significantly removed the possibility of general warfare in the Middle East and, despite a history of wars between Egypt and Israel in 1948–49, 1956, 1967, and 1973 and low-intensity warfare for significant periods during interim periods that seemed like an endless spiral, the two countries did not fight another war against each other for 35 years and counting after 1973.

In August 1979, Carter fired UN Ambassador Young when he violated administration policy and secretly met with a representative from the Palestine Liberation Organization (PLO). After the Iranian hostage crisis began on 4 November 1979 followed by the Soviet invasion of Afghanistan on 25–26 December, Carter admitted that his view of Soviet intentions had been incorrect. Concerned that the Soviet Union was creating a pincer from Afghanistan to the Horn of Africa for grasping or choking Middle Eastern oil, which Brzezinski called the "Arc of Crisis," Carter rejected Vance's counsel and wholeheartedly followed Brzezinski's realist path. Carter now had no time for Africa beyond such cold war concerns as obtaining naval bases in Somalia and Kenya to protect oil shipping lanes, arming the government of Somalia in exchange ostensibly to prevent an Ethiopian invasion, and strengthening North African governments against the threat posed by heavily armed Libya and its cadres of guerillas and terrorists. Vance resigned on 28 April 1980 after Carter rejected his advice and launched an unsuccessful military mission to free the Iranian hostages. The new secretary of state, former Senator Edmund Muskie, largely deferred to Brzezinski's guidance.

Ronald W. Reagan Administration (1981–1989)

The foreign policy shift from Carter to Ronald Reagan was greater even than the shift from Nixon/Ford to Carter. Reagan's goal was to defeat the Soviet Union; his interest in Africa, minimal, seen most famously during a White House visit, when the president called Liberian dictator Samuel Doe "Comrade Moe." Reagan's Africa policy consisted of four parts: stop and then rollback Soviet adventurism, a policy that evolved into the "Reagan Doctrine"; shift from confrontation to rapprochement with South Africa through "Constructive Engagement" that would ease South Africa toward equal rights; use constructive engagement to get South Africa out of southwest Africa (Namibia) while linking this withdrawal to Cuba leaving Angola; and contain or remove Libya's Muammar Qaddafi.

By supporting Jonas Savimbi's UNITA in Angola, just as he was supporting the Mujahedin rebels in Afghanistan and the Contras in Nicaragua, Reagan and his administration hoped to make the cost of defending the Soviet Empire painful or even prohibitive for the inefficient and relatively small Soviet economy. In the long term, Reagan foresaw the Reagan Doctrine as contributing to liberation from the Soviet Union and eventually the overthrow of communism. In the short term, Assistant Secretary of State for African Affairs Chester Crocker believed that it would cause revolutionary change in Southern Africa, although he successfully opposed its application to Mozambique. Blunting or overthrowing communism in Angola by supporting Savimbi's *União Nacional para a Independência Total de Angola*/National Union for the Total Independence of Angola (UNITA), argued Crocker, would allow South Africa to free southwest Africa without fear that independent

Namibia could become a threat to South Africa. This would end South Africa's siege mentality, both by removing the outside threat and by reintegrating South Africa into the West through Constructive Engagement, with the result that South Africa would end repression and allow greater civil rights and equitable treatment for blacks.

Ironically, despite Reagan's personal lack of interest in Africa and the criticism he received for his Southern Africa policy, his hard-line worldwide assault on the Soviet Union did more to change Africa than any other president. By bankrupting and breaking the will of the Soviet Union, Reagan hastened the end of the cold war, which meant that the United States and Soviet Union no longer felt compelled to support unsavory allies like Zaïre's Mobutu or Ethiopia's Mengistu Haile Mariam. Likewise, a major reason that South Africa was willing to end apartheid and move to democratic majority rule was that there was no longer a threat that majority rule could produce a Communist government.

George H.W. Bush Administration (1989–1993)

George H.W. Bush is not known for his Africa policy. A foreign policy realist, during the cold war his focus was decidedly on Europe and Asia. As CIA director, he had good relations with Zaïre's Mobutu Sese Seko, whom he considered a stabilizing force in Central Africa, and honored him by making him the first African leader to be invited to the White House. Otherwise, Africa was very much an afterthought for his administration; indeed, to take African issues off the table, early in his administration he sought negotiated ends to anti-Communist guerilla insurgencies in Angola and Mozambique and encouraged former President Carter to try to foster negotiations between the formerly Communist government of Ethiopia and Eritrean rebels. When these efforts failed, Bush subsequently increased assistance to Angolan rebel Savimbi.

The collapse of the Soviet Empire in late 1989 led Bush to change his Africa policy. When political protests or rebellions subsequently broke out in Zaïre, Liberia, Chad, Kenya, and Somalia, the Bush administration did not intervene despite each having been a close ally or source of foreign policy concern. He went so far as to cut off military support for Liberia's Samuel Doe, who was subsequently overthrown, tortured, and executed. Along with this benign neglect, Bush also launched a little-noticed push for democracy, using public diplomacy and economic pressure to force U.S. allies Mobutu and Kenya's Daniel arap Moi to create multiparty political systems.

Following Bush's November 1992 defeat by Bill Clinton, he ordered U.S. military forces into Somalia as part of a UN operation to feed people who were starving because of the country's civil war and famine. The intervention, called Operation Restore Hope, was restricted to providing food and medical assistance and saved tens of thousands of lives.

Bill Clinton Administration (1993–2001)

Although President Clinton ran as a candidate focused on domestic affairs to contrast himself from Bush, whose interest was clearly on foreign policy at the expense of domestic issues, Clinton's electoral debt to black voters made Africa an early foreign policy priority. What emerged was an ad hoc and inconsistent policy driven by domestic concerns rather than a consistent vision.

During his presidential campaign, Clinton had sharply criticized President Bush for his ostensible failure to support human rights in Haiti and Africa. With the cold war over, Clinton promised a moral and activist foreign policy that would work with the UN in the realms of peacekeeping and nation building. He argued that such policies represented a new U.S. national interest. Among his first foreign policy decisions was to expand the Somalia mission from peacekeeping in order to feed the starving, to peacemaking to create conditions for rebuilding the Somali state. The resulting Battle of Mogadishu, which left 18 U.S. soldiers dead, led Clinton to make a complete change in his policy. At the president's order, National Security Council aide Richard Clarke drew up Presidential Decision Directive 25 (PDD-25), which severely restricted conditions under which the United States would participate in international peacekeeping operations. Although not yet signed by the president when the Rwandan genocide began in April 1994, Clinton's administration closely followed PDD-25 and sought to redeploy every UN peacekeeper out of Rwanda, believing that "mission creep" could eventually force the United States to participate in the operation, but he ultimately agreed to cut the peacekeepers' numbers down to 270. Neither Clinton nor his government would use the term "genocide" to describe the genocide because international law requires that the world intervene to stop the killing. Following the military defeat of the "Hutu Power" *geno-cidaires* who had sought to exterminate the Tutsi, Clinton ordered assistance to be provided to refugee camps in Zaïre, most of which were controlled by Hutu Power extremists.

In 1998, Clinton refocused on Africa. From 22 March to 2 April 1998, the president visited six African countries at a cost of $42.8 million. He was the first president since Carter to visit the continent, and the trip proved popular with Africans. While in Rwanda, Clinton apologized for the world's failure to stop the genocide, and throughout the trip, he echoed South African President Thabo Mbeki, describing an "African Renaissance" brought by what Clinton called "a new generation of leaders," which included Mbeki, Yoweri Museveni of Uganda, Paul Kagame of Rwanda, Laurent-Désiré Kabila of the Democratic Republic of Congo (DRC), Meles Zenawi of Ethiopia, Isaias Afwerki of Eritrea, Joaquim Chissano of Mozambique, and Jerry Rawlings of Ghana. By the end of Clinton's term, all but Rawlings had engaged in political repression and/or gone to war with a neighbor.

On 7 August 1998 al Qaeda bombed U.S. embassies in Kenya, killing 212, and Tanzania, killing 11. All but 12 of the dead were Africans. Clinton responded with Operation Infinite Reach on 20 August, launching cruise missiles on al Qaeda camps in Afghanistan and a pharmaceutical factory in Sudan that was believed to be tied to al Qaeda for the production of nerve gas. Clinton's opponents accused him of launching the attacks to deflect attention from his perjury in the Monica Lewinsky case. Subsequent evidence emerged that the plant was not tied to al Qaeda, causing a Clinton administration split between high-ranking officials such as Secretary of Defense William Cohen, who continued to believe the validity of the charge and mid-level officials, who concluded that the attack had been a mistake.

In October 1998, Clinton sent his special envoy for Africa, Jesse Jackson, to work out a peace settlement in civil war–torn Sierra Leone. Jackson used a constructive engagement policy with Liberian President Charles Taylor, who had launched the war and used guerilla forces to torture and kill hundreds of thousands of Liberians while turning children into drug-besotted killers, and with Sierra Leonean rebel leader Foday Sankoh, who followed the identical child soldier strategy and intentionally maimed or killed tens of thousands. The peace settlement, which made Sankoh vice president and gave him control of

Sierra Leone's diamond mines, quickly failed when Sankoh restarted the civil war with Taylor's assistance, expanding its scope across West Africa. When new peace talks were held in 2000, Sierra Leone's government warned Jackson that his life would be in danger if he entered the country.

Although Clinton often spoke of human rights as a central part of his Africa policy, human rights practices had almost no correlation with foreign aid—much less than the role it had played for Carter, Reagan, or Bush. Instead, Clinton's African focus was expanding trade without regard to internal political conditions. In 2000, he signed the African Growth and Opportunity Act (AGOA), which grants eligible African nations the most liberal trade terms available to countries that are not part of a free trade pact with the United States. In a speech during his last year in office, Clinton said that his Africa policy had resulted in "thousands of triumphs."

George W. Bush Administration (2001–2009)

George W. Bush came into office decrying the "nation building" policy that Clinton had followed in Somalia, Haiti, and Serbia's Kosovo region, promising a "humble" foreign policy. Following the 11 September 2001 al Qaeda attacks, nation building became central to his policy in Afghanistan and Iraq. In Africa, Bush followed a four-pronged policy of fighting terrorism, expanding trade and lowering or erasing African nations' foreign debt, working to eradicate disease, especially HIV/AIDS, malaria, and tuberculosis, and speaking out for human rights in Sudan and Zimbabwe.

Bush administration anti-terror policies in Africa included Operation Enduring Freedom–Horn of Africa (OEF-HOA) and Operation Enduring Freedom–Trans Sahara (OEF-TS), which train local military units as rapid deployment forces, provide air and sea surveillance to interdict terrorist infiltration, and assisted in bombing suspected al Qaeda units retreating from Somalia following Ethiopia's December 2006 invasion. The Trans-Sahara Counterterrorism Initiative (TSCTI) trains African armies across the Sahara and Sahel, a region that policy makers believe could become al Qaeda's primary base. Bush also oversaw creation of the U.S. Africa Command (AFRICOM), which oversees U.S. military operations in Africa except for Egypt.

Bush's debt forgiveness efforts focused initially on his Millennium Challenge Account, created in January 2004, which grants aid to developing nations that meet minimum criteria for good governance, promotion of democracy, investment in people, encouragement of economic freedom, and sound economic policy. Eleven African countries met these criteria in 2007. In 2005, Bush joined the Group of Eight (G-8) leaders of the developed world in agreeing to British Prime Minister Tony Blair's plan to eliminate in totality debt of $40 billion owed by 14 African and four Latin American nations to international development agencies. Four more countries were granted relief by 2007 and ten more were receiving partial relief for a total of $61 billion by the end of 2006. Although Bush preferred foreign trade as a means for development, he also pledged to double African aid by 2010. To that point, his administration had more than tripled African aid to $3.8 billion in 2005 compared to $1 billion provided by the Clinton administration in 2000. Bush also significantly raised the amounts of money contributed to AIDS treatment in Africa and the reduction of malaria, which he made into a foreign aid priority. The President's Emergency Plan for AIDS Relief (PEPFAR) initially was funded with $15 million over five years in 2003, and in 2008 it was reauthorized as part of a five-year, $48 billion omnibus international health bill that included funding for research and assistance for those with tuberculosis and malaria.

In Sudan, Bush walked a tightrope between working with the Sudanese government on terror-related issues—using the vast amounts of information that it had acquired from its long-standing support for al Qaeda and other radical Islamist movements—and using economic sanctions, diplomacy, and public diplomacy to pressure Sudan into reaching agreement with rebels in southern Sudan, and then attempting to end the genocide in Darfur. Bush's Zimbabwe policy was much more direct. In July 2008 he demanded that President Robert Mugabe resign and he proposed international sanctions against the Zimbabwean government that Russia and China vetoed in the UN Security Council.

The Dictionary

– A –

ACHEBE, CHINUA (1930–). Writer whose novels about life in **Nigeria** are used in U.S. high schools and colleges, providing many Americans with one of their first and most compelling sources on African history and culture. Achebe's *Things Fall Apart* (1958), the story of the devastating impact that Western colonialism had on African life and culture, is frequently used in world literature classes. Although used less often, his succeeding novels, especially *No Longer at Ease* (1960) and *Man of the People* (1966), pitilessly show the pressures and hypocrisies young educated Africans experienced after independence and the terrible impact that demagogy and tribalism have had on African political life.

During the war for independence fought by **Biafra**, Achebe served as a roving ambassador and his home was bombed by the government. In 1990 he was paralyzed from the waist down in an automobile accident and moved to the U.S. in semi-exile because of Nigeria's succession of military governments. Since 2004, he has been unable to return to Nigeria after refusing a high national honor from the government in protest against continued misrule.

ACHESON, DEAN G. (1893–1971). U.S. lawyer, secretary of state under President **Harry S. Truman** (1949–53), and statesman. Acheson was a foreign policy realist and Europeanist whose natural inclination was to focus on Europe. For Acheson, Africa was purely an adjunct of **cold war** European policy, and he did not believe African states were prepared for independence.

Egypt was the only African country that Acheson considered worthy of his time because he believed it was the gateway to the Persian

Gulf states' oil wells, because 81,000 troops from **Great Britain** in the Suez Canal Zone were a strategic reserve for European war, and because the Canal Zone's airbases were within range of petrochemical sites in the **Soviet Union**. Acheson strongly opposed U.S. recognition of **Israel** in 1948 as under secretary of state, but acquiesced after President Truman's personal intervention. In 1952, he arranged the sale of a significant quantity of arms to Egypt as a means to strengthen the revolutionary government's moderate President **Muhammad Naguib** against the more radical **Gamal Abdel Nasser** and to encourage Egyptian participation in the Middle East Defense Organization (MEDO), but Truman killed the sale because of concern that it could spur a Middle Eastern arms race and because of political pressure from Jewish American leaders.

ADOULA, CYRILLE (1921–1978). Labor leader and prime minister of **Congo**, 1961–64. Adoula came from a poor family and had little formal education. He became a labor leader thanks to his intelligence and ability to work with people of disparate economic and tribal backgrounds and because he was strongly supported by the powerful U.S. labor union, the **American Federation of Labor–Congress of International Organizations** (AFL-CIO).

Adoula was a founder and vice president of **Patrice Lumumba**'s *Mouvement National Congolais*/Congolese National Movement (MNC) in 1958. Shortly after independence in 1960, he broke with Lumumba over his increasingly dictatorial rule and became Washington's favorite to replace him as prime minister. When Lumumba was assassinated in January 1961, President **Joseph Kasavubu** chose Adoula as prime minister, and the **Central Intelligence Agency** (CIA) outbid the **Soviet Union**'s KGB and radical African governments to win legislative confirmation on 2 August. Adoula was known as hardworking, a nationalist, an opponent of tribalism, and a conciliator. He used his talents to end persecution of Lumumbists but was unsuccessful in negotiations with **Moïse Tshombe**, the president of **Katanga**, to reintegrate his breakaway republic, and with **Antoine Gizenga** to end his Communist-backed rebellion. Adoula turned to the **United Nations** (UN), asking for military assistance in crushing the rebellions, which the UN granted. As UN forces withdrew from Congo in June 1964, a Communist-backed uprising enveloped the eastern half of the country while the Congolese army fled in disarray. Kasavubu fired Adoula, replacing him with Tshombe. Adoula exiled himself, but was brought back by the military government of Joseph-Désiré Mobutu (**Mobutu Sese Seko**), for whom he served as ambassador to the U.S., ambassador to **Belgium**, and briefly as foreign minister in 1969.

AFRICAN AFFAIRS, STATE DEPARTMENT BUREAU OF. U.S. State Department bureau created in 1958 with responsibility for advising the secretary of state on sub-Saharan African affairs. The bureau's predecessor was the Division of African Affairs within the Bureau of Near Eastern, South Asian, and African Affairs, created in 1944.

Under President **Dwight D. Eisenhower**, African Affairs was populated with young Foreign Service officers who had the lowest scores on the departmental examination, poor-performing officers sent into a form of exile, and burned-out officers awaiting retirement. President **John F. Kennedy** completely changed the bureau, making the high profile appointment of former Michigan Governor **G. Mennen "Soapy" Williams** to lead it and replacing officers with many of the department's best young officials.

President **Lyndon B. Johnson** showed little interest in Africa, and the bureau lost its luster. President **Richard M. Nixon** and National Security Adviser **Henry Kissinger** further diminished African Affairs, derisively referring to it as the "Missionary Bureau." After a brief renaissance under President **Jimmy Carter**, subsequent administrations showed little interest in the bureau until President **George W. Bush**, whose second term bureau chief, Jendayi Fraser, played a significant public role on human rights and public health issues and behind the scenes to liberalize markets and push for transparent and honest government.

AFRICAN AMERICANS. People of black African heritage, most of whom are descendants of slaves brought to what is now the United States from Africa or the Caribbean. Throughout most of U.S. history, African Americans have focused on their own problems of political, social, and economic inequality, especially in the segregated South, and have played only a small role in U.S.–Africa policy. The pre-Civil War **American Colonization Society** (ACS) bought the territory that became **Liberia** and paid for several thousand freed slaves to move there. Bishop Henry McNeal Turner led a tiny "back to Africa" movement during the late 19th century that sent 500 African Americans to Liberia, but many returned complaining about the terrible conditions. Jamaican **Marcus Garvey** had greater success in raising money for the cause although less success in actually transporting people to Africa between 1916 and his conviction for mail fraud in 1923.

African Americans played the leading but unsuccessful role in calling for U.S. action against Italy during its invasion of **Ethiopia**. After World War II, the National Association for the Advancement of Colored People (NAACP) engaged in transnational diplomacy in 1948 to prevent Italy from retaking control of its African colonies. The U.S. had pressured Haiti to support Italian restoration, but the NAACP brought the leader of the Somali Youth League to speak with the Haitian delegation about the brutality of Italian rule, which caused the Haitians to ignore U.S. pressure and support the independence of Italy's colonies in the name of solidarity among colored peoples.

The year 1956 saw what historian Thomas Borstelmann called "the Awakening": the confluence of the Bandung Conference of African and Asian nations, the Montgomery bus boycott in Alabama, and the *Brown v. Board of Education* decision. While African Americans focused on the Civil Rights Movement, its tactics of nonviolent resistance spread to Africa as exemplified by the efforts of **Nelson Mandela** and the African National Congress (ANC) in **South Africa**, **Joshua Nkomo** in Southern **Rhodesia (Zimbabwe)**, and **Kenneth Kaunda** in Northern Rhodesia (**Zambia**). Violent repression and imprisonment were the results in South Africa and Southern Rhodesia, most infamously at the Sharpeville Massacre of peaceful demonstrators in South Africa, and it led Mandela and Nkomo to switch from nonviolent to violent tactics.

African Americans had the greatest impact on U.S.–Africa policy during the anti-apartheid movement in the 1980s when **TransAfrica**, a black-led civil rights organization, began the sit-in movement at the South African embassy on 21 November 1984. The protests spread across the country and focused on making universities, businesses, and government entities divest from South Africa.

Since passage of liberalized **immigration** laws in 1965, an estimated 621,000 Africans have moved to the U.S., more people than were imported during slavery. In July 2006, the estimated African American population was 40.2 million. *See also* BUNCHE, RALPH; JACKSON, JESSE; POWELL, COLIN; RICE, CONDOLEEZZA; YOUNG, ANDREW.

AFRICAN GROWTH AND OPPORTUNITY ACT (AGOA). U.S. law passed in 2000 to make importing many products from Africa duty free. AGOA was the culmination of the effort by President **Bill Clinton** to shift U.S. assistance to Africa from **foreign aid** to **trade**. AGOA is applied both to goods that are imported for consumption and some textiles. In 2006, it accounted for $44.26 billion in imports for U.S. consumption, up 16 percent from 2005. Most of these imports, 93 percent, were petroleum products. Almost half of the remaining $3.2 billion in imports (up 7 percent) was minerals and metals, transportation equipment from **South Africa**, and agricultural products, while textile and clothing imports were down 11 percent to $1.3 billion. Oil producers and South Africa have proven to be the leading beneficiaries of AGOA. *See also* EQUATORIAL GUINEA; NIGERIA.

AFRICAN UNION (AU). Successor to the **Organization of African Unity** (OAU) established 9 July 2002 with **Thabo Mbeki**, the president of **South Africa**, serving as its first chairman. The AU was created to replace the OAU in order to provide stronger support for democracy and human rights than its predecessor had done, with constitutional requirements that it follow the African Charter on Human and People's Rights, the Universal Declaration of Human Rights, and the **United Nations** (UN) Charter. Its governing structure includes the Pan-African Parliament, with 265 elected representatives from each of the 53 members (**Morocco** has refused to join because the AU recognizes the Sahrawi Arab Democratic Republic, both of which claim to be the legitimate government of the former Spanish Sahara); the Assembly of the African Union, which consists of Africa's heads of state or heads of government, meets yearly, and makes decisions by a two-thirds vote; and the African Union Commission, which is modeled after the European Union.

The AU has provided **peacekeeping** missions in Burundi in 2003–04 and **Darfur** in **Sudan** 2005 until 2007 when it merged with a **United Nations** (UN) peacekeeping force. It pledged to send peacekeepers to **Somalia** in 2007 although only troops from **Uganda** and Burundi had arrived by mid-2008. The Darfur and Somalia missions were plagued by lack of money and equipment, and the Darfur operation had trouble protecting itself from attacks by both government-backed and rebel forces. The AU saw a military success on 25 March 2008 when AU soldiers from Sudan, **Tanzania**, and Senegal, backed by logistical assistance from **France** and **Libya**, invaded the island of Anjouan and defeated rebel troops after it declared independence from the Comoro Islands. In its effort to foster democracy, the AU protested a military coup in Togo in February 2005, which pressured the government to hold an election in May 2005 that most analysts considered to be fraudulent, and it suspended Mauritania from membership following a military coup in August 2005, which led the government to hold the nation's first free and fair elections in March 2007 although that government was overthrown in August 2008. AU efforts also facilitated a political settlement in **Kenya** following disputed elections in early 2008. In July 2008, the AU heads of state summit saw vehement discussion about whether to bring sanctions against **Zimbabwe** following that country's widely criticized elections, but instead simply passed a resolution calling for the two sides to negotiate a settlement. Zimbabwe's president, **Robert Mugabe**, had served as the AU's vice chairman from 2003–04 despite allegations of past electoral fraud and ongoing human rights abuses. In 2006, President **Omar Bashir** of Sudan was scheduled to be elected chairman, but protests from some African leaders and from the U.S. led the AU to deny him the position.

AFWERKI, ISAIAS (1946–). Guerilla leader and president of **Eritrea** (1991–), who was recognized by President **Bill Clinton** as a leader of the "African Renaissance" just months before he began a disastrous war against **Ethiopia** and ended plans to approve a multiparty constitution. Afwerki was a Communist college student who rebelled in September 1966 against **Haile Selassie**'s Ethiopian monarchy to fight for Eritrea's freedom. His brilliance and doggedness led Eritrea to victory in 1991 against overwhelming odds, but his arrogance as president alienated U.S., African, and European leaders, including erstwhile ally **Meles Zenawi**, Ethiopia's president.

In May 1998, war broke out with Ethiopia. The following month, Afwerki rejected a peace proposal by the U.S. and **Rwanda**. When fighting turned badly against Eritrea, the **Organization of American Unity** (OAU) was uninterested in starting peace talks because of Afwerki's bitter criticism of the OAU as being led by dictators who had done nothing to help his people. Afwerki finally went to the **United Nations** (UN) for help in 2002, and they negotiated a peace similar to the U.S.–Rwandan proposal that he had rejected. The UN sent a **peacekeeping** force that continued to separate the combatants in mid-2008. Eritrea claimed to have lost 19,000 soldiers, but outside estimates range up to 50,000. Afwerki used the war and its continued threat as an excuse to halt implementation of a multiparty constitution and elections, close all independent newspapers, and close the borders to keep Eritreans from leaving the country. When 15 top Eritrean military and political leaders, including lifelong friends, questioned Afwerki's wartime leadership, continued one-man rule, and governing style that included physically attacking cabinet members and generals who angered him, 11 disappeared.

Following the 11 September 2001 attacks, the U.S. consulted Afwerki about using Eritrea's port in Assab as a naval base, but Afwerki refused to free two U.S. diplomats who had been illegally arrested during his crackdown on the opposition. The U.S. rejected the base, opting to locate in Djibouti. Afwerki also antagonized the U.S. by supporting **al Qaeda** and the Islamic Courts Union (ICU) government of **Somalia** in 2006. Afwerki had been a strong proponent of the **Global War on Terror** (GWOT) before supporting the ICU, but the ICU's bitter opposition to Ethiopia made them an automatic Eritrean ally and he provided them with 2,000 fully provisioned soldiers and weapons. After their defeat from an Ethiopian invasion that was supported by the U.S., Afwerki allowed ICU leaders to flee to Eritrea. In mid-2008, the U.S. was considering sanctioning Eritrea by adding it to its list of **terrorism**-supporting governments. *See also* IMMIGRATION; REFUGEES.

AGENCY FOR INTERNATIONAL DEVELOPMENT, UNITED STATES (AID). Foreign assistance agency created by President

John F. Kennedy to consolidate numerous separate aid agencies, coordinate their efforts, and expand U.S. **foreign aid** beyond the technical assistance provided by the administrations of **Harry S. Truman** and **Dwight D. Eisenhower.** Central to AID's mission was centralized long-term national planning based on **modernization theory** to help underdeveloped nations plan national development programs that included such disparate areas as industrialization, labor relations, teacher training, and land reform, as well as macroeconomic analysis. By the 1970s, family planning and environmental stewardship were added to AID's mission.

AID makes contracts with over 3,500 companies and 350 **nongovernmental organizations** (NGOs). For example, it contracts with the **American Federation of Labor–Council of Industrial Organizations** (AFL-CIO) to train African unions in such areas as collective bargaining, and works with the **Centers for Disease Control and Prevention** (CDC) to control diseases such as **AIDS** and malaria, in addition to providing technical assistance. AID has also provided a cover for **Central Intelligence Agency** (CIA) agents to infiltrate third-world countries.

Since the administration of President **Ronald W. Reagan** and particularly since the **Bill Clinton** presidency, AID has shifted its focus to assisting countries with their efforts to liberalize their internal and external markets, working through NGOs instead of working with African governments in order to avoid corruption, and assisting with creation and implementation of projects that promote sustainable development. In fiscal year 2008, President **George W. Bush** requested $5.214 billion for AID to provide development assistance to Africa. In addition, since 2004 AID has led the U.S. government's effort in providing $3 billion for humanitarian programs in the **Darfur** region of **Sudan** and neighboring eastern **Chad**, where many Darfurian refugees have fled. In fiscal year 2008, the Bush administration requested over $579 million for Darfur.

AIDEED, MUHAMMAD FARAH (1930?–1996). Clan leader, warlord, and president of **Somalia** (1995–96), whose forces drove the United States and the **United Nations** (UN) out of Somalia. Aideed served as a police officer, army general, and ambassador under **Muhammad Siad Barré**, who had also jailed Aideed for five years at the beginning of his reign. In 1989, Aideed became leader of a powerful clan and opposed Siad, and in 1991 led the attack that drove Siad out of Mogadishu, the capital.

Like Siad, Aideed intentionally used starvation to crush his opponents, preventing food aid from getting to famine areas and prompting **Operation Restore Hope**, the U.S.-led UN rescue mission to feed Somalia's starving. Aideed initially allowed U.S. forces to feed the hungry, but was threatened by the expanded state-building mission that President **Bill Clinton** and the UN launched to disarm the competing militias. Aideed massacred 24 Pakistani peacekeepers on 5 June 1993, and the UN mission commander, retired U.S. Navy Admiral Jonathan Howe, put a bounty on his head. Aideed ambushed U.S. forces at the Battle of Mogadishu on 3 October. In a two-day battle, 18 U.S. soldiers and as many as 1,000 Somalis died. The battle effectively ended the UN mission when Clinton ordered U.S. forces to avoid combat operations until their withdrawal. Unknown to the world at the time, Aideed was secretly working with **al Qaeda** leader **Osama bin Laden**, whose forces trained Aideed's militia and may have participated in the battle.

After driving out the U.S. and UN, Aideed used the momentum of his victories to take control of Somalia. On 15 June 1995, clan leaders elected Aideed president, but his success bred resentment among his allies and civil war began anew. Aideed was shot in battle and died in his home on 2 August 1996. He was replaced as militia leader by his 34-year-old son, a former U.S. Marine and U.S. citizen who had fought on the U.S. side during Operation Restore Hope.

AIDS (ACQUIRED IMMUNODEFICIENCY SYNDROME). Usually fatal disease native to Central Africa, which has spread throughout the world. AIDS has hit Africa especially hard, with an estimated 25 million people suffering from AIDS or HIV (human immunodeficiency virus), its precursor. **Bill Clinton** was the first U.S. president to push for a worldwide effort to fight the AIDS crisis in Africa, but he made so little progress that in July 2002 he told the International AIDS Conference that he regretted not having done more to fight AIDS. His William J. Clinton Foundation and the Bill & Melinda Gates Foundation have done much work on fighting worldwide AIDS. **George W. Bush** was the first president to make a serious and successful push for dramatically increased U.S. funding for research and treatment.

In mid-2008, Bush's program to fight AIDS, the President's Emergency Plan for AIDS Relief (PEPFAR) supported anti-retroviral treatment for approximately 1.4 million people with HIV/AIDS and care for 10 million, most of them in Africa. PEPFAR initially was funded with $15 million over five years in 2003. In 2008 it was reauthorized as part of a five-year, $48 billion omnibus international health bill that included funding for research and assistance for those with tuberculosis and malaria.

Southern Africa has been the region of the world hardest hit by HIV/AIDS, with 67 percent of the world's HIV cases and 72 percent of the world's yearly AIDS deaths. **Zimbabwe** is believed to have the world's highest HIV/AIDS prevalence rate but the collapse of its medical system makes measurement impossible. **Botswana** has the world's second-highest rate, with 37 percent of the population suffering from HIV/AIDS, which has reduced life expectancy from 67 to 34 years. The rate in **South Africa** is also very high, estimated at 21.5 percent in 2004, and South Africa has more people suffering from HIV/AIDS than any other country, with estimates between 5.7 and 6.4 million people in 2004. The Bush administration used public and behind-the-scenes pressure to push South African President **Thabo Mbeki** away from an AIDS-skeptic position to at least intermittent support for pharmaceutical treatment for HIV/AIDS victims and pharmaceutical treatment to prevent the spread of HIV/AIDS from mother to infant.

Uganda was the first African country to reverse its HIV/AIDS numbers, cutting infections from an early 1990s high of 12 percent to 6 percent in 2006. The Ugandan reversal was not replicated elsewhere in Africa in large part because while **United Nations** (UN) and **non-governmental organizations** (NGOs) working on AIDS in Africa followed Uganda's condom distribution model, they did not seek to apply what Ugandans called "Zero Grazing" and "love Carefully": a "partner reduction strategy" that called on people to avoid indiscriminate sex, an important message in societies where polygamy and concubinage are traditional and accepted practices.

In mid-2007, the UN's chief AIDS researcher revised downward from 40 million to 33 million the number of people worldwide suffering from AIDS, and admitted that the HIV infection rate was 40 percent below what researchers had previously believed. By the end of 2007, thanks to global efforts to fight the disease, new HIV/AIDS infections had declined from 5 million per year in the early 2000s to 2.7 million, and yearly deaths had declined from 2.2 million in 2005 to 2 million.

AKELEY, CARL (1864–1926). U.S. explorer and naturalist, whose natural history museum exhibits of African wildlife played a crucial role in creating American interest in Africa and the conservation of its animals. Akeley created the use of dioramas, exhibits used for science education that display taxidermically preserved animals in artistically rendered examples of their natural habitat. Akeley's work was the basis for the Hall of African Mammals at the American Museum of History in New York. His work in support of mountain gorilla preservation led **Belgium** to create the Parc Nationale Albert, Africa's first national park, in 1925. Akeley died in the Belgian Congo (**Congo**) while collecting specimens.

AL QAEDA. Islamist terrorist organization founded and led by **Osama bin Laden** that has as its immediate goals to create Islamist governments in all Muslim nations, expel Western influences from the Muslim world, and destroy **Israel**. Bin Laden issued a February 1998 *fatwa* proclaiming it a religious duty to kill Americans. Al Qaeda is an Arabic word for "the base" or various synonyms.

Al Qaeda was based in **Sudan**, 1992–96, under the protection of that country's spiritual leader, **Hassan Turabi**, but was expelled to Afghanistan because of **United Nations** (UN) sanctions against Sudan following al Qaeda's attempted assassination of President **Hosni Mubarak** of **Egypt**. Al Qaeda has been active in **Somalia**, assisting **Muhammad Farah Aideed** in his fight against U.S.-led UN forces in August 1993, and infiltrating the Islamist Islamic Courts Union (ICU) government in 2006. Al Qaeda was also responsible for the destruction of U.S. embassies in **Kenya** and **Tanzania** in August 1998.

Following the 11 September 2001 attacks in the United States, President **George W. Bush** ordered the creation of **Operation Enduring Freedom–Trans Sahara** (OEF-TS) and **Operation Enduring Freedom–Horn of Africa** (OEF-HOA) as part of his **Global**

War on Terror (GWOT). OEF-HOA played a significant role in assisting **Ethiopia** to overthrow Somalia's ICU government by providing intelligence and reconnaissance, interdicting al Qaeda efforts to provide sea support, and launching air and sea strikes on suspected al Qaeda positions. *See also* ALGERIA; BLOOD DIAMONDS; TERRORISM; TRANS-SAHARA COUNTERTERRORISM INITIATIVE (TSCTI).

ALBRIGHT, MADELEINE (1937–). U.S. academic, ambassador to the **United Nations** (UN) during the administration of President **Bill Clinton** (1993–97), and first woman to serve as secretary of state (1997–2001), also under Clinton. As UN ambassador, Albright disagreed with the Clinton administration's decision to remove UN **peacekeeping** forces from **Rwanda** at the beginning of the April 1994 genocide. She later reported that she screamed at National Security Council (NSC) aide Richard Clarke that some troops had to stay, and was able to work out a compromise in which the 2,500-man force would only be cut to 550.

As secretary of state, during a December 1997 visit with **Congo**'s President **Laurent-Désiré Kabila**, Albright snubbed opposition leaders in a show of support for Kabila, then was embarrassed at a joint press conference when Kabila furiously responded to a question about longtime opposition leader Étienne Tshisekedi, who had recently been jailed and tortured by Kabila's government, telling reporters that anyone who tried to divide the country would be jailed. Albright supported the July 1999 efforts of **Jesse Jackson**, the president's special envoy for African democratization, to end the civil war in **Sierra Leone** by forcing the government of President Ahmad Kabbah to accept Foday Sankoh's Revolutionary United Front (RUF) in the government with Sankoh as vice president (he was at the time under a death sentence for crimes against humanity), and by giving Sankoh ministerial control over the country's diamond mines.

In April and May 1998, Albright did not respond to urgent personal warnings from U.S. Ambassador to **Kenya** Prudence Bushnell that intelligence sources had repeatedly warned her that **al Qaeda** operatives were targeting the embassy, and that the embassy was physically insecure. On 7 August, the embassy was attacked with car bombs, killing 12 U.S. diplomats and over 200 Kenyans.

ALGERIA. Northwest African nation that fought a bloody and successful war for independence from **France**. Algeria was one of the **Barbary Pirates** states that periodically preyed upon U.S. shipping from the American Revolution until 1815. Algeria was then known as the Regency and had local autonomous power in the Ottoman Empire. Algerian corsairs attacked U.S. ships from 1785 until a treaty was signed in 1795, and then resumed in 1815 before being forced to accept U.S. terms later that year, concluding the Barbary Wars. During World War II, General **Dwight D. Eisenhower** ordered **Operation Torch**, which included Allied invasions of Oran and Algiers on 8 November 1942, laying the groundwork for the invasion of Italy the following year.

During the Algerian war for independence from **France**, begun in 1954, President Eisenhower exerted behind-the-scenes pressure on the French government in an unsuccessful effort to win the colony's freedom. His policy was criticized in two speeches by Senator John F. Kennedy, who called on Eisenhower to push France to surrender Algerian independence. Kennedy's administration was more public in its calls for independence, but Kennedy refrained from pushing too hard on French President Charles de Gaulle, worrying that too precipitate independence for Algeria could lead to his overthrow, which Kennedy said would worsen the position of Algeria and other French colonies. De Gaulle freed Algeria on 3 July 1962.

Algeria's first leader, **Ahmed Ben Bella** was a passionate nationalist, anti-colonialist, and socialist. Kennedy met with Ben Bella at the White House on 15 October 1962. Kennedy had a good opinion of him, but two days later, Ben Bella shocked and infuriated the president when he flew directly to **Cuba** to meet with Fidel Castro and give him a full report about his meeting. Ben Bella warned Castro that the U.S. would use Cuban assistance to Latin American liberation movements as a pretext to invade, and said that Algeria was in a better position to do this internationalist revolutionary duty than was Cuba. Ben Bella also joined Castro in demanding that the U.S. return its Guantánamo naval base to Cuba. When the Cuban missile crisis broke out a few days later, Ben Bella returned to Kennedy's good graces when he assured him that Algeria would not allow airplanes from the **Soviet Union** to refuel on their way to re-supply Cuba.

Thereafter, Ben Bella criticized Kennedy's Vietnam policy and accused the U.S. of supporting imperialism. Nonetheless, the president continued to pay close scrutiny to Algeria and believed that Ben Bella's radicalism would calm as colonialism gave way to independence across the continent. When famine hit Algeria in the winter of 1962–63, Kennedy ordered Food for Peace to be rushed into the country, ultimately feeding one-third of the population, which continued until 1965. Unknown to Kennedy, Ben Bella allowed Fidel Castro to use Algeria as a base for training Latin American revolutionaries, and also provided them with fake IDs and weapons.

Shortly after President **Lyndon B. Johnson** took office, the Algerian ambassador was warned that the new president did not share Kennedy's long-standing interest in Algeria, and so his government should try to tone down its rhetoric. It did not, and Ben Bella began to assist rebels in **Congo**. The U.S. government welcomed the 19 June 1965 military coup that placed Ben Bella under house arrest and elevated Colonel Houari Boumédienne to the presidency because Boumédienne was known as an ardent socialist who wanted to focus on industrialization and improving the dismal Algerian economy rather than emphasizing foreign policy. The following month Johnson met with the Algerian ambassador and angrily told him that his government had to subdue its criticism of U.S. policy in Vietnam, but the Algerians would not, so Johnson personally stopped economic assistance.

During the **Arab–Israeli War of 1967**, Algeria broke relations with the U.S. and nationalized U.S.-owned **oil** companies. Relations were not restored until 1974. Washington again cut off aid. In the months following, Boumédienne so vociferously demanded the war's resumption that he frightened both the U.S. and the **Soviet Union**. Despite his radicalism, Boumédienne sought a middle path between the two superpowers, and at the Fourth Conference of the Non-Aligned Movement, held in Algiers, tried to persuade delegates to declare the U.S. and the Soviet Union the "two imperialisms." He was beaten by Cuba's Castro, who convinced the group to condemn only the U.S. and the West for their "aggressive imperialism."

Boumédienne's successor, Chadli Benjedid, played a facilitating role in the liberation of the U.S. hostages held by Iran, serving as a conduit between the governments. The final agreement that freed the hostages, known as the Algiers Accords, was signed 19 January 1981. The government of President **George H.W. Bush** condemned the Algerian military for suspending elections on 17 January 1992 that the *Front Islamique du Salut*/Islamic Salvation Front (FIS), an Islamist party, was poised to win. Civil war and **terrorism** followed, led by the *Mouvement Islamique Armé*/Islamic Armed Movement (MIA) and the *Groupe Islamique Armé*/Armed Islamic Group (GIA). The administration of President **Bill Clinton** was more sympathetic following the World Trade Center bombing in 1993. Washington provided assistance during the civil war, which lasted until June 2002 and killed as many as 200,000 people.

Algeria was one of the first Arab countries to support the U.S. following the 11 September 2001 attacks by **al Qaeda**, and both countries work together closely on terror-related issues, especially through **Operation Enduring Freedom–Trans Sahara** (OEF-TS) and the **Trans-Sahara Counterterrorism Initiative** (TSCTI). On 9 March 2004, U.S. special forces supported an Algerian operation that killed the second-highest ranking member of a remaining terrorist splinter group, the *Groupe Salafiste pour la Prédication et le Combat*/ Salafist Group for Preaching and Combat (GSPC). In January 2007, the GSPC announced its affiliation with al Qaeda and that it had changed its name to the Al Qaeda Organization in the Islamic Maghreb.

ALI, MUHAMMAD (1942–). U.S. boxer. Ali's reigns as World Heavyweight Champion, his conversion to the Black Muslim religion, and his larger-than-life persona made him one of the world's best-known men. His 30 October 1974 Kinshasa, **Zaïre (Congo)**, fight against George Foreman, known as the "Rumble in the Jungle," marked the high point of **Mobutu Sese Seko**'s effort to make **Zaïre** a center of African culture and political life.

Because of Ali's unique international status and his **African American** heritage, President **Jimmy Carter** sent him to Africa as a special envoy to urge African nations to boycott the 1980 Moscow Olympics in response to the invasion of Afghanistan by the **Soviet Union**. Ali visited five African nations. He frequently received critical treatment because many Africans believed the Carter administration was pandering by sending an African American athlete rather than a key administration foreign policy figure, as had been sent to other regions of the world. Africans also complained about U.S. hypocrisy over its failure to join an African boycott of the 1976 Montreal Olympics in response to participation by racist **South Africa**.

Ali's wounded pride over his reception in Africa played a significant role in his decision to make a boxing comeback against world champion Larry Holmes. The severe beating he received strongly contributed to his early onset of Parkinson's Disease. *See also* SPORTS.

AMERICAN COLONIZATION SOCIETY (ACS). Organization founded on 16 December 1816 with the purpose of sending freed **African Americans** to Africa. The ACS was created in the wake of 18th-century religious revivals in the United States that turned many Americans against slavery, and because of the growing belief that freed slaves could not live peaceably with their former masters. The purpose of the ACS was to buy land in Africa and send freed slaves and those liberated from illegal slaving ships to live there. In this, its leaders were following the example that **Great Britain** had started with **Sierra Leone** in 1787. Among the ACS founders were leading U.S. citizens, including Speaker of the House of Representatives Henry Clay and George Washington's nephew and heir, U.S. Supreme Court Justice Bushrod Washington.

In 1819, President James Monroe persuaded Congress to appropriate $100,000 for the Society. Several expeditions were sent to find an appropriate location, but local African chiefs refused to sell land for a colony until 15 December 1821 when a U.S. naval officer forced a local chief at gunpoint to sell Cape Mersurado, the site of modern Monrovia. The first settlers arrived the next year and named the territory **Liberia**. The great expense of maintaining Liberia ultimately led the ACS to instruct the settlers to declare the colony's independence, which was done on 26 July 1847. From 1847–1892, the ACS continued to assist African Americans to move to Liberia and it operated the only boat that annually sailed there from the U.S. From 1892–1904, it focused its energies on strengthening Liberia by building a public-school system, disseminating information in the U.S., and assisting missionaries' efforts. The ACS ended most of its activities in 1904, although it joined other **non-governmental organiza-**

tions (NGOs) in funding creation of the **Booker T. Washington** Institute in 1929. The ACS dissolved itself in 1963.

In all, the ACS helped over 16,400 African Americans and freedmen in Barbados to immigrate to Liberia and, beginning in 1808, delivered over 5,700 Africans captured on slaving vessels. *See also* AMERICO-LIBERIANS.

AMERICAN FEDERATION OF LABOR–CONGRESS OF INDUSTRIAL ORGANIZATIONS (AFL-CIO). U.S. trade union organization that followed a strongly anti-Communist policy and worked to build anti-Communist trade unions in Africa. The AFL-CIO opposed colonialism and **apartheid** although at times its anti-communism could mute its opposition to each. The union was especially close to **Congo**'s trade union leader and future prime minister **Cyrille Adoula**, and to **Kenya**'s trade union leader and future government minister **Thomas Mboya**. To build up African trade unions' capacity and skills, the AFL-CIO set up the **African American** Institute (AAI) in Kampala, **Uganda**, as a school to train African trade unionists. Most of the institute's early funding was later revealed to have been provided by the **Central Intelligence Agency** (CIA).

During the 1970s, the AFL-CIO was considered to be weak in its opposition to apartheid in **South Africa** until 1978, when **Donald Woods** spoke to the leadership about the life and murder of **Stephen Biko**, the leader of the Black Consciousness Movement. The union's leadership immediately voted to support **divestment** from South Africa and strongly supported the **Sullivan Principles** for equal rights in the workplace. Since the **cold war**, the AFL-CIO has supported workers' rights against the international push for free **trade** and called for multinational businesses in Africa to improve treatment of the environment.

AMERICO-LIBERIANS. Former slaves from the United States who emigrated to **Liberia**, and their descendants. In all, some 16,400 **African Americans** and Barbadians moved to Liberia since 1820, and their descendants continue to dominate Liberian political and economic life. Until President **William Tubman**, the Americo-Liberians did not give the indigenous peoples civil or political rights, and in 1930 the League of Nations found that high government officials were engaged in selling them into forced labor akin to slavery. Every Liberian president except for **Samuel Doe** and **Ellen Johnson-Sirleaf** had at least one parent who was an America-Liberian. In 2008, approximately 150,000 America-Liberians lived in Liberia, 5 percent of the population. *See also* ASHMUN, JEHUDI; IMMIGRATION; SIERRA LEONE; TAYLOR, CHARLES; TOLBERT, WILLIAM.

AMIN DADA, IDI (1925?–2003). Soldier and president of **Uganda** (1971–79). Amin became internationally famous for his buffoonish but often humorous antics and for his brutality that resulted in the deaths of over 250,000 people. As military commander, he came to power on 25 January 1971, overthrowing and forestalling plans by President Milton Obote to arrest him. The coup was greeted happily by Ugandans because Obote's often brutal dictatorship had become unpopular.

By July 1971, Amin began ordering the massacre of opponents or members of those from tribes that had supported Obote. In August 1972, Amin strengthened his popularity at home and across Africa when he ordered the expulsion of Uganda's 80,000 East Indians (Asians) and the confiscation of their property as well as the property of Europeans. This move proved economically disastrous because it robbed the Ugandan economy of its businessmen and merchants, and Amin gave most of the confiscated land and businesses to his cronies, who looted them. Amin also derisively but amusingly attacked Western political leaders. His elevation to the chair of the **Organization of African Unity** (OAU) in 1975–76 did much to harm the credibility of the organization in the United States, and U.S. commentators were shocked when he received a hero's welcome from the other heads of state.

Amin developed close relations with President **Muammar Qaddafi** of **Libya** and with the Palestine Liberation Organization (PLO). When Palestinian terrorists hijacked an airplane to Entebbe Airport in Uganda, Amin gave assistance to the hijackers, and was stunned when Israeli paratroopers rescued most of the hostages. Amin retaliated by ordering the execution of an elderly woman hostage who had been hospitalized. As Uganda's economy collapsed and reports emerged that Amin had killed over 200,000 Ugandans, the U.S. Congress passed a **trade** embargo in October 1978. Days later, rebellious Ugandan troops invaded **Tanzania**. Tanzanian President **Julius Nyerere** called Amin "a murderer, a liar and a savage," and ordered a counterinvasion that overthrew Amin on 11 April 1979. Nyerere restored to power Obote, who was subsequently overthrown by guerilla forces led by **Yoweri Museveni**. Amin fled to Libya and then Saudi Arabia, where he remained until his death. Amin's final toll is generally estimated to have been over 250,000 dead Ugandans, but exile organizations assisted by Amnesty International put the total at 500,000.

ANGOLA. Southwestern African nation that fought a successful war for independence from **Portugal** followed by a 28-year civil war. Three guerilla movements fought for independence, **Agostinho Neto**'s *Movimento Popular de Libertação de Angola*/Popular Movement for the Liberation of Angola (MPLA), backed by **Cuba** and the Eastern Bloc, **Holden Roberto**'s *Frente Nacional de Libertação de Angola*/National Liberation Front of Angola (FNLA), and **Jonas Savimbi**'s *União Nacional para a Independência Total de Angola*/National Union for the Total Independence of Angola (UNITA), both of which were backed by **Zaïre**, **South Africa**, **Zambia**, **China**, the United States, and several other African countries. Following its Carnation Revolution in April 1974, Portugal announced that it would grant its colonies their independence, with Angola's freedom coming on 11 November 1975. The civil war and outside interference increased tremendously as each side fought for control of the country. The MPLA won the civil war in December 1975 thanks to the intervention of 12,000 Cuban troops.

Until his death in 1979, Neto proceeded to communize Angola, except for **oil** fields owned by Gulf Oil (which became part of Chevron in 1984). His successor, José Eduardo dos Santos, continued along the Communist path and allowed tremendous corruption. The MPLA's repression led to resurgence by the resilient Jonas Savimbi, whose UNITA continued to receive covert support from South Africa and Zaïre. In the 1980s, Savimbi became a darling of U.S. conservatives such as Senator **Jesse Helms** and received millions of dollars of support from President **Ronald W. Reagan** in pursuit of his **Reagan Doctrine** of rolling back third-world communism, and from the administration of **George H.W. Bush**, an estimated $250 million in all. Reagan even unsuccessfully sued Gulf in an attempt to stop it from doing business with the MPLA.

Cuban troops were removed in stages between 1 April 1989 and 26 May 1991 as part of the **New York Accords** signed by Angola, Cuba, and South Africa at the **United Nations** on 22 December 1988. The accords were the result of pressure by the U.S. and the Soviet Union as part of their joint effort to end the **cold war**. They required South Africa to give **Namibia** its independence in exchange for the Cuban withdrawal from Angola. Following the accords, continued U.S. and Soviet cooperation forced the Angolan government and Savimbi to sign a peace agreement in May 1991. The UN sent **peacekeeping** troops but lacked money and the troops' mission was circumscribed. Savimbi ran for president against dos Santos in September 1992, came in second in the first round of voting, claimed that the election was stolen, and returned to the bush after he and his advisers fought their way out of the capital, Luanda, but thousands of his supporters were killed.

President **Bill Clinton** refused to resume funding UNITA, and South Africa's transition to majority rule in 1994 left Savimbi almost bereft of outside assistance, so he agreed to peace again in November 1994. The UN committed itself to melding a national unity government, but the MPLA worked to undermine Savimbi politically while murdering UNITA leaders in the countryside, and Savimbi resumed the war. The fall of Zaïre's **Mobutu Sese Seko** in 1997 and the accession to power with Angolan assistance of **Laurent-Désiré Kabila** squeezed Savimbi. The Angolan government launched a major offensive against him in December 1998, which was supported by the U.S., including U.S. government experts providing military assistance in the form of advice on counterinsurgency. At the same time, the U.S. role in Angolan oil expanded at the expense of European competitors. Savimbi was finally ambushed, hunted down, and killed on 22 February 2002. UNITA surrendered weeks later. Following Savimbi's death, government repression and corruption continued with elections scheduled for 2008 and 2009.

ANNAN, KOFI (1938–). Diplomat and first secretary-general of the **United Nations** (UN) from sub-Saharan Africa (1997–2007). Born and raised in **Ghana**, Annan received much of his education in the United States, earning his bachelor's degree from Macalaster College in St. Paul, Minnesota, and a master's degree in management from the Massachusetts Institute of Technology. He held numerous positions for the UN and in Ghana beginning in 1962.

From 1993–94, Annan was UN assistant secretary-general for **peacekeeping** operations. As such, he oversaw peacekeeping in **Rwanda**, which had been suffering civil war. He ignored reports from the commander of UN forces in Rwanda, General Roméo Dallaire, that the "Hutu Power" government planned to launch the Rwandan Genocide against the Tutsi minority, and he refused to allow Dallaire to confiscate weapons caches that leaders of the government-backed **Interahamwe** paramilitary planned to use to execute the genocide. The resulting mass murder killed over 937,000 people. Dallaire later reported that Annan slowed down UN assistance to his forces after the genocide began. Following the genocide, Annan said that he had followed proper procedures and in hindsight, would have done nothing differently.

Annan became secretary-general on 1 January 1997 with the strong support of the U.S. after the U.S. vetoed a second term for Secretary-General **Boutros Boutros-Ghali** of **Egypt**. As secretary-general, Annan made fighting HIV/**AIDS** and other infectious diseases a major priority and pushed through creation of the Global Fund to Fight AIDS, Tuberculosis, and Malaria in January 2002. Under his leadership, the UN oversaw a notably successful peacekeeping operation in East Timor and generally expanded its peacekeeping duties.

In 2003, Annan worked to prevent the U.S. and **Great Britain** from invading Iraq. The following year, it was revealed that the UN's "oil for food" program in Iraq, which was in operation between the two Gulf Wars, had been used to funnel $17 billion illegally to Iraqi President Saddam Hussein by, among others, UN officials including Annan's close aide, Benan Sevan, and officials from several governments, including Russia and **France**. The final report on the UN's investigation made an "adverse finding" against Annan, showing that he had known about the "kickback scheme" as early as February 2001 but had not informed the Security Council or the public. Also under Annan's tenure, peacekeeping forces in several countries, including **Guinea**, **Congo**, **Sudan**, and **Sierra Leone**, were involved in corruption and sexual exploitation of refugees, but the UN took no action against the perpetrators.

Annan was a strong supporter of increased **foreign aid** from the developed world to the third world, and was particularly critical of the U.S for lagging in this area. He also was responsible for establishing the UN's Millennium Development Goals in September 2000, which call for wealthy countries to provide enough foreign aid that by 2015, the world will have eradicated extreme poverty and hunger, achieved universal primary education, promoted gender equality and the empowerment of women, reduced mortality of children under five years old by two-thirds, improved maternal health, combated deadly infectious diseases like HIV/AIDS and malaria, ensured development that maintains a sustainable environment, and developed a global partnership for development. The following year, Annan and the UN shared the Nobel Peace in recognition of their work "for a better organized and more peaceful world."

Annan made strong statements against corruption and tyranny in Africa when speaking at African summits. In July 2000, he told African leaders at the **Organization of African Unity** (OAU) heads of state summit that they were to blame for most of the continent's problems because of their failures to promote development and peace, which led to the developed world's withdrawal of foreign aid. Afterwards, he said that Africa took up 60 to 70 percent of his time. In retirement, Annan has continued to work on international issues, and in 2008 he brokered a successful settlement to the political crisis in **Kenya**.

APARTHEID. Policy of "separate development" by the white-minority government of **South Africa**, which began in 1948 with the coming to power of the Afrikaner-dominated National Party, and lasted until shortly before black-majority rule in 1994. The goal of apartheid (Afrikaans, apartness) was for each black tribe to receive its own independent tribal homeland, known as *Bantustans*. The *Bantustans* were tiny, noncontiguous, overcrowded, and mostly farmed out, populated primarily by women, children, and old people. Despite blacks making up approximately 75 percent of South Africa's population, *Bantustans* consisted of only 13 percent of South Africa's total land area and included no harbors, mines, or major cities.

Blacks were kept on the *Bantustans* through the "pass law" system, which required every black over the age of 15 to carry a pass, like an internal passport, which included the person's tribe and whether or not they had the legal right to reside in white-reserved areas. By legally requiring that every black reside in a tribal homeland, the government could control the population while keeping black labor in white-reserved areas illegal, migratory, and thus cheap and easily controlled. Periodically, police swept into shantytowns built on the edge of cities to check residents' passes. Sometimes thousands of people without the legal right to live in the shantytown would be rounded up, put on buses, and shipped to their homelands, often a place that they had never even visited before. A second means of enforcing apartheid was "banning" prominent people who spoke out against apartheid. Banned whites would be restricted to their home towns, banned blacks to their *Bantustans* for a legally determined period during which they would be unable to speak in public or to the press and would be restricted in the number of nonfamily members that they could see at one time.

Although apartheid kept the price of most unskilled labor low, it was primarily created in 1948 to protect poor and uneducated Afrikaners, which was done by making it illegal for businesses to hire cheap black labor when white labor was available to do the job, reserving some types of jobs for whites only, and making it illegal to promote blacks above whites. The added expense of apartheid ultimately turned South African businessmen against the system.

Along with separate development, apartheid included "petty apartheid," the *de jure* practice of enforced separation in everything from marriage to separate restrooms, water fountains, and beaches, as well as segregated schools. Because these were an obvious and easily understood target for protest by anti-apartheid activists at home and abroad, including the movement for economic sanctions, President **P.W. Botha** ended petty apartheid in the early 1980s, and repealed the pass laws in 1986, responding also to the **Constructive Engagement** policy of President **Ronald W. Reagan**. The combination of economic damage caused by economic sanctions, the increasing economic dysfunction that apartheid caused South African business, public weariness at being an international pariah, and the defeat of the **Soviet Union** in the **cold war**, led President **F.W. de Klerk** to "unban" the African National Congress (ANC) and the South African Communist Party, free **Nelson Mandela**, and begin negotiating with Mandela for the transition to majority rule, which was achieved in May 1994. *See also* COMPREHENSIVE ANTI-APARTHEID ACT; DIVESTMENT (DISINVESTMENT) FROM SOUTH AFRICA MOVEMENT; FILM; PATON, ALAN; TRANSAFRICA; VORSTER, BALTHAZAR JOHANNES (JOHN).

ARAB–ISRAELI WAR OF 1948–49. Attempt by five Arab states (**Egypt**, Jordan, Syria, Lebanon, and Iraq) to destroy **Israel**, launched on 15 May 1948, the day after the Jewish state declared independence. The Israeli army defeated its opponents on 7 January 1949 following a series of three campaigns that expanded Israeli territory, providing strategic depth and access to the Red Sea. Peace negotiations were overseen for the **United Nations** (UN) by **Ralph Bunche**, an **African American** diplomat who worked for the secretary-general. Although Bunche could only get the belligerents to agree to armistices rather than a peace treaty and recognition of Israel's right to exist, he won the Nobel Peace Prize in 1950 for his work. *See also* ACHESON, DEAN G.; FAROUK I; NAGUIB, MUHAMMAD; NASSER, GAMAL ABDEL; TRUMAN, HARRY S.

ARAB–ISRAELI WAR OF 1967. Known to the West as the Six-Day War and to the Arabs as "the Setback," this war, which lasted from 5–10 June 1967, was a devasting defeat for **Egypt** and President **Gamal Abdel Nasser**'s dream of Pan-Arab nationalism. Egypt, Syria, and Jordan lost strategically important territory to **Israel**, including Egypt's loss of the Gaza Strip and Sinai Penninsula. Nasser was forced to rely much more closely on the **Soviet Union** to rebuild his destroyed military power, and he gave the Soviets access to Egyptian military bases for the first time. He also accused the United States of having participated in the Israeli attack, severed relations, and expelled thousands of U.S. citizens. In May 1971, Nasser's successor, **Anwar Sadat**, signed a Treaty of Peace and Cooperation with the Soviets. The Israeli government concluded that Egypt and its allies had been irremediably weakened by the war, and proved obdurate in the face of Egyptian and occasional U.S. efforts to restart the peace process. *See also* JOHNSON, LYNDON B.; RUSK, DEAN; UNITED NATIONS (UN).

ARAB–ISRAELI WAR OF 1973. Also known as the Ramadan War, the War of the Crossing, the October War, and the Yom Kippur War. Although it ended in defeat for **Egypt**, this 20-day war reestablished Egypt's military reputation, showed **oil**-producing Arab states their economic power when they precipitated a worldwide recession by cutting off oil sales to the West, forced **Israel** to realize that military power alone would not guarantee peace, and jolted U.S. President **Richard M. Nixon** and National Security Adviser **Henry Kissinger** into taking the lead in bringing the parties together through "**shuttle diplomacy.**" *See also* SADAT, ANWAR AL-.

ARMSTRONG, LOUIS ("SATCHMO") (1901–1971). African **American** musician who was one of the key figures in jazz **music**. A brilliant trumpeter and singer, Armstrong was considered the greatest jazz performer of all time. He was known as "Ambassador Satch" because of his role in bringing jazz to all parts of the world, including Africa. After a hugely successful tour of the Gold Coast (**Ghana**) in 1956, the U.S. Information Agency (USIA) sent Armstrong on a 15-country, 27-concert African tour in 1960–61 as a cultural ambassador to newly independent Africa. The purpose of the visit was to show racial progress in the United States and deflect charges of racism in U.S. treatment of African Americans. Contrary to the wishes of Armstrong's State Department handlers, he preached a message that said that while the goal of U.S. policy was freedom, it was not always the reality.

The tour was a great success, helping to improve America's image in the wake of **Patrice Lumumba**'s overthrow in **Congo** and ongoing racial turmoil in the U.S. South. Armstrong's successful tour helped to spur other tours by "jazz ambassadors," which led to greater musical fusion between jazz and African styles, while unintentionally giving authority to public policy statements by jazz musicians.

ASHMUN, JEHUDI (1794–1828). American Colonization Society (ACS) agent whose determination and organizational skill saved the

Liberia colony in its early days. Ashmun was a white Presbyterian minister who went to Liberia to lead the colony in 1822. The colony's approximately 120 people were poorly supplied and impoverished, ill led, and under frequent attack by native tribes. Ashmun immediately reorganized the colony's finances and defeated local tribes. In 1824, **Americo-Liberians** rebelled over the authoritarian government insisted upon by the ACS, and Ashmun was forced to retreat to the Cape Verde islands. Ashmun returned and won back the loyalty of the Americo-Liberians by creating a legal code and constitution that gave effective power to blacks instead of whites. Thereafter, he combined with U.S. naval forces to defeat local slave-trading chiefs, ending the slave **trade** in the region, and expanded the colony into the interior. He contracted a deadly case of malaria and returned to the U.S. to die in 1828.

ASWAN HIGH DAM. Dam built by the government of **Egypt** near the city of Aswan on the Upper Nile in the vicinity of the southern border with **Sudan**. The question of who would pay for the dam led to revolutionary changes in the **cold war**, colonialism, and the Middle East.

The first serious planning for the dam began in 1952 shortly after General **Muhammad Naguib** and Lieutenant Colonel **Gamal Abdel Nasser** came to power following a coup. Despite Nasser buying $200 million worth of weapons from the **Soviet Union** by way of Czechoslovakia on 27 September 1955, U.S. Secretary of State **John Foster Dulles** believed that funding the dam would tie Egypt to the West, so the United States, **Great Britain**, and the **World Bank** agreed on 14 December 1955 to finance the first stage of building the dam through grants and loans at an estimated cost of $270 million. Nasser responded to Western largesse with virulent anti-Western rhetoric and recognition for the People's Republic of **China**. The British accused him of masterminding riots and attempted coups against conservative pro-Western Arab opponents, although U.S. President **Dwight D. Eisenhower** and his administration reserved judgment.

Faced with rebellious congressmen who supported **Israel**, or came from cotton-growing states that did not want to help expand Egypt's cotton crop, or opposed **foreign aid** on principle, or were outraged by the anti-American, pro-Soviet Bloc turn in Nasser's foreign policy,

Dulles killed the agreement on 19 July 1956. He had no fear that the Soviet Union would step in to build the dam because he believed they could not afford it, which would have the added benefit of undercutting the Soviets' claim that they offered an economic alternative to the West. If they did pay for it somehow, Dulles believed that the funds would have to come from squeezing Eastern Bloc countries for the money, which would spark the sort of anti-Soviet rebellions that had broken out in Poland during the previous month.

On 26 July, Nasser shocked Dulles and the other foreign-policy makers in the Eisenhower administration by nationalizing the Suez Canal and announcing that he would use the profits to pay for the dam. Great Britain and **France** were humiliated when Eisenhower stopped them from retaking the canal in conjunction with Israel during the **Suez Crisis** of October–November 1956. In 1958, Soviet Premier Nikita Khrushchev announced that the Soviet Union would build the dam. Construction began in 1960 and it was completed on 21 July 1970.

ATLANTIC CHARTER. Plan by President **Franklin Delano Roosevelt** and Prime Minister Winston Churchill of **Great Britain** for creation of a new post–World War II international order. The Atlantic Charter was negotiated at the Atlantic Conference (9–12 August 1941, before the United States had entered the war) on warships off the coast of Newfoundland, Canada. It was issued 14 August 1941. Roosevelt saw the Charter's purpose was to avoid the errors that followed World War I by expanding the New Deal to the rest of the world.

The Charter was important for Africa because Roosevelt successfully pressured Churchill into accepting Article 3, under which the U.S. and Great Britain agreed to "respect the right of all people to choose the form of government under which they will live; and they wish to see sovereign rights and self-government restored to those who have been forcibly deprived of them." Although the Charter was a clear statement in favor of decolonization, Churchill told the British Parliament that it referred only to those nations conquered by the Axis powers.

To fulfill Article 3, Roosevelt ordered the State Department to create the Committee on Colonial Policy (CCP) during the fall of 1943, which laid out U.S. postwar policy for colonies and League of Nations mandate territories. The CCP called on colonial powers to give dependent peoples the opportunity for independence if they wished it and to set dates for independence. It also proposed an international trustee system through a **United Nations** (UN). Roosevelt's death, the accession of **Harry S. Truman** to the presidency, and the beginning of the **cold war** caused the U.S. to back away from many of the goals of the Atlantic Charter, and adhere to a policy of practical support for the colonial powers.

– B –

BAGHDAD PACT. Middle Eastern anti-Soviet military alliance created by U.S. Secretary of State **John Foster Dulles**. President **Gamal Abdel Nasser** of **Egypt** refused to join because he considered the alliance a neo-colonial trap since it included **Great Britain**. Dulles had considered Egypt to be the alliance's central player, but instead of dropping the idea, he re-centered it on Iraq, Nasser's most important rival for influence in the Middle East. The Pact of Mutual Cooperation, popularly known as the Baghdad Pact, was signed on 24 February 1955 although the United States was not a signatory. Nasser considered the increased U.S. military support for Iraq to be threatening to Egypt, and moved closer to the **Soviet Union** in consequence. *See also* EISENHOWER, DWIGHT D.

BALEWA, ABUBAKAR (1912–1966). First prime minister of **Nigeria** (1960–66). Balewa was a close ally of President **John F. Kennedy**, who appreciated Balewa's public claims of neutrality in the **cold war** combined with his refusal to join the often anti-American Neutral Bloc. Under Balewa, Kennedy made Nigeria an "emphasis state," which would receive special U.S. economic development assistance to provide a model for African development. Balewa entered office with a reputation for honesty, but was caught up in the massive economic and political corruption that produced the 15 January 1966 coup in which he was brutally assassinated and the government overthrown. *See also* AGENCY FOR INTERNATIONAL DEVELOPMENT (AID); FOREIGN AID.

BARBARY PIRATES. More accurately described as privateers, the Barbary Pirates were corsairs based in modern **Morocco**, **Algeria**, **Tunisia**, and **Libya**, who preyed on shipping from the Christian world, stealing cargoes and imprisoning sailors, ransoming officers and enslaving enlisted men. The American Revolution removed the protection provided by the British navy for American ships, prompting treaties with Morocco including a treaty of friendship that is the longest continuous relationship between the United States and another state. From 1785–96, Algerian Pirates captured 13 U.S. ships and held over 100 American sailors as slaves. In March 1786, U.S. envoys Thomas Jefferson and John Adams met with Tripoli's envoy, Abd al-Rahman, who told them that it is Muslims' "right and duty" to fight and enslave infidels.

The U.S., like most European nations, agreed to pay tribute to the local rulers, but as the price increased to 20 percent of the U.S. budget at the turn of the 19th century ($1.25 million), President Thomas Jefferson sent the U.S. Navy to fight the pirates, enforcing peace by 1805. Attacks began again during the War of 1812, apparently with the connivance of **Great Britain**. When the war ended, President James Madison sent the U.S. fleet on a successful mission to free U.S. hostages and force the Barbary states to pay compensation. Madison famously said, "The United States, while they wish for war with no nation, will buy peace with no one." U.S. Mediterranean commerce increased dramatically thereafter. The defeat shattered the Pirates' international image as a sea power, and the end of the Napoleonic Wars allowed Europeans to unite against them. By 1830, the strongest Barbary power, Algeria, had been conquered and annexed by **France**.

BASHIR, OMAR AL- (1944–). Army officer and leader (1989–) of **Sudan**, responsible for the genocide in **Darfur**. Bashir led a coup by middle-ranking officers, who were Arab and Muslim, against Sudan's democratically elected government because of its poor performance in the country's civil war against black Christian and animist southern Sudanese. He and his men acted because high-ranking officers had forced the government to begin negotiations with the guerilla Sudan People's Liberation Movement (SPLM), but Bashir and his men demanded total war against the south, which they proceeded to unleash, contributing a significant share of the estimated two million people who died by the time the war ended on 9 January 2005. Black slavery played a significant part in the war, and Bashir himself reportedly owned several slaves.

For the first decade of his rule, Bashir was under the sway of Islamist scholar **Hassan Turabi**, who made Sudan a center of Islamic **terrorism**, allowing **Osama bin Laden** to move there in 1991 and organize **al Qaeda**. International pressure from the United States, which placed Sudan on its list of "state sponsors of terrorism" following the 1993 World Trade Center bombing that killed six and wounded over 1,000, and from the **United Nations** (UN), which placed economic sanctions on Sudan in April 1996 following an unsuccessful al Qaeda–backed attempt on the life of President **Hosni Mubarak** of **Egypt** in June 1995, led the military part of Bashir's government to moderate. In May 1996, Bashir's defense minister ordered bin Laden to leave Sudan after being rebuffed by the administration of **Bill Clinton** when he offered to turn bin Laden over to the U.S., and Bashir removed Turabi from power in December 1999.

Bashir was quick to denounce the 11 September 2001 al Qaeda attacks in the U.S. Thereafter, he reportedly provided the U.S. with valuable intelligence in the **Global War on Terror** (GWOT) and, under strong economic and political pressure from the government of **George W. Bush**, negotiated a peace settlement with the SPLM that went into effect on 9 January 2005. The settlement ended the civil war and created a constitution that gave the southern Sudanese autonomy, significant control over their **oil**, and the option to vote for independence in 2015.

At almost the same time that the peace negotiations began in 2003, Bashir launched genocide against the rebellious black Muslim population of **Darfur**, Sudan's poorest and least developed province. Militia horsemen known as the **Janjaweed**, backed by the Sudanese army and air force, have followed a policy of rape, murder, poisoning of waterholes, and burning of villages to displace an estimated 2.5 million people, with between 200,000 and 400,000 deaths. As of mid-2008, Bashir had made almost impossible the work of **African Union** (AU) and UN **peacekeeping** forces. Despite protest by the governments of **China** and **South Africa**, on 14 July 2008, the chief prosecutor of the International Criminal Court, Luis Moreno-

Ocampo, asked judges to issue an arrest warrant on Bashir for his government's crimes against humanity in Darfur. Sudanese officials warned that the government could not guarantee the safety of UN and AU peacekeeping forces if Bashir were to be indicted, although they emphasized that this was not a threat. *See also* IMMIGRATION; REFUGEES.

BATTLE OF KASSERINE PASS. World War II battle fought during the **Tunisia Campaign** between United States and Axis forces from Germany and Italy, 19–25 February 1943. The battle was preceded by a series of defeats suffered by U.S. forces at the hands of German Field Marshall Erwin Rommel, which led U.S. forces to withdraw to Kasserine Pass, a strong defensive position. Poor training and inept U.S. command led to loss of the pass on the first day of battle, but strong Allied resistance, particularly by troops from **Great Britain**, prevented the Axis victory from turning into a rout. The pass was re-taken on 25 February following a strategic retreat by Rommel. After the Battle of Kasserine Pass, the Allied commander in North Africa, General **Dwight D. Eisenhower**, replaced incompetent officers and ordered significant changes in how American soldiers were trained for battle. The result was a transformed army that performed credibly by the end of the Tunisia Campaign. *See also* OPERATION TORCH.

BELGIUM. European colonial power, whose disastrously rapid de-colonization in **Congo** and subsequent support for the rebellious **Katanga** province created a brutal civil war and produced sub-Saharan Africa's first confrontation between the United States and the **Soviet Union**. Belgium's divide-and-rule policy between the Tutsi and Hutu in **Rwanda** helped to lay the groundwork for the Rwandan Genocide. *See also* KASAVUBU, JOSEPH; LUMUMBA, PATRICE; MOBUTU SESE SEKO; RWANDA, GENOCIDE IN; TSHOMBE, MOÏSE.

BEN BELLA, AHMED (1918?–). First prime minister and president of **Algeria** (1962–65). Ben Bella was one of the "historic chiefs" of Algeria who created the *Front de Libération Nationale*/National Liberation Front (FLN) that began Algeria's revolution and war for independence. Ben Bella emerged as the FLN's external political leader, working closely with the external military leader, Houari Boumédienne. On 22 October 1956, **France** hijacked his airplane when he and other FLN leaders were flying to peace talks, jailing them until 1962. At independence, he and Boumédienne emerged triumphant over the internal party leadership, and Ben Bella was appointed the country's first prime minister in 1962. He was promoted to be its first president in 1963.

Ben Bella's government led a one-party state with an ideology that was agrarian socialist, Pan-Arab, and secular. He brutally put down several rebellions during his reign, ordered the execution of former compatriots, created a cult of personality, became increasingly erratic and authoritarian in his behavior toward colleagues, and seemed to lose interest in domestic affairs as his focus shifted to foreign policy, where he traded off Algeria's revolutionary cachet to take for himself a prominent international role. He was particularly close to **Cuba**'s Fidel Castro, who provided Algeria with tanks and troops that helped stop **Morocco** from taking Algerian territory in the October 1963 "Sand War." President **John F. Kennedy** also sought to work with Ben Bella, which paid off for Washington during the Cuban missile crisis when Ben Bella told Kennedy that the **Soviet Union** would not be allowed to land Cuba-bound airplanes in Algeria for refueling.

Boumédienne overthrew Ben Bella on 19 June 1965, placing him under house arrest. After Boumédienne died in 1978, his successor, Chadli Benjedid, freed Ben Bella in July 1979. Ben Bella has since been a strong supporter of a multiparty state with a peaceful Islamist orientation.

BIAFRA. The name given by rebels in the predominately Ibo eastern region of **Nigeria** during their 1967–70 unsuccessful secession rebellion. Creation of Biafra followed a 15 January 1966 military coup that overthrew Nigeria's Muslim-led government and replaced it with an Ibo general, Johnson Aguiyi-Ironsi. The coup angered Muslims who lived in the north and were probably a majority of the population, because while northern leaders were assassinated along with Yoruba leaders from western Nigeria, Ibo leaders were not. Ironsi exacerbated the situation by dissolving the federal constitution and replacing it with a powerful unitary government. He was assassinated on 29 July 1966 and pogroms were launched across the north against

Ibo who had moved to the north as traders and civil servants. An estimated 30,000 Ibo were killed and over one million fled to Iboland. Despite efforts to reconcile the country by the new military ruler, Lieutenant Colonel **Yakubu Gowon**, the Ibo seceded as the nation of Biafra on 30 May 1967.

After initial Biafran victories, the Nigerian army began slowly pushing back the Biafrans and Gowon ordered the blockade of Biafra. The Biafrans paid for a sophisticated lobbying effort, especially in the United States, which pressured President **Lyndon B. Johnson** into providing relief aid, antagonizing Gowon. President **Richard M. Nixon** expanded the assistance and even considered recognizing Biafra, but did not out of concern that it would alienate other governments, for which colonial borders were sacrosanct, and might lead to secession movements across Africa.

Biafra surrendered on 15 January 1970. The estimated number of deaths, mostly from starvation and disease, is as high as three million. Although the Nixon administration worried that Nigeria would brutally punish the Ibo, Gowon immediately ordered the army to treat them well and to begin bringing relief supplies into the territory.

BIKO, STEPHEN (STEVE) (1946–1977). Charismatic black intellectual and political leader in **South Africa** whose murder by the South African government did much to raise consciousness in the United States about the brutality of **apartheid**. Biko was a medical student until 1972 when he gave up his studies for full-time organizing of black South Africans on the basis of color. Biko's vision of black self-assertion was strongly influenced by the work of **Frantz Fanon** and he sought a dramatic break with the psychologically debilitating self-hatred engendered by apartheid in order to lead blacks to recognize their ability and potential power. For the mass of people, Biko's message filtered down to "Black is beautiful." Unlike Fanon, Biko said that this change must be nonviolent. South African whites and people around the world became familiar with Biko's message thanks to the newspaper reportage of his friend, **Donald Woods**, a white South African newspaper editor.

For his efforts, the government banned Biko and harassed him with repeated arrests. His jailers beat him to death on 12 September 1977. His death led to violent protest that was crushed by mass arrests and the banning of Black Consciousness groups. In the U.S., Biko's killing received extensive press coverage that emphasized the death of a nonviolent activist at the hands of his government. Five of the police officers who killed Biko applied for amnesty with South Africa's Truth and Reconciliation Commission, but were denied. *See also* TUTU, DESMOND.

BIN LADEN, OSAMA (1957–). Founder and chief of the Islamist **al Qaeda terrorism** organization. His tie to Africa began following his participation in the successful war by Afghanistan's Mujahedin to overthrow the Communist government and drive out troops from the **Soviet Union** that were propping it up. In 1989, bin Laden was invited to move his operation to **Sudan** by that nation's de facto leader, **Hassan Turabi**, but instead he returned to Saudi Arabia a hero. Bin Laden bought various Sudanese properties over the next three years and moved to Khartoum in 1992 after alienating the Saudi royal family. From Sudan, he oversaw al Qaeda's first terror attack on 29 December 1992, an unsuccessful bombing of a Yemeni hotel where U.S. troops were staying while on their way to **Somalia** as part of **Operation Restore Hope**. Years later, bin Laden admitted that he had also trained and supplied the militia of Somali warlord **Muhammad Farah Aideed** with weapons and fighters who participated in the Battle of Mogadishu.

In 1996, under international pressure for their mutual terrorist attacks, the Sudanese offered to send bin Laden to Saudi Arabia, and also offered to turn him over to the U.S. The Saudi government refused to take him, and President **Bill Clinton** later explained that the U.S. could not take bin Laden because Justice Department officials did not believe there was enough evidence to make a case against him. Bin Laden then moved back to Afghanistan, where he issued a February 1998 *fatwa* proclaiming it a religious duty to kill Americans. Bin Laden oversaw the August 1998 bombing of the U.S. embassies in **Tanzania** and **Kenya**, among other worldwide terrorist acts that culminated in the 11 September 2001 attacks in New York, Washington, and Pennsylvania. Following the invasion of Afghanistan by the U.S. and its allies, bin Ladin fled, allegedly to Pakistan's ungovernable Waziristan tribal province. There have been periodic reports of bin Laden's death as well as videos and tapes believed to be authentic.

BLOOD DIAMONDS. Also known as "conflict diamonds." Diamonds mined primarily in **Sierra Leone**, **Angola**, and **Congo** during the 1990s and sold to finance wars by rebel movements. In Sierra Leone, slaves who were often children or kidnap victims excavated the diamonds, which were smuggled into **Liberia** and sold to middlemen, who smuggled them to Europe and India for cutting. Liberian President **Charles Taylor** took a cut from the sales, a portion of which he used to fund the Revolutionary United Front (RUF) in Sierra Leone as well as guerilla movements in Ivory Coast and **Guinea**. One of Taylor's chief middlemen was an **al Qaeda** agent, who earned hundred of millions of dollars for the organization.

Diamond merchants claimed that there was no way to trace if a diamond was from a conflict region or not, but as international pressure built on the diamond industry, DeBeers Corporation, the most important diamond mining and marketing company, discovered a means for doing so. In 2003 it became known as the Kimberley Process Certification Scheme. The 2006 **film** *Blood Diamond* played a significant role in bringing the issue to public consciousness.

BOTHA, PETER WILLEM (P.W.) (1916–2006). Prime minister and president of **South Africa**, whose "total strategy" sought to crush African National Congress (ANC) and South West Africa People's Organization (SWAPO) rebels, and bludgeon neighboring countries into leaving South Africa alone. As defense minister for Prime Minister **John Vorster** (1966–78), Botha argued that South Africa faced a "total onslaught" from the **Soviet Union**, which was responsible for the rise of Communist governments in Southern Africa, the basing of ANC guerillas in nearby non-Communist countries, and black protest within South Africa. In response, he called for a "total strategy" that would force regional compliance to South Africa's will through military attacks on infrastructure and ANC camps, economic pressure by cutting off the illegal **trade** with South Africa that was necessary for other African governments' survival, and a diplomatic offensive to follow up on these gains.

Botha implemented this policy when he became prime minister in 1978, supporting the *Resistência Nacional Moçambicana*/Mozambican National Resistance (RENAMO) in its civil war against the Communist **Mozambique** government, **Jonas Savimbi**'s *União Nacional para a Independência Total de Angola*/National Union for the Total Independence of Angola (UNITA) against **Angola**'s Communist government and, allegedly, dissident elements of **Joshua Nkomo**'s Zimbabwe African People's Union (ZAPU). Botha also sent South African troops into Angola, creating a 25-mile-wide buffer zone to keep out SWAPO guerilla infiltration into Southwest Africa (**Namibia**), and approved targeted assassinations of ANC leaders. On 16 March 1984, Mozambique capitulated, signing the Nkomati Accord under which both sides agreed to end support for guerilla movements against the others, which both largely did although the South Africans violated the treaty more often than the Mozambicans.

At home, Botha followed through on Vorster's unfulfilled promise to end petty **apartheid**, and ended the pass law system in 1986. But international pressure against apartheid, spurred in large part by Nobel Peace Prize winner Archbishop **Desmond Tutu**, led to international sanctions, including by the United States in 1986, which severely damaged the South African economy. Massive Cuban intervention in Angola—57,000 troops by 1988—halted South African aggression and most analysts believe threatened defeat that could lead to increased attacks on Southwest Africa, a major war with Cuba, and destruction of vital South African infrastructure. With public opinion dramatically turning against the war, Botha agreed to peace negotiations led by the U.S. and signed the Treaty of Ruacana, which ended the war in August 1988, and the **New York Accords** in December, which created the mechanism for South African withdrawal from Southwest Africa, elections and independence for the colony as Namibia, and withdrawal of Cuban troops from Angola. With the "total strategy" broken and the Soviet Empire collapsing, Botha was forced to resign by reform-minded colleagues on 15 August 1989. Under the black-majority rule government that followed, he was called to testify before the Truth and Reconciliation Committee, but refused. Botha was put on trial for human rights crimes committed during his rule, but was released on a technicality.

BOTSWANA. Landlocked and largely desert Southern African nation that despite being one of the world's five poorest countries at independence in 1966, has had the continent's fastest economic growth since that year and the world's fastest economic growth since 1970. Botswana is one of two African nations to receive independence between 1957 and 1975 that has had a democratically elected government throughout its history, and is Africa's only nation with "A" credit ratings from international stock and bond analysts Moody's and Standard & Poor's. Transparency International rates it the least corrupt nation in Africa. While this economic dynamism has been fueled by the discovery of diamonds shortly after independence in 1966, Botswana has not fallen into the "resource trap" of corruption and dictatorship. It has been so economically successful that the U.S. ended **foreign aid** in 1996, although it was later resumed to help fight HIV/**AIDS**.

Botswana's unique status as a democratic, capitalist, and economically dynamic country that has improved the standard of living even in remote villages has made it a favorite of U.S. government officials and for scholars who point to it as the great exception to Africa's troubled history. President **Bill Clinton** visited Botswana in 1998, and Botswana is considered the leading site for the Southern African base of the **U.S. Africa Command** (AFRICOM) if and when its basing structure is transferred to the African continent from Germany. The two nations also jointly manage an International Law Enforcement Academy, located outside Gaborone, the capital. The academy, which trains law enforcement officials from across Africa, is one of four in the world that are joint ventures with the U.S.

The U.S. works closely with Botswana to assist with treatment and control of HIV/AIDS and tuberculosis. Botswana faces a demographic crisis because of a devastating AIDS epidemic, the world's second-highest rate of AIDS infection, which has slashed life expectancy from 67 years to 34 years in 2007.

President Ian Khama, who took office 1 April 2008, has been one of the strongest critics of President **Robert Mugabe** of **Zimbabwe**. He called for **African Union** (AU) sanctions against Zimbabwe during a July 2008 AU Summit.

BOURGUIBA, HABIB (1903–2000). Moderate prime minister (1956–57) and president (1957–87) of **Tunisia** and close U.S. ally.

Bourguiba was a lawyer and anti-colonial leader who had been educated in **France**. The French jailed him three times for his nationalist activities, but he spoke out against collaboration with Nazi Germany after the fall of France in 1940.

In 1946, Bourguiba traveled to the U.S. to build support for Tunisian independence. Although he developed close ties with the American Federation of Labor (AFL) and Congress of Industrial Organizations (CIO) labor unions (later consolidated as the **AFL-CIO**), he found the administration of **Harry S. Truman** sympathetic but more concerned about supporting France. The war for independence in **Algeria** and scattered but increasing violence in Tunisia led France to negotiate internal autonomy with Bourguiba in 1955, followed by full independence in 1956. Bourguiba was elected prime minister and, in 1957, had parliament remove the bey (king) and appoint himself president. He quickly consolidated full power and in 1975 had himself legislatively voted president for life.

Bourguiba followed a moderate foreign policy, although he provided strong support for Algerian independence, and followed a moderate socialist policy to modernize Tunisia. These policies appealed to President **John F. Kennedy**, who invited Bourguiba to be the first African ruler to visit him at the White House. Bourguiba became known as Kennedy's favorite African leader, and Kennedy's favor helped to make Tunisia Africa's recipient of the greatest per capita **foreign aid** provided by the U.S. At home, Bourguiba allowed little dissent, jailed or exiled several thousand political opponents, and ordered the assassination of a few of the most important exiles.

Bourguiba shifted to a rigidly socialistic policy in 1964, leading to cuts in U.S. and **World Bank** assistance. Dire economic straits forced him to turn to the Bank and **International Monetary Fund** (IMF) for assistance in 1970, and thereafter he oscillated his economic policy between accepting international pressure from financial lenders to end subsidized prices for necessities and to sell off inefficient socialized businesses, and giving in to public protest against higher prices and unemployment by restoring low prices and jobs.

In 1982, under pressure from the U.S., Bourguiba allowed the Palestine Liberation Organization (PLO) to relocate to Tunis from Beirut, following the invasion of Lebanon by **Israel**. Israeli attacks on Palestinian targets in and around Tunis in 1985 and 1988 led to mass protests against Israel and the U.S. The attacks, combined with economic unrest, also sparked the rise of radical Islam in Tunisia. Bourguiba cracked down on the Islamists with such force that Prime Minister Zine al-Abidine Ben Ali concluded that he had developed a senility-based obsession with crushing the Islamists, so on 7 November 1987 Ben Ali had a panel of doctors declare Bourguiba unfit, and the president was constitutionally removed from power. He was retired to his home village where he died in 2000.

BOUTROS-GHALI, BOUTROS (1922–). Professor, diplomat for his native **Egypt**, and first African secretary-general of the **United Nations** (UN) (1992–97). Boutros-Ghali took office as UN secretary-general on 1 January 1992. His relationship with the administration of President **Bill Clinton** suffered on a personal level because U.S. leaders considered him secretive and intellectually arrogant. This was especially true of U.S. ambassador to the UN **Madeleine Albright**, whom Boutros-Ghali considered to be a nonentity and treated with special hauteur.

Boutros-Ghali's downfall as secretary-general came as a result of the UN's role in **Somalia** in 1993. Following **Operation Restore Hope**, an ostensibly UN operation ordered by President **George H.W. Bush** to use the U.S. military to feed Somalia's starving people in the wake of civil war and government collapse, President **Bill Clinton** expanded the mission to encompass nation building and disarming clan-based militias. Clinton turned over formal control of the operation to the UN, although **peacekeeping** forces remained under U.S. military command. After the changeover, Somali warlords were suspicious of the UN due to Boutros-Ghali's close relationship with former President **Muhammad Siad Barré**, overthrown in 1991. When a militia led by **Muhammad Farah Aideed** attacked and killed 24 Pakistani peacekeepers, the U.S. and Boutros-Ghali were determined to defeat Aideed. The ensuing Battle of Mogadishu, fought 3–4 October 1993, killed 18 U.S. soldiers and led Clinton to withdraw U.S. forces. Clinton and Albright blamed Boutros-Ghali for the disaster and in 1996 vetoed his reappointment for a second term despite the other 14 members of the Security Council supporting him. Instead of Boutros-Ghali, the U.S. pushed forward his deputy, **Kofi Annan** of **Ghana**, who became sub-Saharan Africa's first secretary-general in 1997.

In retirement, Boutros-Ghali continued to work in the fields of diplomacy and human rights and wrote an autobiography that excoriates Albright and the Clinton administration.

BOWLES, CHESTER (1901–1986). U.S. politician, author, and diplomat. After his appointment as ambassador to India by President **Harry S. Truman**, Bowles immersed himself in the problems of third-world countries, writing numerous books and essays during the 1950s. Among the most important was *Africa's Challenge to America* (1956). Bowles argued that by accepting Africa's political and economic diversity while building mutual cultural understanding through exchange programs, the U.S. would strengthen national security by drawing the continent into shared values, thus making African nations into willing partners.

Even without the long-term benefit this would provide to U.S. security, Bowles believed that the U.S. had a moral responsibility to help African nations to develop through economic assistance in what he saw as a global New Deal. This assistance would be especially important in the years immediately after independence, he argued, when new governments would be at their weakest and least competent. Once this initial rocky period was over, Bowles said that African nations would begin rapid development with the help of the U.S. Bowles' book had a strong influence on Senator **John F. Kennedy**, who as president saw to it that many of these ideas became policy. For Bowles, the U.S. relationship with Africa and the third world was of greater long-term consequence than the **cold war**, a view that Kennedy did not share.

As Kennedy's under secretary of state, Bowles reorganized the Bureau of African Affairs, which the **Dwight D. Eisenhower** administration had created but used as a dumping ground for inept or burned out foreign-service officers. He replaced them with highly ranked young officers, academics, and journalists. Likewise, he sought ambassadors for Africa who were young, creative, and energetic. Unfortunately for Bowles, his voluble cheerleader nature grated on the laconic Kennedy, his administrative skills were very poor in a position that oversaw the department's day-to-day operations, and he leaked to numerous reporters that he had advised the president against the Bay of Pigs operation. On 26 November 1961, Bowles and other State Department officials were removed in the "Thanksgiving Day Massacre." He was reassigned as the president's adviser on third-world issues, a position without responsibility or power, and Kennedy eventually appointed him to a second tour as ambassador to India.

BRZEZINSKI, ZBIGNIEW (1928–). U.S. scholar and national security adviser under President **Jimmy Carter** (1977–81). Brzezinski was a refugee from Poland who became a strong opponent of communism. His scholarly career focused on the cold war, especially U.S. relations with the **Soviet Union** and Soviet foreign policy. His *Africa and the Communist World*, which he edited in 1963, was an early and influential look at Soviet policy in Africa.

As Carter's national security adviser, he and Secretary of State **Cyrus Vance** focused attention on the East–West relationship, but Brzezinski was much more hawkish than Vance. While Brzezinski was a global thinker who saw Soviet policy in Africa as part of an overall Soviet plan, Vance saw Africa as a regional problem that should be handled by Africans whether or not the Soviets involved themselves. This view was held even more strongly by **United Nations** (UN) Ambassador **Andrew Young**.

Brzezinski disagreed with Vance and other members of the administration, including the president, over the Horn of Africa. Brzezinski concluded that Soviet support for **Ethiopia** combined with expansion of its military presence in South Yemen put U.S. Persian Gulf interests in danger. When **Somalia** invaded Ethiopia's Ogaden Desert to launch the **Ogaden War**, Brzezinski argued that Washington should provide Somalia's government with assistance, but Carter agreed with Vance and Young that it was a regional problem and refused to assist the Somalis. When evidence emerged in mid-January 1978 that troops from **Cuba** had been transported from **Angola** to Ethiopia, Brzezinski pushed in February for an aircraft carrier task force to be sent off the coast as a show of strength, but Vance strongly disagreed and the president again rejected Brzezinski's counsel. This began what became a severe split between Brzezinski and Vance, particularly over the question of whether areas like the Horn of Africa should be linked to U.S. ratification of the second Strategic Arms Limitation Treaty (SALT II).

Brzezinski later concluded that U.S. failure to stand up to the Soviets in the Horn of Africa probably led to their December 1979 invasion of Afghanistan, which forced Carter's withdrawal of the SALT II treaty from the Senate, ending détente. He also believed that it encouraged **Libya**, **Algeria**, and Cuba to behave more aggressively. He later concluded that another consequence was that it led to future overreaction by Washington to bold new Soviet initiatives. For these reasons, Brzezinski famously concluded, "SALT lies buried in the sands of the Ogaden."

Brzezinski's role in dealing with **Egypt** and Middle East peace was circumscribed by Carter's personal efforts to bring the sides together, and his role in Southern Africa was also limited. Afghanistan and the Iranian hostage crisis, which began in November 1979, effectively ended high-level U.S. concern with sub-Saharan Africa.

BUNCHE, RALPH (1903–1971). **African American** professor and diplomat whose work in the Middle East for the **United Nations** (UN) earned him the Nobel Peace Prize following the **Arab–Israeli War of 1948–49.** After the **Suez Crisis,** Bunche created the **peacekeeping** method by which UN soldiers acted as a neutral "peace force," which only fires its weapons in self-defense, rather than a "fighting force" that imposes peace through the barrel of a gun.

Bunche was the first African American to earn a doctorate in government from Harvard University and became a professor of political science at Howard University. During World War II, when he joined the Office of Strategic Services (OSS), the U.S. government's hastily created intelligence agency, Bunche's dissertation on West Africa and subsequent field research made him a logical choice to lead the OSS's African research and analysis division. He was so successful that he was transferred to the State Department and in 1945 was appointed acting chief of the Division of Dependent Areas, the first African American to lead such a unit. Bunche was assigned to work on the UN Charter, and was primarily responsible for its sections on colonialism. The UN recruited him, and he spent the remainder of his career with the organization, becoming its chief troubleshooter.

In 1947, Bunche was assigned as the secretary-general's representative to a UN committee on the future status of Palestine with full power to investigate any issue dealing with its future. He negotiated a series of truces during the Arab–Israeli War of 1948–49, and concluded an armistice between **Israel** and five Arab nations including **Egypt** in 1949, which demarcated new borders that remained intact until the **Arab–Israeli War of 1967**. For this latter effort, Bunche was awarded the Nobel Peace Prize in 1950. Bunche later played a major role in creating the UN Emergency Force (UNEF), a multinational buffer between Egypt and Israel after the Suez Crisis in 1956, the first ever UN peacekeeping operation.

Bunche served as the UN representative at the 30 June 1960 ceremony that gave **Congo** its independence from **Belgium**, and stayed to discuss future development aid. The eruption of the **Congo Crisis**, during which he was briefly detained by Congolese troops who believed he was Belgian because of his light skin, forced him to stay two months to try to work out a peace settlement. When the Congolese government requested peacekeepers and the UN Security Council agreed to send them, Bunche found himself commanding the *Opération des Nations Unies au Congo*/UN Organization in the Congo (ONUC), several thousand international soldiers and bureaucrats sent to restore order. Despite his force's limited mandate of peacefully restoring order and not interfering in internal Congolese affairs, Prime Minister **Patrice Lumumba** continuously and ever more angrily insisted that Bunche order ONUC to attack the secessionist **Katanga** province, which Bunche said his mandate did not allow him to do. Bunche's dealings with Lumumba turned remarkably bad; privately he called Lumumba a "madman" who was the "*lowest* man I have ever encountered. . . . I hate Lumumba." Bunche left Congo at the end of August 1960, believing that he needed to be replaced since he and Lumumba could no longer work together.

In the spring of 1967, Bunche worked with UN Secretary-General U Thant to try to stop Egyptian President **Gamal Abdel Nasser** from forcing UNEF to withdraw from the Egyptian border with Israel, but the agreement with Nasser that had created the peacekeeping force gave Egypt the unilateral right to end the mission. Even if the UN had ignored Nasser's demand, there would have been no way for it to continue to supply the peacekeepers. Their withdrawal and Egypt's violation of international law by blockading the Strait of Tiran led Israel to attack on 5 June, commencing the Arab–Israeli

War of 1967. Thereafter, Bunche negotiated a cease-fire, which took effect on 15 July.

BUSH, GEORGE H.W. (1924–). U.S. president (1989–93), whose administration presided during the collapse of the **Soviet Union**. Bush was a political "realist," whose concern when he became president was almost wholly on Great Power politics. As the Soviet Empire collapsed, his administration sought to create what he called a "New World Order" that would ensure international peace, assist in economic development, and provide greater protection for human rights. In keeping with this new vision, Bush's administration did not try to shore up faltering U.S. allies that were dictatorships in Africa including **Chad**, **Liberia**, and **Somalia**, pressured the government of **Kenya** to democratize, took the lead in negotiating peace in **Ethiopia**, **Sudan**, and **Mozambique**, successfully pressured King **Hassan II** of **Morocco** to liberalize his government and release political prisoners, and launched **Operation Restore Hope** at the end of his administration, sending 25,000 marines to **Somalia** to feed starving people.

Bush did continue realist policies in **Angola**, providing tens of millions of dollars worth of weapons and supplies to the rebel *União Nacional para a Independência Total de Angola*/National Union for the Total Independence of Angola (UNITA) guerilla movement led by **Jonas Savimbi**, which forced the Angolan government to negotiate a peace settlement while assuaging conservative U.S. foreign political intellectuals and politicians, who criticized Bush for his efforts to shore up the Soviet Union in the interest of realist stability. *See also* CLINTON, WILLIAM J. (BILL); HELMS, JESSE; REAGAN DOCTRINE.

BUSH, GEORGE W. (1946–). U.S. president (2001–09). During the 2000 presidential campaign, Bush downplayed Africa's significance for U.S. foreign policy and repeatedly said that there were no national security issues that would warrant U.S. military intervention on the continent.

Upon taking office, Bush's Africa policy goals were the same as those of his predecessor, **Bill Clinton**: foster **trade** and economic growth, promote democratization, fight corruption, and stop the spread of **AIDS**. Secretary of State **Colin Powell**, an **African American**, pushed the president to take greater interest in Africa, and in May 2001, Bush met with President **Olusegun Obasanjo** of **Nigeria** at the White House and, along with **United Nations** (UN) Secretary-General **Kofi Annan**, announced that the U.S. had pledged $200 million to the UN's global trust fund for fighting HIV/AIDS.

Fighting disease in Africa remained a Bush priority, and he was instrumental in changing interpretations of intellectual property rules that allowed production of cheaper drugs for treating AIDS, a policy that Clinton had talked about doing throughout his administration. Bush also differed from Clinton in that his administration successfully pressured President **Thabo Mbeki** of **South Africa** to change from denying the connection between HIV and AIDS to using the government to import drugs to treat the disease and prevent its spread from mother to infant. In international organizations, the Bush administration has pushed for programs in support of abstinence and marital faithfulness. In mid-2008, Bush's program to fight AIDS, the President's Emergency Plan for AIDS Relief (PEPFAR) supported anti-retroviral treatment for approximately 1.4 million people with HIV/AIDS and care for 10 million, most of them in Africa. PEPFAR initially was funded with $15 million over five years in 2003. In 2008 it was reauthorized as part of a five-year, $48 billion omnibus international health bill that included funding for research and assistance for those with tuberculosis and malaria.

In **foreign aid**, the Bush administration created the **Millennium Challenge Corporation** (MCC) to provide assistance to impoverished countries if they reach benchmarks on economic reform, educational funding, democratization, and fighting corruption. Economic aid for Africa doubled the totals of Bush's predecessor, and his 2009 budget proposal called for it to double again by 2010. Bush himself made week-long trips to Africa in 2003 and 2008.

The 11 September 2001 attacks made Africa much more important to the Bush administration as a significant front in the **Global War on Terror** (GWOT) because of their vulnerability to infiltration by **al Qaeda**. The U.S. government began **Operation Enduring Freedom–Horn of Africa** (OEF-HOA) and **Operation Enduring Freedom–Trans Sahara** (OEF-TS) to train African armies in counterterrorist techniques, and OEF-HOA has played a significant role in projecting U.S. power and interdicting terrorists and pirates in the Persian Gulf region. To coordinate U.S. military policy in Africa, the **U.S. Africa Command** (AFRICOM) was created in 2006. The Bush administration has strongly supported the governments of **Ethiopia, Uganda**, and **Rwanda**, which it sees as regional bulwarks against **terrorism** in east and Central Africa and as islands of stability and economic development in a war-torn region that includes civil war–plagued **Congo, Sudan**, and **Somalia**. Bush's invasion of Iraq and the capture of Saddam Hussein were probably instrumental in **Muammar Qaddafi** of **Libya** giving up his weapons of mass destruction (WMD) program.

Diplomatically, the Bush administration's pressure and diplomacy helped push Sudan into ending its civil war with southern Sudan, and Bush himself was the first world leader to call Sudan's policy in **Darfur** genocide. Bush, who had written "not on my watch" in the margin of a report on President Clinton's response to the Rwandan Genocide, reportedly sought military intervention in Darfur, but was talked out of it by National Security Adviser **Condoleezza Rice**, who argued that after the invasions of Afghanistan and Iraq, there could be a dangerous worldwide reaction by Muslims against a third U.S. intervention in a Muslim country. His administration has played the leading international role in pressuring the Sudanese government and Darfurian rebel groups into peace talks, but he has not pressed Sudan as hard as he might because its government has provided Washington with important information on Islamist terrorist organizations since 11 September, and out of concern that Sudan would renege on its settlement with southern Sudan. Bush was also criticized for failing to play an active role in bringing peace to **Liberia** in 2003, when he sent a small contingent of troops to protect U.S. citizens instead of intervening in the civil war. U.S. pressure did help to force the Liberian president, **Charles Taylor**, to step down and exile himself to Nigeria, and in 2006 Bush successfully pressured Nigeria's Obasanjo to extradite Taylor to **Sierra Leone** for trial on war crimes charges.

Secretary of State Rice played a significant role in pressuring Mwai Kibaki, the president of **Kenya**, to form a coalition government with opposition leader Raila Odinga following disputed elections. Bush and his administration have also been world leaders in pressuring President **Robert Mugabe** of **Zimbabwe** to step down. *See also* RWANDA, GENOCIDE IN.

BUTHELEZI, MANGOSUTHU (GATSHA) (1928–). Zulu leader of **South Africa** whose moderate opposition to **apartheid** won him support among conservatives in the United States. Buthelezi was a member of the Zulu royal family and served as chief adviser to the Zulu king. Although he opposed the creation of South Africa's *Bantustan* policy, he accepted the post as chief minister of KwaZulu in 1972, but refused to accept independence. Buthelezi opposed the African National Congress (ANC) and its support for economic sanctions against South Africa such as **divestment**, arguing that they hurt South African workers, and he strongly supported the **Sullivan Principles**, which called on U.S.-based corporations with business in South Africa to adhere to equal employment practices. Buthelezi also broke with the ANC over its support for violent resistance against apartheid.

Buthelezi's Zulu-based Inkatha Freedom Party violently fought against student protests during the Soweto riots and in street warfare against the ANC in the 1980s and early 1990s that killed an estimated 10,000 people. Inkatha was later shown to have been assisted by South African security forces. As it became clear in the 1990s that Buthelezi was no longer the leader of black South Africans except for the Zulu, he grew obstructionist in the transition to majority rule. He opposed the majority-rule constitution negotiated between President **F.W. de Klerk** and ANC leader **Nelson Mandela** because of its strong centralization, but after secret negotiations that continued until days before the election, he agreed to participate. Although Inkatha only received 10 percent of the vote, Mandela appointed Buthelezi home affairs minister to reconcile the parties. He was fired in 2004 by Mandela's successor, **Thabo Mbeki**, because of differences over **immigration** policy.

BYRD AMENDMENT. November 1971 amendment to a U.S. defense appropriations bill proposed by Virginia Senator Harry F. Byrd Jr., a Democrat who left the party to become an independent in 1970. The Byrd Amendment allowed the U.S. to import chrome from **Rhodesia (Zimbabwe)**, thus violating mandatory **United Nations**

(UN) sanctions against the illegal government of Prime Minister **Ian Smith**. Byrd argued that the exemption was necessary because chrome was a strategic resource that could only be obtained from Rhodesia or the **Soviet Union**. Opponents argued that Byrd was simply pushing a racist policy. The law harmed relations with black African nations although there is debate over its practical impact other than strengthening African opposition to U.S. policies in the UN. President **Jimmy Carter** made ending the law a foreign policy priority, and he signed its repeal on 18 March 1977.

– C –

CAMP DAVID ACCORDS. Agreements between **Egypt** and **Israel** brokered by President **Jimmy Carter**, which laid the foundation for peace between the two nations. Carter's proposal for a Middle East "all-parties conference" in Geneva, Switzerland, which would include the **Soviet Union**, prompted Egyptian President **Anwar Sadat** to take the dramatic step of going to Israel himself in order to prevent the Soviets from reemerging as a central player in the Middle East, which would have ruined the work that Sadat and U.S. Secretary of State **Henry Kissinger** had done to marginalize them following the **Arab–Israeli War of 1973**. Thereafter momentum for peace bogged down, and Carter invited Sadat and Israeli Prime Minister Menachem Begin to the "weekend White House" at Camp David in Maryland.

Carter famously negotiated, argued, and prayed with Sadat and Begin until both agreed to frameworks for comprehensive Middle East peace, which was rejected by the other Arab states, and for peace between Egypt and Israel. The agreements were signed 17 September 1978. Carter continued often intense negotiations to bring the framework to a signed treaty that formalized the peace and established diplomatic relations on 26 March 1979. There followed massive U.S. economic and military assistance to Egypt, making it the largest **foreign aid** recipient in Africa. Sadat and Begin won the 1978 Nobel Peace Prize for their work.

CARTER, JAMES E. (JIMMY) (1924–). President of the United States (1977–81), who tried to move U.S. Africa policy from the peripheral adjunct to the West–East struggle that it had been during the administrations of **Richard M. Nixon** and **Gerald R. Ford** to an area of intrinsic importance to the U.S. World events waylaid Carter's policy, especially intervention in the Horn of Africa by **Cuba** and the **Soviet Union**, the Iranian hostage crisis, and the Soviet invasion of Afghanistan.

Carter's Africa policy goals were interrelated: deemphasize the **cold war** in Africa, push **Rhodesia (Zimbabwe)**, **South Africa**, and Southwest Africa (**Namibia**, illegally occupied by South Africa) into majority rule, and improve relations with black Africa. One of Carter's first legislative successes was the March 1977 repeal of the **Byrd Amendment**. Carter followed this victory with a speech at the **United Nations** (UN), where he told cheering delegates that the U.S. now supported UN sanctions on Rhodesia. In September 1977, Carter announced his Anglo-American plan for Rhodesia. The plan called for restoration of colonial control over Rhodesia by **Great Britain** that would be supported by UN **peacekeeping** forces during a transition to one man–one vote universal suffrage within one year. Whites would be protected by allotting them 20 of the 100 parliamentary seats, and the guerillas would be protected by integrating their armies with the Rhodesian army. Rhodesian Prime Minister **Ian Smith** responded by reaching an internal settlement with black leaders who had rejected violence, and giving whites greater legislative protection than proposed under the Anglo-American plan. In the interim, U.S. voters, worried in part by Carter's seemingly weak foreign policy, ousted several liberal senators, who had been leading opponents of Rhodesia's internal settlement, in the November 1978 congressional elections.

After the renamed Zimbabwe–Rhodesia held an April 1979 election with universal suffrage won by Bishop **Abel Muzorewa**, Congress passed the Case–Javits Amendment, which compelled Carter to lift sanctions if Rhodesia held free and fair elections and made a good-faith effort to negotiate with the guerilla leaders. Fearing the impact that lifting sanctions would have on U.S. standing with other African nations, Carter managed to push through a new bill that broadened his power to keep sanctions intact if he believed them to be in the national interest. Continued civil war and UN sanctions supported by London and Washington forced the Zimbabwe–Rhodesia government to attend the British-sponsored Lancaster House negotiations, where Carter broke an impasse by suggesting that the U.S. could provide economic assistance to pay for independent Zimbabwe's government to purchase white-owned farms, transport Commonwealth peacekeepers to Zimbabwe, and assist in returning and resettling **refugees**. Guerilla leader **Robert Mugabe** won the ensuing election.

Carter showed his new policy of separating Africa from the cold war when he took minimal action to support U.S. ally **Mobutu Sese Seko** of **Zaïre** following a March 1977 invasion of Shaba province (**Katanga**) by former Katangan *gendarmerie* based in Communist-led **Angola**. Carter's shift to a tougher cold war policy was evident in his much stronger reaction to a second invasion by the Katangans in May 1978.

The cold war made its major intrusion in Africa during the Carter years in the Horn of Africa. **Ethiopia**'s conversion to communism under **Mengistu Haile Mariam**, the worsening human rights situation, and **Somalia**'s invasion of Ethiopia's Ogaden Desert region that started the **Ogaden War**, potentially turned the Horn into an area of Great Power confrontation. Carter avoided this by evenhandedly cutting support to Ethiopia in response to the human rights abuses and refusing to aid Somalia until it withdrew from the Ogaden. Carter refused to act even when the Soviet Union intervened by flying 15,000 Cuban troops to Ethiopia, which repelled the Somalis, despite National Security Adviser **Zbigniew Brzezinski** telling him that the U.S. had to make a stand against Soviet adventurism, which he saw as part of a Soviet master plan to create an "Arc of Crisis" across the Persian Gulf and Middle East. Instead, the State Department's Anthony Lake made a speech calling on the Soviets to follow the U.S. lead in Africa and withdraw from the Horn and from Angola. The Soviets declined. Brzezinski wrote in his memoirs that détente was buried under the sands of the Ogaden.

The Carter administration also played a significant role in Southwest Africa (Namibia), creating the **Western Five Contact Group**, which used a combination of diplomacy and political pressure to foster negotiations between South Africa and the Southwest Africa People's Organization (SWAPO). Intransigence by both sides at key moments plus South Africa catching the Contact Group making a secret agreement with SWAPO stalled negotiations, and the Iranian hostage crisis and Soviet invasion of Afghanistan ended U.S. focus on the problem.

Since his defeat for reelection by **Ronald W. Reagan** in 1980, Carter has been involved in Africa policy through the Carter Center, a **non-governmental organization** (NGO) founded in 1982 that monitors elections to ensure that they are free and fair, although Carter is frequently accused of turning a blind eye to electoral abuses. The Carter Center also works to eradicate debilitating diseases or parasites like the guinea worm. While visiting Zimbabwe in 1986, Carter attended a Fourth of July celebration with Mugabe, who proceeded to attack the U.S. and Reagan's foreign policy. Carter walked out of the dinner and the Reagan administration cut off **foreign aid** to Zimbabwe after Mugabe refused to apologize. *See also* SHABA, INVASIONS OF; VANCE, CYRUS; YOUNG, ANDREW.

CARTER DOCTRINE. Name given to two different foreign policy initiatives by President **Jimmy Carter**. When he became president, Carter proclaimed that support for human rights was now central to U.S. foreign policy. Journalists initially dubbed this fundamental reorientation from the realpolitik of President **Richard M. Nixon** and Secretary of State **Henry Kissinger** the Carter Doctrine, but the name did not stick. Carter changed the direction of his foreign policy following the late 1979 Iranian hostage crisis and invasion of Afghanistan by the **Soviet Union**, accepting National Security Adviser **Zbigniew Brzezinski**'s analysis of an "Arc of Crisis" from Afghanistan to the Horn of Africa that threatened Persian Gulf **oil** by land and sea. Carter announced this new foreign policy in his State of the Union Address on 23 January 1980, when he said: "An attempt by any outside force to gain control of the Persian Gulf region will be regarded as an assault on the vital interests of the United States. It will be repelled by the use of any means necessary, including military force." Journalists immediately called his policy the Carter Doctrine, and this time the name stuck. *See also* ETHIOPIA; OGADEN WAR; SOMALIA; VANCE, CYRUS; YOUNG, ANDREW.

CENTERS FOR DISEASE CONTROL AND PREVENTION (CDC). Established in 1946 as the Communicable Disease Center with the responsibility for eradicating malaria in the United States, which it did by 1951, the CDC's mission subsequently expanded to include global health. The CDC's Coordinating Office for Global Health seeks to enhance global health through sharing knowledge and resources, assisting with prevention and detection of disease, and using state-to-state diplomacy to assist with medical response to infectious disease epidemics.

The CDC has focused much of its international work on Africa because of public health crises from indigenous diseases like HIV/**AIDS** and malaria, and such poverty-related health care problems as maternal and infant health. President **George W. Bush** gave the CDC responsibility for implementing the President's Emergency Plan for AIDS Relief (PEPFAR), created in 2003 with an initial five-year budget of $15 billion over five years. In mid-2008, PEPFAR supported anti-retroviral treatment for approximately 1.4 million people with HIV/AIDS and care for 10 million, most of them in Africa. In 2008 it was reauthorized as part of a five-year, $48 billion omnibus international health bill that included funding for research and assistance for those with tuberculosis and malaria. The CDC also works with the **Agency for International Development** (AID) to implement the President's Malaria Initiative (PMI), created in 2005 with an initial five-year commitment of $1.5 billion to cut in half malaria deaths in 15 African countries.

PEPFAR builds off the Global AIDS Program, established by the CDC in 2000 to assist impoverished nations with HIV prevention, improvement in care and treatment of HIV victims, and building capacity and infrastructure for controlling HIV/AIDS. In 2008, the Global AIDS Program had over 100 staffers stationed in third-world countries and worked with over 1,000 local staff. By March 2008, PEPFAR had provided antiretroviral treatment for more than 1.73 million people in 15 third-world countries (13 of them in Africa, constituting over 90 percent of the people treated), and drugs to prevent mother-to-child transmission of HIV to 12.7 million women. It has also provided care for 6.6 million people and counseling for 33 million.

PMI focuses on protecting pregnant women and small children from malaria through provision of 5.4 million treated mosquito nets, short-term preventive treatment for pregnant women, and treatments for pregnant women with malaria. The first study of the program's impact, in **Zanzibar**, showed a 90 percent drop in malaria cases among children under two years of age. *See also* FOREIGN AID.

CENTRAL INTELLIGENCE AGENCY (CIA). U.S. intelligence agency created in 1947 with responsibility for overseas collection of information and covert political operations. The CIA did not create an African division until mid-1959. Because the U.S. government is slow to declassify documents on CIA activities, much of the information available on CIA activities in Africa has came from journalists and revelations by former CIA agents like Miles Copeland, John Stockwell, David W. Doyle, and **Larry Devlin**.

The CIA played its most significant roles in **Egypt**, where it assisted **Gamal Abdel Nasser** in coming to power and had close ties with **Anwar Sadat**; in **Congo**, where it worked with the Congolese government and especially with military commander Joseph-Désiré Mobutu (**Mobutu Sese Seko**) during the **Congo Crisis** and throughout Mobutu's subsequent rule; in **Angola**, where it supported the *Frente Nacional de Libertação de Angola*/National Liberation Front of Angola (FNLA) off and on beginning in 1961 until 1975, and the *União Nacional para a Independência Total de Angola*/National Union for the Total Independence of Angola (UNITA), in 1975 and 1985–91; in **Libya**, where it worked to overthrow president **Muammar Qaddafi** by creating an exile army made up of Libyan soldiers captured in the war with **Chad**; and in Chad, where it provided military assistance to support president **Hissene Habré** and keep Libyan-supported Chadians out of power from 1981–90. The CIA's role in Africa was so great during the **Ronald W. Reagan** administration that the National Security Council (NSC) official responsible for Africa was a CIA agent until 1986.

Numerous reports of the CIA's role in the overthrow of President **Kwame Nkrumah** of **Ghana** are based on very thin evidence including CIA documents that show a careful monitoring of the prospective coup makers but no actual CIA role in the coup. A key source for reports about a CIA role is forged documents created as part of a disinformation campaign by the **Soviet Union**. The Soviets also successfully used fake documents to harm U.S. relations with **Algeria, Guinea**, Mali, and **France** (over Algeria), and to make the world think that the U.S. was assisting **South Africa** with its nuclear weapons program during the 1980s. *See also* CONGO, CENTRAL INTELLIGENCE AGENCY INVOLVEMENT IN; EGYPT, CENTRAL INTELLIGENCE AGENCY INVOLVEMENT IN; STANLEYVILLE (KISANGANI) HOSTAGE RESCUE.

CHAD. Landlocked Central African nation with a population of 10 million divided into 200 separate ethnic groups, religiously divided between northern Muslims and southern Christians and animists, racially divided between northern Arabs and southern Blacks, economically divided between northern pastoralists and southern farmers, and historically divided between northern slavers and southern enslaved. The result is a nation that is one of the world's poorest, which has suffered constant rebellion almost since its creation in 1960 that has left it open to the machinations of outsiders, especially **France**, its colonial ruler, **Libya**, **Sudan**, and the United States.

Like most of former French Africa, Chad's relations with the U.S. were friendly but distant because France jealously guarded its premier standing against the "Anglo-Saxons." This was reinforced by the Chadian government's reliance upon French economic assistance to prop up the economy and French soldiers to prop up the regime. U.S. interest in Chad was triggered in May 1980 when, following the collapse of Chad's government into a Hobbesian civil war of 11 factions, Chadian President Goukouni Oueddei allied with Libya's **Muammar Qaddafi**, who sent 4,000 troops to help Goukouni take control of the country. A mutual defense pact signed in June deepened suspicion, which was confirmed when Goukouni signed a national unification agreement with Qaddafi on 6 January 1981, just days before the inauguration of U.S. President **Ronald W. Reagan**.

Reagan was determined to oust Qaddafi, whom he saw as the Soviet Union's proxy who funded terrorists and destabilized neighbors and distant African nations. African nations also feared Qaddafi's thrust into the heart of Equatorial Africa, and provided assistance to facilitate overt and covert **Central Intelligence Agency** (CIA) assistance to Goukouni's chief opponent, **Hissene Habré**. Diplomatic pressure compelled Goukouni to remove the Libyans in favor of **Organization of African Unity** (OAU) troops. The OAU forces did nothing to stop Habré's subsequent attack, and Goukouni was overthrown.

Subsequent Libyan efforts to assist Goukouni led the U.S. to provide Habré with assistance worth $10 million in mid-July 1983, and another $15 million in early August. An aircraft carrier was stationed off the Libyan coast and AWACS spy planes were sent to Sudan to monitor Libya's military. French troops followed on 9 August and created a line demarcating the boundary between the two sides at the 16th parallel. At the behest of the CIA, Chad allowed former Libyan prisoners of war, who had formed the Libyan National Army (LNA), to establish a base in 1987, and the CIA reportedly funded mercenaries in the Chadian armed forces. During the last phase of the fight with Libya, known as the "Toyota War," Chadian soldiers received international fame for attaching machine guns to Toyota trucks, which they used to drive the Libyans from all but Chad's extreme north. The Libyans lost at least $1 billion worth of weapons and supplies. Habré's total funding from the Reagan administration reportedly reached $500 million. The **George H.W. Bush** administration did not consider Libya the threat that Reagan had because the **cold war** was ending and Qaddafi had moderated his behavior. Habré also lost French assistance because his regime had turned too brutal and narrow in its base of support. He was overthrown by Idriss Déby, a former lieutenant, who received Libyan assistance. The U.S. evacuated the LNA on 7 December.

With Déby's government providing relative stability, **oil** companies began to follow up on discoveries in southern Chad near the town of Doba, finding reserves estimated at 900 million barrels. When during the late 1990s bankers refused to finance $4.2 billion in oil infrastructure and a 650-mile pipeline to port facilities in Cameroon because of Chad's history of civil disorder and corruption, the U.S. offered to provide significant assistance in 2000, backing $293 million in funds through the Export-Import Bank and another $193 million loan from the **World Bank**. The **Bill Clinton** administration, the World Bank, and the **George W. Bush** administration were determined that this would be a new type of developmental assistance, with guarantees to prevent it from becoming the sort of corrupt white elephant that had been the common result of World Bank loans. Therefore, the loan was conditioned upon the Chadian government's agreement to spend 95 percent of the profits on developmental projects, conditions that Déby said he found acceptable.

The oil consortium that won the right to do the work, which included ChevronTexaco and Exxon Mobil, also agreed to maintain high environmental standards and to work with local peoples to ensure that they benefited with minimal negative disruption. The Bush administration authorized the deal in 2003 with hopes that it would provide a model for other developing countries, especially Iraq. Instead, the Déby government, already corrupt, grew more so (in 2005 it was rated the world's most corrupt by Transparency International), and rebels saw that the prize of winning power was much greater or, if they could not win power but could make trouble, the government would pay them not to make trouble. The result was more rebellions, which are often little more than brigandage. On 13 April 2006 and 1 February 2008, Chadian rebels supported by Sudan attacked the Chadian capital, N'Djamena, but failed to overthrow Déby's government. In response to these and other attacks, Déby increased defense spending and the World Bank withdrew its employees.

In April 2006, World Bank President Paul Wolfowitz agreed to decrease required developmental spending to 70 percent of the national budget, but the government made no effort to meet that requirement. In August 2006, Déby nationalized ChevronTexaco's share of the business and threatened to do the same to Exxon Mobil, with China prospectively taking over and giving Déby a bigger cut of the profits. As a result of these machinations, the **United Nations** (UN) ranks Chad as the world's fifth-poorest country.

Along with its internal disorder, which has created 180,000 internally displaced people, Chad suffers from humanitarian crises in Sudan, where the UN estimates that over 250,000 **refugees** have fled the **Darfur** region into eastern Chad, and the Central African Republic, where 57,000 refugees have fled civil war into southern Chad. Most of these people live in refugee camps and are dependent on **foreign aid** for survival. *See also* BASHIR, OMAR AL-; NON-GOVERNMENTAL ORGANIZATIONS (NGOs).

CHINA. Communist nation that is the world's most populous country. China has seen three periods of engagement in Africa, the first during the early years of independence as an ideological crusade, the second in Angola during the mid-1970s to stop the expanding power of the **Soviet Union**, and the last beginning in the mid-1990s in a worldwide search for natural resources and markets. China's relationship with Africa began in 1958 when it was one of the first countries in the world to recognize the provisional government of the *Front de Libération Nationale*/National Liberation Front (FLN) rebels in **Algeria** who were fighting **France** for their independence. China provided guerilla training and arms assistance for rebels in **Congo** during the **Congo Crisis** of 1960–65. The relationship began in earnest in 1963 as part of Communist Party Chairman Mao Zedong's effort to supplant the Soviet Union and make China the leader of worldwide communism.

From December 1963 to January 1964, Prime Minister Zhou Enlai traveled to 10 African countries during which he laid the groundwork for recognition from 14 African countries that cut relations with Taiwan by the end of 1964, and began long-term relationships with African liberation movements, including the Zimbabwe African National Union, the Pan-Africanist Congress in **South Africa**, and the *Frente de Libertação de Moçambique*/Front for the Liberation of Mozambique (FRELIMO). The Soviets grew so paranoid about Chinese advances that they ordered KGB agents in Africa to count the number of portraits of Chairman Mao on public display and to deface them. The Chinese diplomatic offensive was largely aborted in 1965 when Kenyan security forces captured Chinese arms bound for Congolese rebels, and in June, when the normally dexterous Zhou declared that Africa was "ripe for revolution" while he was visiting **Tanzania**, after which he was refused entry by every other African country, five of which subsequently suspended or broke relations.

The Sino-Africa relationship waned during the Cultural Revolution (1966–76) although China did build the Tanzam Railway (1970–75) between Tanzania and **Zambia**, a $500 million project that is China's largest **foreign aid** project. The railway's purpose was to assist Zambia by giving it a way to get its copper to international markets without having to cross the territory of white racist governments in **Rhodesia**, **Mozambique**, or **South Africa**, and to improve Tanzania's economy by providing revenue-generating **trade** for its port at Dar es Salaam. The railway was a failure because Tanzania was unable to manage its port effectively. China also heavily involved itself with **Zaïre** beginning in 1973 when President **Mobutu Sese Seko** launched a cultural revolution based on the Chinese model, and in **Angola**, where it coordinated with the U.S. and apparently, South Africa, to use Zaïrian territory to train *Frente Nacional de Libertação de Angola*/National Front for the Liberation of Angola (FNLA) and *União Nacional para a Independência Total de Angola*/ National Union for the Total Independence of Angola (UNITA) guerillas in their unsuccessful civil war against the Soviet-backed *Movimento Popular de Libertação de Angola*/Popular Movement for the Liberation of Angola (MPLA).

After Mao's death in 1976, the Chinese government again turned inward as it liberated its economy. In 1996, China reemerged as a much more important force in Africa when President Jiang Zemin toured the continent seeking to create new relationships. The only precondition that he laid down for aid and trade with African nations was that they accept the "One China" policy, which says that Taiwan is a province of China. From 1995 to 2006, Africa's trade with China increased from $4 billion per year to $55.5 billion. By 2007, China had supplanted **Great Britain** as Africa's third-largest trade partner and was poised to pass **France** in 2009. An energy crisis in 2003 dramatically spurred Chinese investment in Africa, focusing on **oil** exploration and development of new oil fields. The Chinese government's refusal to criticize African governments for human rights abuses and its willingness to sell weapons even to pariah governments has opened many doors to Chinese trade and investment. China has invested heavily in Sudanese oil fields and **Sudan** is its second-largest oil supplier after Angola. The Chinese have been Sudan's primary arms supplier since the mid-1990s despite a **United Nations** (UN) Security Council arms embargo, China threatened to veto proposed UN sanctions against Khartoum for its policy in **Darfur**, and in mid-2008 it consulted with other Security Council members about blocking the International Criminal Court's genocide indictment against Sudanese President **Omar Bashir**. In 2008 China also continued to sell arms including warplanes to **Zimbabwe** despite myriad human rights abuses by its government, but during the electoral crisis of April 2008, Southern African labor unions and governments blocked the unloading of a Chinese cargo ship filled with munitions, which finally was forced to return to China. China again exerted its influence in the UN in July 2008 when it joined Russia in vetoing sanctions against Zimbabwe following contested elections won by President **Robert Mugabe**.

China passed the **World Bank** as a lender to Africa during the early 2000s, and by 2006 it was lending African governments three times more money than the Bank. As a result, African governments are less reliant on international organizations for assistance and the Bank and **International Monetary Fund** (IMF) have begun shifting their lending priorities from good governance and fighting corruption to seeking to induce governments to improve their business climate. In late 2007, 750,000 Chinese were working in Africa. Estimates in 2007 said that Chinese trade with Africa would grow to $100 billion by 2010. *See also* GBENYE, CHRISTOPHE; GIZENGA, ANTOINE; KABILA, LAURENT-DÉSIRÉ; MULELE, PIERRE; SAVIMBI, JONAS.

CLARK AMENDMENT. Amendment to the International Security Assistance and Arms Control Act of 1976, which made permanent the **Tunney Amendment**'s ban on U.S. covert or overt aid for antigovernment guerillas in **Angola**. The amendment was made by Senator Dick Clark, an Iowa Democrat who was chairman of the Senate Foreign Relations Subcommittee on Africa. The Clark Amendment was repealed in 1985 in order to allow renewed U.S. support for anti-Communist guerillas led by **Jonas Savimbi** as part of the **Reagan Doctrine** of rolling back gains by the **Soviet Union** in the third world. *See also* CUBA; SOUTH AFRICA.

CLINTON, WILLIAM JEFFERSON (BILL) (1946–). U.S. politician, president (1993–2001), and international philanthropist. Clinton entered office demanding a much more vigorous Africa policy than his predecessor, **George H.W. Bush**, which would work through the **United Nations** (UN) and the **Organization of African Unity** (OAU) to bring democracy and economic development across the continent, and would provide vigorous **peacekeeping** and nation building where needed.

Shortly after taking office, Clinton expanded the mission and duration of **Operation Restore Hope**, the Bush administration's intervention in **Somalia**. Clinton transformed a brief peacekeeping operation charged with feeding a starving populace into a peacemaking and nation-building operation that began trying to disarm competing Somali militias, focusing on that of the most powerful warlord, **Muhammad Farah Aideed**. Clinton followed his multilateralist perspective by placing U.S. forces under nominal UN command although they remained under U.S. commanders. A series of violent confrontations culminated in the 3–4 October 2001 Battle of Mogadishu in which 18 U.S. soldiers were killed, at least in part because the Clinton administration turned down an earlier request by Joint Chief of Staff **Colin Powell** for heavy armor. It was later revealed that the **al Qaeda** terrorist organization had trained Aideed's forces and may have participated in the ambush itself. After Clinton withdrew U.S. forces from Somalia, **Osama bin Laden** reportedly concluded that he could launch acts with impunity against the U.S. Al Qaeda bombed U.S. embassies in **Kenya** and **Tanzania** in August 1998 despite repeated warnings to the State Department from the U.S. ambassador to Kenya that the embassy was dangerously vulnerable. Clinton responded by attacking al Qaeda camps in Afghanistan and bombing an aspirin factory in **Sudan**, al Qaeda's former base.

Somalia made Clinton very skeptical about the UN's role in peacekeeping. On 27 September 1993, he told the UN General Assembly: "The United Nations must know when to say no." When genocide began in **Rwanda** during early April 1994, the president ordered the State Department to work behind the scenes to kill the UN peacekeeping mission already on the scene, eventually agreeing to a compromise by UN Ambassador **Madeleine Albright** that cut its troop strength by 90 percent while Rwanda's "Hutu Power" government killed 947,000 mostly Tutsi in three months. National Security Adviser Anthony Lake later called the Clinton administration's response "truly pathetic."

In October 1997, Clinton appointed civil rights leader **Jesse Jackson** to be his special envoy for Africa. Jackson was point man for U.S. policy in **Sierra Leone**, heavily pressuring its government to share power with Revolutionary United Front (RUF) leader Foday Sankoh, who was at the time sentenced to death for tens of thousands of crimes against humanity. Sankoh resumed Sierra Leone's civil war until his capture in May 2000. Jackson also persuaded Clinton to telephone President **Charles Taylor** of **Liberia** from Air Force One during Clinton's Africa visit in March–April 1998, giving what was seen as U.S. support for a man responsible for the deaths of over 100,000 Liberians and for launching the RUF and guerilla movements in Ivory Coast and **Guinea**. Jackson was later quietly dismissed.

Clinton frequently spoke of an African Renaissance, identifying its leaders at various times as **Yoweri Museveni** of **Uganda**, **Paul Kagame** of **Rwanda**, **Meles Zenawi** of **Ethiopia**, **Isaias Afwerki** of **Eritrea**, Joaquim Chissano of **Mozambique**, **Laurent-Désiré Kabila** of **Congo**, **Thabo Mbeki** of **South Africa**, and **Jerry Rawlings** of **Ghana**. By 2000, all of these men except for Rawlings and Mbeki oversaw or were personally responsible for increased corruption, undemocratic policies, human rights violations, and even warfare against other Renaissance leaders. Even Mbeki had begun to draw international opprobrium for his skepticism about scientific claims that HIV causes **AIDS** and his refusal to allow his government to pay for discount-priced drugs that prevent HIV from becoming AIDS and prevent its transmission from mother to infant.

Clinton's 22 March–2 April 1998 visit to six African countries, making him the first president to go to Africa since **Jimmy Carter**, was extremely popular among Africans and **African Americans**. He made a second trip in 2000. By the end of his administration, Clinton had stripped down U.S. goals for Africa to fostering **trade** and economic growth, promoting democratization, fighting corruption, and stopping the spread of AIDS. **Foreign aid** had been reduced to below the final year of the Bush administration. In early 2000, Clinton told the National Summit on Africa that his Africa policy had resulted in "thousands of triumphs, large and small."

In November 2000, African Affairs Bureau Director Susan Rice traveled to southern Sudan, the country's rebellious black-dominated region, in an unsuccessful effort to prod the administration to take action against the Arab-dominated government of Sudan, which allowed government-backed Arab militias to conduct slave raids and sell them in slave markets.

After leaving the presidency, Clinton created the William J. Clinton Foundation, a **non-governmental organization** (NGO), which has made its primary goals providing cheap drugs for the treatment of AIDS and alleviating mass poverty in Africa through programs that create sustainable growth. *See also* AFRICAN AFFAIRS, STATE DEPARTMENT BUREAU OF; BASHIR,

OMAR AL-; PRESIDENTIAL DECISION DIRECTIVE 25; RWANDA, GENOCIDE IN.

COLD WAR. Worldwide struggle between the West, the United States and its allies, versus the East, the **Soviet Union** and its allies and satellites. Known as the cold war because it was not a "hot war"—a violent military conflict—the cold war was an ideological, political, economic, and cultural competition for world power. In broad outline, it was Western democratic capitalism or social democracy versus Communist totalitarianism, but in Africa after the first few years of independence, it was usually a contest to woo support from dictatorships that tended to follow various degrees of socialism. Following Vladimir Ilich Lenin's classic theory of imperialism, Soviet leaders believed that breaking the third world from the West was a crucial step toward overthrowing capitalism in the West.

The cold war first came to Africa following World War II when Soviet ruler Josef Stalin sought control of **Tripolitania**, a province of formerly Italian-controlled **Libya**, but was blocked by the United States. Although the Soviets lost a base on the Mediterranean Sea, failure to win an African colony gave them credibility with decolonizing third-world countries in the **United Nations** (UN), where the Soviets led the decolonization movement against the Western colonial powers. Conversely, Washington's need to support its colonialist allies in the North Atlantic Treaty Organization (NATO) forced it to mute its historic opposition to colonialism, providing the Soviets with a long-term advantage in the UN as African nations tended to side with Soviet foreign policy throughout the 1970s and 1980s.

Cold war rivalry in Africa grew after Stalin's death in 1953 because he had shown little interest in the continent after his failure in Libya. Stalin's successor, Nikita Khrushchev, broke into the third world in 1955 when he traded a huge trove of Soviet weapons to **Egypt** through Czechoslovakia in exchange for cotton. His success in working with President **Gamal Abdel Nasser** led him to change Soviet ideological doctrine and foreign policy the following year, arguing that the Soviets could work with "bourgeois nationalists" because decolonization would hurt the colonial powers and mark a first step on the former colonies' path to communism. Soviet support for **Algeria**'s war for independence from **France**, which also began in

1956, put this theory into practice. The **Congo Crisis**, which began in July 1960, created a new opening for Soviet propaganda against the West. It also briefly showed opportunity for the Soviets when Prime Minister **Patrice Lumumba** of **Congo** sought Soviet military intervention in the months before his overthrow and assassination.

Soviet support for Leftist governments, especially **Guinea**, led by **Ahmed Sékou Touré**, **Ghana**, led by **Kwame Nkrumah**, Algeria, led by **Ahmed Ben Bella**, and Mali, led by Mobido Keita, was initially successful thanks to ideological sympathy and significant aid programs. The U.S. responded to these efforts with **foreign aid** based on **modernization theory** and with efforts to show moral commitment to third-world progress through the **Peace Corps**. Both sides sought to build influence through military assistance and both used their intelligence services to support their friends and destabilize their opponents. The Soviet effort in these countries was undermined by low-quality assistance (including two snowmobiles for Guinea, an equatorial nation), overreaching by pushing too hard for radical transformation in Guinea, which alienated Touré, and by the corruption and general failure of these governments to provide a better life for their people, which led to Ben Bella's overthrow in 1965, Nkrumah's overthrow in 1966, and Keita's in 1968.

The Soviets' greatest defeat came in Egypt after the death of Nasser. His successor, **Anwar Sadat**, personally despised them and believed that they had nothing to offer Egypt except weapons. Before the **Arab–Israeli War of 1973**, he expelled most of the Soviet advisers and technicians from the country and removed the rest after the war, realigning with the U.S.

The Soviets concluded that the first wave of pro-Soviet leaders had failed because they were not Communists who were leading Marxist–Leninist parties and because they came to power peacefully. The Soviets launched a second wave of African intervention in the mid-1970s when colonial wars for independence brought to power Communist regimes in **Mozambique** and **Angola**, a coup brought to power a Communist regime in **Ethiopia** that ruthlessly set about implementing Marxist–Leninist policies, and civil war brought to power a Leftist government in **Zimbabwe**. The Soviets concluded that Africa had reached a tipping point and would now inexorably turn Communist. Instead, these governments' repressive policies produced civil wars supported by the **apartheid** government of **South Africa** and, in the mid-1980s, by the U.S. in Angola as part of the **Reagan Doctrine** of support for anti-Communist rebels. Soviet support for these governments, which ran into the tens of billions of dollars, also damaged the weak Soviet economy.

The Soviet Union's Mikhail Gorbachev and President **Ronald W. Reagan** worked together to end the cold war in Africa beginning in 1988. The U.S. pressured South Africa to grant independence to Southwest Africa (**Namibia**), and the Soviets pressured Angola and **Cuba** to withdraw Cuban troops. The Soviet Union itself collapsed 25 December 1991. *See also* ACHESON, DEAN G.; BOTHA, PETER WILLEM (P.W.); BRZEZINSKI, ZBIGNIEW; BUSH, GEORGE H.W.; CARTER, JAMES E. (JIMMY); CARTER DOCTRINE; CHINA; CLARK AMENDMENT; CONGO, CENTRAL INTELLIGENCE AGENCY INVOLVEMENT IN; DEVLIN, LARRY; DULLES, ALLEN W.; DULLES, JOHN FOSTER; EGYPT, CENTRAL INTELLIGENCE AGENCY INVOLVEMENT IN; EISENHOWER, DWIGHT D.; EISENHOWER DOCTRINE; FORD, GERALD R.; GIZENGA, ANTOINE; HAILE SELASSIE I; JOHNSON, LYNDON B.; KASAVUBU, JOSEPH; KENNEDY, JOHN F.; KISSINGER, HENRY; LIBYA; MACHEL, SAMORA; MENGISTU HAILE MARIAM; MOBUTU SESE SEKO; MUGABE, ROBERT; NETO, AGOSTINHO; NEW YORK ACCORDS; NIXON, RICHARD M.; NIXON DOCTRINE; NKOMO, JOSHUA; NUJOMA, SHAFILSHONA SAMUEL ("SAM"); OGADEN WAR; OPERATION IAFEATURE; OPERATION WIZARD; QADDAFI, MUAMMAR AL-; ROBERTO, HOLDEN; RUSK, DEAN; SAVIMBI, JONAS; SIAD BARRÉ, MUHAMMAD; SIMBAS; STANLEYVILLE (KISANGANI) HOSTAGE RESCUE; TERRORISM; TRUMAN, HARRY S.; TSHOMBE, MOÏSE; TUNNEY AMENDMENT; VANCE, CYRUS; YOUNG, ANDREW.

COMPREHENSIVE ANTI-APARTHEID ACT (CAAA). Law passed 2 October 1986 by the U.S. Congress over the veto of President **Ronald W. Reagan**, which required U.S. sanctions on **South Africa** until its government ended the state of emergency, ended **apartheid**, released from jail African National Congress (ANC) leader **Nelson Mandela** and all other political prisoners, lifted bans on political parties, and began serious negotiations with the ANC toward majority rule. The CAAA banned U.S. businesses from new investments in South Africa, banned the import of many South African goods including Krugerrand gold coins, and ended flights between South Africa and the U.S. It was the first time in the 20th century that Congress overrode a president's veto on a foreign policy issue.

Analysts believed the CAAA would have little impact on the South African economy since other countries would take advantage of the investment opportunities it presented, but other Western countries instead followed the U.S. lead and began sanctions on South Africa. Combined with the **divestment (disinvestment) from South Africa movement**, the impact on the South African economy was dire, and helped to force the South African government to move from apartheid to black-majority rule. *See also* BOTHA, PETER WILLEM (P.W.); HELMS, JESSE; TRANSAFRICA; TUTU, DESMOND.

CONFLICT DIAMONDS. *See* BLOOD DIAMONDS.

CONGO. Central African nation that has played a central role in U.S. Africa policy since its independence in 1960. Congo is the size of the U.S. east of the Mississippi and is bounded by nine countries: the Central African Republic, **Sudan**, **Uganda**, **Rwanda**, Burundi, **Tanzania**, **Zambia**, **Angola**, and Congo–Brazzaville. From its Kamina airbase (refurbished by the **Central Intelligence Agency** [CIA] during the 1980s for operations in Angola), nonstop, roundtrip flights can be made to any place in Africa. Congo is endowed with vast mineral wealth, including gold, diamonds, copper, cobalt, and uranium (which the U.S. relied upon for building its first atomic bombs), as well as rubber and hard woods. Its huge size, central location, and strategic minerals placed it at the center of the **cold war** from almost the first day of independence. In the post–cold war period, it was the site of Africa's first continental war, with nine countries (Angola, **Zimbabwe**, **Namibia**, **Chad**, Sudan, and **Libya** sending troops in support of Kabila, and Burundi, Rwanda, and Uganda against him) fighting for its spoils.

Congo had a brutal history under colonialism, with King Léopold II of **Belgium** personally owning the Congo Free State from 1885 to

1908 (the U.S. was the first nation to recognize his control on 22 April 1884) and renting concessions to often rapacious Belgian businesses, which instituted deadly forced labor enforced with mutilations such as cutting off the hand of people who resisted. Léopold's policies led to demands by the U.S. and other countries for Congo to be taken from Léopold, and the Belgian parliament took control in 1908, ending the worst abuses.

While the Belgians provided better housing and services for a greater percentage of the population than did any other colonizers, Congolese society was controlled by the combined power of business, church, and government—Congo's famous "three pillars"—which controlled every aspect of workers' lives in an excruciatingly totalitarian system. This was combined with a strict system of segregation that humiliated blacks. A few, who had assimilated to European mores (known tellingly as *évolués* [evolved]), sought equality for themselves but tended to ignore everyone else. Included in this group had been **Patrice Lumumba**, **Joseph Kasavubu**, and Joseph-Désiré Mobutu (**Mobutu Sese Seko**), although each moved to a nationalist position. As late as the 1950s, the Belgians believed they would control Congo for at least 100 years, and did not prepare the colony for independence. Education was broadly based compared to the rest of Africa, but stopped at sixth grade for all but the most highly talented. The first Congolese undergraduate matriculated in 1954 and at independence there were less than 30 black college graduates, no doctors, lawyers, or army officers. Pro-independence riots broke out in 1959, surprising the Belgians, and by January 1960 they had capitulated, agreeing to free Congo as the Republic of Congo on 30 June 1960. Kasavubu was elected president and Lumumba prime minister although the former supported a weak union and the latter a powerful centralized state.

Five days after independence, the Congolese army rebelled over the government's failure to grant pay raises or to promote a single Congolese to the officer corps despite its having done both for civil servants. This began the **Congo Crisis**. After Lumumba expressed support for the rebels, fired the Belgian commanders, and promoted and granted raises to the soldiers (resulting in the Congolese army having no privates), Belgium promptly intervened militarily to protect its citizens and to assist rebels in the mineral-rich **Katanga** province, which declared independence. The administration of President **Dwight D. Eisenhower**, which had planned to make Congo into a showcase for its capitalism-based economic development policies and considered Lumumba the best and strongest possible leader, quickly concluded that Lumumba's erratic actions and immaturity threatened to destroy the country, a view seconded by **United Nations** (UN) officials. Lumumba's rhetoric, which increasingly supported positions held by the **Soviet Union**, led Eisenhower to conclude that he was, at best, a dupe whom the Soviets would ultimately control. With **Operation Wizard**, the **Central Intelligence Agency** (CIA) sought to discredit him personally and destabilize his position, and CIA Director **Allen Dulles** ordered his assassination, perhaps on Eisenhower's orders. The Congolese themselves killed Lumumba with the assistance of the Belgians.

On 24 November 1965, Mobutu unexpectedly overthrew the government of the renamed **Democratic Republic of Congo**, ending a political stalemate between Kasavubu and Prime Minister **Moïse Tshombe**, just as Mobutu had done from September 1960–February 1961 following a similar stalemate between Kasavubu and Lumumba. This time Mobutu did not return to the barracks, ruling until he was overthrown in 1997. During his almost 32 years in power, Mobutu bankrupted Congo, stealing billions of dollars in national income and foreign assistance; began "authenticity" and "Zaïrianization" movements that changed the country's name to **Zaïre**, changed the name of many provinces and cities, forced Zaïrians to take African names such as his own Mobutu Sese Seko, and nationalized most foreign businesses with the spoils going to himself and his cronies. Mobutu quit paying the civil service and army, forcing them to live off the land through bribes and robbery, tried but failed to turn himself into a regional power broker by intervening in Angola, and supported U.S. and Western cold war policy in Africa in exchange for **foreign aid** and periodic interventions to stop rebellions against his rule.

The end of the cold war led the U.S. government to stop assisting Mobutu in order to force him to reform. The 1994 genocide by the "Hutu Power" government of Rwanda against its Tutsi minority and the government's subsequent defeat and exile to northeastern Zaïre led to Mobutu's fall. His refusal or inability to take action against the *génocidaires,* who were waging guerilla war against Rwanda, led the Rwandan government to attack the camps and create a buffer zone along its border. When Mobutu's army fled, the Rwandans pressed their attack and, in the name of a rebel movement led by **Laurent-Désiré Kabila**, defeated Mobutu and drove him into exile.

Kabila proved to be even more brutal and incompetent than Mobutu. He broke with the Rwandans, who responded by creating a new rebel force supported by Uganda and Burundi that almost succeeded in removing Kabila until his opponents were stopped by intervention from Angola, Namibia, Zimbabwe, Sudan, Chad, and Libya. The war, called Africa's "first world war" by many and "the Second Scramble for Africa" by President **Julius Nyerere** of **Tanzania**, grew even worse when the Rwandans and Ugandans fought each other along with rebel militias that each backed. UN **peacekeeping** forces and foreign aid were sent in 2002 at a cost of $2 billion per year. The peacekeepers, with a very limited mandate restricting their ability to use force to separate the combatants, themselves engaged in smuggling and child sexual exploitation.

Kabila was killed by a bodyguard in 2001 and was succeeded by his son, **Joseph Kabila**. Negotiations, strongly pushed by the United States, led to an agreement that significantly lessened fighting, produced a transitional government in 2003, and elections in 2006 won by the younger Kabila. In January 2008, the International Rescue Committee, a respected non-governmental organization, estimated that 5.4 million people had died in the fighting and from starvation and disease caused by the war between 1998 and 2007. *See also* ADOULA, CYRILLE; CONGO, CENTRAL INTELLIGENCE AGENCY INVOLVEMENT IN; DEVLIN, LARRY; GBENYE, CHRISTOPHE; GIZENGA, ANTOINE; MULELE, PIERRE; SIMBAS; STANLEYVILLE (KISANGANI) HOSTAGE RESCUE.

CONGO CRISIS. Term generally given to a period of recurring crises in **Congo** lasting from 1960–65, which brought the **cold war** to Africa. The Congo Crisis was precipitated by the 5 July 1960 army rebellion that followed 30 June independence, the ensuing intervention by **Belgium**, the secession of **Katanga** province by **Moïse Tshombe**, **United Nations** (UN) intervention, and the assassination of **Patrice Lumumba**. The secessions, army intervention, revolving door governments, wars, outside interventions, political assassinations, and urban terrorism were only brought to an end with a November 1965 military coup by Joseph-Désiré Mobutu (**Mobutu Sese Seko**). *See also* ADOULA, CYRILLE; CONGO, CENTRAL INTELLIGENCE AGENCY INVOLVEMENT IN; DEVLIN, LARRY; DULLES, ALLEN W.; EISENHOWER, DWIGHT D.; GBENYE, CHRISTOPHE; GIZENGA, ANTOINE; KASAVUBU, JOSEPH; MULELE, PIERRE; OPERATION WIZARD; PEACEKEEPING; SIMBAS; STANLEYVILLE (KISANGANI) HOSTAGE RESCUE.

CONGO–KINSHASA. Name frequently used for **Congo**, the former colony of **Belgium**, from 1966–71.

CONGO–LÉOPOLDVILLE. Name frequently used for **Congo**, the former colony of **Belgium**, from 1960–66.

CONGO, CENTRAL INTELLIGENCE AGENCY INVOLVEMENT IN. U.S. government involvement in **Congo** by the **Central Intelligence Agency** (CIA) was extensive and varied, particularly during the series of crises collectively known as the **Congo Crisis**. CIA intervention commenced with independence from **Belgium** on 30 June 1960 until the crushing of the **Simbas'** rebellion in November 1965. The most important CIA figure in Congo was **Larry Devlin**, who served as station chief from 1960–63 and 1965–67, and retired to Zaïre where he served as a key CIA liaison with president Joseph-Désiré Mobutu (**Mobutu Sese Seko**).

The CIA's first Congo project was **Operation Wizard**, started in late August 1960, with the purpose of politically marginalizing Prime Minister **Patrice Lumumba**. Devlin and his men bribed newspapermen to plant negative stories about Lumumba, organized demonstrations against him, and Devlin advised, cajoled, and bribed Congolese leaders to oppose him. CIA headquarters finally ordered Devlin to kill Lumumba, and the order may have come from President **Dwight D. Eisenhower** (some of those present at an 18 August National Security Council [NSC] meeting believed Eisenhower made a veiled order to assassinate Lumumba, which would preserve plausible deniability on his part, while others believed he was simply calling for Lumumba's political neutralization).

The first assassination attempt called for slipping Lumumba poisoned toothpaste, but Devlin did not do it for moral reasons and because he believed it would be a political mistake. A second attempt was to be carried out by a contracted non-American assassin, whose name has never been revealed, but Lumumba was arrested by the Congolese government on 1 December 1960, which aborted the mission. Congolese later executed him in the presence of Belgian police. A 2002 investigation by the Belgian government established that Devlin and the CIA played no role. After civil government was restored in 1961, the CIA bought legislative support for its preferred prime ministerial candidate, **Cyrille Adoula**. The State Department questioned whether purchasing elected officials was a sound basis for creating a stable government, but concluded that there was no other feasible way in Congo.

The CIA's most important Congolese contact was Army Chief of Staff Mobutu. Mobutu recognized the crucial role that the CIA could play in his ascending to power, and Devlin recognized Mobutu's ambition and ability. Devlin had briefly met Mobutu two times before an early September 1960 meeting when Mobutu sought out Devlin and told him that if he could be immediately assured of U.S. support, he would temporarily overthrow Lumumba and President **Joseph Kasavubu** to install a government of technocrats to restore stability. Without time to consult Washington, Devlin risked his career by reluctantly telling Mobutu that the U.S. would back the coup, which was successful. They became close friends and Devlin dined with Mobutu several times a week thereafter, advising him on any aspects of his rule and twice blocking assassination plots against him. Devlin has also been accused of encouraging Mobutu's November 1965 coup, after which Mobutu kept power, but Devlin denies it, claiming that Mobutu kept plans for the coup a secret, although the next day Mobutu asked Devlin to vet his list of cabinet nominees and Devlin suggested removing two, which Mobutu did.

The CIA also played a significant role in helping the central government put down rebellions. When Lumumba left **United Nations** (UN) protective custody to join a rebel government in Stanleyville (Kisangani) established in his name, the CIA allegedly provided the Congolese with information that assisted with his capture. During 1964, with Simba rebels based in eastern Congo controlling two-thirds of the national territory, the CIA set up an "instant air force" of Italian jets converted into fighters and World War II vintage U.S. bombers that were piloted by non–U.S. citizen Cuban exiles, who had participated in the Bay of Pigs. CIA pilots continued to man Mobutu's air force through 1969. The CIA may have paid for mercenary soldiers that led the government's counterattack and did provide special forces soldiers to act as advisers. The CIA also used more subtle tactics such as when agents learned that Czechoslovakia was shipping arms through **Sudan** in boxes marked as Red Cross refugee supplies, they paid Sudanese stevedores to drop one of the boxes from a crane, breaking it open to reveal Soviet-made rifles, thus forcing the Sudanese government to stop the weapons flow. When a source in **Egypt** told Devlin that a Congolese would be flying into Sudan from the **Soviet Union** carrying several hundred thousand dollars for Lumumbist **Antoine Gizenga**'s forces during the spring of 1961, the CIA arranged to steal the money while the man was meeting with customs officers. Gizenga's armed forces had a reputation for being the best paid in Congo, but this loss of funding severely damaged morale.

In the mid-1970s, **Zaïre** served as a base for the CIA to train **Holden Roberto**'s *Frente Nacional de Libertação de Angola*/National Front for the Liberation of Angola (FNLA) rebels, and in the 1980s, it was a conduit point for the CIA to arm **Jonas Savimbi**'s *União Nacional para a Independência Total de Angola*/National Union for the Total Liberation of Angola (UNITA). *See also* GBENYE, CHRISTOPHE; STANLEYVILLE (KISANGANI) HOSTAGE RESCUE.

CONGO, DEMOCRATIC REPUBLIC OF. Official name of **Congo** from 1964–71 and 1997–present.

CONGO, REPUBLIC OF. Official name of **Congo** from 1960–64.

CONSTRUCTIVE ENGAGEMENT. U.S. policy toward **South Africa** during the presidency of **Ronald W. Reagan**. Early in his administration, Reagan argued that in light of South Africa's vital mineral wealth and support for the West, the U.S. could not abandon it to possible Communist takeover. Constructive Engagement was therefore formulated by Assistant Secretary of State for African

Affairs Chester Crocker as a way to treat South Africa as a valued anti-Communist ally rather than a pariah state while working behind the scenes with quiet diplomacy to express U.S. abhorrence for **apartheid** and to persuade the government to end repression and grant its black population civil rights. The policy may have born some fruit, as the South African government dismantled so-called petty apartheid, the sort of segregation used in the Jim Crow American South, and ended pass laws, which required blacks to carry internal passports. Nonetheless, the South African government strengthened the central apartheid policy of "separate development" through the institutionalization of autonomous or independent *Bantustans* (so-called tribal homelands) as the sole legal nationalities for blacks.

U.S. public opinion began to turn against Constructive Engagement beginning on Thanksgiving weekend, 1984, when protesters led by **TransAfrica** held a sit-in at the South African embassy to protest apartheid. The sit-in movement spread to colleges across the U.S., augmented by student demands that their colleges divest portfolio stock held in corporations doing business with South Africa. The pressure hit its peak with passage over Reagan's veto of the **Comprehensive Anti-Apartheid Act** (CAAA) in October 1986, despite the president's arguments that black African nations engaged in **trade** with South Africa and black South African leaders like **Mangosuthu Buthelezi** said that sanctions would hurt South African blacks.

The U.S. role in negotiating the December 1988 **New York Accords** that gave independence to **Namibia** and removed **Cuban** and South African troops from **Angola** may have been facilitated by the relationship fostered by the Constructive Engagement policy. *See also* AFRICAN AFFAIRS, STATE DEPARTMENT BUREAU OF; DIVESTMENT (DISINVESTMENT) FROM SOUTH AFRICA MOVEMENT.

CUBA. Caribbean island nation, whose longtime president, Fidel Castro, provided **foreign aid** and military assistance including intervention to African nations out of a spirit of fraternal revolutionary solidarity and as a means of keeping the United States occupied in theaters away from the Western Hemisphere and thus unable to focus its might on Cuba.

To improve social development, Castro provided socialist African nations with doctors and technical experts while providing their students with free college educations, which sometimes included guerilla training in addition to standard courses in dialectical materialism. Militarily, Cuba provided soldiers and armaments to many nations, but most importantly to **Algeria**, where they prevented **Morocco** from taking disputed territory in 1963; **Congo**, where Che Guevara failed in his 1965 effort to bring to power **Laurent-Désiré Kabila**; **Angola**, where 17,000 troops defeated two competing rebel armies and **South Africa**, bringing to power Communist leader **Agostinho Neto** in 1976, then 57,000 defended Angola from the South Africans again in 1987, helping to force South Africa to free Southwest Africa (**Namibia**), the last African colony; and in **Ethiopia**, where 15,000 intervened in its **Ogaden War** with **Somalia** and drove the Somali army out of the Ogaden Desert, then helped to crush indigenous rebel movements around the country (although not in **Eritrea**).

The end of the **cold war** and pressure from the **Soviet Union** led to withdrawal of Cuban troops from the continent, which precipitated the collapse of Ethiopia's Communist government in 1991, and forced the Angolan government to negotiate a short-lived peace settlement with opposition guerilla leader **Jonas Savimbi** in 1992. In mid-2008, Cuba continued to provide African governments with humanitarian support and educational opportunities. *See also* BOTHA, PETER WILLEM (P.W.); MENGISTU HAILE MARIAM; NUJOMA, SHAFILSHONA SAMUEL ("SAM"); ROBERTO, HOLDEN.

– D –

DARFUR. A western region of **Sudan** that is the site of genocide perpetrated by the Sudanese government. Darfur is the size of Texas and is Sudan's poorest and least developed region. Its population is primarily black and Muslim, but with a significant nomadic Arab population. The region has suffered neglect and occasional repression since Sudan achieved independence.

Fighting began in February 2003 when guerillas from the Sudan Liberation Movement/Army (SLM/A) and the Justice and Equality Movement (JEM) attacked Sudanese military bases in retaliation for government-supported militia attacks on black Darfurian farmers. The government responded in April 2003 with a campaign that seems designed to exterminate the region's black population. Government army officers led Arab-based militias known as the **Janjaweed**, which were supported by the Sudanese air force. They attacked and burned villages, slaughtering indiscriminately, poisoned wells, and raped women who are subsequently ostracized by their own people. By mid-2008, 2.2 million Darfurians out of a population of six million had been displaced to camps in Sudan or eastern **Chad**, with between 200,000 and 400,000 killed or dying from starvation by mid-2008. Civil unrest spread to Chad and the Central African Republic.

U.S. Secretary of State **Colin Powell** called Darfur genocide on 9 September 2004, the first world leader to do so, and was seconded by President **George W. Bush**, but the **United Nations** (UN), **African Union** (AU), and European Union (EU) disagreed. U.S. efforts to persuade the UN to declare genocide, which would have necessitated UN intervention, were blocked by the government of **China**, which had extensive commercial ties with the Sudanese government, especially with its nascent **oil** industry. The AU sent **peacekeepers** in August 2004. They were to be replaced by a "hybrid" peacekeeping force of AU and UN forces, the United Nations–African Union Mission in Darfur (UN-AMID) authorized in July 2007, but by mid-2008 the UN reported that it was "severely under-resourced," with only 9,000 soldiers and police deployed out of a mandated 26,000.

In 2007, U.S. activists began a divestment campaign against the Sudanese government. By mid-2008, 60 colleges and 24 states had divested, led by Harvard University. In 2008, the movement focused its efforts on TIAA-CREF, a $400 billion provider of financial services to employees of universities, **nongovernmental organizations** (NGOs), and government employees. Despite having divested from **South Africa** because of apartheid in 1986, TIAA-CREF refused to divest its $67 million in shares from the four oil companies that provided the Sudanese government with 70 percent of its revenue as of mid-2008.

From 2004 to 2008, the U.S. contributed over $3 billion for aid programs in Sudan and refugees and displaced people in eastern Chad, including $600 million appropriated for fiscal year 2008. In 2007, Congress passed the Sudan Accountability and Divestment Act, which authorizes state and local governments to divest from businesses with operations in Sudan and prohibits the U.S. government from contracting with them. On 28 May 2008, the three major U.S. candidates for president released an unprecedented joint statement that said each would take immediate action against the government of Sudan if "peace and security" were not restored to Darfur by the time that one of them took office in January 2008. On 14 July 2008, the chief prosecutor of the International Criminal Court, Luis Moreno-Ocampo, asked judges to issue an arrest warrant for Sudanese leader **Omar Bashir** on charges of crimes against humanity in Darfur. Sudanese officials warned that they could not guarantee the safety of UN and AU peacekeeping forces if Bashir is indicted, but emphasized that this was not a threat.

DE KLERK, FREDERICK WILLEM (F.W.) (1936–). President of **South Africa** (1989–94) and co-winner of the Nobel Peace Prize with **Nelson Mandela** for having negotiated South Africa's transition to democratic majority rule. De Klerk succeeded the hard-line **P.W. Botha** as South Africa's president and immediately set out in a new political direction. The confluence of the fall of the **Soviet Union**'s empire, South African war weariness over fighting in **Angola** and Southwest Africa followed by relief over its successful decolonization to independent **Namibia**, economic difficulties caused by worldwide economic sanctions, and a general malaise over being an international pariah created an atmosphere in which de Klerk had the opportunity to move boldly toward systemic reform.

In February 1990, de Klerk freed Mandela, the African National Congress (ANC) leader, and began negotiations. At the same time, violence broke out between the ANC and **Mangosuthu Buthelezi**'s Zulu Inkatha Party, with perhaps 10,000 people dying by 1994. Inkatha was later proven to have been secretly funded by South African intelligence. A secret unit of South African intelligence also grew increasingly violent, targeting ANC leaders for assassination. Mandela blamed de Klerk for the violence and for his failure to stop it, and de Klerk blamed the ANC. Despite their differences, de Klerk and Mandela shared the 1993 Nobel Peace Prize, and the following year Mandela was elected president. De Klerk's goal was to negotiate a system of power sharing, but Mandela refused to compromise on majority rule. Combined with the increasing ethnic violence and ungovernability in the impoverished black townships that was ordered by the ANC, Mandela's refusal to yield forced de Klerk to agree to complete majority rule.

Following Mandela's April 1994 election, De Klerk served as one of the government's deputy presidents until 1996, when he went into opposition. De Klerk appeared before South Africa's Truth and Reconciliation Committee three times and apologized for **apartheid** without taking responsibility for abuses under his rule. The commission concluded that he had done little to rein in the security services and had not told the commission about gross human rights abuses of which he had knowledge.

DEVLIN, LARRY (1924–). Central Intelligence Agency (CIA) station chief in **Congo** (1960–63, 1965–67), chief for East Africa (1963–65), and for the Africa Division. Devlin became a crucial figure in U.S. relations with Congo because he quickly recognized the ambition and talent of Congolese Army Chief of Staff Joseph-Désiré Mobutu (**Mobutu Sese Seko**), and because Mobutu recognized the crucial role that the CIA could play in advancing his career.

Devlin had concluded that Congo's first prime minister, **Patrice Lumumba**, was dangerously erratic and had surrounded himself with Leftist advisers, thus making him a target for the **Soviet Union**. The administration of President **Dwight D. Eisenhower** was so concerned about Lumumba that CIA Director **Allen Dulles** ordered Devlin to kill him, on Eisenhower's specific orders, he was told. Devlin believed that murdering Lumumba would be immoral and a dangerous policy error, although he agreed that Lumumba had to be removed, so he used bureaucratic delay while working to erode Lumumba's power and public standing through the CIA's **Operation Wizard**. Although historians have frequently blamed Devlin for killing Lumumba or at least disposing of his body, a commission of inquiry by the government of Belgium exonerated him and the U.S. government in 2002.

Devlin has also been blamed for plotting Mobutu's 1965 coup, which he denies, although he admitted having breakfasted most mornings with Mobutu for months prior to the coup and having helped choose Mobutu's cabinet in the days following. Devlin retired from the CIA in 1974 and went to work in diamond merchant Maurice Tempelsman's **Zaïre** office, also working as a CIA conduit to Mobutu. State Department officials complained that Mobutu continued to treat him as the real source of U.S. power. *See also* ADOULA, CYRILLE; CONGO, CENTRAL INTELLIGENCE AGENCY INVOLVEMENT IN; GIZENGA, ANTOINE; SIMBAS.

DIVESTMENT (DISINVESTMENT) FROM SOUTH AFRICA MOVEMENT. Movement begun on 13 March 1966 to end U.S. business investment in **South Africa** in order to pressure its government to end **apartheid** and begin black-majority rule. Divestment had little success until critical mass was achieved following news media coverage of the violence resulting from South Africa's 1983 effort to create a constitution that gave legal rights to Asians (East Indians) and Coloreds (mixed race) and took away the citizenship of black South Africans, making them citizens of their ethnic *Bantustans* (tribal homelands) without legal rights outside their *Bantustans*. A key moment in the divestment campaign was a 1986 threat to divest by TIAA-CREF, one of the largest financial services corporations in the U.S., which handled pension funds for universities and organizations in the medical, research, cultural, and nonprofit fields.

Student involvement was also intense, with sit-ins that followed the example of a Thanksgiving 1984 sit-in at the South African embassy by **TransAfrica**, a lockout of administrators at Columbia University, and the building of "shantytowns" on campuses to simulate life in the illegal black townships that surrounded South African cities. Students pressured Harvard University to make a small partial divestment from its portfolio of businesses with branches in South Africa, which was followed on 18 July 1986 by the University of California, which voted to divest completely, selling $3.1 billion in stock and bonds with ties to South Africa. On 26 August, the California State Senate voted to divest pension funds for the entire state of California. On 6 October, General Motors, which had begun the **Sullivan Principles** to bring civil rights to South African workers at the workplace, reluctantly voted to divest, followed by IBM on 21 October 1986. Western European nations and Japan followed the U.S. lead. Each of these actions hurt South Africa's economy and created among white South Africans a sense that the West had abandoned them, both of which would have long-term consequences in pushing South Africa toward ending apartheid and instituting black-majority rule. *See also* BOTHA, PETER WILLEM (P.W.); COMPREHENSIVE ANTI-APARTHEID ACT (CAAA); CONSTRUCTIVE ENGAGEMENT; TUTU, DESMOND.

DODD, THOMAS (1907–1971). U.S. statesman and senator from Connecticut (1959–71). Dodd was a liberal Democrat and one of the most strongly anti-Communist U.S. senators. Known for his withering questioning of administration foreign policy officials—he had been an outstanding prosecutor at the Nuremburg War Crimes Trial of former Nazis—Dodd strongly supported the rebel government of **Moïse Tshombe** in **Katanga**, the rebel government of **Ian Smith** in **Rhodesia (Zimbabwe)**, and the **apartheid** government of **South Africa**. He argued that Tshombe's government was the best example of multi-racial democracy in Africa and that blacks had higher standards of living in Rhodesia and South Africa, and often more civil rights, than anywhere else in Africa. Dodd's ability to mobilize anti-Communist public opinion, such as through the **Katanga Lobby**, often forced Presidents **John F. Kennedy** and **Lyndon B. Johnson** to weaken their positions against these countries' governments, causing tensions between the U.S. and African countries. Dodd was censured by the Senate for conversion of campaign funds for personal use in 1967, and was defeated for reelection in 1970. *See also* CONGO.

DOE, SAMUEL (1951–1990). Army sergeant and first indigenous tribesman to rule as president of **Liberia**, (1980–90). Although barely literate, Doe came to lead a group of native enlisted men who were unhappy with the **Americo-Liberian** domination of Liberia's political, economic, and social life. The international recession of the 1970s forced President **William Tolbert** to talk about cutting the army's economic special privileges. After Tolbert used the army in April 1979 to suppress protests over increased prices for rice, the country's staple crop, Doe and his men launched a 12 April 1980 coup. Tolbert was brutally murdered: it was reported that Doe personally disemboweled him in his bed and ritualistically ate pieces of his body to gain his strength. Doe took over as president and, at age 28 and an enlisted man, was the youngest and lowest-ranking soldier to come to power in Africa to that time.

Within days, kangaroo courts with nonsensical proceedings sentenced Tolbert's top advisers to firing squads, which were botched but executed. Ecstatic crowds celebrated. The celebrations quickly turned to fear on a scale never before seen in Liberia as brutality and incompetence became the hallmarks of Doe's rule. Doe's Krahn tribe supplanted the Americo-Liberians as Liberia's rulers and brutally repressed the other indigenous tribes. Despite the depravities of his rule, Doe became an American client when he went to the U.S. embassy for advice after the failures of the first months of his rule threatened to destroy the country's economy.

Thereafter, Doe was a strong anti-Communist—he closed the embassy of the **Soviet Union**—and repeatedly promised to return to the barracks, winning him strong support from the administration of **Ronald W. Reagan**. Doe also allowed the U.S. to maintain vital communications equipment by the **Central Intelligence Agency (CIA)** and other government agencies. In return, his government received vast American patronage, some $500 million, which he squandered. Doe's buffoonery and continued reneging on pledges to return to the barracks finally pushed the U.S. to use its **foreign aid** leverage to compel him to hold elections in October 1985, but Washington did nothing to ensure that the results were fair. After several weeks of creative accounting while holding up announcement of the results, Doe emerged victorious with 51 percent of the vote. The U.S. took no steps to punish him although diplomats believed that the kind of pressure that was at that time being put on Philippines' President Ferdinand Marcos would have forced Doe out of office.

In December 1989, a charismatic half Americo-Liberian gangster and political opportunist, **Charles Taylor**, launched a tribal rebellion against Doe and the Krahn. The U.S. no longer had need to support a regime such as Doe's because the Soviet Union's empire was collapsing, so the **George H.W. Bush** administration ignored Doe's calls for help. Troops from **Nigeria** intervened and Doe surrendered to them. They turned him over to their favored rebel leader, Taylor's former military commander, Prince Johnson. Johnson wanted Doe's stolen millions and, to make him talk, personally oversaw his torture. After cutting off Doe's ears, nose, lips, tongue, and genitalia (which were shoved in his mouth), he was murdered, and pieces of his body eaten, all of which was videotaped at Johnson's orders. Until the election of President **Ellen Johnson-Sirleaf**, the videotape was easily available from Monrovia street vendors.

DU BOIS, WILLIAM EDWARD BURGHARDT (W.E.B.) (1868–1963). African American teacher, scholar, and civil rights leader. Du Bois was one of the earliest African Americans to earn a doctoral degree. His scholarship initially focused on African American history and sociology, and his doctoral dissertation on the **transatlantic slave trade** was of seminal importance. Du Bois argued against the "industrial education" ideas associated with **Booker T. Washington**, which focused on improving African American life from the bottom up while ignoring civil rights. Instead, Du Bois said that the "Talented Tenth" of African Americans should pull up the race through rigorous education in the liberal arts, as was done at such **historically black colleges and universities** (HBCUs) as Howard and Lincoln. Du Bois was also an integrationist, particularly in the first half of his long life, and bitterly opposed the black separatist ideas of **Marcus Garvey**.

In 1909, Du Bois helped found the National Association for the Advancement of Colored People (NAACP) and the following year became editor of its newspaper, *The Crisis*, until his resignation in 1934. As editor, Du Bois combined reportage with hard-hitting and often inflammatory editorials, increasing circulation to over 100,000 by 1920. He placed a far greater emphasis on Africa than the editor of any other publication in the United States, which continued after he left the newspaper. As a result, from 1910 to 1945, *The Crisis* published more articles and editorials on Africa than all other national magazines and newspapers combined.

Du Bois' interest in modern Africa may have begun when he attended a Pan-African conference in London in 1900, although the participants made almost no mention of Africa itself. Du Bois organized a series of Pan-African conferences beginning in 1919, with a much greater emphasis on Africa. Suggestions made at the 1919 Pan-

African conference may have influenced the victorious World War I Allies to create the League of Nations mandate system for conquered colonies included in the Treaty of Versailles. In 1930, Du Bois published two books about African history and culture, and in 1946, 1960, and 1965 he published books on Africa's foreign relations and its international role. In 1923–24, Du Bois went to Africa for the first time. While visiting **Liberia**, he is believed to have persuaded President Charles D.B. King to announce that Liberia would accept no immigrants from the U.S. traveling with Garvey's Universal Negro Improvement Association (UNIA), which killed Garvey's movement.

As early as 1915, Du Bois' ideas on Africa in the world system were much more radical than was his work on the U.S., and were a precursor to the Leninist theory of imperialism. By 1961, he had concluded that capitalism was as evil at home as it was abroad, and he became a Communist. In October 1961, Du Bois moved to **Ghana** when President **Kwame Nkrumah** agreed to sponsor creation of an *Encyclopedia Africana* under the direction of Du Bois. In 1963, Du Bois took Ghanaian citizenship when the U.S. embassy refused to renew his passport. He died in Ghana at the age of 95 on 27 August 1963, the day before the March on Washington.

DULLES, ALLEN W. (1893–1969). Central Intelligence Agency (CIA) director under Presidents **Harry S. Truman, Dwight D. Eisenhower**, and **John F. Kennedy** and brother of Eisenhower's secretary of state, **John Foster Dulles**. Allen Dulles was a strong supporter of covert operations as a means of quietly projecting U.S. power. The CIA's most important African interventions under Dulles were in **Egypt** and **Congo**. In Egypt, the CIA assisted **Muhammad Naguib** and **Gamal Abdel Nasser** of the Free Officers Movement in overthrowing King **Farouk**, and then tried to overthrow Nasser during the summer of 1957 in Operation SIPONY, which may have included sending assassination teams to kill him. In Congo, **Operation Wizard** tried to destabilize and bring down Prime Minister **Patrice Lumumba**. It was superseded by Dulles' direct order to CIA Station Chief **Larry Devlin** to kill Lumumba, an order that Devlin delayed in executing until Congolese and officers on loan from **Belgium** together killed him. The CIA also played an ambiguous role during **Algeria**'s war for independence, apparently supporting both **France**

and the rebels. President **John F. Kennedy** fired Dulles following the Bay of Pigs fiasco, although officially Dulles resigned a few months later.

DULLES, JOHN FOSTER (1888–1959). Strongly anti-Communist secretary of state under President **Dwight D. Eisenhower** and brother of Central Intelligence Agency (CIA) Director **Allen Dulles.** John Foster Dulles was the Republican Party's top foreign affairs specialist when Eisenhower was elected in 1952. Said to make foreign policy with "a sword in one hand and a Bible in the other," Dulles' anti-Communist rhetoric obscured a careful lawyer's mind.

Dulles' primary goals for **Egypt** and the Middle East were conflicting and proved untenable. He sought Middle East peace with a systematic program: work closely with Egyptian President **Gamal Abdel Nasser**, whom many already considered a dangerous character; treat **Israel** the same as Egypt instead of maintaining President **Harry S. Truman**'s pro-Israel tilt; and freeze arms sales to all sides to avoid a regional arms race. At the same time, Dulles tried to put together a Middle East anti-Soviet alliance that would prevent Soviet expansionism. Nasser wanted no part of the alliance, which became the **Baghdad Pact**, and was enraged when Egypt's chief Arab opponent, Iraq, replaced Egypt as its cornerstone. Nasser also wanted modern weapons in quantity, so he turned to the **Soviet Union** in 1955, and received over $200 million worth through Czechoslovakia. Dulles tried to rekindle relations with an offer to provide significant assistance in building the **Aswan High Dam**, but Nasser's continued enmity led him to cancel the project in July 1956, precipitating the **Suez Crisis**. Although hospitalized with the cancer that killed him, Dulles argued forcefully to Eisenhower that the United States must force **Great Britain, France**, and Israel to stop their attacks on Egypt and withdraw, which Eisenhower did.

Dulles was a strong opponent of colonialism, and was especially tough on the French for refusing to free **Algeria** and instead fighting the Algerian civil war. Although he considered sub-Saharan Africa to be vital to the West, it played only a small part in his calculations. Despite his anti-colonialism, Dulles worried that Africa was a troubled place open to Soviet machinations and, if Africa were lost to the Communists, the economic consequences would be so great that

Western Europe would not be able to defend itself. As a result of this analysis, in 1956 he said that the U.S. would only support independence in those colonies that were ready for it, but he also began work to increase U.S. **foreign aid** to Africa. *See also* EURAFRICA.

– E –

EGYPT. Located at the confluence of Arab North Africa and the Arab Middle East, Egypt is the most populous and powerful Arab country and played an important role in U.S. foreign policy from almost the first days of the **cold war**. President **Harry S. Truman**'s unexpected and undiplomatically quick recognition of **Israel** in May 1948 and U.S. support for Israel in the subsequent Arab invasion created a difficult hurdle for good U.S. relations with Egypt. Equally as difficult was the U.S. alliance with **Great Britain** and **France**, which jointly controlled the Suez Canal while the British also had a series of military bases with 81,000 men in the Suez Canal Zone. Neither U.S. ally would give up its interest in the canal because of fear that the Egyptians either lacked the capability to run it or would intentionally block them from using it, which would put Western Europe's **oil** supply in jeopardy. Just as important, the British and French were determined to maintain their position as Great Powers. Relations improved and a deal was worked out in which the British evacuated the bases and left behind only technicians to run the canal following the **Central Intelligence Agency** (CIA)–backed 23 July 1952 overthrow of Egyptian King **Farouk** by the Free Officers Movement, a "colonel's coup" led by Lieutenant General **Muhammad Naguib** and Colonel **Gamal Abdel Nasser**.

Truman's successor, **Dwight D. Eisenhower**, was much less accommodating of the U.S. European allies and Israel because he hoped to win Nasser's support for making Egypt the foundation for a Middle Eastern alliance against the **Soviet Union**. Historians agree that this goal led Eisenhower to have the least "special" relationship with Israel of any president. U.S. policy failed because Nasser considered Great Britain and Israel to be Egypt's greatest threats, not the Soviets. Nasser's goals were to unite the Arabs into one nation under his control, destroy Israel, and impose socialism.

When Nasser bartered a huge arms deal with the Soviets in exchange for cotton in September 1955, the U.S. first offered then reneged on a promise to fund at least the first stage of building the **Aswan High Dam**. Nasser surprised the Eisenhower administration when he retaliated by nationalizing the Suez Canal. British intelligence had also learned that Egypt was using covert operations to try to overthrow the monarchs of Jordan, **Libya**, and Iraq, prompting Prime Minister Anthony Eden to demand armed intervention. Eisenhower instead cautioned patience, diplomacy, and allegedly a joint U.S.-British intelligence effort to discredit Nasser, arguing that more vigorous measures would alienate the Arab masses, which would endanger conservative Arab governments. Eden ignored him and secretly conspired with the French and the Israelis to retake the canal and overthrow Nasser. Israel invaded Egypt on 29 October 1956 with the British and French joining on 5 November. The U.S. aborted the **Suez Crisis** through uncompromising political and economic pressure, leaving Nasser more popular and influential among the Arab people than ever before as the man who had defeated the colonialists. Despite diplomacy, efforts to subvert his opponents, and armed intervention in Yemen, Nasser was unable to capitalize on his prestige to unite the Arab states except for a brief union with Syria (1958–61) during which he changed Egypt's name to the United Arab Republic. His successor, **Anwar Sadat**, changed the name back in 1971.

President **John F. Kennedy** moved U.S. policy much closer to Israel than Eisenhower's had been, including the sale of sophisticated weapons, but he and Secretary of State **Dean Rusk** concluded that neither the Israelis nor the Arabs were prepared to compromise on a peace agreement, so they left the issue alone. Nasser's intervention in the Yemeni civil war on the side of pro-Soviet forces prevented Kennedy from improving relations with Egypt. President **Lyndon B. Johnson** was too engrossed in domestic issues and then Vietnam to make Egypt or the Middle East a priority. This changed on 18 May 1967 when Nasser ordered the **United Nations** (UN) to remove the UN Emergency Force (UNEF) peacekeepers that had separated Egypt from Israel since the end of the Suez Crisis. He also blockaded Israeli access to the Red Sea, an act of war. Without a buffer between the two countries, Israel launched what became the **Arab–Israeli War of 1967**, which cost Egypt the Sinai and Gaza Strip along with much of Nasser's international prestige and his air force. Nasser broke relations with Washington, accusing the U.S. of having been the true perpetrator of the attack on his air force. Military recovery required Nasser to have still closer relations with the **Soviet Union**. Nasser's death in September 1970 produced national and regional hysteria.

President Sadat wanted to break Egypt's tie with the Soviets and secretly sought an opening with the U.S. and Israel, but was rebuffed. To show them that Egypt remained consequential, Sadat launched the **Arab–Israeli War of 1973** on 6 October 1973. Although the Egyptians were defeated and their forces would have been crushed had not the U.S. intervened to stay the Israelis, the significant initial Egyptian successes shook the administration of **Richard M. Nixon** and the Israeli government out of their complacent disdain for Arab power and provided Sadat with the prestige to remove the Soviets from Egypt. Secretary of State **Henry Kissinger**'s "**shuttle diplomacy**" worked out a settlement to the war, and his "step-by-step" diplomacy slowly moved the parties toward a larger peace.

Jimmy Carter's election as president in November 1976 ended Kissinger's careful movement toward peace, replaced by Carter's call for a Geneva conference that would solve all the Middle East's problems at once. To prevent the conference, Sadat went to Jerusalem to meet with the new Israeli prime minister, Menachem Begin. Initial euphoria gave way to intransigence from both sides and rejection by the other Middle East powers and the Soviets, so Carter matched Sadat's dramatics by bringing him and Begin to the Camp David presidential retreat to work out a peace treaty in September 1978. After 12 days of intense negotiation, argument, and prayer at meetings held together by a steadfastness of purpose that belied the rest of Carter's foreign policy, Sadat and Begin signed the **Camp David Accords**. Carter broke another impasse in early 1979 when he flew to Egypt and Israel for talks. A treaty was signed on 26 March 1979 that returned the Sinai to Egypt in exchange for peace between the two nations and mutual recognition. Carter also promised to increase aid to Egypt, which peaked at $4 billion annually in **foreign aid** and $2 billion in military assistance. There would have been no treaty without Carter's efforts.

In March 1980, Sadat assisted the U.S. by agreeing to give the deposed shah of Iran a place to live following the 4 November 1979

Iranian invasion of the U.S. embassy and ensuing hostage crisis, which ostensibly had been launched when the U.S. allowed the shah to come to New York for medical treatment. Carter hoped that Sadat's action would lead to release of the hostages, but was disappointed. Sadat was assassinated by Egyptian Islamic Jihad during celebration of the anniversary of the 1973 war. His successor, **Hosni Mubarak**, joined the U.S. in the first Gulf War in January–February 1991, reportedly receiving $20 billion in economic aid and $20 billion in debt forgiveness as compensation. Mubarak opposed the second Gulf War that began in March 2003 but has worked closely with the U.S. in the **Global War on Terror** (GWOT). In 2004, he began an economic liberalization program overseen by his son, Gamal Mubarak, which has led to impressive economic growth of 7 percent per year and increased foreign direct investment from $450 million in 2003 to $10 billion in 2008, but high inflation combined with stagnant wages for the poor produced a slight growth in poverty from 2005 to 2008. Many analysts believe that Mubarak is grooming Gamal to be his successor as president. *See also* ACHESON, DEAN G.; BAGDAD PACT; DULLES, ALLEN W.; DULLES, JOHN FOSTER; EGYPT, CENTRAL INTELLIGENCE AGENCY INVOLVEMENT IN; FORD, GERALD R.

EGYPT, CENTRAL INTELLIGENCE AGENCY INVOLVEMENT IN. U.S. intelligence began its work in **Egypt** during World War II when the **Central Intelligence Agency**'s (CIA) precursor, the Office of Strategic Services (OSS), set up its Middle Eastern headquarters in the capital, Cairo, during early 1943. The CIA apparently began serious **cold war** operations in Egypt during late 1951, working to avoid upheaval in Cairo, which the U.S. government feared could lead to a Communist takeover. The Egyptian army had performed disastrously in the **Arab–Israeli War of 1948–49**, poverty was endemic, and instability had become chronic due to Egyptian demands that the governments of **Great Britain** and **France** turn over the Suez Canal, which they were loathe to do for strategic and prestige reasons. Egyptian King **Farouk**'s lack of interest in affairs of state allowed the problems to fester until fighting broke out between Egyptian and British troops in January 1952.

The CIA sought to support an alternative to Farouk, and agent Kermit Roosevelt, grandson of President **Theodore Roosevelt**, recommended the Free Officers Movement, a nationalist group of primarily colonels led by Lieutenant Colonel **Gamal Abdel Nasser** and General **Muhammad Naguib**. On 2 February 1952, CIA Director **Allen Dulles** approved U.S. support for a coup, and the Free Officers successfully overthrew Farouk on 23 July 1952. The CIA has not released information about what assistance it actually provided. It continued to support the Free Officers' government, especially its intelligence unit, in order to crush a rebellion by the Islamist Muslim Brotherhood. The CIA also reportedly supplied Nasser with the bulletproof vest that saved his life during an attempted assassination by the Brotherhood in October 1954.

Nasser's 26 September 1955 agreement to **trade** cotton for Eastern Bloc weapons severely damaged relations with the U.S., and Secretary of State **John Foster Dulles** met with his British counterpart to discuss how to bring Nasser back or, if necessary, overthrow him. By the summer of 1956, the U.S. and Great Britain had launched Operation Omega, a covert operation designed to bring down Nasser. Most information about the operation remains classified, and apparently President **Dwight D. Eisenhower** sought to have it postponed as the Suez situation worsened in October. Despite forcing Great Britain, France, and **Israel** to halt their November invasion of Suez and withdraw from Egypt, probably saving Nasser and ending the **Suez Crisis**, the Eisenhower administration continued to talk about removing him. In late 1956 or early 1957, Allen Dulles told a State Department briefer, "If that colonel of yours pushes us too far, we will break him in half." The U.S. sought British assistance for a new effort to bring down Nasser during the summer of 1957, called Operation SIPONY, which they hoped would result in a military coup. A CIA source has reported that Secretary of State Dulles called for Nasser's assassination and that three hit teams were sent to Egypt, but nothing happened. U.S. Senate investigators were unable to confirm these rumors in 1975.

In March 1958, U.S. intelligence apparently tried to prevent Egypt from unifying with Syria to form the United Arab Republic by persuading Saudi Arabian King Saud to pay Syria's Abdul Hamid Sarraj $5 million to back out. Instead, Sarraj reportedly turned the money over to Nasser and told him that he had learned that the U.S. had played a role in the plot. Nasser came to blame the U.S. for every subsequent setback, including the brilliant Israeli performance in the **Arab–Israeli War of 1967** and the expulsion of the Palestine Liberation Organization (PLO) from Jordan by King Hussein in 1970.

The CIA became very close to Nasser's successor, **Anwar Sadat**, after his turn to the West following the **Arab–Israeli War of 1973**. By 1979, the CIA reportedly began to provide Sadat with protection, including electronic and human intelligence to provide warnings of coup plots, but it was unable to stop Muslim extremists from assassinating him on 6 October 1981.

EISENHOWER, DWIGHT D. (1890–1969). U.S. military leader and president (1953–61). Eisenhower's National Security Council (NSC) created the first official U.S. foreign policy toward sub-Saharan Africa, **NSC Memorandum 5719/1**, in 1957.

Eisenhower had more personal experience in the third world and Africa than any other president, having served in the Philippines with responsibility for creating a professional Filipino army, and in North Africa as commander of **Operation Torch** and the **Tunisia Campaign**. His experience left him with a generally poor opinion of third-world peoples. Nonetheless, Eisenhower believed that colonialism's time had passed and that its continuation would alienate the third world from the West and drive it to the **Soviet Union**, resulting in disastrous loss of access to strategic resources for the U.S. and the West. At the same time, Eisenhower worried that U.S. support for decolonization could lead Europe's colonial powers to lessen support for the North Atlantic Treaty Organization (NATO), the Western bulwark against the Soviet Bloc.

Although Eisenhower used his presidential "bully pulpit" to argue that the U.S. was the leader of the anti-colonial movement because of its history as the first colony to win its independence, many Africans and their leaders saw the U.S. as a racist country that provided economic and military support to the colonizers while violently repressing the civil rights of **African Americans**' Civil Rights Movement as vigorously as Europeans were repressing independence movements.

Eisenhower and Secretary of State **John Foster Dulles** used gentle public diplomacy combined with often brutally frank behind-the-scenes talks in an effort to push the Europeans toward a measured decolonization with gradual, phased movement to self-government. The

Eisenhower administration especially pushed this approach for Africa, where the president and his advisers believed that few colonies were ready for independence because they had minuscule educated elites and middle classes, huge numbers of illiterates, and few sources of national income. His government's position was often based as much on racist notions about Africans as it was on demographic and economic data. On more than a few occasions, records of administration discussions about Africa showed that officials, including the president himself, referred to Africans as "barely out of the trees." Vice President **Richard M. Nixon** also used such language, and he was the administration's strongest supporter of African independence and **foreign aid**.

Nixon's leadership on Africa policy within the administration followed a 1957 Africa tour centered on attending **Ghana**'s independence celebration. Nixon convinced Eisenhower that the Communist threat to Africa was so great that the administration needed a comprehensive Africa policy and greater economic assistance to Africa. Eisenhower was also pushed into a more vigorously anti-colonial stance by Senator **John F. Kennedy** of Massachusetts, who in 1956 and 1957 speeches attacked the Eisenhower administration for its failure to pressure **France** to end the civil war in **Algeria** and grant independence. Kennedy also said that Eisenhower should support the efforts of all colonized peoples to win their freedom. Eisenhower also began to follow Nixon's advice and push for greater economic assistance to Africa based on national security grounds, abandoning his previous policy of "**trade**, not aid." Congressional refusal to fund foreign aid in the amounts that he considered necessary prompted Eisenhower repeatedly to complain that Congress and the people of the U.S. did not understand foreign policy.

Eisenhower's most controversial Africa policy was in **Congo**, which was given its independence from **Belgium** on 30 June 1960. In the months prior to independence, Eisenhower's State Department had determined that Congo would become the most important recipient of U.S. foreign aid because of its vast mineral resources and its strategic position at the center of Africa. Eisenhower reversed his policy when the Congolese army mutinied and civil war broke out five days after independence, and Prime Minister **Patrice Lumumba** responded in an erratic and apparently pro-Soviet manner. Following

United Nations (UN) intervention and the threat of Soviet intervention in support of Lumumba, Eisenhower told his advisers that the U.S. would ensure that the UN was not driven from the country even if it meant a fight with the Soveits. In August, **Central Intelligence Agency** (CIA) Director **Allen W. Dulles** and perhaps Eisenhower himself ordered Lumumba's assassination, but declassified U.S. and Belgian government documents show that the U.S. played no role in his execution.

Egypt saw the most striking example of Eisenhower's anticolonialism, when he used overwhelming economic pressure combined with strident public diplomacy at the UN to force **Great Britain**, France, and **Israel** to end the **Suez Crisis**. Despite having saved the government of President **Gamal Abdel Nasser**, Eisenhower's **cold war** focus on such policies as the **Baghdad Pact** and his decision to withdraw funding for Egypt's **Aswan High Dam** had disastrous consequences, as they either alienated Nasser and drove him to the Soviets, or gave him a pretext for making the informal alliance. *See also* ADOULA, CYRILLE; BELGIUM; DEVLIN, LARRY; MOBUTU SESE SEKO; OPERATION WIZARD; PORTUGAL.

EISENHOWER DOCTRINE. Proclamation by President **Dwight D. Eisenhower** that the United States would use its armed forces to defend any Middle Eastern country that requested assistance while under attack or imminent attack by any country under the control of "International Communism." The doctrine also says that the U.S. would provide economic and military assistance to any Middle Eastern country threatened by internal Communist forces. Eisenhower made the announcement in a special address to Congress on 5 January 1957.

Eisenhower issued his doctrine two months after the **Suez Crisis**, during which the **Soviet Union** threatened to intervene against **Great Britain**, **France**, and **Israel** for their attack on **Egypt**, and after which the British lost much of their will to project power into the Middle East. Eisenhower also sought to check growing Egyptian prestige and self-confidence that followed the failed invasion by putting the world on notice that he would intervene instantly in the event of a Soviet invasion or an attack by the Egyptians, acting as their proxy. In fact, Eisenhower knew that subversive Communist influence in Middle Eastern countries was negligible and that the real danger was Arab nationalism fostered by President **Gamal Abdel Nasser**, the radical and charismatic Egyptian leader who, supplied by Soviet military assistance and **foreign aid**, threatened the Persian Gulf's **oil** sheikdoms. It was at Nasser and his ambition that the doctrine was truly directed.

When the U.S. sent 14,000 soldiers and Marines into Lebanon to pacify communal violence at its government's request on 15 July 1958, Eisenhower told the American people that the purpose was to prevent a Communist takeover, but he secretly told congressional leaders that he was bolstering the confidence of conservative Arab leaders, who believed that the Lebanese situation was related to the recent bloody Egyptian-backed Arab nationalist coup against the Hashemite monarchy in Iraq and an attempted coup against Jordan's moderate Hashemite King Hussein. He wrote in his memoirs that the purpose was to show an increasingly arrogant Nasser that the U.S. was willing and able to protect its vital national interests. International reaction was extremely negative, but Eisenhower wrote that the intervention had a salutatory impact on Nasser's attitude toward Washington. *See also* COLD WAR.

ENDURING FREEDOM–HORN OF AFRICA (OEF-HOA), OPERATION. *See* OPERATION ENDURING FREEDOM–HORN OF AFRICA (OEF-HOA).

ENDURING FREEDOM–TRANS SAHARA (OEF-TS), OPERATION. *See* OPERATION ENDURING FREEDOM–TRANS SAHARA (OEF-TS).

EQUATORIAL GUINEA. West African nation that has become important to U.S. foreign policy due to the discovery of **oil** in 1996. From 1996 to early 2008, U.S. oil companies invested $10 billion in Equatorial Guinea's oil industry.

Analysts for **non-governmental organizations** (NGOs) that monitor human rights and good government in Africa rank Equatorial Guinea as having the worst human rights situation in Africa and President Teodoro Obiang Nguema as its most brutal dictator. Obiang came to power in 1979 when he overthrew and executed his uncle,

Francisco Macias Nguema, who himself had killed or driven into exile one-third of the country's population, ordered all of the nation's currency brought to his palace, and was widely considered insane. Obiang eased the worst aspects of Macias' repression but continues to rule as a dictator. In May 2008 elections, Obiang's party won 99 out of 100 parliamentary seats in elections almost universally deemed fraudulent.

Countering the general policy of President **George W. Bush** to push for greater political democracy and economic liberation in Africa, Secretary of State **Condoleezza Rice** met with Obiang on 12 April 2006 and called him "a good friend." In 2007, Equatorial Guinea was the twenty-fifth leading exporter of oil to the United States and in January 2007 it possessed 1.1 billion barrels of proven reserves.

ERITREA. Horn of Africa nation that, while under the rule of **Ethiopia**, engaged in a 30-year war for independence, which was achieved in 1993. Eritrea was an Italian colony before World War II. After Italy's defeat, heavy U.S. pressure on the **United Nations** (UN) resulted in it being made an autonomous part of a federation with Ethiopia on 15 September 1952 instead of being assigned as a colony to another European country or becoming a UN trusteeship. Ethiopian Emperor **Haile Selassie** used coercion, bribery, and divide-and-rule tactics to annex Eritrea with the agreement of Eritrea's legislature on 14 November 1962. The previous year, rebels had begun to fight for independence. The guerillas splintered into factions ranging at various times from conservative Muslim to various competing strands of Communist. They received assistance and training from Saudi Arabia, the **Soviet Union**, and **China**, among others.

In July 1977, the Soviets broke with the Communist Eritrean People's Liberation Front (EPLF) guerillas and gave full support to the Communist Ethiopian government of **Mengistu Haile Mariam**, who launched a military campaign against the rebels, although **Cuba**'s Fidel Castro refused Mengistu's requests to use his 15,000 troops in Ethiopia against the Eritreans. Soviet generals conducted operations and by April 1978 had taken over complete control of the military operation. Over 200 Soviet combat pilots and hundreds of technical advisers manned heavy weapons against the Eritreans. Moscow also sent billions of dollars worth of armaments, but Ethiopia could not defeat the guerillas.

After Mikhail Gorbachev took power at the Kremlin in 1985, he began to question his government's massive spending in Africa. In 1989, he ordered that the effort wind down. In February 1990, the U.S. announced that it supported Eritrea's right to self-determination. The now-united Eritreans threw in their lot with Ethiopian rebels and defeated Mengistu on 21 May 1991. The U.S. assisted with peace negotiations and Ethiopia's new president, rebel leader **Meles Zenawi**, immediately agreed to let the Eritreans vote for their independence, with elections set for April 1993. Independence was supported by 99.8 percent of the Eritreans, and Ethiopia promptly granted it with rebel leader **Isaias Afwerki** appointed president.

Relations between the two leaders quickly deteriorated personally and nationally, and war broke out in May 1998. An estimated 500,000 soldiers fought one another and 600,000 people were displaced or became **refugees**. In June, Afwerki rejected a peace agreement proposed by the U.S. and **Rwanda**, and Eritrea was defeated on 18 June 2000, accepting terms similar to the U.S.–Rwandan peace plan. When Eritrea surrendered, the UN sent emergency **foreign aid** to the estimated 12 million people in the Horn of Africa who were facing imminent starvation. Officially, 19,000 Eritreans died in the fighting. The Algiers Agreement of December 2000 created a temporary security zone along the border patrolled by the UN. The UN continued to keep the two sides apart in early 2008 at a cost of $220 million per year and the food crisis continued. Former U.S. Ambassador to the UN John Bolton inadvertently revealed in his autobiography that the U.S. secretly but unsuccessfully asked the boundary commission to revise its decision to give Ethiopia part of the disputed territory.

Eritrean support of the Islamist Islamic Courts Union (ICU) in **Somalia**, which defeated the country's Ethiopian-backed provisional government in 2006, led to threats by the U.S. to add Eritrea to its list of State Sponsors of Terror, harming U.S. assistance and **trade**. The U.S. supported an Ethiopian invasion of Somalia in December 2006 that defeated the ICU. Several ICU leaders fled to Asmara, Eritrea's capital. In mid-2008, Eritrea's army had 300,000 soldiers, one in 14 Eritreans. It had also mobilized its forces to the border with Djibouti.

Immigration was outlawed although many Eritrean refugees escaped to the U.S. Because of the wars and recurring droughts across the Horn of Africa, the UN estimated in mid-2008 that 14.5 million people required humanitarian assistance.

ETHIOPIA. East African nation on the Horn of Africa that was a key U.S. **cold war** ally until the 1974 overthrow of Emperor **Haile Selassie**. The post–cold war government of **Meles Zenawi** has been a strong U.S. ally in the **Global War on Terror** (GWOT). Ethiopia was the only African country to avoid colonialism through force of arms during the Scramble for Africa, defeating the Italians at the Battle of Adowa in 1896. Italian Prime Minister Benito Mussolini avenged the defeat when he ordered his army to attack Ethiopia on 3 October 1935. Although **African Americans** strongly supported Ethiopia, U.S. President **Franklin Delano Roosevelt** responded with an arms embargo against both countries, which harmed the Ethiopians, many of whose soldiers fought with spears, but did not harm the Italians, who used the war to test their warplanes, tanks, and poison gas. The resulting slaughter ended with Ethiopia's conquest and annexation on 7 May 1936, and the U.S. lifted the embargo on 20 June. U.S. sentiment shifted to the Ethiopian cause following Emperor Haile Selassie's moving and dignified 30 June 1936 speech before the League of Nations in which he predicted, "It is us today. It will be you tomorrow." *Time* magazine responded by choosing him "Man of the Year."

Following Ethiopia's liberation on 28 November 1941, **Great Britain** tried to run the country as a conquered territory, but the U.S. forced the British to relax control of Ethiopian foreign policy and, in 1946, stopped them from annexing the ethnically Somali Ogaden Desert region and giving it to a Greater Somaliland colony. In 1945, Haile Selassie's government granted **oil** exploration contracts in the Ogaden to Sinclair Oil, a U.S. company. The emperor also demanded **Eritrea**, formerly an Italian colony, which the British had hoped to divide with the Italians. Haile Selassie argued that control of Eritrea was a vital national interest since the Italians had used it as a jumping off point for invasions in 1896 and 1935. U.S. pressure at the **United Nations** (UN) helped Ethiopia acquire the colony as a federal province that would retain some local autonomy, but the agreement's terms were vague. In 1953, Haile Selassie granted the U.S. a secret communications base in Asmara, the Eritrean capital, and Washington began to provide Ethiopia with economic **foreign aid** and military assistance. Over the next 10 years, Haile Selassie eroded Eritrea's independent powers until he ended the treaty in 1962 and annexed the province, sparking a rebellion that continued until 1991, when Eritreans were promised the right to vote for their independence in 1993.

Ethiopia was a charter member of the UN. Because of its close relationship with the U.S. and Haile Selassie's support for collective security based on his country's experience prior to World War II, Ethiopia sent a battalion to fight in the Korean War under UN auspices and U.S. military command. Washington's support for Haile Selassie continued into the 1970s accompanied by concern that he was losing his grip. The 1973 oil price shock, separatist rebellions, drought accompanied by inept or malevolent government response in the rebellious Wollo province that may have killed 200,000 people, and general dissatisfaction among the middle class, college students, and junior army officers about the slow pace of modernization and political reform led to a military coup that removed Haile Selassie from power on 12 September 1974. He was replaced by a military government of mostly junior officers called the Dergue (Amharic, "Committee").

One of the Dergue's key figures was **Mengistu Haile Mariam**, who publicly called himself a Marxist–Leninist, moved Ethiopia closer to the **Soviet Union**, slaughtered his opponents, and pushed the government into Communist policies such as a 1975 land nationalization that created Soviet-style collective farms. On 12 April 1976, Mengistu announced a national political program, "The National Democratic Revolution," based on the principles of scientific socialism. Despite these dramatic moves to the Left, Secretary of State **Henry Kissinger** decided that the U.S. could keep the Dergue from breaking with the West if it dramatically increased military aid. Therefore, from mid-1974 until the fall of 1976, Washington sent Ethiopia $180 million worth of arms, almost three times more than had been sent during the Haile Selassie years, and Ethiopia was one of only five nations for which Kissinger recommended increased military aid during this post-Vietnam period of military and diplomatic retrenching.

In a 3 February 1977 coup, Mengistu massacred his moderate colleagues and launched what he called "Red Terror" against civilian opponents, killing an estimated 500,000. Newly inaugurated President **Jimmy Carter** broke with Kissinger's realist policy on 24 February 1977 when he ordered Secretary of State **Cyrus Vance** to inform Congress that the U.S. was cutting some assistance to Ethiopia due to the regime's deplorable human rights record. Many Africa specialists, who had opposed Kissinger's foreign policy as cold war–driven without concern for local African problems, nonetheless believed that Carter's policy was a mistake that drove Ethiopia into the Soviet camp. In fact, Soviet documents reveal that Mengistu was a Communist convert intent upon joining Ethiopia with the Eastern Bloc, and that he had signed a secret agreement with the Soviets on 14 December 1976, which provided his government with over $100 million in weapons. Mengistu continued his march leftward on 23 March 1977, when he ordered the U.S. to close its communications base at Asmara, remove the **Peace Corps**, close consulates and remove aid staff, and reduce the U.S. embassy to almost a skeleton crew. In mid-April, he abrogated Ethiopia's military assistance agreement with Washington.

In mid-February 1977, **Somalia**'s President **Muhammad Siad Barré** saw opportunity in Ethiopia's chaos and infiltrated approximately 1,500 soldiers into the Ogaden to assist the Western Somali Liberation Front, which his government had supported with weapons for several years. Mengistu began to ask the Soviets for huge amounts of military aid and **Cuba** for troops. After unsuccessfully trying to mediate a peace agreement, Cuban President Fidel Castro recommended that the Soviets provide Mengistu with more military aid, concluding that he was a true Communist while Siad, a close Soviet ally, was not. The Soviets' realist calculation said that Ethiopia was a better investment with its population almost 10 times greater than Somalia and its excellent strategic placement at the mouth of the Red Sea, which could provide a choke point for Persian Gulf oil headed to Western Europe. Soviet ideology also said that a genuine Marxist–Leninist government, saved by the force of Soviet Bloc arms, could provide the spark that would set off Communist revolutions across the continent. On 1 May 1977, the Ethiopians signed an agreement with the Soviets that brought Soviet total arms expenditure to $300 million by the end of 1978. The Somalis responded by launching the **Ogaden War** on 13 July 1977. By November, the Somalis controlled 90 percent of Ethiopia's Ogaden Desert, prompting Castro and the Soviets to airlift the first of 15,000 Cuban troops to Ethiopia from **Angola** on 25 November. The Cubans stopped then reversed the Somali advance, driving out the Somali army on 8 March 1978.

Mengistu's continued brutality produced regional rebellions among the Tigrayans and Oromo, among others, as well as continued fighting by the Eritreans. In April 1978, the Soviets took over complete control of the Eritrean operation and Soviet and Cuban military commanders led the other fronts. Ethiopia was the Soviets' largest military intervention since the Korean War and their most significant effort to modernize a country since China in the 1950s. The Soviets' goal was to make Ethiopia an example for all of Africa of the benefits of a Communist system. They provided over 7,000 Soviet and Eastern European advisers to oversee the communization of the country, and they ran many of the country's economic and technical ministries.

Mengistu used a 1984–85 drought centered in Tigray and Eritrea to try to break rebel resistance by withholding food except to those who moved to government-controlled concentration camps. Although the UN and **non-governmental organizations** (NGOs) sent foreign aid, the UN estimated that one million people died. Western celebrities did not understand the Ethiopian government's malign purpose, and raised millions of dollars for famine relief through the "Live Aid" concert and sales of the "We are the World" and "Do They Know It's Christmas?" albums. The Ethiopian government stole much of the money and relief supplies or used the aid to force people into collectivized villages.

By the late 1980s, the Soviet Union's reforming leader, Mikhail Gorbachev, had concluded that its African allies were not worth the money, which was costing the Soviet Union's weak economy billions of dollars per year. In June 1989, Herman Cohen, the State Department's Bureau Chief for African Affairs, met with his Soviet counterpart in Rome to discuss collaborating in ending the cold war in Africa. The Soviets agreed to cut off aid to Ethiopia, which precipitated Cuban withdrawal as well. Mengistu's government collapsed on 19

May 1991, under rebel attack. The U.S. provided logistical assistance to facilitate guerilla leader **Meles Zenawi** (himself a former Communist) taking power.

Meles allowed an Eritrean referendum on independence and granted it on 24 May 1993. Relations deteriorated quickly thereafter and war resumed in May 1998, which Ethiopia won on 18 June 2000 at the cost of perhaps 100,000 soldiers. The Algiers Agreement of December 2000 created a temporary security zone along the border patrolled by the UN. In the interim, an estimated 12 million people on the Horn of Africa, many of them **refugees**, faced starvation from famine and displacement. A UN commission demarcated the boundary between the nations in April 2002, ruling that disputed territory belonged to Eritrea, but Ethiopia refused to recognize the result, and UN forces continued to separate the combatants in mid-2008. Former U.S. Ambassador to the UN John Bolton inadvertently revealed in his autobiography that the U.S. secretly but unsuccessfully asked the boundary commission to revise its decision to give Ethiopia part of the disputed territory.

Meles became a close U.S. ally in the GWOT. He ordered 5,000 to 10,000 soldiers to invade Somalia in December 2006 with tacit U.S. support to overthrow the Islamist and Eritrean-supported Islamic Courts Union (ICU) government. His men restored Somalia's transitional government, which Meles had been instrumental in bringing to power. By July 2008, Ethiopia continued to occupy Somalia. With 2.5 million Somalis requiring food aid, the UN estimating that one million Somalis were displaced or refugees and faced going hungry because of fighting and difficulty in shipping emergency food into the country because of attacks by pirates. Across the Horn of Africa, the UN estimated that 14.5 million people required humanitarian assistance in 2008. *See also* AFRICAN AFFAIRS, STATE DEPARTMENT BUREAU OF; AFWERKI, ISAIAS; IMMIGRATION; ISRAEL; MUSIC; YOUNG, ANDREW.

EURAFRICA. Idealized conception of future relations between the former colonial powers and their former African colonies after independence. Creating Eurafrica was the goal of U.S. policy makers, especially President **Dwight D. Eisenhower** and Secretary of State **John Foster Dulles**. Dulles foresaw European integration with

Africa bringing cooperative economic success through development of Africa's natural resources. He argued that creating Eurafrica was predicated on good relations between North and South, which required deliberate but rapid decolonization. Dulles worried that **France**'s futile military struggle to hold onto **Algeria** would prevent such an outcome. *See also* BELGIUM; GREAT BRITAIN.

– F –

FANON, FRANTZ (1925–1961). Martinican psychiatrist and radical philosopher famous for *The Wretched of the Earth*. Fanon moved to **Algeria** and became a leading figure among the *Front de Libération Nationale*/National Liberation Front (FLN) rebels who were fighting for independence from **France**. Fanon's work argued that racism and colonialism robbed the colonized of their manhood, which could only be restored through cathartic violent revolution and liberation. Peaceful transition to independence, he wrote, meant neo-colonialism and continued psychological oppression. Fanon also argued that the peasant mass was ready for liberation, an idea that Portuguese Guinea's rebel leader Amilcar Cabral accepted but discovered was wrong, almost leading to his death and the extirpation of his movement. In late 1961, the **Central Intelligence Agency** (CIA) arranged for Fanon to be flown to Washington to receive treatment for leukemia. After his death on 6 December, a CIA officer accompanied his body to **Tunisia** where the FLN transported it across the border to Algeria for burial. The incident infuriated France's President Charles de Gaulle.

FAROUK I (1920–1965). King of **Egypt** famous for his gluttony. Farouk was crowned at age 16 in 1936. During World War II, he refused to declare war on Germany and appointed a pro-German government. When German Field Marshall Erwin Rommel took El Alamein, only 60 miles from Cairo, **Great Britain** surrounded Farouk's palace with tanks, marched into his private study, and forced him to appoint an anti-German premier under threat of forced abdication. This embarrassment made Farouk much less willing to deal with the British in the postwar years. More important, it humiliated many Egyptian army officers, including **Muhammad Naguib**

and **Gamal Abdel Nasser**, who concluded that the army had to replace Farouk, and British influence in Egypt had to end.

The 25 January 1952 British attack on Egyptian forces near the Suez Canal Zone and the "Black Saturday" riot that followed the next day, combined with Farouk's well-known debauchery, destroyed his popularity and political influence. The **Central Intelligence Agency** (CIA) tried to work with him to stabilize the situation, but he was not interested. Fearful that continued Egyptian chaos could lead to a Communist takeover, the CIA began to support the Free Officers Movement of nationalist soldiers led by Lieutenant Colonel Nasser and General Naguib. On 23 July 1952, the Free Officers took over Cairo. Farouk appealed to the United States for assistance, but was rebuffed. On 26 July, in a move reminiscent of the British during World War II, troops surrounded Farouk's Alexandria palace and ordered him to abdicate and leave the country immediately, which he did. Farouk continued his gluttonous ways and died of a heart attack in Rome at age 46. *See also* ARAB–ISRAELI WAR OF 1948–49.

FILM. There have been relatively few mass-market movies about Africa that have played in the United States and most have focused on white people, primarily foreign. In the great majority of these movies, black or Arab Africans have served in roles similar to African wildlife, providing exotic backdrops to the action. Even movies about African historical events or contemporary social problems have been about whites, or at least have had important white characters. Perhaps as a result, movies about Africa have done little to increase Americans' understanding of Africa, and have frequently reinforced preexisting prejudices, although the portrayal of black Africans has improved considerably since early depictions as cannibals and savages in the *Tarzan* and *Jungle Jim* series. In the 21st century, black Africans are generally portrayed as victims, whether of their own governments or malign outside forces. African actors and movies have also had difficulty breaking through to mass audiences in the U.S.

The biggest grossing films about Africa have been cartoons or cartoonish adventure/comedies, with *The Lion King*, *The Mummy Returns*, *Madagascar*, and the 1999 version of *Tarzan* the top money makers. Another successful theme is white people confronting

African wildlife, including such films as *Hatari*, *Born Free*, *Gorillas in the Mist*, *The Ghost and the Darkness*, and *I Dreamed of Africa*. Each of these movies has also been associated with or spawned conservation efforts, supported primarily by Western governments or **non-governmental organizations** (NGOs).

Movies about North Africa have tended to be biblical epics, like the *Ten Commandments*; adventures, such as *Raiders of the Lost Ark*; war movies focusing on taming desert nomads, including the several versions of *Beau Geste*, or fighting the Nazis, as in *Casablanca*; or horror movies, like the various *Mummy* incarnations.

Movies about politics and social problems in sub-Saharan Africa have focused on the struggle against **apartheid** in **South Africa**, **Idi Amin** of **Uganda**, the Rwandan Genocide, U.S. relations with Africa, and social issues including **blood diamonds** and the role of pharmaceutical companies. Apartheid spawned several films during the anti-apartheid movement of the late 1980s and early 1990s, including *Cry Freedom*, *A Dry White Season*, *Sarafina!*, *The Wilby Conspiracy*, *The Power of One*, *Master Herald and the Boys*, *A World Apart*, and the made-for-television *Mandela*. None of these movies was a commercial success despite each having featured a major star, and *Cry Freedom* lost $20 million. As a result, they probably had little success in turning the U.S. public against apartheid.

Of the anti-apartheid movies, only *Sarafina!* and *Mandela* are centered almost exclusively on black South Africans, and *Cry Freedom*, ostensibly about Black Consciousness leader **Stephen Biko**, instead focuses on his friend, **Donald Woods**, a white journalist whom Biko converted to opposing apartheid. *Cry, the Beloved Country*, a 1951 film based on the famous novel by **Alan Paton**, was a commercial and artistic success, unlike the 1995 remake. The most commercially successful movie against apartheid was the surprising *Lethal Weapon 2*, a traditional Hollywood summer blockbuster in which the villains are racist and brutal agents of the South African government. Subsequent movies about apartheid, including *Amandla!* and *Catch a Fire*, have not been commercially successful in the U.S.

The movies about Africa with perhaps the greatest impact on U.S. foreign policy were 1970s depictions of Idi Amin, Uganda's murderous president. Although criticized at the time for seemingly over-the-top portrayals of Amin, these movies, which include *Operation*

Entebbe and *Raid on Entebbe* (dealing with a rescue of hostages who were being held with Amin's assistance) proved to be quite accurate in tone if not always in fact. A documentary, *General Idi Amin Dada: Self Portrait*, was devastating. These works did much to turn U.S. public opinion against Amin, resulting in a U.S. embargo against Uganda that may have contributed to Amin's overthrow. Forest Whitaker's portrayal of Amin in *The Last King of Scotland* earned him the Academy Award for best actor.

Movies about the Rwandan Genocide have been critical successes, including *Hotel Rwanda*, *Sometimes in April*, *100 Days*, and *Beyond the Gates* (released overseas as *Shooting Dogs*). Like the other social conscience movies, these films and the less critically successful *Shake Hands with the Devil* (a dramatization of the far better received documentary and autobiography of **United Nations** [UN] General Roméo Dallaire's experience leading **peacekeepers** in **Rwanda**) have had as themes or sub-themes the ethical dilemma faced by good white people trapped in an evil circumstance.

U.S. relations with Africa are the subject of *Black Hawk Down*, which covers the Battle of Mogadishu in **Somalia**, *The Wind and the Lion*, an almost unrecognizable account of **Theodore Roosevelt**'s intervention in **Morocco**, and *Amistad*, about an 1839 African slave mutiny followed by a successful court case in which the Africans were allowed to return to Africa. U.S. foreign policy failings are touched upon in movies about apartheid and the Rwandan Genocide, and in Raoul Peck's *Lumumba*.

Movies that seek to raise awareness about contemporary African problems include *Blood Diamond* and *The Constant Gardener*, which manages to deal with alleged abuses by the pharmaceutical industry and with the genocide in the **Darfur** province of **Sudan**. Although both were only moderately successful at the box office, *Blood Diamond* prompted the De Beers mining company to launch a "consumer education" media advertising campaign to mitigate the potential damage, explaining that the Kimberley Process for certifying the origin of diamonds ended the legitimate sale of blood diamonds.

Few African actors have been successful stars in the U.S., and even fewer African movies have been commercially successful. Those actors who have broken through tend to be remarkably successful, including, Omar Sharif of **Egypt**, Charlize Therzon of South Africa, and Benin's Djimon Hounsou, all of whom have been nominated for or won Academy Awards. The most successful African movie in the U.S. is *The Gods Must Be Crazy*, an idyllic comedy about the hunter–gatherer San (Bushmen) confronting modern South African civilization and civil war. *See also* RWANDA, GENOCIDE IN.

FIRESTONE NATURAL RUBBER COMPANY. Subsidiary of Firestone Tire & Rubber Company (today Bridgestone/Firestone). Firestone Natural Rubber Company oversees the one-million acre Firestone Plantation in **Liberia**. The genesis of Firestone Natural Rubber Company was Secretary of Commerce Herbert Hoover's activist approach to improving U.S. business during the 1920s. Hoover sought to guarantee U.S. access to vital natural resources that were being restricted by colonial governments. **Great Britain** and Netherlands controlled the rubber market, a vital product for automobile tires. Hoover's department worked with U.S. rubber companies to find a rubber source that could be controlled by U.S. business interests and thus break the colonial monopoly. A worldwide search, subsidized in part by the Commerce Department, led rubber magnate Harry S. Firestone, owner of Firestone Tire & Rubber Company, to send experts to Liberia in December 1923. Promising soil conditions prompted the U.S. government to appropriate $500,000 to subsidize a successful Firestone soil survey.

In 1926, the Liberian government granted Firestone the right to lease up to one million acres at 6 cents per acre for 99 years. Firestone did so, creating the world's largest plantation in Harbel, Liberia. In addition, Firestone agreed to pay an export tax and provided a $5 million loan to retire the country's previous onerous debt. While the terms were remarkably generous to Firestone, especially from the 21st-century perspective, they were better than most such agreements with third-world countries at the time. Rubber money probably saved the Liberian government from colonial takeover by a European power in the wake of revelations that the vice president and probably the president were involved with trafficking in forced labor that was akin to a slave **trade**.

Along with the rent, export tax, and loan, Firestone agreed to make further internal improvements to get the rubber to market more quickly, to make conditions safer for its management staff, and to improve productivity of labor. These included building roads and a modern harbor, and hiring experts from Harvard and Yale Universities to conduct health surveys of local diseases and the country's forest resources, then using the data to build a hospital, sanitation plant, electric power plant, and telephone system. The plantation became a company town, although the cost of housing and prices in company stores were set within the workers' wage levels in order to avoid charges of forced labor.

Plummeting rubber prices during the Great Depression halted Firestone's development of the property, thus depriving the Liberian government of export revenues, which forced it to miss debt repayment beginning in 1931. In 1933, Firestone asked the U.S. government to send a warship to Monrovia to enforce payment, but President **Franklin Delano Roosevelt** refused, rejecting "gunboat diplomacy" by explaining to the State Department that Firestone had taken a risk by investing in Liberia and it was not the job of the U.S. government to protect his investment if it went bad. Firestone's fortunes and Liberia's were turned around by the desperate need for rubber supplies during World War II. Liberia became relatively prosperous, which funded a patronage system that allowed President **William Tubman** to begin integrating indigenous Liberians into the national mainstream.

In 2005, Firestone Natural Rubber and the government of Liberia signed a 37-year agreement that raised the lease to 50 cents per acre. On 17 November 2005, workers at the Harbel plantation filed a lawsuit in U.S. federal court under the Alien Tort Claims Act, charging Firestone with using forced labor and child labor. A May 2006 report by the **United Nations** (UN) Mission in Liberia (UNMIL) supported many of the plaintiffs' claims. On 26 June 2007, a judge rejected Firestone's motion for summary judgment, and depositions began in April 2008. The following month, witnesses accused Firestone of intimidation. The **American Federation of Labor–Council of Industrial Organizations** (AFL-CIO) assisted the 4,000 plantation workers to receive independent union representation in December 2007.

FORD, GERALD R. (1913–2006). U.S. politician and the only unelected president (1974–77). Ford had been Republican leader in the House of Representatives when President **Richard M. Nixon** selected him as vice president following the resignation of Spiro Agnew. He assumed the presidency when Nixon resigned on 9 August 1974. Although it is a cliché that Ford left foreign policy to **Henry Kissinger**, his national security adviser whom he also appointed secretary of state, it is also generally true.

Ford's interest in sub-Saharan Africa began in April 1975 when he joined President **Kenneth Kaunda** of **Zambia**, President **Mobutu Sese Seko** of **Zaïre (Congo)**, and Prime Minister **John Vorster** of **South Africa** in working to stop the **Soviet Union**–backed and Communist-led *Movimento Popular de Libertação de Angola*/Popular Movement for the Liberation of Angola (MPLA) from taking power in **Angola**. Ford ordered the CIA to begin **Operation IAFEATURE**, which provided $48 million in covert assistance to opposition guerilla movements. Ford and Kissinger saw the intervention as an opportunity to demonstrate U.S. resolve while halting Soviet expansionism. The operation was defeated because Fidel Castro of **Cuba** sent 12,000 soldiers to support MPLA's **Agostinho Neto**, and because Ford was forced to withdraw support from the guerilas after U.S. newspapers reported on the CIA operation and the South African intervention, which prompted the U.S. Congress to pass the **Tunney Amendment** and the **Clark Amendment**, banning further U.S. intervention in Angola. Ford strongly but unsuccessfully resisted the amendments, arguing that they were an unconstitutional usurpation of presidential power.

Ford and Kissinger feared that defeat in Angola could precipitate a domino-producing race war that would lead to the Communist overthrow of South Africa and **Rhodesia (Zimbabwe)** and the collateral losses of Zaïre and Zambia, ultimately resulting in a superpower confrontation. To prevent this scenario from occurring, Ford authorized Kissinger to engage in a **"shuttle diplomacy"** across Southern Africa in an unsuccessful effort to broker the transition to majority rule in Rhodesia.

In the Middle East, Ford allowed Kissinger to continue shuttle diplomacy, which culminated in the September 1975 Sinai II agreement between **Egypt** and **Israel**. Both belligerents agreed to solve their differences peacefully, Israel returned important strategic territory and oil wells, and the U.S. built and staffed monitoring stations at crucial border positions on Egyptian territory. Ford was defeated for a new term of office by **Jimmy Carter**, who promised a foreign policy with a greater emphasis on human rights. *See also* ROBERTO, HOLDEN; SADAT, ANWAR AL-; SAVIMBI, JONAS.

FOREIGN AID. U.S. foreign aid for Africa and the third world began during the administration of President **Harry S. Truman** when he announced the **Point Four** program in his 1949 inaugural address. Point Four sought to make U.S. science and industrial progress available to the third world through grants and technical assistance. Foreign aid was expected to help third-world countries develop economically, end mass poverty, and prevent the hopelessness and misery that could create openings for the **Soviet Union** to gain influence or even produce Communist revolutions.

President **John F. Kennedy** expanded the mission of U.S. foreign aid from building infrastructure and providing technical advice into a development program based on **modernization theory**, which included assisting with centralized national planning and providing assistance and support for reform in areas of basic human needs such as agricultural reform, education, and public health. In pursuit of these goals, he called on the world to fund a "decade of development." To coordinate the U.S. effort more efficiently, Kennedy created the **Agency for International Development** (AID), which centralized several foreign assistance bureaucracies. At the same time that he expanded the mission, Kennedy was frustrated by strong congressional resistance to foreign aid programs that many Americans considered wasteful. This became a common trope thereafter in light of corruption by foreign governments, estimates in 2004 were that 40 percent of African savings were held abroad and the **African Union** (AU) estimated that corruption cost African governments $148 billion per year; ungratefulness, as shown by third-world criticism of the U.S. and votes against it at the **United Nations** (UN); immorality, by the U.S. government spending money abroad when poverty continued at home; and simple failure, with the world providing Africa with foreign aid valued at $568 billion between 1965 and 2006 but most African countries' economies and standards of living experiencing only minimal progress or often regress. By the end of Kennedy's administration, foreign aid was below the level spent in the last year of the administration of his predecessor, **Dwight D.**

Eisenhower, whom Kennedy had strongly criticized for not providing enough aid to the third world.

During the **cold war**, U.S. aid to Africa overwhelmingly went to U.S. allies **Tunisia, Liberia, Ethiopia, Congo (Zaïre)**; to **Nigeria**, which President Kennedy had sought to use as a prototype of democratic development; to **Guinea** and **Ghana**, which Kennedy and his successors sought in essence to bribe to keep neutral; and **Tanzania**, home of a much praised experiment in "African Socialism" called *Ujamaa*. All of these aid recipients were dwarfed by assistance to **Egypt**, which received $53 billion in U.S. assistance from 1971–2001, and also surpassed by **Morocco**, a key U.S. ally and moderate force in the Middle East.

With the cold war's end, President **George H.W. Bush** sought to create a New World Order by including a country's form of government as a criterion for assistance, and by military intervention in **Somalia** to feed a starving populace. President **Bill Clinton** ran for office criticizing Bush's failure to move more strongly in the direction of multilateral support for development and foreign aid, but quickly pulled back in both areas after the Battle of Mogadishu in Somalia where 18 U.S. soldiers were killed. Instead Clinton focused on encouraging **trade** and supporting governments that he said were part of the "African Renaissance" of democracy and development. By the end of his administration, Clinton had actively worked to prevent UN intervention to stop the Rwandan Genocide and provided a greater percentage of foreign aid to African dictatorships than had George H.W. Bush. Foreign aid reached its post-1960 nadir in constant dollars during the Clinton administration, with a $14 billion appropriation in 1997.

Foreign aid has continued to face congressional resistance although President **George W. Bush** had much greater success than his predecessors by emphasizing its importance in the **Global War on Terror** (GWOT), and by working with conservative religious organizations. His administration tripled the amount of assistance to Africa that had been provided by the Clinton administration. Following Clinton's lead, Bush has continued to focus foreign aid on encouraging business and investment, liberalization of markets, fighting disease, and working through **non-governmental organizations** (NGOs) as a way to reach the grassroots and strengthen civil society while avoiding giving the money to often-corrupt governments. Bush also created the **Millennium Challenge Corporation** (MCC), which assists countries in the effort to democratize, fight corruption, improve social conditions, and improve governance. The MCC negotiates to provide expensive projects for those countries that meet these criteria. Bush has made fighting disease such as HIV/**AIDS** and malaria a priority, working through AID and the **Centers for Disease Control** (CDC). The President's Emergency Plan for AIDS Relief (PEPFAR) initially was funded with $15 million over five years in 2003 and was reauthorized as part of a five-year, $48 billion omnibus international health bill that included funding for research and assistance for those with tuberculosis and malaria. Bush's foreign aid priorities were distracted by the war on terror, with **Uganda**, Ethiopia, and **Rwanda** continuing to receive significant foreign aid because they supported this effort despite oppressive and undemocratic governments.

The U.S. government annually provides more foreign aid than any other country, $27.3 billion in 2005, but as a percentage of national income, the U.S. government has been among the lowest if not the lowest since the 1970s, 0.22 percent in 2005, 20th out of the 22 largest donor nations. Of this amount, a large percentage has gone to **Israel** and Egypt as an incentive to keep Middle East peace and to reconstruction in Afghanistan and Iraq. Many defenders of U.S. assistance point out that this measurement does not include military assistance in the form of relief during natural disasters, providing transportation and logistical support to aid providers, and providing security for aid workers in conflict zones. Other assistance not included in traditional measurements, according to the Index to Global Philanthropy compiled by the Center for Global Prosperity at the Hudson Institute, is charitable assistance from U.S. NGOs such as religious organizations, which provided $33.5 billion in 2005; money sent by individuals to family who live in developing countries, $61.7 billion; and loans and investment by U.S. corporations, $69.2 billion.

Critics of U.S. government foreign aid point out that it is frequently tied to a requirement that recipients spend the money on U.S.-produced goods, reducing the value of the support while serving as indirect welfare for U.S. businesses. Critics of government-provided foreign aid in general argue that foreign aid creates "moral hazards" by promoting improvident borrowing and discouraging government thrift. Previous foreign assistance regimes, particularly during the 1960s and 1970s, have also promoted inefficient centralized planning and grandiose government-owned and politically inspired building projects.

In 1996, Clinton joined with the Group of 7 (G7) leaders to create the Heavily Indebted Poor Countries (HIPC) plan, which organized and coordinated the world's industrial nations with international financial organizations, including the **World Bank**, the **International Monetary Fund** (IMF), the African Development Fund, and private banks, to create conditions to reduce the external debt of the HIPCs to sustainable levels. To be eligible, a country had to show a track record of reform and sound policies under the tutelage of the World Bank and the IMF over a six-year probationary period. In 1999, the probationary period was accelerated under HIPC-2 so that some countries became immediately eligible. That year, Clinton announced that the U.S. would unilaterally cancel the entire $5.7 billion that these 42 countries owed the nation. In 2005, Bush agreed to bring the U.S. into the Multilateral Debt Relief Initiative (MDRI), which allows the poorest countries to receive 100 percent relief of eligible debt after completing the HIPC process. Bush also joined the leaders of the Group of 8 (G8) (the major industrial powers plus Russia) in their pledges to double economic aid from $25 billion to $50 billion by 2010 with $25 billion for Africa, and to cancel the debts of 18 of the world's poorest countries, estimated at $42 billion of which $34 billion was owed by African countries. By mid-2008, the HIPC had cut external debt for 33 countries by $45.5 billion and the MDRI had cut an additional $21.1 billion. In the period 1965–2006, Africa received an estimated worldwide total of $568 billion in foreign aid. *See also* PEACE CORPS; RWANDA, GENOCIDE IN.

FOSSEY, DIAN (1932–1985). American naturalist whose book about her research on gorillas in **Rwanda**, *Gorillas in the Mist*, became a best seller and was made into a successful **film**. Fossey opposed tourism as exploitive of wildlife and disruptive of habitat, and she opposed zoos as the equivalent of animal prisons that often required the killing of many animals to facilitate the capture and transport of a few. Fossey's international prestige combined with her radical anti-tourism stance, personal leadership of anti-poaching patrols, and often irascible nature led her to have many powerful enemies in Rwanda, who envisioned her costing them potentially vast sums of money following the success of her film. She was brutally murdered 26 December 1985, allegedly at the order of Rwandan government officials.

FRANCE. Western European colonial power that continues to play a significant role in its former African colonies. Following its humiliating defeat and occupation in World War II, France lost much of its credibility as a leading international power. France's chaotic postwar governments, which experienced constant crisis and turnover, had one constant belief about their colonies: their continued possession made France important internationally. For this reason, the French were loath to give them up. Paris was outraged by a May 1950 speech by the State Department's George McGhee in which he gently called for eventual independence for the world's colonies. The United States began to back away from this view with the start of the Korean War, as **cold war** necessity trumped Washington's vision of decolonization. The crisis in **Algeria** during the 1950s and early 1960s created difficulties for the **Dwight D. Eisenhower** and **John F. Kennedy** administrations, as both sought to maintain good relations with their North Atlantic Treaty Organization (NATO) ally and the decolonizing world.

Since decolonization, U.S. and French Africa policy have tended not to intersect as France has jealously guarded its relationship with its former colonies, having regarded "the Anglo-Saxons," the U.S. and **Great Britain**, as representing a threat as dire to their African interests as the **Soviet Union** during the cold war, while playing a generally minimal role outside Francophone Africa. This came to the fore most directly in **Rwanda**, a former colony of **Belgium** that had entered the French sphere of influence. During the 1994 Rwandan Genocide, French fear that the Tutsi-led *Front Patriotique Rwandaise*/Rwandan Patriotic Front (RPF) was a stalking horse for Britain and the U.S. led it to continue support for the *génocidaires* until the RPF overthrew the murderous "Hutu Power" government. *See also* BOURGUIBA, HABIB; CHAD; GUINEA; HASSAN II; MOROCCO; MUHAMMAD V; NASSER, GAMAL ABDEL; RWANDA, GENOCIDE IN; SUEZ CRISIS (1956); TUNISIA.

– G –

GARVEY, MARCUS M., JR. (1887–1940). African nationalist from Jamaica who moved to the United States and organized a mass movement to "return" **African Americans** to Africa. Garvey's battle with civil rights leader **W.E.B. Du Bois** and his own lax control over his organization's finances resulted in no African Americans emigrating to Africa and Garvey going to jail.

Garvey was heavily influenced by the work of **Booker T. Washington**, whom he saw as a black separatist. He claimed that reading Washington's *Up From Slavery* made him realize that he had to be a race leader. He moved to the U.S. in 1916 and quickly organized the Universal Negro Improvement Association (UNIA). He had a genius for pageantry and public speaking, using parades, uniforms, and rallies to win huge support among African Americans, especially the poor, while inspiring millions around the world with his vision. He declared himself provisional president-general of Africa and was quite public about the UNIA's central mission, which was to transport 20,000 to 30,000 families of educated and technologically skilled African Americans to **Liberia**, where they would work to undermine colonialism and accelerate Africa's economic development. In addition to raising money to buy ships to transport African Americans to Liberia, Garvey also sought $2 million by subscription to buy land for resettlement and to pay off Liberia's foreign debt, which was so far in arrears that it threatened the country's independent existence. In 1920, he announced the Declaration of Rights of the Negro Peoples of the World, in which he called for "Africa for the Africans."

Although a remarkable promoter—the UNIA had more members worldwide than all previous black organizations combined—Garvey was a terrible administrator and his enterprise was rife with corruption. Liberian government officials also took advantage of Garvey to take significant amounts of money for themselves while giving Garvey and the UNIA nothing in return.

Du Bois was a bitter opponent of Garvey's racial exclusivist policies, and used his position as editor of *The Crisis*, the newspaper of the National Association for the Advancement of Colored People's (NAACP), to try and bring down Garvey. Garvey was imprisoned for fraud in 1923 and while out on bail the following year, made a final push to move African Americans to Liberia. His effort ended in July 1924, when the Liberian government announced that it would not accept anyone transported to Liberia by the UNIA. In the months preceding the announcement, Du Bois had met with Liberian President Charles D.B. King, and is believed to have played a significant role in persuading King to make the announcement. Garvey lost his legal appeal later that year and returned to jail until 1927 when he was released and deported to Jamaica. He died in London, almost forgotten, in 1940.

GBENYE, CHRISTOPHE (1927–). Congolese politician and rebel leader during the **Congo Crisis**. Gbenye was one of the strongest political allies of **Congo**'s first Prime Minister, **Patrice Lumumba**. Because Gbenye had spent considerable time in the **Soviet Union** and had close ties to the Chinese, the United States considered him one of the most dangerous Congolese leaders. Gbenye was instrumental in helping Lumumba leave **United Nations** (UN) protective custody, was captured with him as they fled, but escaped, joining the rebel Stanleyville government and succeeding fellow Lumumbist **Antoine Gizenga** as its president just before its collapse on 14 January 1962.

In 1964, Gbenye met with President **Gamal Abdel Nasser** of **Egypt**, who helped him begin a rebellion in eastern Congo. Despite chaotic leadership and no central control, within months the rebels took almost two-thirds of Congolese territory. Government troops regained the initiative under the leadership of **Moïse Tshombe** but, on 7 September, Gizenga declared himself president of a rump state, the secessionist People's Republic of the Congo. Following Gizenga's capture, Gbenye declared himself president, serving as the regime's public face. Possibly at his order, rebel **Simba** warriors collected foreigners from across the region to Stanleyville as hostages, including the U.S. consul and four other consulate staffers. The Simbas frequently threatened the hostages' lives and randomly slaughtered a few. This proved Gbenye's government's undoing because it gave the United States and **Belgium** cause for direct intervention and to launch the **Stanleyville (Kisangani) hostage rescue**, with U.S. transport planes carrying in 340 Belgian soldiers to liberate the hostages and assist the mercenary-led Congolese army in taking Stanleyville. Thereafter, mopping up continued until the rebels' final defeat in November 1965. Gbenye went into exile, returning after a 1983 amnesty. *See also* CONGO CRISIS; CONGO, CENTRAL INTELLIGENCE AGENCY IN; DEVLIN, LARRY; MULELE, PIERRE.

GHANA. The first sub-Saharan colony to receive its independence thanks to the charismatic leadership of **Kwame Nkrumah**, which forced a reorientation of U.S.–Africa policy. Nkrumah, a U.S.-educated socialist, strove to liberate and unite the African continent into a Pan-African union under his leadership, to socialize and industrialize Ghana, and ultimately all of Africa. Upon receiving independence on 6 March 1957, Ghana was one of the wealthiest third-world nations or colonies, with reserves of over $500 million, the largest in sub-Saharan Africa. It was the world's largest exporter of cocoa, supplying one-third of the world's crop, possessed one of the world's most productive gold mining industries, the fifth biggest in the world, and had Africa's best-educated bureaucracy. There followed economic catastrophe brought on by the collapse of cocoa prices, disastrous socialist economic policies, and corruption. For 25 years, the economy contracted at an average rate of 1 percent per year.

Central to Nkrumah's plans for Ghana was building the **Volta River Dam** and aluminum works, for which President **John F. Kennedy** pledged U.S. **foreign aid**. His foreign policy began with a pro-Western tilt, which was at odds with his ideology, but he briefly unified Ghana with the radical West African governments of **Guinea** and **Mali**, and in 1960, secretly signed a union with Prime Minister **Patrice Lumumba** of **Congo** shortly before Lumumba's assassination. Nkrumah had been growing dictatorial, but following Lumumba's assassination, he made himself Ghana's absolute ruler and steadily moved toward the **Soviet Union** in foreign and domestic policy. His rhetoric turned anti-American, accusing the U.S. of backing attempts to assassinate him and of using the **Peace Corps** to subvert his government. Despite his Leftism, Nkrumah had a high opinion of President Kennedy, who met with him in March 1961, before any other sub-Saharan African leader. During the Cuban missile crisis, Nkrumah refused Soviet requests to refuel **Cuba**-bound cargo airplanes in Ghana, thus helping to keep the U.S. blockade intact.

Nkrumah's increasingly pro-Soviet stance almost cost him the $370 million U.S.-built Volta River Dam project, which Kennedy and his successor, **Lyndon B. Johnson**, both seriously considered aborting. Johnson did cut food assistance and refused to provide Ghana with additional long-term credits. When the Soviets could not provide the billions of dollars necessary to develop the dam's electrical and industrial capabilities, Nkrumah turned back to the United States for assistance. At the same time, he published *Neo-Colonialism*, a profoundly anti-American book, which killed any lingering desire in the Johnson administration to assist him.

Nkrumah was overthrown on 24 February 1966 while on his way to Beijing on a quixotic journey to negotiate peace in Vietnam. Documents later released by the U.S. government showed that for over a year, the U.S. embassy had been in contact with the officers who overthrew Nkrumah, although the documents also indicate that Washington only monitored the situation, doing nothing to encourage or discourage the conspirators. Claims that **Central Intelligence Agency** (CIA) station chief Howard T. Banes played a role in organizing the coup have not been proven. Former CIA agent John Stockwell claimed that the embassy was so well informed about the coup that afterwards it worked with the new government to confiscate several pieces of Soviet military equipment.

The military government, which called itself the National Liberation Council (NLC), immediately expelled Eastern Bloc representatives and ordered the Soviets to cut their embassy staff by two-thirds. Soldiers also reportedly shot a group of Soviet advisers at the presidential castle, who were allegedly managing the country in Nkrumah's absence. Washington immediately promised to provide the new government with the food aid that it had denied Nkrumah.

The NLC quickly returned to the barracks in 1969, but President Kofi Busia was unable to stop the economic slide begun under Nkrumah. Busia's growing authoritarianism and a plan to reduce military pay and perquisites led to his overthrow in 1972. Corruption, inefficiency, and rapid economic decline led to a second coup in 1978 followed quickly by an unsuccessful junior officers' revolt led by Flight Lieutenant **Jerry Rawlings**. While Rawlings waited in jail for his execution, junior officers led a mob that released him and appointed him president. Rawlings ordered the execution of three former military heads of state, the public whipping of market women accused of charging extortionate prices, and the destruction of the

Accra marketplace. He then returned to the barracks and allowed elections. Continued corruption and economic decline led to a second Rawlings coup in 1981.

Rawlings governed as a socialist until the mid-1980s when **International Monetary Fund** (IMF) pressure forced him to begin liberalizing the economy. Rapid economic growth turned him into a committed capitalist and, after he won power in a democratic election in 1992, President **Bill Clinton** called him a leader of the "African Renaissance." Rawlings retired in 2001, his anointed successor was defeated in national elections, and Rawlings stepped aside for John Kufuor to take office, one of the first instances of an African opposition party being allowed to take power after it won an election, although there have been tensions, including Rawlings implying that he might have to launch a third coup and calls for Rawlings to be tried for the execution of his predecessors.

GIZENGA, ANTOINE (1925–). Vice prime minister (1960), first vice prime minister (1961–62), and prime minister (2006–) of **Congo** and a significant figure during the **Congo Crisis**. A schoolteacher, Gizenga became a Leftist political leader prior to independence and, although a member of different political parties, became **Patrice Lumumba**'s closest collaborator. In early 1960, Gizenga spent three months in the **Soviet Union**, where the **Central Intelligence Agency** (CIA) believed he set up arms shipments to Congo. Because he supported Lumumba's late-August 1960 push for Soviet assistance, President **Joseph Kasavubu** fired Gizenga along with Lumumba on 5 September 1960. In November, Gizenga planned to rendezvous with Lumumba in Lumumba's Stanleyville power base. Gizenga arrived safely and launched a rebellion on 19 November, but Lumumba was captured days after his 26–27 November escape from **United Nations** (UN) protective custody.

Gizenga proclaimed himself the legitimate president of Congo with his capital at Stanleyville after Lumumba's death was announced on 13 February 1961. His government was recognized by Communist and radical African countries, which provided significant military assistance. Although his forces won control of half of Congo, Gizenga could not capitalize on his success owing to an autocratic nature combined with a morbid fear of assassination that kept him from leaving his official residence for months at a time. Chaos, tribal warfare, and purges grew so terrible in his territory that people who wore glasses were murdered because this implied they were members of the elite.

When the Congolese parliament met to choose a new prime minister in July 1961, the U.S. government worried that Gizenga might win, and he was reportedly offered the support of nationalist politicians, but Gizenga's suspicion that it was a trap and his refusal to leave Stanleyville and meet with the legislators alienated those that had not yet been bribed by the CIA, KGB, or radical African governments, and he was defeated by **Cyrille Adoula**. Gizenga was selected as an officer in the new government but continued to lead the Stanleyville rebels until late 1961. The rebellion was defeated by the Congolese army on 14 January 1962, Adoula jailed Gizenga on 16 January, and he was not freed until **Moïse Tshombe** took power as prime minister in July 1964. Gizenga returned to Stanleyville and seceded from Congo on 7 September, calling his country the People's Republic of Congo. Thirteen Leftist governments recognized this government, but Gizenga was captured and jailed in October, and in 1965 his government was overthrown by Tshombe's old **Katangan** *gendarmarie*, mercenaries, a CIA-run air force, and Belgian paratroopers flown in by the U.S. to free 3,000 foreign hostages in the **Stanleyville (Kisangani) hostage rescue**.

Joseph-Désiré Mobutu (**Mobutu Sese Seko**) freed Gizenga following his 24 November 1965 coup and sent him into a 27-year exile. Gizenga returned following a 1990 amnesty. He ran for president in 2006, finishing third. In the runoff, he supported the victorious **Joseph Kabila**, who appointed Gizenga prime minister on 30 December. *See also* CONGO, CENTRAL INTELLIGENCE AGENCY INVOLVEMENT IN; DEVLIN, LARRY; GBENYE, CHRISTOPHE; MULELE, PIERRE.

GLOBAL WAR ON TERROR (GWOT). Name given by President **George W. Bush** to the U.S.-led international struggle against Islamist **terrorism**. In Africa, the GWOT has focused on the Horn of Africa and the trans-Sahara region. On the Horn, the U.S. launched **Operation Enduring Freedom–Horn of Africa** (OEF-HOA) with military bases in Djibouti, naval picket lines set up to prevent terrorist infiltration by sea, and reconnaissance and military assistance given to **Ethiopia** in its war against the Islamist Islamic Courts Union (ICU) in **Somalia**. In the Sahara and Sahel, the U.S. launched **Operation Enduring Freedom–Trans Sahara** (OEF-TS), which provides regional governments with training, reconnaissance, and other forms of assistance. To coordinate U.S. military policy in Africa, Washington created the **U.S. Africa Command** (AFRICOM) in 2006. Critics have alleged that military assistance provided by the U.S. to African nations for fighting the GWOT has strengthened regimes against their regional and domestic opponents more than it has improved fighting against **al Qaeda** and Islamist al Qaeda–affiliated movements, and that support for Ethiopia against the ICU has alienated many Somalis, who traditionally oppose Ethiopia. *See also* ALGERIA; CHAD; ERITREA; MOROCCO; TUNISIA.

GOWON, YAKUBU (JACK) (1934–). Military ruler of **Nigeria**, who crushed secession by the country's Eastern Region. Following the second Nigerian military coup of 1966, Gowon emerged as an ethnic and religious compromise choice for leadership because he was from the predominantly Northern Region, like most surviving generals, but was a Christian, like most southerners. Gowon sought to restore national unity, but massacres of an estimated 30,000 Christian Ibos in the north led the Ibo-dominated Eastern Region to secede on 29 May 1967, calling itself **Biafra** and starting a civil war. Gowon's efforts to blockade Biafra and starve the Ibo into submission were matched by Biafran President Chukwuemeka Ojukwu's effort to make it difficult for his breakaway republic to receive relief supplies in order to use pictures of starving Biafrans as propaganda to win international sympathy and intervention against Nigeria. President **Lyndon B. Johnson** suspended military assistance to Nigeria and ordered an arms embargo against both sides, angering Gowon.

As the sophisticated Biafran propaganda effort took hold in the United States, Johnson faced pressure from the Left and Right to help the Biafrans, but at the same time, the State Department emphasized that this would antagonize most African nations, for whom the former colonial borders were sacrosanct. Frustrated, Johnson reportedly demanded that his staff come up with a way to "get these nigger babies off my TV set." Johnson finally ordered food to be sent in June

1968, which continued under **Richard M. Nixon**, who briefly considered recognizing Biafran independence, but in the end only increased the relief assistance. When Biafra surrendered on 12 January 1970 after Ojukwu fled the country, Gowon shocked the world by immediately allowing **foreign aid** to enter the province and acting to ensure that there would be no retribution against the Ibo. His anger at the U.S. led him to push Nigeria into a truly nonaligned policy, which contributed to Nixon's washing his hands of Africa. Economic relations continued undisturbed and by 1979 Nigeria was the second-largest supplier of **oil** to the U.S.

Gowon was unable to manage Nigeria's economy effectively in peacetime, especially after the tremendous and continuing rise in oil prices that began in 1973. Government corruption was endemic, spurred in large part by his order that some sectors of the economy would be off limits to foreign investment and taken over by Nigerians, most of whom received the windfall through political connections rather than merit. Indiscriminate and uncoordinated government spending on white elephant projects wasted billions of dollars as the port of Lagos became infamous for having hundreds of ships waiting for months to offload. When Gowon decided on 1 October 1974 to postpone indefinitely the scheduled 1976 transition to democracy, public dissatisfaction led to his 29 July 1975 overthrow by General **Murtala Muhammad** while Gowon attended an **Organization of African Unity** (OAU) summit.

Thereafter, Gowon retired to **Great Britain**, where he earned a doctorate in political science. Following Muhammad's assassination, the government of General **Olusegun Obasanjo** accused Gowon of complicity, stripped him of his military rank and pension, and issued an indictment against him. He was later pardoned and returned to Nigeria where he taught political science and was elected to the Senate.

GREAT BRITAIN. European colonial power that strongly moved to a policy of decolonization following the **Suez Crisis** in **Egypt**. With Suez showing the British they were no longer a Great Power, they began their withdrawal from the Middle East. That knowledge and growing demands for independence led the government of Prime Minister Harold Macmillan to speed up decolonization, although not as fast as the administration of **John F. Kennedy** demanded in international forums such as the **United Nations** (UN). Despite decolonization, the United States generally deferred to British leadership in sub-Saharan Africa on issues that did not impinge on the **cold war**. **Rhodesia (Zimbabwe)** was a rare exception when Secretary of State **Henry Kissinger** launched "**shuttle diplomacy**" in the summer of 1976 in a failed attempt to end the civil war and bring majority rule.

In the post–cold war era, the British government has largely deferred to U.S. leadership of the **Global War on Terror** (GWOT), but has played a leading role in encouraging the developed world to provide African nations with **foreign aid** and international debt relief. London has also maintained at least a symbolic status in Africa through periodic meetings of the Commonwealth, which includes all former British African colonies and **Mozambique**. Zimbabwe was suspended as of mid-2008. *See also* BOTSWANA; FRANCE; GHANA; ISRAEL; KENYA; NASSER, GAMAL ABDEL; NIGERIA; SIERRA LEONE; SOMALIA; SOUTH AFRICA; SUDAN; TANZANIA; UGANDA; ZAMBIA.

GUINEA. West African nation, which voted for independence from **France** in 1958, the only French sub-Saharan African colony to do so. Guinea's last colonial prime minister was **Ahmed Sékou Touré**, a radical labor leader. Touré earned the enmity of French President Charles de Gaulle when he called on Guineans to reject de Gaulle's plan for limited sovereignty and to vote for full independence. After 95 percent of the population voted for independence, de Gaulle granted it on 2 October 1958 and the French immediately withdrew, taking with them everything they could and destroying what they could not. De Gaulle threatened U.S. President **Dwight D. Eisenhower** that if the United States provided any assistance to Guinea, he was prepared to withdraw France from the North Atlantic Treaty Organization (NATO), so Eisenhower refused even to acknowledge Guinea's request for **foreign aid** and did not send an ambassador for eight months following independence.

Touré, a radical socialist, turned to the **Soviet Union** for economic assistance. He supported Soviet policy in **Congo** during the **Congo Crisis**—withdrawing Guinean troops from the **United Nations** (UN) **peacekeeping** operation, blaming the death of former Prime Minister

Patrice Lumumba on imperialist powers, and demanding the dismissal of UN Secretary-General **Dag Hammarskjöld** and his advisers. Touré also visited the Soviet Union and declared that Guinean foreign policy marched in step with the Soviets; accepted 1,500 Eastern Bloc technicians; signed black Africa's first **trade** agreements with the Soviets; moved toward collectivizing agriculture and nationalizing mines, businesses, banks, and foreign trade; and began receiving over $100 million in projects, assistance, and military equipment. Many leading Leftist African national liberation movements also made Conakry their base.

Touré's totalitarian mix of black nationalism and socialism, which he called "Pan-Africanism," briefly made Guinea a favored destination of Black Power advocates, who had become disenchanted with the U.S. Most famously, singer Harry Belafonte and former Student Nonviolent Coordinating Committee (SNCC) leader Stokely Carmichael, who renamed himself Kwame Touré, relocated to Guinea with his wife, South African singer Miriam Makeba. Touré also briefly unified Guinea with the radical West African governments of **Ghana** and Mali.

U.S. Senator **John F. Kennedy** had been impressed with Touré during a 1959 meeting. Following reports from U.S. Ambassador to Guinea William Attwood that Touré was unhappy with the Soviets and their aid, President Kennedy began coaxing Touré and Guinea out of the Soviet camp toward the Non-Aligned Movement. Kennedy ordered Guinea a small economic assistance package and sent his brother-in-law, **Peace Corps** Director Sargent Shriver, to meet with Touré. Much impressed, Touré stopped public attacks against the Peace Corps and the U.S. and accepted a Peace Corps mission. Following Soviet-backed unrest during December 1961, Touré expelled the Soviet ambassador, continued to accept economic assistance from the Soviets, and began to move Guinea closer to the U.S., culminating in an October 1962 White House meeting with President Kennedy. Days later, the Cuban missile crisis began. At Kennedy's request, Touré refused to give the Soviets permission to use Guinea as a refueling stop for Cuba-bound airplanes that could have broken the U.S. blockade, despite the Soviets having paid to lengthen an airstrip to accommodate long-range jets.

The mercurial Touré turned against the U.S. in 1966, blaming the **Central Intelligence Agency** (CIA) for overthrowing his friend, President **Kwame Nkrumah** of **Ghana**. In 1974, Touré reconciled with President Fidel Castro of **Cuba**, allowing Cuban transport airplanes to use Guinea's airfield to refuel before heading south for **Angola** to assist the *Movimento Popular de Libertação de Angola*/Popular Movement for the Liberation of Angola (MPLA) forces fighting the civil war. Touré ignored U.S. threats to retaliate against Guinea if he continued to work with the Cubans. Four years later, he cancelled many of the concessions he had granted to the Soviets after concluding that they were not providing enough assistance, and reestablished good relations with the U.S. and France.

Touré's pox on both houses approach to dealing with the East and West paid dividends in the form of significant economic assistance from the U.S., Western Europe, **China**, and the Soviet Bloc. The money was wasted though, swallowed by his Stalinist economic system and its concomitant corruption. Between 20 and 40 percent of Guinea's population fled Guinea's poverty and repression during Touré's rule. By the time of his death from heart problems at a Cleveland, Ohio, hospital on 26 March 1984, Guinea was one of the world's poorest, least developed, and most isolated countries. *See also* MUSIC.

– H –

HABRÉ, HISSENE (1936?–). Warlord, prime minister (1978–79), and president (1982–90) of **Chad**. Habré's fierce Chadian nationalism made him a bitter opponent of **Libyan** leader **Muammar Qaddafi** and his attempts to annex northern Chad, which led to Habré becoming the recipient of significant assistance from the governments of President **Ronald W. Reagan** beginning in 1981 and **George H.W. Bush** until 1990. Habré combined intelligence, outstanding organizational ability, ruthlessness, egoism, and a powerful nationalism to emerge from Chad's myriad civil wars as president and drive the Libyan army out of his country, but these same characteristics caused the disaffection and rebellion that led to his ouster and exile in Senegal.

Habré's brutality, he is alleged to have been responsible for the deaths of 40,000 Chadians, made him the first former African president to be indicted for war crimes. Following attempts to extradite him to **Belgium** in November 2005 where he would be tried under that nation's "universal jurisdiction" law for crimes against humanity, the **African Union** (AU) ordered Senegal to create a special human rights court to conduct his trial. Preparations were still being made in mid-2008.

HAILE SELASSIE I (1892–1975). Emperor of **Ethiopia** (1930–74) whose call for the world to assist his country against Italy's invasion prior to World War II made him an international symbol of anti-Fascism and later, a leader in Africa's decolonization movement. After World War II, he was the closest U.S. **cold war** ally in Africa.

Ethiopia was a feudal society mired in the 16th century when Haile Selassie took power as emperor in 1930. He worked to modernize it, but was limited by the power of the aristocracy and the Ethiopian Orthodox Church. His army was unprepared when Italy attacked on 3 October 1935, and many of Haile Selassie's men were armed with spears against Italian tanks, warplanes, and mustard gas. The U.S. and the rest of the world did nothing to help despite organized protests by **African Americans**, and Haile Selassie fled into exile on 2 May 1936. He spoke before the League of Nations on 30 June 1936, calling on the world to assist Ethiopia and stand up to Fascism. The speech made Haile Selassie an international hero, especially in the U.S. Thereafter, every U.S. president sought close ties with Haile Selassie because of the prestige in which Africans held him. Haile Selassie used the support of President **Franklin Delano Roosevelt** to prevent **Great Britain** from taking Ethiopia or carving it up after the British drove out the Italians in October 1941, and he persuaded the **Harry S. Truman** administration to work in the **United Nations** (UN) to give him control over **Eritrea**. In 1953, Haile Selassie signed a defense treaty with the U.S. that guaranteed diplomatic support and arms, and he sent troops to join UN forces in the Korean War.

Haile Selassie's goal was to make Ethiopia "the capital of Africa." He was a key figure in creating the **Organization of African Unity** (OAU) on 25 May 1963, bringing radical and conservative state leaders together in Addis Ababa to create an organization with the purpose of mediating problems between nations and liberating the continent from imperialism. His prestige and tireless efforts ensured that the organization would be based in his capital. By the 1970s, the emperor was losing his mental abilities and was cut off from reality by his advisers. Mishandling and cover-up of a famine in 1972–73 that killed between 40,000 and 80,000 in Wollo province contributed to the erosion of his authority. The situation grew so dire that President **Richard M. Nixon** ordered the U.S. embassy to begin cultivating possible successors.

Haile Selassie was removed from office and placed under house arrest on 12 September 1974, although he continued to be officially recognized as emperor. He was formally removed the following year, and was probably murdered, allegedly by his successor, **Mengistu Haile Mariam**, on 12 August 1975.

HAMMARSKJÖLD, DAG (1905–1961). Second secretary-general (1953–61) of the **United Nations** (UN), who died while trying to end the **Congo Crisis**. By trying to keep the UN neutral, Hammarskjöld earned the enmity of the leaders of **Congo**, radical African states, the **Soviet Union**, the United States, and **Belgium**.

Hammarskjöld first became involved with Africa during the **Suez Crisis**. He worked with his assistant, **Ralph Bunche**, to create a buffer between **Egypt** and **Israel** by creating the UN Emergency Force (UNEF), the first UN **peacekeeping** force. The UN was immediately involved in the Congo Crisis through Bunche, who was on the scene when the army mutinied five days after its 30 June 1960 independence. On 14 July, the UN responded to the Congolese government's request for UN troops to restore order, creating the *Opération des Nations Unies au Congo*/UN Operation in the Congo (ONUC) and sending the first troops the next day. Its mandate did not allow ONUC to force the breakaway **Katanga** province to rejoin Congo. Prime Minister **Patrice Lumumba** soon demanded that it do so, but Hammarskjöld refused, leading Lumumba to begin frequent denunciations of the secretary-general and the UN as imperialist tools and to call for help from the Soviets. This brought the U.S. more deeply into the crisis. In September, the Soviets demanded that Hammarskjöld be fired because of his handling of the Congo Crisis and the secretary-general position be replaced by a troika. Nonetheless,

Hammarskjöld went to Congo four times and met with Lumumba in New York.

When army commander Joseph-Désiré Mobutu (**Mobutu Sese Seko**) overthrew Lumumba in October, Lumumbists and President **Joseph Kasavubu** sent delegations to the UN, each claiming to represent the legitimate Congolese government. Although Hammarskjöld neither liked nor trusted Lumumba, he nonetheless strove to prevent the U.S. from pushing neutralist countries into voting to seat Kasavubu's delegation, but was unsuccessful. After Lumumba's capture, beating, and humiliation by Mobutu's forces in late November, Hammarskjöld demanded that he be treated humanely, but was ignored and Lumumba was murdered on the orders of Katangan President **Moïse Tshombe** in January 1961.

Hammarskjöld died on 17 September 1961 when his airplane crashed on his way to negotiations between Tshombe and **Cyrille Adoula**, Congo's new prime minister. Investigators ruled that the crash was probably caused by pilot error, but the Soviet Union accused **South Africa** of having been involved, which it denied.

HASSAN II (1929–1999). Moroccan king, moderate leader, and close U.S. ally. Hassan, like all Moroccan sultans, was both political and religious leader by dint of the Moroccan belief that he was a direct descendant of the Prophet Muhammad and was thus the Prince of the Faithful. Hassan was a key adviser for his father, King **Muhammad V**, both of whom **France** sent into exile from 1953–55. After independence in 1956, Muhammad appointed Hassan the military's chief of staff and Hassan led the army in putting down rebellions in the Rif Mountains. He became king following the death of his father on 26 February 1961.

Hassan created North Africa's first parliament in 1963, but by 1965 he had dissolved it and thereafter ensured his dominance through rigged elections. During this period until 1991, and especially the years following two attempts to kill Hassan by military leaders in 1971 and 1972, Morocco saw the "years of lead," during which political opponents were murdered. Perhaps hundreds disappeared with 70 of the most important sent to Tazmamart Prison, a top secret facility, where half died, thousands more were jailed and tortured, hundreds of Polisario Front leaders from the former Spanish Sahara were murdered or disappeared, and labor and political unrest were crushed by violence that killed several hundred.

At the end of the **cold war**, President **George H.W. Bush** pressured Hassan to close Tazmamart, free political prisoners, and democratize, all of which Hassan did beginning in 1991. Opposition parties were allowed to appoint prime ministers under Hassan's "*alternance*" (French, "rotation") policy beginning in 1997, and Hassan allowed them to govern, unprecedented in the Arab world (although they were accused of allowing themselves to be co-opted). Hassan's liberalization policies have been expanded by his son and successor, Muhammad VI, who has allowed freedom of speech on most subjects and created an Equity and Reconciliation Commission in 2006, which is investigating and compensating victims of human rights violations committed between 1956 and 1999.

HELMS, JESSE (1921–2008). Conservative U.S. senator from North Carolina (1973–2003) who played a significant role in Africa policy during the presidencies of **Ronald W. Reagan**, **George H.W. Bush**, and **Bill Clinton** because of his leadership of the Senate Foreign Relations Committee during the Clinton years, and his skillful use of parliamentary rules when he was not the chairman. From the start of the Reagan administration, Helms pushed for support of rebels against Communist regimes in **Angola** and **Mozambique**, a policy that later came to be known as the **Reagan Doctrine**. Helms successfully pushed for the repeal of the **Clark Amendment** that prohibited U.S. support for **Jonas Savimbi**'s guerillas, but failed to get U.S. support for the *Resistência Nacional Moçambicana*/Mozambican National Resistance (RENAMO). Helms had also been a supporter of the illegal white regime in **Rhodesia**, arguing that it was fighting Communist guerillas, and supported the international settlement that led to creation of short-lived **Zimbabwe**–Rhodesia. Helms also backed **constructive engagement** with **South Africa**.

In 2000, Helms met with Rock music singer **Bono** to discuss HIV/**AIDS** in Africa. Bono convinced Helms to reverse his long-standing opposition to **foreign aid** and funding treatment for AIDS, and he became a key Senate leader in the effort to fight AIDS in Africa.

HEMINGWAY, ERNEST (1899–1961). American writer whose novels, short stories, and autobiographical pieces about his African exploits significantly increased Americans' interest in the continent.

HISTORICALLY BLACK COLLEGES AND UNIVERSITIES (HBCUs). U.S. colleges and universities created for **African Americans** during the segregation era. HBCUs provided African Americans and visiting Africans and West Indians with higher education at a time when opportunities in Europe were few and when segregation in the U.S. prevented them from attending most American universities. HBCUs were initially created by religious organizations in the North before the Civil War, but their numbers dramatically increased in the South after the Civil War to provide opportunity and leadership for the Freedmen. Most focused on educating teachers or providing an ostensibly practical, industrial education, following the example of Samuel Chapman Armstrong at Hampton Institute (Hampton University) and his student **Booker T. Washington** at the Tuskegee Normal and Industrial Institute (Tuskegee University). Northern HBCUs tended to follow the liberal arts model espoused by Washington's leading opponent, African American leader **W.E.B. Du Bois**.

For African students, the most important universities were Lincoln University, founded in Pennsylvania by the Presbyterian Church in 1854, Howard University, founded in Washington, D.C., by General O.O. Howard in 1867, Wilberforce University, the oldest HBCU, founded in Ohio by the Methodist Episcopal Church in 1856, and Tuskegee, founded in 1881. Lincoln's tie to Africa was obvious from its inception as the Ashmun Institute, named for **Jehudi Ashmun**, the man who saved the **Liberia** colony following his appointment as its leader by the **American Colonization Society** (ACS). By 1900, Lincoln had 35 African students, the most of any U.S. college, of whom 33 were Liberians. Wilberforce had a dozen students from **South Africa** in the 1890s.

During the 1930s, HBCUs became a crucial source of African leadership, with 35 Lincoln graduates holding high positions in African colonies. The most important HBCU-educated African leaders were **Kwame Nkrumah**, the first president of **Ghana**, **Nnamdi Azikiwe**, the first president of **Nigeria**, both of whom were Lincoln graduates, Hastings Banda, the first president of Malawi, who studied at Central Ohio College (Central State University) and Meharry Medical College in Tennessee, and A.B. Xuma, 1940s president of South Africa's African National Congress (ANC), who studied at Tuskegee. Many of Nkrumah's advisers were also HBCU graduates. Nkrumah's fame as the face of African nationalism led many African students to attend HBCUs. Azikiwe also played an important role as a recruiter through news stories in his newspaper, the *West African Pilot*, during the 1930s and 1940s.

After World War II, Howard became the leading HBCU among Africans as it worked to maintain its "romantic historical tie" to Africa. By 1960, it had the largest international student body in the U.S., with most of these students coming from Africa and the Caribbean. African heads of state regularly made speeches at Howard, and several received honorary degrees. Integration and the ensuing diminution of purpose for HBCUs has significantly decreased their role in creating African leaders. Today African leaders are much more likely to have attended Harvard than Lincoln or Tuskegee, although Howard continues to be an important educational destination.

– I –

IAFEATURE, OPERATION. *See* OPERATION IAFEATURE.

IMMIGRATION. Immigration of Africans to what would become the United States was unfree and in chains from at least 1619 until emancipation by the U.S. Civil War (1861–65). It has been rapid since 1980. Immigration from the U.S. to Africa, primarily to **Liberia**, has been historically minimal.

The first recorded instance of Africans being brought to **Great Britain**'s North American colonies was 20 black indentured servants brought to Jamestown in the Virginia colony in 1619. At the time, there were 32 black indentured servants already in the colony, but the date of their settlement is unknown. Few Africans were brought to the 13 colonies until the 1660s, when African peoples' status legally changed from serving fixed-term indentureships to permanent chattel slavery. Slave imports from the West Indies and from Africa in the

trans-Atlantic slave trade grew more rapidly after Bacon's Rebellion in 1676, when white indentured servants rebelled against the colonial government. Slaves primarily worked on plantations, mostly in the South, growing tobacco, rice, and indigo. Slave imports grew still more rapidly following the 1793 invention of the cotton gin, which made growing American cotton one of the world's most lucrative businesses. Importing slaves to the U.S. was made illegal on 1 January 1808, although a trickle were illegally imported thereafter. In all, approximately 500,000 Africans were brought to what is now the U.S. until the Thirteenth Amendment to the U.S. Constitution ended slavery in 1865.

Immigration to the U.S. by free Africans was minimal until the late 20th century. The first legal immigrants were Cape Verdeans who fled a drought in the late 19th century to come to the southeastern New England coast to work in the whaling industry. At the same time, dozens of Africans began to come to the U.S. to study, primarily at **historically black colleges or universities** (HBCUs), and a few stayed rather than return home. The number of students and those who illegally remained slowly increased until the 1950s when the numbers began comparatively rapid growth as it became clear that Europe would soon be decolonizing Africa. The number of people expanded still further with the first wave of independence in the 1960s.

Since the mid-1960s, African immigration to the U.S., both legal and illegal, has been fueled by the pull of economic opportunity and the push of endemic political instability and economic mismanagement in many African countries. Beginning in 1980, the number of African immigrants rapidly expanded because of the Refugee Act of 1980, which has brought more than 200,000 African **refugees** to the U.S. for permanent resettlement, resulting in influxes of people from Liberia, **Sierra Leone**, **Somalia**, **Ethiopia**, **Eritrea**, and **Sudan**. The numbers increased still more rapidly beginning in 1986 because of the Immigration Reform and Control Act (the Simpson–Mazzoli Act), which granted amnesty to 30,000 African illegal aliens. The Immigration Act of 1990 created a lottery system that randomly distributed visas and expanded the number of Africans eligible to enter the country by creating "diversity visas" for areas of the world such as Africa that had not traditionally been allowed to immigrate to the U.S. Economic and political instability has led to significant recent immigration from **Nigeria**, **Zimbabwe**, and **South Africa**. In one noted instance, a young woman was granted asylum from Togo after she fled that country rather than undergo a family-ordered clitoridectomy. Once a person has been legally admitted, U.S. law makes it much easier for members of the family to immigrate with "family reunification visas."

The 2000 census showed 612,548 Africans legally living in the U.S., more people than were taken from Africa under slavery. Most analysts agree that the number of illegal immigrants is at least equal to the number of legal residents. Of legal African immigrants, 48.9 percent hold a college diploma, the highest percentage for immigrants from any continent.

U.S. immigration to Africa began in 1822 under the auspices of the **American Colonization Society** (ACS), which sought to remove free **African Americans** from the U.S. Some 13,000 former slaves or their descendants moved to Liberia by 1867. The collapse of the post–Civil War Reconstruction policy in the American South, under which the U.S. Army had protected the rights of African Americans, and the intense negrophobia and violence that followed, spurred two African American–led efforts to go "back to Africa." The first began in 1878 with creation of the Liberian Exodus Joint Stock Steamship Company, which delivered one shipload of 183 migrants to Liberia before going bankrupt. Bishop Henry McNeill Turner took over leadership of the movement in the 1880s but lack of funding meant that only about 800 more people were able to make the move.

The second "back to Africa" movement, led by **Marcus Garvey** and his Universal Negro Improvement Association (UNIA), was far larger but resulted in no African Americans moving to Liberia. A final small flow of people moved to Africa, primarily **Ghana** and **Guinea**, following their independence in 1957 and 1958. These African Americans, numbering in the hundreds, moved for idealistic reasons: to provide needed skills to uplift Africa, in support of socialism, and in pursuit of an idealized vision of Africa as a place where black people would be free from the segregation and prejudice they experienced in the U.S.

INTERAHAMWE. Kinyarwanda: variously translated as "Those who stand together" or "Those who fight together," but colloquially as

"Those who kill together." The Interahamwe was **Rwanda**'s "Hutu Power" paramilitary organization that served as shock troops for the genocide. *See also* ALBRIGHT, MADELEINE; CLINTON, WILLIAM J. (BILL); CONGO; FRANCE; KAGAME, PAUL; MOBUTU SESE SEKO; RWANDA, GENOCIDE IN.

INTERNATIONAL BANK FOR RECONSTRUCTION AND DE-VELOPMENT. *See* WORLD BANK.

INTERNATIONAL MONETARY FUND (IMF). Organization created along with the **World Bank** (International Bank for Reconstruction and Development) following their proposal at the July 1944 Bretton Woods, New Hampshire, international conference that was planning the post–World War II international economic order. The IMF was established on 27 December 1945. It was part of President **Franklin Delano Roosevelt**'s postwar vision for using **foreign aid** as a way to prevent a second Great Depression and the international instability and warfare that came in the Depression's wake. The IMF was created to work in tandem with the World Bank by guaranteeing stability in global currency markets through surveillance (monitoring economic and financial developments, and providing policy advice to prevent economic crises), lending money to countries with balance of payments shortages, advising countries how to correct the policies that led to the balance of payments crisis, and providing technical assistance.

In the third world, while the Bank focused on providing economic development loans for specific programs or functions, the IMF would assess the performance of national economies and offer advice and, during emergencies, provide short-term support for a country's balance of payments. When World Bank Director Robert McNamara created structural adjustment programs (SAPs) in September 1979 to bail out economies that could no longer meet their debt payment obligations, the IMF worked with the Bank in providing short-term assistance to get countries past the immediate emergency while the Bank sought to fix the long-term situation.

Since 2000, the IMF has followed the Bank's lead in trying to retain a significant role in international economic development at a time when both wealthy and impoverished countries have rejected SAPs, national planning, and large-scale economic projects in favor of debt forgiveness and encouraging international economic liberalization. *See also* **TRADE.**

ISRAEL. Middle Eastern Jewish state that has been victim or aggressor in the **Arab–Israeli Wars of 1948–49, 1967**, and **1973**, as well as the **Suez Crisis** of 1956. Israel signed a peace treaty with **Egypt** in 1979 following **Anwar Sadat**'s dramatic 19 November 1977 trip to Israel, President **Jimmy Carter**'s shepherding of the 1978 **Camp David Accords**, and Carter's 1979 intervention to ensure that the peace process did not come unstuck.

Israel also played a significant role in supporting sub-Saharan African nations in the early years of independence, providing agricultural and military technical assistance and training. Most African nations broke relations with Israel during the 1973 Arab–Israeli War in third-world solidarity with the Arab aggressors and in the usually unmet hope of receiving economic assistance from the Arab oil-producing states in the face of skyrocketing oil prices. Thereafter, Israel sometimes worked with **South Africa**, another international pariah, particularly in the field of nuclear weaponry. In 1977, Israeli paratroopers rescued 256 hostages from Palestinian and Baader–Meinhof terrorists at Entebbe Airport in **Uganda** with the loss of one soldier and four hostages.

Israel has been a strong supporter of the government of **Ethiopia** as a counterweight to Arab and Muslim states in the Horn of Africa region and to keep in check Muslim governments in **Somalia** and **Eritrea**. During the reign of **Mengistu Haile Mariam**, Israel secretly negotiated to evacuate approximately 50,000 Ethiopian Jews (Falasha) to Israel in exchange for money and military assistance totaling over $50 million, including U.S.-made cluster bombs until the U.S. ordered the Israelis to stop sending them. *See also* AMIN DADA, IDI; BOURGUIBA, HABIB; TUNISIA.

– J –

JACKSON, JESSE (1941–). U.S. civil rights leader and President **Bill Clinton**'s special envoy for the president and secretary of state for the promotion of democracy in Africa. Jackson was a longtime friend of General Ibrahim Babangida, the military ruler of **Nigeria**, and Jackson's son received **oil** concessions for work he had done on Babangida's behalf. Jackson was a strong supporter of Babangida's creation of a limited democratic system. Following Babangida's annulling of the 1993 presidential election and his subsequent ouster in favor of General Sani Abacha, Clinton sent Jackson to help resolve the crisis, but human rights leaders refused to meet with Jackson due to his relationship with Babangida.

With the encouragement of **Liberian** president **Charles Taylor**, Jackson helped broker the July 1999 **Sierra Leone** peace agreement between Ahmad Tejan Kabbah, the democratically elected president, and Foday Sankoh, leader of the Revolutionary United Front (RUF), a group without a political agenda but known for its massacres, use of child soldiers, and random amputations of civilians' arms or legs. Sankoh was backed by Taylor, and both were politically supported by Jackson's friend Donald Payne, the leader of the Congressional Black Caucus. Jackson said he could reform Taylor and Sankoh the way he had Chicago gang leaders, so he followed a policy of constructive engagement in which he offered friendship rather than criticism for their human rights records. In July 1999, Jackson hammered out a Sierra Leone power-sharing agreement that was made thanks to strong pressure on Kabbah from Jackson and the White House. It released Sankoh from a Sierra Leonean jail, where he was awaiting execution for mass murder, elevated him to vice president, and gave him control of Sierra Leone's diamond mines. Smuggling of **blood diamonds** to Liberia dramatically increased.

In May 2000, Jackson tried to bring the parties back together, but was advised not to go to Sierra Leone for his own safety after favorably comparing Sankoh's RUF with **Nelson Mandela**'s African National Congress (ANC) at a press conference on 12 May. Instead Jackson met with Taylor. In the course of their meeting, Jackson reassured Taylor that the U.S. had no position on a proposed **United Nations** (UN) human rights tribunal for Sierra Leone and he advised Taylor to refute reports that he was behind the violence in Sierra Leone and in his own country. The Clinton administration had initially lauded its success in Sierra Leone following the Jackson agreement, but when the RUF continued its brutality and newspaper stories appeared about how the RUF disfigured children, on 5 June 2000 a State Department spokesman denied any U.S. role in the settlement. Jackson was quietly dismissed as special envoy shortly thereafter. In December 2000, Secretary of State **Madeleine Albright** cabled the U.S. embassy in Liberia that the U.S. government now considered Taylor a uniquely bad actor in Africa.

JANJAWEED. Government-supported Arab horse militias used by the government of **Sudan** to commit genocide against the black residents of **Darfur**, the poorest and least developed province in that country. The Janjaweed (colloquial Arabic, often translated as "evil horse-men") attack and burn villages, slaughter indiscriminately, poison wells, and rape women who are subsequently ostracized by their own people. By mid-2008 they had displaced 2.5 million Darfurians out of a population of six million to camps in **Sudan** or **Chad**, with between 200,000 and 400,000 people killed or dying from starvation. *See also* BASHIR, OMAR AL-; IMMIGRATION; REFUGEES.

JOHNSON, LYNDON B. (1908–1973). U.S. senator, vice president (1961–63) and, following the assassination of **John F. Kennedy**, president (1963–69). Johnson's initial policy focus on domestic affairs and subsequent immersion in the Vietnam War left him without time or interest to involve himself in Africa. His Africa policy primarily consisted of using **foreign aid** to try to force countries into supporting his Vietnam policy. When African leaders such as Houari Boumédienne of **Algeria** and **Gamal Abdel Nasser** of **Egypt** refused, he personally ordered that aid, including food, be withheld.

Johnson's logistical support for the November 1964 **Stanleyville (Kisangani) hostage rescue** by **Belgium** in **Congo** angered African leaders, despite the Congolese government having supported the mission. Their reaction further alienated Johnson from Africa. A second Congolese intervention, in June 1967, angered Congress. A visit to **South Africa** by Robert F. Kennedy in May 1966 roused Johnson to make his first speech on Africa and to talk about a Johnson Doctrine in Africa, but the effort was quickly abandoned. Johnson provided emergency aid to **Nigeria**'s rebel **Biafra** province after telling his advisers to "get these nigger babies off my TV set."

Johnson also showed little interest in the Middle East until Nasser ordered the removal of **United Nations** (UN) peacekeepers on its border with **Israel** and blockaded Israel from entering the Gulf of Aqaba. Secretary of State **Dean Rusk** began a frantic series of meetings with the UN, Israel, Egypt, the **Soviet Union**, and Western European nations, but was unable to avert the **Arab–Israeli War of 1967**. Israel's victory was so rapid and complete that it allowed the Middle East again to recede as an issue. *See also* DODD, THOMAS; GHANA; MCNAMARA, ROBERT S.; SOUTH AFRICA; ZAMBIA; ZIMBABWE.

JOHNSON-SIRLEAF, ELLEN (1938–). President of **Liberia** and the first woman to be elected president of an African nation. Johnson-Sirleaf is a Harvard University–educated economist who worked for numerous **non-governmental organizations** (NGOs) during several periods of exile from Liberia. Johnson-Sirleaf is known as the "Iron Lady" for her toughness in the face of two imprisonments and multiple periods of lengthy exile. She is the second president of Liberia without **Americo-Liberian** ancestors, although one grandfather was a German. Both of her grandmothers were illiterate.

As a young woman, Johnson-Sirleaf exiled herself to the United States to avoid prison after she called the government of **William Tubman** a "kleptocracy" during an international development meeting in Liberia. It was during this period that she received most of her higher education. She returned to Liberia after Tubman's death and worked for the administration of **William Tolbert**. Following his assassination, she went into exile again, returning in 1985 to run for the Senate as an opponent of President **Samuel Doe**. Doe twice imprisoned her and she left the country again. She briefly supported the ultimately successful civil war by warlord **Charles Taylor** that led to Doe's ouster and murder. In 1997, Johnson-Sirleaf ran for president and was defeated by Taylor. She went into exile again when he charged her with treason.

After Taylor's overthrow in 2003 and creation of the **United Nations** (UN) Mission in Liberia (UNMIL), a military and police force of 15,000 sent to keep the peace, Johnson-Sirleaf returned to Liberia and was elected president on 8 November 2005, taking office on 16 January 2006. Secretary of State **Condoleezza Rice** and First Lady Laura Bush represented the U.S. at the inaugural. Two months later,

Johnson-Sirleaf addressed a joint session of the U.S. Congress and asked for U.S. assistance to rebuild her country. Her rule has been characterized by ethnic reconciliation, emphasis on good government, encouragement for business and investment, creation of a Truth and Reconciliation Commission, an international effort to acquire **foreign aid**, emphasis on economic growth (8 percent in 2007) and work with international lenders to have Liberia's $3.4 billion foreign debt cancelled.

Johnson-Sirleaf's effort to have the debt forgiven has resulted in the **World Bank**, the **International Monetary Fund** (IMF), and the African Development Bank raising $1.5 billion for debt relief through mid-2008, and the U.S. canceling Liberia's bilateral debt of $391 million. As of mid-2008, the U.S. had provided her government with $750 million in reconstruction and development assistance administered through the **Agency for International Development** (AID) and $750 million to the UN to help pay for UNMIL. A further $342 million was appropriated for fiscal year 2008. The U.S. also overhauled and trained the Liberian army while the UN trained the police. In Monrovia, the capital, some vestiges of civilization such as electricity and running water began to be restored. President **George W. Bush** acknowledged Liberia's progress by visiting the country in February 2008. *See also* FIRESTONE NATURAL RUBBER COMPANY; REFUGEES.

– K –

KABILA, JOSEPH (1971–). Military commander and president (2001–) of **Congo**. Primarily raised in **Uganda** and **Tanzania**, Kabila speaks accented French and Lingala (the army's lingua franca) and did not have excellent command of either language when his father, **Laurent-Désiré Kabila**, appointed him armed forces commander following the **Rwanda**-backed invasion that brought him to power on 29 May 1997. Joseph became president following his father's assassination on 16 January 2001. Known as a far kinder and humbler man than his egotistical and often brutal father, Kabila has a reputation for pliability, which may have served him well in peace negotiations that ended Congo's brutal civil war and led to 2006 elections, which he won. *See also* GIZENGA, ANTOINE.

KABILA, LAURENT-DÉSIRÉ (1939–2001). Congolese rebel and president (1997–2001), who was briefly a favorite of the U.S. government. Kabila was a follower of **Congo**'s first prime minister, **Patrice Lumumba**, and became a rebel following the 13 February 1961 announcement of Lumumba's assassination. Kabila's forces were part of **Antoine Gizenga**'s Soviet bloc–supported rebellions, but he broke with Gizenga in 1964, forming his own Lake Tanganyika–based organization in the Kivu region. At various times he received military training in **China**, and he was heavily influenced by Cultural Revolution ideology.

Ernesto "Che" Guevara and 120 guerillas from **Cuba** went to fight with Kabila in April 1965. Guevara found Kabila's **Simba** warriors ill-disciplined and brutal. In his posthumously published journals, Guevara criticized Kabila for leading his movement from luxury hotels and their bars in foreign cities. Despite his frequent absences, Kabila was able to maintain control over a small enclave west of the Mitumba Mountains throughout the 32-year government of **Mobutu Sese Seko**, creating a Communist government that was supported by mining and smuggling gold and diamonds, drug-running, and prostitution. Kabila outlawed the use of money and retained power through witchcraft and grisly murders, which included the burning of an estimated 2,000 elderly people who were accused of sorcery.

When the government of **Rwanda** decided to overthrow Mobutu for allowing **refugee** camps to be taken over by the **Interahamwe**, the "Hutu Power" paramilitary organization that had led the genocide in Rwanda, they sought out Kabila to serve as the rebels' leader, allegedly finding him passed out in one of his saloons. Rwanda's army put him in power on 29 May 1997. Kabila promised reforms, civil rights, and elections in April 1998, and he changed **Zaïre**'s name back to the Democratic Republic of Congo. President **Bill Clinton** called Kabila a leader of the "African Renaissance" and met with him in **Uganda** during his 1998 tour of Africa. Afterwards Kabila broke his promises, creating a dictatorship as corrupt and even more brutal than Mobutu's. He imposed a Maoist cultural revolution, created "People's Committees" charged with spying on neighbors, and jailed and tortured political opponents. Thereafter, the Clinton administration kept its distance.

On 2 July, a rebellion among Rwanda-backed Banyamulenge tribesmen and former Kabila supporters broke out in eastern Congo. On 27 July 1998, as protests mounted about "foreign occupation" by Rwandan soldiers, Kabila expelled the 100 Rwandan soldiers who were leading his army. Kabila turned for support to the Interahamwe. He also received outside assistance from **Angola,** which sought revenge for Mobutu's support of guerilla leader **Jonas Savimbi, Namibia,** and **Zimbabwe** in exchange for mineral and timber concessions, and even **Chad** and **Libya.** The rebels were supported by Rwanda, Uganda, and Burundi, which also took concessions. The result was Africa's first continental war, which ended in 2002, and civil war that continued on a low level into mid-2008. An estimated 5.4 million people died from the violence and dislocation by 2008. Kabila was assassinated by one of his bodyguards on 16 January 2001, and was succeeded by his son, **Joseph Kabila.** *See also* IMMIGRATION; RWANDA, GENOCIDE IN.

KAGAME, PAUL (1957–). Rwandan rebel leader, vice president, and president (2000–), who overthrew Rwanda's genocidal "Hutu Power" government in 1994. Kagame had trained at the U.S. Command and General Staff College at Fort Leavenworth, Kansas, and hundreds of his soldiers had been trained in everything from psychological operations to tactical special forces exercises.

Kagame and a group of Rwandan Tutsi exiled to **Uganda** had fought for **Yoweri Museveni**'s National Resistance Army, which overthrew the Milton Obote dictatorship in 1986. Following Museveni's victory, Kagame began to organize the *Front Patriotique Rwandaise*/Rwandan Patriotic Front (RPF), which started a guerilla war against Rwanda's radical Hutu government. The RPF was spectacularly successful, and as it reached the outskirts of the capital, Kigali, the Rwandan government agreed to power sharing in 1994. When the airplane carrying the presidents of Rwanda and Burundi was shot down as it returned to Rwanda from peace talks, the **Rwanda genocide** began, which ended only when Kagame's forces defeated the "Hutu Power" government and drove its followers into exile in **Zaïre** and **Tanzania.**

Zaïrian leader **Mobutu Sese Seko** refused or was unable to prevent Hutu terrorists from infiltrating Rwanda, so Kagame ordered the Rwandan army to attack the refugee camps to stop it. When the Zaïrian army fled, Kagame continued the advance with the goal of overthrowing Mobutu, which he did on 16 May 1997, installing longtime Zaïrian rebel **Laurent-Désiré Kabila** as his successor. Six weeks before he invaded Zaïre, Kagame had been in Washington discussing the dangers posed by the Hutu refugee camps. Many people assumed from his Washington ties that the U.S. was behind the invasion, and President Bill Clinton called Kagame a leader of the "African Renaissance." When Kabila subsequently turned on Kagame, the resulting war brought nine countries into **Congo**, Rwanda fought former ally Uganda, and an estimated 3.8 million people were killed by the time it officially ended in 2002. Kagame and Rwanda were accused of human rights violations in the attacks on the refugee camps that began the war.

Domestically, Kagame jailed his leading opponent, Pasteur Bizimungu, a Hutu in a country that is 90 percent Hutu. Kagame has also criticized Paul Rusesabagina, the hero of the **film** *Hotel Rwanda*, who is considered a possible presidential candidate. Kagame has expelled businesses based in **France** and **Belgium**, replacing them with U.S. and Indian businesses. His management of the economy has led to tremendous economic growth in pursuit of his goal of transforming Rwanda into the Singapore of Africa, and he has made Rwanda a banking and high tech center for Central and East Africa.

KASAVUBU, JOSEPH (1917–1969). First president of **Congo** (1960–65). Kasavubu's moderation and, U.S. officials believed, pliable and lazy personality made him a valuable U.S. ally against the radical nationalists, secessionists, and Communists who threatened Congolese unity and the country's Western political and economic orientation during the **Congo Crisis**. Kasavubu was one of Congo's few university graduates, having earned a degree in theology, and became a teacher and civil servant. As one of the founders and the first president of the *Confédérations des Associations Tribales du Katanga*/Association of Bakongo (ABAKO), an ethnic organization that demanded independence for the Bakongo people into a supranational Bakongo state, Kasavubu became a national hero when he was the first black African Congolese political figure to stand up to **Belgium**. Much of Kasavubu's political strength came because the Bakongo were the dominant tribe in Léopoldville, Congo's capital.

Belgian authorities jailed Kasavubu for two months in early 1959, accusing him of having fomented riots that followed a speech in which he called for independence. Following inconclusive Congolese national elections held shortly before independence was to be granted on 30 June 1960, Kasavubu worked out a compromise with **Patrice Lumumba**, the highest vote-getter and a nationalist politician, under which Kasavubu was chosen as president and Lumumba took the more powerful position of prime minister. It was a poor match as Kasavubu sought a federal government while Lumumba strongly supported a powerful unitary government.

Seen by many in Washington as weak, lazy, and lacking political skills, and by his enemies as being sleepy like a crocodile, Kasavubu broke with Lumumba over Lumumba's demands that the **United Nations** (UN) crush resistance in the breakaway **Katanga** republic (Kasavubu agreed with UN officials that this was not part of its mandate), Lumumba's increasingly erratic and autocratic behavior, and Lumumba's calls for assistance from the **Soviet Union**, which Kasavubu had originally supported. On 5 September 1960, Kasavubu fired Lumumba, in a controversial move that followed the letter if not the spirit of the Congolese constitution, and then Lumumba fired Kasavubu. The stalemate was broken on 14 September by army Chief of Staff Joseph-Désiré Mobutu (**Mobutu Sese Seko**), who overthrew them both. Under U.S. pressure, Mobutu restored Kasavubu to office in order to provide greater legitimacy for the coup. When Lumumba persuaded soldiers holding him captive to release him in January 1961, Kasavubu joined Mobutu and other political leaders in rushing to the camp in a successful effort to persuade the soldiers to throw him back in jail. Kasavubu joined the others in concluding that Lumumba was too great a threat to their rule and agreed to turn Lumumba over to his enemy, Katanga's **Moïse Tshombe**, who murdered him. Mobutu returned to the barracks on 9 February 1961. Kasavubu spent the next three years trying to keep a politically moderate and anti-Communist coalition in power.

Military gains by radical government opponents in eastern Congo led Kasavubu to surprise the world, including the U.S., by appointing

Tshombe prime minister in 1964. Tshombe's success in crushing the rebellion with assistance from the U.S., Belgium, and a mercenary-led army and air force that they funded prompted him to declare his intention to run for president in 1965, leading Kasavubu to fire him. Continued stalemate caused Mobutu to overthrow the government a second time in November 1965. Kasavubu retired to his tiny home village, where he was kept in internal exile until his death. *See also* ADOULA, CYRILLE; CONGO, CENTRAL INTELLIGENCE AGENCY INTERVENTION IN; GIZENGA, ANTOINE; HAMMARSKJÖLD, DAG; STANLEYVILLE (KISANGANI) HOSTAGE RESCUE.

KATANGA. Richest and most prosperous province in **Congo**, which seceded from 11 July 1960 to 14 January 1963. Katanga's secession contributed significantly to the **Congo Crisis** of 1960–65. One week after the Congolese army's rebellion of 5 July 1960, Katangan provincial President **Moïse Tshombe** declared Katanga an independent country. The **United Nations** (UN) quickly responded by sending a **peacekeeping** force to restore order and prevent a Superpower conflict between the United States and the **Soviet Union**. The Katangan government was backed by **Belgium** in the form of Belgian administrators, who were told that they would lose their jobs if they went home (those in the rest of Congo had the right to go home and receive new jobs), and security personnel, by the copper-mining consortium Union Minière du Haut Katanga, one of the famous "pillars" of the Belgian Congolese state, and by several hundred foreign mercenaries, who had at their disposal a single jet fighter, with which the Katangans easily repulsed the Congolese army's attempts to retake the province.

UN Secretary-General **Dag Hammarskjöld** resisted demands by Congolese Prime Minister **Patrice Lumumba** that UN troops forcibly reintegrate Katanga, arguing that this exceeded the mandate given to him by the Security Council. Lumumba's response, publicly charging that Hammarskjöld was backing the Katangans in league with the Belgians, put UN administrators and soldiers in jeopardy, which badly harmed relations and ultimately prompted Lumumba to make public calls during August 1960 for the Soviet Union to provide military assistance. The Soviets quickly answered with cargo planes full of equipment, ammunition, and advisers. Lumumba's actions destroyed any remaining sympathy that the administration of **Dwight D. Eisenhower** had for his cause and prompted **Central Intelligence Agency** (CIA) orders for his assassination. Congolese President **Joseph Kasavubu** fired Lumumba on 5 September and Army Chief of Staff Joseph-Désiré Mobutu (**Mobutu Sese Seko**) overthrew them both on 14 September. Congolese leaders collectively turned Lumumba over to Tshombe on 17 January 1961, who participated in beating him and personally oversaw his execution.

Following another failed effort by the Congolese army to retake Katanga in September 1961, the UN, armed with an expanded Security Council mandate, began an offensive that went awry, and Kennedy pressured the UN to stand down and negotiate, which Tshombe used to stall and keep his province independent. Kennedy finally agreed to a new offensive in late 1962, which was supported by U.S. cargo planes, and Katanga's military quickly collapsed. On 14 January 1963, Tshombe surrendered Katanga back to Congo and went into exile in Madrid. *See also* DODD, THOMAS; KATANGA LOBBY.

KATANGA LOBBY. Informal alliance of conservative U.S. activists and politicians spearheaded by publicist Marvin Liebman, the man behind the China Lobby, and Democratic Senator **Thomas Dodd** of Connecticut, in support of the illegal separatist government of **Moïse Tshombe** in **Katanga** province of **Congo**. The lobby argued that because Katanga was the freest, best run, and most genuinely multiracial government in Africa, the administration of President **John F. Kennedy** and the **United Nations** (UN) should leave it alone. The lobby's efforts played a part in Kennedy pressuring the UN to negotiate rather than exploit its military successes against Katanga in late 1962. The lobby dissolved following Katanga's defeat and reintegration into Congo on 12 January 1963.

KAUNDA, KENNETH (1924–). Zambia's first president (1964–91). Known for his public decency and humanitarianism, Kaunda was famous for carrying an oversized handkerchief to use when his speeches moved himself to tears, but he was also a tough political fighter who created a one-party state and was not afraid to jail and even torture his opponents during his 27-year rule. Prior to independence, Kaunda was internationally known for his opposition to British colonial rule in Zambia, then known as Northern Rhodesia. **Great Britain** twice jailed him and tried to prevent his election, but prison increased Kaunda's popularity and made him more uncompromising in his quest for unfettered independence and power. After independence on 24 October 1964, Kaunda sought to rule under an ideology he called Zambian Humanism, a socialist policy that combined traditional African agriculture with **Soviet Union**–style socialism. A long-term, dramatic, and sustained drop in copper prices starting in 1974 and the cost of the economic and sometimes military struggle for independence and majority rule in **Rhodesia** badly hurt the Zambian economy, and his government's large network of inefficient parastatals combined with a generally bloated and corrupt bureaucracy ruined what was left of the economy. Kaunda himself was known for an austere lifestyle that included vegetarianism and teetotaling.

Kaunda's diplomacy, publicly sworn to oppose colonialism, neocolonialism, and racialism, frequently saw him in unusual alliances. In April 1975, he pleaded with Secretary of State **Henry Kissinger** for the U.S. to intervene to stop the Soviet-backed *Movimento Popular de Libertação de Angola*/Popular Movement for the Liberation of Angola (MPLA) from coming to power in **Angola**; he supported guerilla leader **Jonas Savimbi** in **Angola** despite knowing that he was receiving covert military aid from **South Africa**; he tried to starve residents of a Zimbabwe African National Union (ZANU) refugee and guerilla training camp into joining the Zimbabwe African People's Union (ZAPU), which was led by his friend, **Joshua Nkomo**; and he worked with South African Prime Minister **John Vorster** in an unsuccessful effort to achieve a Southern African détente. Perhaps his most famous diplomatic statement occurred after **Cuba**'s intervention in the Angolan civil war, when he warned of a new imperialism in Africa from "a plundering Tiger [the Soviet Union] with its deadly Cubs [Cuba]."

Kaunda's rule grew harsher over time so that by the 1980s, his jails were filled with political prisoners accused variously of plots to overthrown and assassinate him or involvement in the illegal drug market. Food riots and political protests led Kaunda to allow multiparty elections in 1991, in which he received less than 20 percent of the vote for president. The government of Frederick Chiluba subsequently banned Kaunda from making a political comeback. Kaunda's son, Wezi, considered his political heir, was murdered in November 1999, but it was never determined if the murder was political or criminal. Kaunda continued to play a leading role in the political opposition in mid-2008.

KENNEDY, JOHN F. (1917–1963). U.S. politician and president (1961–63). During the 1950s, Kennedy was one of the few members of the U.S. Senate to take a forceful public position in favor of decolonization. He was greatly influenced by **modernization theory** and was a strong supporter of increased **foreign aid** to Africa. Kennedy adviser W.W. Rostow characterized as "timid" economic aid policy under **Dwight D. Eisenhower**, and Kennedy vowed to revolutionize U.S. foreign aid. Kennedy was one of the few presidents to take a personal interest in African affairs and he symbolically showed this by making African Affairs Bureau chief **G. Mennen Williams** the first State Department appointment of his administration, preceding even Secretary of State **Dean Rusk**. Kennedy was much affected by a 6 January 1961 speech by the **Soviet Union**'s leader, Nikita Khrushchev, which pledged support for third-world revolutions, and the speech heightened the sometimes contradictory nature of Kennedy's twin goals for Africa of assisting the continent's economic development in order to improve people's lives and using foreign aid as a **cold war** tactic to prevent Africans from being seduced by communism. Kennedy's **Peace Corps** was particularly popular in Africa.

On 2 July 1957, Senator Kennedy made a speech to the U.S. Senate in which he called on **France** to grant independence to **Algeria**. Apparently Kennedy had been in secret contact with representatives of the *Front de Libération Nationale*/National Liberation Front (FLN), whom the Eisenhower administration had refused to meet. Kennedy's speech was blunt in calling for independence as the only way to retain influence in Algeria and all of North Africa and in telling the Eisenhower administration that it must not let friendship for France stand in the way of telling the French what had to be done. The speech was terribly unpopular in U.S. foreign policy circles and in

Paris, but it was very popular with Africans and Arabs. Kennedy subsequently became chairman of the Foreign Relations Committee's African Affairs Subcommittee, although he took the position under the condition that the committee would not have to meet.

As president, Kennedy met with Algerian President **Ahmed Ben Bella** at the White House on 15 October 1962. Two days after their meeting, Ben Bella shocked and infuriated the president when he flew directly to **Cuba** to see Fidel Castro and give him a report about the meeting. Ben Bella warned Castro that the U.S. would use Cuban assistance to Latin American liberation movements as a pretext to invade, and offered to work as a conduit to assist Cuba's revolutionary efforts, which Castro accepted. When the Cuban missile crisis broke out a few days later, Ben Bella returned to the president's good graces when he assured him that Algeria would not allow airplanes from the **Soviet Union** to refuel to re-supply Cuba. Thereafter, Ben Bella criticized U.S. policy in Vietnam and accused Washington of supporting imperialism. The president nonetheless continued to pay close attention to Algeria and believed that Ben Bella's radicalism would calm as colonialism gave way to independence across the continent. When famine hit Algeria in the winter of 1962–63, Kennedy ordered Food for Peace to be rushed into the country, ultimately feeding one-third of the population, which continued until it was cut off in 1965 by President **Lyndon B. Johnson** in retaliation for Algerian support of North Vietnam.

Kennedy was able to move other Leftist rulers away from the Soviet orbit and more firmly into the neutralist camp, including **Ahmed Sékou Touré** of **Guinea**, **Kwame Nkrumah** of **Ghana**, and **Gamal Abdel Nasser** of **Egypt**. Touré and Nkrumah joined Ben Bella in refusing to allow the Soviets to use their airfields during the missile crisis. He was able to maintain good relations with Nasser and provided Egypt with significant quantities of food through the Food for Peace program despite Kennedy selling advanced warplanes to **Israel** and Nasser supporting rebels in **Congo** and North Yemen, but the Yemeni intervention proved too great a roadblock for Kennedy to attempt to organize Middle East peace negotiations. The **Congo Crisis** was Kennedy's most difficult foreign policy problem in Africa, and his support for **United Nations** (UN) intervention sometimes wavered due to the opposition of Senator **Thomas Dodd** and the **Katanga**

Lobby. In **South Africa**, Kennedy declared a unilateral U.S. embargo on arms sales and subsequently voted for such a resolution at the UN.

Kennedy reorganized the foreign aid bureaucracy, combining several agencies into a new **Agency for International Development (AID)** in order to create a more coherent policy. His government worked closely with the governments of **Nigeria** and **Tunisia**, providing generous foreign aid in order to make these countries the equivalent of demonstration projects for the black and Arab worlds, and Tunisian President **Habib Bourguiba** was reputed to be his favorite African leader. Economic support for neither country bore fruit, with Nigeria's government wiped out in a violent 1966 coup and Tunisia requiring bailout by the **World Bank** and the **International Monetary Fund** (IMF) in 1970. Congressional support for foreign aid also rapidly diminished so that by the final year of his presidency, it was lower than in the much criticized final year of the Eisenhower administration.

The ambivalent nature of Kennedy's two-strand Africa policy of modernization and fighting the cold war came through strongly in his policy toward **Portugal**. In early 1961, he ordered his representatives at the UN to vote for a resolution condemning Portugal's colonial policy, but the U.S. military's need for Portugal's Azores Islands air and sea bases led him to begin abstaining on such resolutions in 1963 and he told Portugal's UN ambassador that the 1961 vote had been a mistake. *See also* AFRICAN AFFAIRS, STATE DEPARTMENT BUREAU OF; KATANGA; VOLTA RIVER DAM.

KENYA. East African nation and U.S. ally since independence in 1963. The relationship grew closer during the **Ogaden War** between **Somalia** and **Ethiopia**, when the government of **Daniel arap Moi** gave the U.S. military basing rights and the U.S. provided him with significant military assistance. Relations declined during the **George H.W. Bush** administration, when U.S. Ambassador Smith Hempstone worked against Moi and pressured him into multiparty rule, but improved under President **Bill Clinton**, who took off the pressure. Following the 11 September 2001 **al Qaeda** attacks, Kenya became an important U.S. ally in the **Global War on Terror** (GWOT).

The U.S. was quick to recognize the 22 December 2007 reelection of Moi's successor, Mwai Kibaki over Raila Odinga, but backed away as evidence mounted that the election had been stolen. The ensuing inter-ethnic violence was the worst in Kenya's history, killing as many as 1,500 and displacing 350,000, with economic losses estimated at $550 million per week for two months. The U.S. joined the European Union (EU) and **African Union** (AU) in a successful effort to pressure both sides to accept former **United Nations** (UN) Secretary-General **Kofi Annan** as mediator. On 18 February 2008 and again on 23 February, Secretary of State **Condoleezza Rice** went to Kenya and bluntly and publicly said that Kibaki must agree to "genuine power sharing." Annan completed an agreement with both sides on 27 February, and Odinga became prime minister on 17 April 2008. *See also* KENYATTA, JOMO; MBOYA, THOMAS; ODINGA, OGINGA.

KENYATTA, JOMO (1896?–1978). Kenyan political activist and alleged terrorist, whose pro-Western policies as prime minister (1963–64) and president (1964–78) made him an ally of the United States. Kenyatta did doctoral work in anthropology in **Great Britain** and published his Oxford University doctoral dissertation on the customs of his native Kikuyu people. He also trained as a Communist revolutionary in the **Soviet Union**, but quickly despised the Russians and their system. His return to Kenya in 1946 made him leader of the Kikuyu and the nationalist anti-colonial movement. In 1952, the British accused Kenyatta of masterminding a growing Kikuyu radical movement called Mau-Mau and jailed or detained him for nine years. Kenyatta had publicly opposed and repudiated Mau-Mau, but the British believed he was using his skills as an anthropologist and Communist to create atavistic tribal rebellion. In fact, Soviet records were so poor, because of Josef Stalin's purges, that there was no institutional memory of Kenyatta having trained in Moscow.

As prime minister, he called for racial reconciliation, allowed whites to keep their plantations, followed capitalist economic policies, and maintained a pro-Western foreign policy. In this, Kenyatta was influenced by his minister of economic planning and development, **Thomas Mboya**, a labor leader who had strong ties to the **American Federation of Labor–Congress of Industrial Organiza-**

tions (AFL-CIO). Kenyatta's vice president, **Oginga Odinga**, a Communist secretly supported by both Moscow and Beijing, had worked to move Kenyatta to the Left, and then worked to undermine him. Recognizing a Communist from personal experience, and tipped off by the **Central Intelligence Agency** (CIA) to Odinga's subversive activities, Kenyatta used Mboya, a Luo, to marginalize Odinga, also a Luo, thus also strengthening Kenyatta's Kikuyu.

By the late 1960s, Kenyatta began to show signs of senility, and his policies became more Kikuyu-centric. In 1969, Mboya was assassinated, allegedly by order of Kenyatta's entourage, Odinga and other opposition figures were jailed, and the constitution was changed to make Kenya a one-party state. Corruption also grew alarmingly. Kenya's economy, once one of the best and fastest growing in Africa, began to slow. Kenyatta died on 22 August 1978, and was succeeded by Vice President **Daniel arap Moi**, a member of the politically unimportant Kalenjin tribe.

KISSINGER, HENRY A. (1923–). Professor, national security adviser under Presidents **Richard M. Nixon** and **Gerald R. Ford** (1969–75) and secretary of state under Ford (1973–77), the only man to serve in these roles simultaneously. During most of his tenure, Kissinger showed little knowledge of or interest in sub-Saharan Africa, which he saw as having minimal geo-strategic value. Early in the Nixon administration, Kissinger reportedly took a stack of cables and memoranda about the region and threw them across his office, yelling, "Bring me something important!" He commonly derided the State Department Bureau of African Affairs as populated with "missionaries," a strong insult for someone with his realist foreign policy views. Kissinger instead focused on *détente* with the **Soviet Union**, extricating the U.S. from Vietnam, and creating a *de facto* alliance with China against the Soviets. He even ignored the Middle East, concluding that **Egypt** had been irremediably weakened by the **Arab–Israeli War of 1967**. He did not follow up Egyptian President **Anwar Sadat**'s attempts to draw the U.S. into discussions about the region, and apparently scuttled efforts by Secretary of State William Rogers to begin a Middle East peace process.

Egypt's 6 October 1973 attack on **Israel**, launching the **Arab–Israeli War of 1973**, dramatically reoriented Kissinger's interest, and he was instrumental in saving Israel with a massive airlift, and then in saving the Egyptian army by cutting off aid to the Israelis to force them into a cease-fire. During the war, Nixon was often intellectually and physically debilitated by the Watergate scandal. At war's end, Kissinger's **"shuttle diplomacy"** restarted peace talks and froze the Soviet Union out of the peace negotiations.

Kissinger's interest in sub-Saharan Africa only arose when it entered the **cold war** in 1975 thanks to the civil war in **Angola** that followed the announcement by **Portugal** that it would grant independence on 11 November 1975. Although he apparently saw Angola as having minimal strategic value, Kissinger believed that stopping the *Movimento Popular de Libertação de Angola*/Popular Movement for the Liberation of Angola (MPLA), backed by **Cuba** and the Soviets, was necessary to show U.S. resolve following Washington's failure to prevent the defeat of South Vietnam. He believed that he had the support of black African nations when President **Kenneth Kaunda** of **Zambia** visited Washington and reported that Africans wanted the U.S. to stop the MPLA from coming to power, although Kissinger later learned that Kaunda had exaggerated other African governments' opposition. Kissinger oversaw the **Central Intelligence Agency**'s (CIA) **Operation IAFEATURE**, launched in July 1975, which provided the *Frente Nacional de Libertação de Angola*/National Front for the Liberation of Angola (FNLA) and the *União Nacional para a Independência Total de Angola*/National Union for the Total Liberation of Angola (UNITA) with a total of $48 million in military training and assistance. Strong circumstantial evidence indicates that the operation was in conjunction with the government of **South Africa**, which launched an almost simultaneous covert operation in Angola. Congress aborted IAFEATURE when it passed the **Tunney** and **Clark Amendments**, which cut off all U.S. operations in Angola in the wake of newspaper reports about the U.S. operation and the South African intervention. South Africa's angry protests buttress the contention that the intervention was a joint effort.

Worried that **Rhodesia** would be the next domino, Kissinger sought to stabilize Southern Africa by pressuring the illegally established white government of Prime Minister **Ian Smith** to abdicate power to a moderate black government. In March 1976, Kissinger warned Cuba to stay out of Rhodesia. The following month, in

Lusaka, Zambia, during his first tour of Africa, he announced that Washington supported black majority rule in Rhodesia, a turnaround from the previous policy laid out in **National Security Study Memorandum 39** (NSSM 39), which had set out a policy of working with Southern Africa's white governments because it was believed they would rule for the indefinite future and would respond best to quiet appeals for civil rights rather than public criticism. Kissinger used the sort of shuttle diplomacy across the region that had been so successful in the Middle East, meeting with Smith and rebel leader **Joshua Nkomo**, but not rebel leader **Robert Mugabe** or Bishop **Abel Muzorewa**, the leading internal opposition leader. The effort failed after the leaders of the surrounding Front Line States rejected Kissinger's plan when they learned that Rhodesian whites would continue to control defense and internal security during a two-year transitional period. Kissinger's efforts did spur **Great Britain** into convening a conference in Geneva, Switzerland, on 28 October 1976, attended by the major black and white leaders, but Nkomo and Mugabe rejected Kissinger's proposals and the conference failed. *See also* AFRICAN AFFAIRS, STATE DEPARTMENT BUREAU OF; CAMP DAVID ACCORDS; CARTER DOCTRINE; ETHIOPIA; MENGISTU HAILE MARIAM; MOBUTU SESE SEKO; MUHAMMAD, MURTALA; NIGERIA; NIXON DOCTRINE; NYERERE, JULIUS; OBASANJO, OLUSEGUN; SOUTH AFRICA; TAR BABY OPTION; VORSTER, BALTHAZAR JOHANNES (JOHN).

– L –

LIBERIA. West African nation created as a home for freed U.S. slaves. During the **cold war**, Liberia became one of the most important U.S. allies in sub-Saharan Africa. Liberia was founded by the **American Colonization Society** (ACS) as a way to solve the perceived problem of free blacks living in a white society. After several failed attempts, land was purchased in December 1821 and the first settlers arrived in the following year. Liberian life was precarious due to disease and attacks by indigenous tribes. In 1826, management of the colony was taken over by a white evangelical Christian, **Jehudi Ashmun**. Ashmun attacked and defeated local slaving tribes, forcing them to leave the colony alone and to renounce slavery. When he left in 1828, the Liberians began to enslave the local indigenous people in all but name because the **Americo-Liberians** considered them inferior since they were not Christians and did not behave in "civilized" ways. Liberia expanded following the 1831 Nat Turner slave rebellion in Virginia, which caused several states to encourage freed slaves to emigrate. Between 1820 and 1843, 4,571 freedmen arrived in Liberia, but only 1,819 remained alive in Liberia in 1843. The ACS granted independence in 1847, but pressure from U.S. Southerners prevented U.S. recognition until June 1862 during the U.S. Civil War. By 1867, approximately 13,000 **African Americans** had immigrated to Liberia.

The U.S. prevented European powers from colonizing Liberia during the "Scramble for Africa" in the late 19th century. Liberia became a symbol of freedom for Africans living under colonialism, although in reality it was a badly run feudal society constantly on the verge of collapse. Its government only granted indigenous peoples citizenship at the turn of the 20th century. In 1908, with **Great Britain**, **France**, and Germany working to take control of Liberian finances and perhaps to colonize the country after it defaulted on loan payments, African American leader **Booker T. Washington** intervened with President **Theodore Roosevelt** and persuaded him to send a delegation to Liberia to assess what could be done to restore the country to solvency. In order to keep the Europeans at bay, Roosevelt ordered three warships to accompany the delegation and to remain until the group had finished. The study group recommended and the U.S. government agreed to loan the Liberian government money to pay off the country's foreign debts, appoint an American financial adviser to oversee customs and budget making, and send three African American U.S. soldiers to train the army.

In the late 1910s and early 1920s, **Marcus Garvey** sought to use Liberia as the foundation for his unrealized plan to create a united and free Africa. U.S. business interest in Liberia emerged at that time because of the tremendous need for rubber in the automobile industry. In 1926, the Liberian government granted Firestone Tire & Rubber Company the right to lease up to one million acres at 6 cents per acre for 99 years. Firestone did so, creating the world's largest plantation in Harbel, Liberia, as part of a Firestone subsidiary, **Firestone**

Natural Rubber Company. In addition, Firestone agreed to pay an export tax, provided a $5 million loan to retire the country's previous debts, and made numerous internal improvements.

In 1926, Liberian government officials, including the vice president, were accused of engaging in a slave **trade** with surrounding colonies. As reports to the U.S. government increased, on 8 June 1929 Secretary of State Henry L. Stimson sent the Liberian government a note demanding an end to the trade and dismissal of those involved, while making a veiled threat of outside intervention if nothing was done. An international committee appointed by the Liberian government, known as the Johnson–Christie Committee for its leaders, Charles S. Johnson, a leading African American academic, and Cuthbert Christy, a British doctor and expert on Africa, found that the accusations were correct, which forced the vice president and president to resign. The U.S. worked with the League of Nations to reform the system, but when the new president, Edwin Barclay, refused to give financial control of the country to the League, President Herbert Hoover suspended diplomatic relations as did other major powers. At the same time, plummeting rubber prices caused by the Great Depression deprived the Liberian government of export revenues, which forced it to miss debt payments beginning in 1931. The combination put the country's survival in jeopardy.

The 1934 appointment of a U.S. financial manager to act virtually as proconsul led President **Franklin Delano Roosevelt** to restore relations and prevented European powers from taking *de facto* control of the country. During the late 1930s, Fascist Italy and Nazi Germany each sought control of Liberia as a League of Nations mandate, prompting Roosevelt to send a warship to Monrovia in 1938 as a sign of U.S. support for its continued independence.

U.S. economic interest in Liberia was rekindled by World War II because of the desperate need for rubber in the war effort. In 1942, the U.S. signed a mutual defense pact with Liberia. It dredged and improved Monrovia's harbor, built what remains the longest landing strip in Africa, and set up two military bases and supply depots in preparation for **Operation Torch**, the invasion of North Africa. In January 1943, Roosevelt visited Liberia and persuaded Barclay to expel German nationals and declare war on Germany, which his government did in 1944. Barclay and Vice President **William Tubman**, the president-elect, visited the U.S. in 1944, and Barclay was the first black man to spend the night at the White House as a guest.

Liberia's rubber boom and President Tubman's decision in 1948 to allow shipping lines to use Liberia as an official ship registry gave Barclay the money to use patronage to begin greater integration of indigenous peoples. He also ordered government officials to respect indigenous customs during his 27-year rule. Tubman successfully worked with the U.S. government to pressure Firestone into improving wages and working conditions, and treating Liberian government officials with respect. Despite Tubman's reforms, Americo-Liberians continued to run the country when he died in 1971 and longtime Vice President **William Tolbert** took office. After eight ineffectual years in power during which he did manage to steal $200 million, Tolbert was brutally murdered in a coup, allegedly by its leader, **Samuel Doe**, a member of the indigenous Krahn tribe.

Despite his brutality, buffoonery, massive corruption, and economic mismanagement, the U.S. government supported Doe and provided his government with $500 million in **foreign aid** during his 10 years in power because he allowed the U.S. to continue military use of the airfield and to maintain control of the **Central Intelligence Agency**'s (CIA) Liberian-based African communications network, which Tubman had granted. Liberia also became the leading recipient per capita of U.S. foreign aid. The collapse of the **Soviet Union** freed the United States from the need to support unsavory dictators, and the **George H.W. Bush** administration cut off military assistance in mid-1990 and did nothing to stop a civil war that led to Doe's defeat and murder. As the civil war continued, troops sent by **Nigeria** intervened in 1990 and restored a semblance of order but the war continued in the bush. **Charles Taylor**, who was half Americo-Liberian, emerged as the strongest warlord. Taylor had created a child army and turned rural Liberia into a criminal state from which he smuggled illegal drugs and diamonds, the latter with the secret assistance of **al Qaeda**. He also spread civil war across West Africa in pursuit of what he called "Greater Liberia."

A West African **peacekeeping** force called the Economic Community of West African States Monitoring Group (ECOMOG), 3,000 men primarily consisting of troops from **Nigeria**, intervened in 1990, but with little assistance from the U.S. or other Western powers. The

United Nations (UN) sent a contingent of 368 military observers known as the UN Observer Mission in Liberia (UNOMIL) in 1994 to oversee and assist ECOMOG, but the forces worked badly together and several times guerillas captured UNOMIL forces and held them hostage. A settlement was reached in 1995 and elections were held in 1997, which Taylor stole through intimidation while election monitors did nothing out of fear that he would relaunch the civil war. Taylor expanded his West African guerilla wars in **Sierra Leone**, **Guinea**, and Ivory Coast, but they responded in kind and a new Liberian civil war broke out in 1999. Taylor's army was defeated, and on 27 June 2003, President **George W. Bush** called on Taylor to resign. He added pressure by sending a U.S. Navy contingent off the Liberian coast. Bush was instrumental in persuading Nigeria to reenter Liberia as a peacekeeping force on 4 August, and in exerting the pressure that forced Taylor to go into exile to Nigeria on 11 August 2003. Bush briefly sent a contingent of 200 Marines to help restore order and UN Secretary-General **Kofi Annan** convinced the Security Council to create the United Nations Mission in Liberia (UNMIL), a well-trained and armed force of 15,000 soldiers and police, to take over peacekeeping duties on 1 October 2003. On 29 August 2006, Nigeria and Liberia acceded to U.S. and international pressure and extradited Taylor to Sierra Leone to be tried for crimes against humanity. He was transferred to the International Criminal Court at The Hague in 2006 and the trial began the following year, continuing into 2008.

Liberia's civil wars and Taylor's rule caused the death of 200,000 Liberians, and 300,000 people across the region died from the wars Taylor had generated. One half of Liberia's population became **refugees** or displaced people. By the time Taylor left office, there was no electric power in the country outside of a few generators for the wealthy and well connected, no running water, no sewer service, and no garbage collection. Tropical disease was rampant and HIV/**AIDS** infection neared 7 percent of the population. Unemployment was 85 percent and life expectancy had fallen to 42.5 years.

Elections for Taylor's successor were won by **Ellen Johnson-Sirleaf**, who had lost to Taylor in 1997. A Harvard University–educated economist, Johnson-Sirleaf has sought to rebuild Liberia by encouraging ethnic reconciliation, good and open government, and business investment. Some revenue sources already existed because, despite the chaos, neither Taylor nor Doe had interfered with the Firestone rubber plantation or abused Liberia's standing as providing a reputable "flag of convenience" for shippers. Economic growth was 8 percent in 2007 and a consortium of the **World Bank**, the **International Monetary Fund** (IMF), and the African Development Bank began raising money to remove Liberia's $3.4 billion foreign debt, themselves cutting it by $1.5 billion through mid-2008. The U.S. also cancelled Liberia's entire bilateral debt of $391 million. As of mid-2008, the U.S. had provided $750 million in reconstruction and development assistance administered through the **Agency for International Development** (AID) and $750 million to help pay for UNMIL. A further $342 million was appropriated for fiscal year 2008. The U.S. also overhauled and retrained the Liberian army while the UN trained the police. In Monrovia, the capital, some vestiges of civilization such as electricity and running water began to be restored. Bush acknowledged Liberia's progress by visiting the country in February 2008. *See also* CLINTON, WILLIAM J. (BILL); JACKSON, JESSE.

LIBYA. North African country whose president, **Muammar Qaddafi**, became a leading supporter of worldwide **terrorism** as an unsuccessful means to leadership of the Arab and African worlds. Libya was an Italian colony until World War II when it was liberated by forces from **Great Britain** and **France** in 1943. As the war ended, the **Soviet Union**'s premier, Josef Stalin, sought a trusteeship over Libya's **Tripolitania** region, but was blocked by the British, French, and United States. Unable to decide how to govern Libya under European rule or **United Nations** (UN) trusteeship, the UN granted Libya its independence under King Idriss I on 24 December 1951. In 1954, Idris signed a 16-year agreement allowing the U.S. to use an airbase in exchange for rent and a large and wide-ranging economic development package, together providing the country with most of its revenue until the discovery of significant **oil** deposits in 1959.

Idris was overthrown on 1 September 1969 by young army officers who were followers of the Pan-Arab socialist policies of President **Gamal Abdel Nasser** of **Egypt**. Qaddafi, a 27-year-old signals officer, quickly emerged as leader. A charismatic mystic, Qaddafi sought to unite all Arabs under his leadership. He expounded his vision of

Former President Theodore Roosevelt poses while hunting in Kenya, circa 1909. Extensive newspaper coverage of Roosevelt's safari did much to heighten U.S. interest in Africa. The animals he killed were preserved in several U.S. natural history museums. Photo courtesy of the Library of Congress, Washington, D.C.

U.S. soldiers land on the beach near Algiers during Operation Torch, 8 November 1942. Photo courtesy of the Franklin D. Roosevelt Presidential Library, Hyde Park, N.Y.

President Franklin D. Roosevelt with Sultan Muhammad V of Morocco during the Casablanca Conference, 22 January 1943. Muhammad claimed that Roosevelt promised to support Moroccan independence after WWII, although no official comment was made to that effect. The meeting did highlight Roosevelt's support for colonial peoples and infuriated Free French leader Charles de Gaulle. Photo courtesy of the U.S. Embassy, Rabat, Morocco.

Vice President Richard M. Nixon and his wife, Pat, attend Ghana's independence celebration with Finance Minister K.A. Gbedeman, March 1957. Nixon successfully encouraged President Dwight D. Eisenhower to focus greater attention on sub-Saharan Africa but showed almost no interest during his own administration (1969–1974). Photo courtesy of the National Archives, College Park, Md.

President John F. Kennedy greets Peace Corps volunteers at the White House, 9 August 1962. Kennedy created the Peace Corps as a nonpolitical missionary-like organization, which proved to be a tremendous boon to the U.S. image abroad and U.S. foreign policy in Africa. Photo courtesy of the John F. Kennedy Presidential Library, Columbia Point, Mass.

President Jimmy Carter and UN Ambassador Andrew Young greet President Julius Nyerere of Tanzania, 4 August 1977. Carter and Young embarked on a new but unsuccessful U.S. foreign policy in sub-Saharan Africa that tried to separate the continent from the cold war. Photo courtesy of the Jimmy Carter Presidential Library, Atlanta, Ga.

President Jimmy Carter with Egypt's President Anwar Sadat at the beginning of the Camp David Summit, 6 September 1978. Carter's intervention was crucial in negotiating the Camp David Accords between Sadat and Israel's Prime Minister Menachem Begin. Photo courtesy of the Jimmy Carter Presidential Library, Atlanta, Ga.

President Ronald Reagan receives a National Security Council briefing on the bombing of Libya, 15 April 1986, launched in retaliation for a Libyan terrorist attack on a disco in West Berlin, West Germany, which killed two U.S. soldiers and a Turkish woman. Photo courtesy of the Ronald W. Reagan Presidential Library, Simi Valley, Calif.

President Bill Clinton meets with Nelson Mandela, the future president of South Africa, on 4 July 1993. The Clinton years marked the nadir of U.S. interest in Africa. Photo courtesy of the National Archives, College Park, Md.

President George W. Bush greets patients and family members at a hospital in Dar es Salaam, Tanzania, 17 February 2008. Bush dramatically increased U.S. focus on sub-Saharan Africa, particularly funding for the prevention and treatment of communicable disease and assistance for countries that democratized, liberalized their economies, and met social development goals. Photo courtesy of www.whitehouse.gov.

Secretary of State Condoleezza Rice meets with President Teodoro Obiang Nguema of Equatorial Guinea, 12 April 2006. Close relations with Obiang, one of the world's most notorious despots, went against the Bush administration's human rights policy in Africa, but Equatorial Guinea has become a significant source of U.S. oil. Photo courtesy of www.state.gov.

Arab nationalism, Islam, and socialism in his *Green Book*, which many Islamists consider sacrilegious. Qaddafi quickly began using Libya's oil money to create a Pan-Arab nation. When this failed, he turned his attention to sub-Saharan Africa, undermining governments and deeply involving himself in the politics of **Chad**, Libya's southern neighbor, until his army was driven out in 1987. Qaddafi also supported terrorism against his opponents, funding and training terrorists and liberation movements from every Arab country, as well as countries in sub-Saharan Africa, Western Europe, Asia, and Latin America: over 80 groups in all. Among the liberation groups he supported were the African National Congress (ANC) in **South Africa** and Leftist guerillas such as the Sandinistas in Nicaragua, which especially antagonized President **Ronald W. Reagan**.

While every president before Reagan had opposed Qaddafi, Reagan concluded that Qaddafi was the "most dangerous man in the world." He considered Libya to be a Soviet satellite that played both a key international role as a weapons depot and training ground for terrorist organizations, and a regional role through aggression in Chad, Egypt, and **Sudan**, and subversion throughout the continent. Reagan sent the U.S. Navy into international waters claimed by Qaddafi in 1981, 1986, and 1989, each time using lethal force against Libyan military challenges. Qaddafi responded by sending assassination squads to kill Reagan in 1981; backing terrorist attacks on commercial airports in Rome and Vienna in December 1985, and a West Berlin nightclub frequented by U.S. soldiers in April 1986; sending an assassination team in 1987 to kill Lieutenant Colonel Oliver North of the National Security Council, who had planned the 1986 attack; and bombing a passenger flight over Lockerbie, Scotland, on 21 December 1988, killing 270. Reagan responded by ordering the bombing of terrorist camps and Qaddafi's tent, allegedly killing his adopted daughter. The Lockerbie bombing prompted President **George H.W. Bush** and the British to push sanctions through the UN on 1 January 1992, which were tightened on 11 November 1993. After Qaddafi gave up for trial two intelligence agents implicated in the crime, Washington began to ease sanctions it had imposed in addition to the UN's. Following the conviction of one of the agents and acquittal of the other on 31 January 2001, Qaddafi opened negotiations to improve relations with the U.S. Following the 11 September 2001 attacks, Qaddafi began to exchange information with the U.S. about **al Qaeda**.

In March 2003, Libya began discussions with U.S. and British officials about dismantling its weapons of mass destruction (WMD) program and its terrorist-support structure. In August, Qaddafi agreed to pay $2.7 billion to the families of the Lockerbie victims and, on 12 September, the UN lifted all sanctions. On 19 December, Libya announced that it was giving up all WMD and ending ties to terrorist organizations, and quickly did so. The March announcement came days before the U.S.-led invasion of Iraq and the December announcement came days after Saddam Hussein was captured, but many analysts do not see a connection between the events. In May 2006, the U.S. restored full diplomatic relations with Libya and removed Libya from the State Sponsors of Terrorism list. In January 2008, Congress passed a law that allows victims of previous Libyan-sponsored terrorist attacks to seize Libyan property in the U.S. or place liens on companies that do business with Libya, including oil companies. Qaddafi complained to Bush in March 2008 that these were new economic sanctions, so on 31 October Bush added $1.5 billion to the fund to compensate all victions.

LUMUMBA, PATRICE (1925–1961). Politician and first prime minister of **Congo** (1960). A charismatic orator and nationalist, Lumumba's erratic behavior brought on by addiction to drugs and alcohol, his state business dealings with a well-known international swindler, and his flirtation with the **Soviet Union** helped precipitate the **Congo Crisis** and caused the United States to move quickly from strong support to issuing orders for his assassination.

Although unable to attend college, by his late twenties Lumumba was a leader of assimilated Congolese known as *évolués* (French, "evolved"), who pushed for their rights and privileges in the important eastern city of Stanleyville (Kisangani). Jailed by **Belgium** for fraud (1956–57), allegedly on trumped up charges, Lumumba's public standing was much enhanced. In December 1958, Lumumba went to **Ghana** to attend the All African People's Conference, organized by **Kwame Nkrumah**, where he was seduced by radical nationalism and Pan-Africanism. The Belgians did not allow his rival, **Joseph Kasavubu**, to attend, making Lumumba the most prominent attendee from Congo and the recipient of a good deal of Nkrumah's time. When Lumumba returned to Congo, he helped found the *Mouvement National Congolaise*/Congolese National Movement (MNC), Congo's first nationalist political party rather than a regional or tribal grouping. At a political rally on 28 December 1958, Lumumba may have been the first black Congolese to make a public call for national independence. Riots followed a 28 October 1959 rally, and the Belgians again jailed Lumumba. Continued riots and protests grew in intensity, forcing Belgium to release Lumumba to attend a conference in Brussels to discuss Congolese decolonization. He presented the intransigent demand for almost immediate independence, and the Belgians capitulated, agreeing to grant it on 30 June 1960.

Lumumba's MNC won a plurality of the votes and was the only party to take seats in a majority of Congo's provinces, but its total vote was only 24 percent, forcing him to form a coalition with several parties, the largest of which was Kasavubu's *Confédérations des Associations Tribales du Katanga*/Bakongo Alliance (ABAKO). Lumumba and Kasavubu almost excluded southern parties from the government, most importantly **Moïse Tshombe**'s *Confédérations des Associations Tribales du Katanga*/National Confederation of Tribal Associations of **Katanga** (CONAKAT) and Albert Kalonji's *Mouvement National Congolaise/Kalonji*/Congolese National Movement/Kalonji (MNC/Kalonji), a breakaway party created following a split with Lumumba the previous year.

Lumumba's speech at the 30 June 1960 independence-day celebration began the series of events that led to his ouster and assassination. Following a speech by Belgian King Baudouin I self-congratulating the Belgian people for their work in civilizing Congo, Lumumba made a brilliant but scathing and unscheduled rebuttal. Contrary to legend, Lumumba's speech was written in the days prior to the celebration and was not an off-the-cuff response delivered in the heat of the moment. The speech was so critical that Baudoin's colleagues almost physically restrained him from walking out. Lumumba personally told him, "We are no longer your dirty monkeys," (the worst and most common Belgian insult against black Africans), then he spent the rest of the day behind the scenes trying to apologize to Baudoin, who refused to accept. Lumumba's speech changed the atmosphere in Congo, where even Lumumba had assumed that the Belgians would remain behind the scenes to do the technical work of running a country that had only a handful of black college graduates and no black army officers.

Lumumba's first order of business as prime minister was to push through promotions, pay raises, and other perquisites for black government officials. He did nothing for the armed forces, which rebelled five days after independence. To stop the mutiny, Lumumba sent home most of the Belgian army officers and replaced them with Congolese, who were elected by their men. He granted across-the-board promotions and pay raises (leaving the army without privates), appointed his uncle, Victor Lundula, commander of the army, and his longtime personal assistant, Joseph-Désiré Mobutu (**Mobutu Sese Seko**), chief of staff. Whites fled the country in a panic and civil order collapsed. Lumumba publicly blamed the Belgians for purposely causing the unrest. On 10 July, the Belgians rushed armed forces to Congo, ostensibly to protect Belgian lives and property, and on the following day, with Belgian encouragement, Tshombe announced Katanga's secession to prevent the chaos from spreading into his province. The following month, Kalonji led South Kasai into secession. On the evening of 10 July, Lumumba and Kasavubu called on the **United Nations** (UN) to help restore civil order but explicitly said that their government did not need assistance in putting down the secessionists. The UN immediately agreed, and the first 3,000 troops of the *Opération des Nations Unies au Congo*/UN Organization in the Congo (ONUC) arrived on 15 July with approximately 20,000 in place shortly thereafter. When UN Secretary-General **Dag Hammarskjöld** refused Lumumba's request to attack Katanga, pleading that it was outside the UN's mandate, UN representative **Ralph Bunche** wrote, "Lumumba was crazy and he reacted like a child."

On 17 July, Lumumba threatened to call in the Soviets to drive out the UN force if it did not remove the Belgian military within 48 hours. Such behavior became the norm as Lumumba reportedly began to drink a bottle of gin per day and use large quantities of marijuana. Sometimes in the course of a day he would harshly attack the UN or the U.S. in public then, later that day, publicly praise them. By late July, the **Central Intelligence Agency** (CIA) had concluded that Lumumba had been bought by the Communists. On 22 July, he signed a 50-year development agreement worth $2 billion with Louis Edgar Detwiler, a shady U.S. businessman, despite warnings from the U.S. ambassador and key officials from Ghana and **Guinea**. Under intense outside pressure, the Congolese legislature did not ratify the deal. A few days later, Lumumba met with Secretary of State Christian Herter following a series of acrimonious meetings in New York with Hammarskjöld. When he arrived in Washington, he requested that a blonde white prostitute be brought to Blair House, where he was staying, which the CIA procured. Such a request of the socially conservative administration of President **Dwight D. Eisenhower** could not have been well received, and Eisenhower officials concluded after meeting with him that Lumumba was a "psychotic." On 18 August 1960, CIA Director **Allen Dulles** ordered CIA Station Chief **Larry Devlin** to kill Lumumba, claiming that the order came from President Eisenhower, but Devlin stalled long enough that he did not have to execute the order.

When Lumumba returned to Congo in early August, he ignored the objections of Kasavubu, Mobutu, and other key figures and called on the Soviets to provide military support, which they did, and used the support to attack the secessionist government in South Kasai. Government forces won the battle but followed with a massacre of over 1,000 people that frightened 250,000 people into flight. Hammarskjöld compared the violence to genocide, Mobutu broke with Lumumba, and on 5 September, Kasavubu fired Lumumba. That evening, Lumumba went on national radio and publicly fired Kasavubu and called on the Congolese army to rise up in support. Mobutu overthrew both on 14 September, and Lumumba obtained UN protection. Despite this, Lumumba called on the Soviets "to brutally expel the UN from our Republic." Four days later, he wrote to Hammarskjöld asking for full UN assistance in implementing a deal that he and Kasavubu had made, which Lumumba claimed effectively ended the crisis, and he promised the UN his full support.

After the UN voted to seat Kasavubu's new government, Lumumba fled UN protection for Stanleyville, where a government had been set up in his name, but stopped in every village along the way to rouse the citizenry. He was captured three days later with two colleagues at a riverbank that demarked the point of his freedom. Physically beaten and humiliated, Lumumba and his colleagues were taken to an army base outside Léopoldville, where they remained for a month and a half. On 13 January 1961, Lumumba fomented or took advantage of an uprising among soldiers demanding higher pay. The Congolese leadership flew to the camp to talk the soldiers back to the barracks. Concluding that Lumumba was a constant threat to return to power and wreak vengeance, Kasavubu, Mobutu, and others sent Lumumba and his colleagues to Katanga, reportedly as a peace offering for Tshombe. On the six-hour flight, Lumumba and the others were almost beaten to death. After arrival, the beatings continued, joined this time by Tshombe and his ministers, who drunkenly ordered their execution. Lumumba and the others were shot and buried in shallow graves. Belgians who were present remarked on his courage. The next day, two Belgians and their black African assistants exhumed the bodies, cut them up, and destroyed them in sulphuric acid. Lumumba's skull was crushed into powder and his teeth scattered along the road.

In death, Lumumba became a potent symbol of resistance to colonialism and neo-colonialism that then was appropriated by the Soviets, who named after him a university and guerilla training facility for foreign students. *See also* PEACEKEEPING.

– M –

MACHEL, SAMORA (1933–1986). Guerilla leader and president of **Mozambique**. Machel was a doctrinaire Communist whose experience as president turned him into a pragmatic socialist who began to abandon Marxism–Leninism in the years before his death.

Machel was the semi-educated son of a successful farmer. He attended nursing school but did not have the money to finish his training. He came from a family with a history of rebellion against colonial **Portugal**, and in 1962 he was one of the first to join the *Frente de Libertação de Moçambique*/Front for the Liberation of Mozambique (FRELIMO). After receiving military training in **Algeria**, he became a guerilla leader and eventually military commander. Following the assassination of FRELIMO's leader, Eduardo Mondlane, an act for which Machel was accused by some opponents, Machel became leader of FRELIMO and moved the party sharply to the Left. He accepted military aid from the **Soviet Union** and **China**.

FRELIMO's civil war contributed to the crisis in Portugal that produced the 25 April 1974 coup that overthrew the Portuguese government and led to Mozambique's independence on 25 June 1975. At independence, Mozambique lacked skilled black managers and technicians because of Portuguese policy to send whites to the colonies to fill these roles and to educate only the tiniest minority of blacks. Machel's government created economic catastrophe when it nationalized most large private and church holdings and gave white Mozambicans the "24/24 order"—leave in 24 hours with 24 kilos of belongings. Machel called on the Soviet Union and East Germany in an unsuccessful effort to fill this gap with military assistance and technicians. The East Germans also created a secret police, which especially persecuted northern tribes, the Catholic Church, and traditional leaders, killing between 10,000 and 100,000 people.

As president, Machel supported the efforts of the **Zimbabwe** African National Union (ZANU), led by **Robert Mugabe**, to overthrow the white government of **Rhodesia**. He allowed ZANU to infiltrate guerillas at any point along the border, but the economic consequences for Mozambique were so dire that he forced Mugabe to abort a planned final military offensive in late 1979 and instead join negotiations to bring the guerillas into the political process. When Zimbabwe became independent, Machel warned Mugabe not to destroy his economy as Machel had done by getting revenge and driving out the whites. Mugabe heeded Machel's advice during the first two decades of his rule.

Machel's support for ZANU led to a Mozambican civil war when Rhodesia helped to create the *Resistência Nacional Moçambicana/* Mozambican National Resistance (RENAMO) guerillas. After Zimbabwe's independence, RENAMO moved to **South Africa**, whose government used it to counter Mozambican support for the African National Congress (ANC). Because of RENAMO's reported brutality, the administration of President **Ronald W. Reagan** did not follow the **Reagan Doctrine** of supporting anti-Communist guerillas in Mozambique and did not supply RENAMO with weapons to overthrow FRELIMO.

On 16 March 1984, Washington persuaded Machel and pressured South African President **P.W. Botha** to sign the Nkomati Accord peace agreement in which Mozambique agreed to throw out the ANC and South Africa agreed to stop supporting RENAMO. Neither party lived up to the letter of the agreement, but each substantially cut support. By this time Machel did not trust the Soviets—he had warned Oliver Tambo, Communist Party leader of South Africa, that they sought to dominate Africa (Tambo then told the Soviets what Machel had said)—and he did not forewarn the Soviets that he was negotiating the accord.

Thereafter, relations with the U.S. continued to improve. Washington began to provide Mozambique with economic assistance in January 1985, and Reagan had a friendly White House meeting with Machel on 19 September 1985. Thereafter, the State Department unsuccessfully pushed to supply his government with military assistance against RENAMO. That year Machel also began liberalizing the economy. He died in an airplane crash on 19 October 1986, probably due to pilot error, although South Africa and the Soviet Union have been accused of causing it. Machel's successor, Joaquim Chissano, slowed down Machel's reforms, but in 1990, under heavy U.S. and **International Monetary Fund** (IMF) pressure, sped up liberalization and announced the end of the Marxist system. In October 2006, the South African government announced that it was re-investigating the crash that killed Machel, but has issued no further reports.

MANDELA, NELSON ROLIHLAHLA (1918–). Resistance leader and first president of **South Africa** under majority rule (1994–99). Mandela was from an aristocratic Xhosa family and became a lawyer, quickly rising through the ranks of the African National Congress (ANC). At first he was a black exclusivist and anti-Communist, but his admiration for the steadfastness of white South African Communists led him to support a multi-racial approach. The South African government charged him with treason in 1956, but he was acquitted. The 1960 Sharpeville Massacre convinced Mandela that nonviolent resistance had failed. In 1961, he helped to found *Umkhonto we Sizwe* ("Spear of the Nation"), the ANC's guerilla wing, and was its first leader. He was arrested in August 1961 and sent to Robben Island prison for a life term.

In prison, Mandela almost became a forgotten man as the government repressed the ANC and other resistance groups. **Stephen Biko**'s Black Consciousness movement and the Soweto riots of 1976–77 raised black awareness and put South Africa on the news and front pages around the world. Ironically, the South African effort to take him out of the public mind by imprisoning him on an island served as a perfect symbol among newly radicalized South Africans and for the world at large. Demands for his release sparked protests against **apartheid**. In 1984, the government removed him from Robben Island to a mainland prison, but protests continued.

The collapse of the **Soviet Union** and its empire convinced South African President **F.W. de Klerk** that it would be safe to release Mandela, which he did on 11 February 1990. Mandela and de Klerk negotiated the transition to democratic majority rule, which took place with Mandela's inauguration as president on 19 May 1994. For their efforts, they jointly shared the Nobel Peace Prize in 1993. As president, Mandela's focus was racial and ethnic reconciliation. Mandela's government had good relations with the U.S. except for Mandela's insistence that South Africa would maintain good relations with **Libya** and **Cuba** as thanks for their support during apartheid. Unlike most African leaders, he decided to retire from office after a single term and was succeeded by **Thabo Mbeki** in 1999.

In retirement, Mandela has been an African elder statesman and activist. In 1999, he served as mediator to end the political/ethnic crisis in Burundi following the death of mediator **Julius Nyerere**, and on 25 June 2008 he criticized the "tragic failure of leadership" by President **Robert Mugabe** in **Zimbabwe**. Among the causes that Mandela has worked for are ending poverty, providing for children particularly orphans, and the fight against **AIDS**, admitting that he should have paid more attention to the HIV/AIDS crisis while president. The 46664 AIDS organization, which stages fundraising concerts for AIDS research, is named for his prison identification number. Mandela's son died of AIDS in January 2005. On 1 July 2008, the U.S. removed Mandela from its **terrorism** watch list, a carry-over from the **cold war**. *See also* BUTHELEZI, MANGOSUTHU.

MAZRUI, ALI A. (1933–). African history professor whose Public Broadcasting Service (PBS) television series, *The Africans: A Triple Heritage*, served as an introduction to the continent for many Americans. Mazrui is also the author of several major works on African history.

Mazrui was born in **Kenya**, received his bachelor's and doctoral degrees from universities in **Great Britain**, and his master's degree from Columbia University. He was a professor at Makerere University in **Uganda** until forced into exile to the University of Michigan by President **Idi Amin**. Mazrui subsequently worked for numerous universities in North and South America, Africa, Europe, Asia, and Australia. He has also served as a special adviser to the **World Bank**.

Mazrui's work has rejected both capitalism and all varieties of socialism, which he considers impositions on Africa by Western imperialism. His *The Africans* explores the influences of Africa's indigenous heritage, Western culture, and Islam on Africa's people.

MBEKI, THABO (1942–). Anti-**apartheid** leader who became the second president of **South Africa** under majority rule (1999–2008). Mbeki served as an ambassador for the African National Congress (ANC) in a variety of key postings, then as deputy president under President **Nelson Mandela**. A South African Communist Party leader before the fall of apartheid, thereafter he shed Communist ideology and supported free market policies. President **Bill Clinton** said that Mbeki was one of the "new breed" of African leaders. During his presidency, South Africa has experienced impressive economic growth, expanded international **trade**, and low inflation, but one-quarter of the population is unemployed and half the country lives in poverty. Archbishop **Desmond Tutu** criticized Mbeki in 2004 for economic policies that he said have benefited a small elite while ignoring the overwhelming majority of South Africans. Corruption also became extensive under his rule, with government officials themselves taking advantage of Black Economic Empowerment (BEE) under which well-connected black businessmen receive significant shares of South African big business. At the turn of the millennium, Mbeki alienated much of the world by acting on his belief that HIV does not cause **AIDS**, refusing to allow his government to buy drugs that were offered by pharmaceutical companies at much-reduced rates. International pressure, including by President **George W. Bush**, and a South African Supreme Court decision compelled him to allow the drugs into the country.

Mbeki also followed a policy of "constructive engagement" with President **Robert Mugabe** of **Zimbabwe** as Mugabe persecuted his opponents and destroyed Zimbabwe's economy. The **African Union**

(AU) appointed Mbeki mediator for Zimbabwe in 2007, and he repeatedly said that it was up to Zimbabweans to solve their own problems. At the same time, Mbeki defended Mugabe in international forums, earning another sharp rebuke from Tutu. In May 2008, riots against foreigners, primarily Zimbabwean **refugees**, killed 42 and left thousands homeless. Mbeki was out of the country at the time and waited several days before he cut short his trip to confront the crisis. On 21 July, Mbeki oversaw signing of a preliminary agreement between Mugabe and opposition leader **Morgan Tsvangirai** that lays out terms for negotiations to end Zimbabwe's political crisis. Political division in the ANC forced Mbeki's resignation on 24 September 2008.

MBOYA, THOMAS (TOM) (1930–1969). Labor leader and cabinet minister from **Kenya** who worked closely with the **American Federation of Labor–Congress of Industrial Organizations** (AFL-CIO) and the **Central Intelligence Agency** (CIA). A charismatic orator and outstanding organizer with the ability to win over opponents, Mboya vaulted to secretary-general of the Kenya Federation of Labor (KFL) in 1953, one year after joining. Although he was a member of the Luo tribe, his skills made him a leading figure during the Kikuyus' Mau-Mau Rebellion. Mboya helped win the release of Kikuyu leader **Jomo Kenyatta** from detention in 1961 and played a significant role in negotiating independence in 1963.

Mboya served as Kenyatta's minister of economic planning and development, overseeing Kenya's move to capitalism although it was proclaimed as socialism, including continued support for white-owned plantations. Mboya was also a strong anti-Communist who skillfully marginalized **Soviet Union**–backed Vice President **Oginga Odinga**, causing him to resign in frustration. Mboya was obviously ambitious to succeed Kenyatta as president, flaunted his U.S. connections, and often traveled with a praetorian guard of union muscle. When he was assassinated on 5 July 1969, most Kenyans concluded that these factors combined with his Luo heritage had led powerful Kikuyus to order the assassination, although the official judgment was that he was killed by a lone gunman.

MCNAMARA, ROBERT S. (1916–). U.S. business and political leader who served as president of the Ford Motor Company, secretary of defense under Presidents **John F. Kennedy** and **Lyndon B. Johnson** (1961–67), and president of the **World Bank** (1968–81). Soon after his appointment as World Bank president in 1967, McNamara announced his goal of doubling the amount of Bank loans to third-world countries ("loan volume"), and refocusing the Bank's resources from infrastructure to assisting with industrialization and improving global standards of living. To do this, McNamara successfully pushed for the Bank to create a five-year plan that promoted expensive nationally owned factories and expanded Bank activities to include social programs that would have a direct impact on people's lives. His next five-year plan expanded the Bank's loan volume again by adding agricultural projects.

McNamara virtually turned **Tanzania** into an international demonstration project for the use of **foreign aid**, sharing with many other lenders great enthusiasm for the humane socialist vision of President **Julius Nyerere** embodied in his *Ujamaa* ("familyhood") policy of villagization. McNamara ensured that grants and loans totaling in the billions of dollars were provided to Tanzania in support of this vision. McNamara also moved the Bank into industrial policy, providing assistance for gigantic state-owned industrial plants, including hundreds of millions of dollars in loans for paper and shoe factories in Tanzania and billions of dollars for a steel plant in **Nigeria**. These policies failed, the Tanzanian factories never worked at more than 5 percent of capacity and the Nigerian steel plant never produced any steel.

Such gigantic and failed projects came to be known as "black elephants," an African play on the term "white elephant." Although standards of living improved in Tanzania, in 1981 it came to symbolize the failure of McNamara's vision when the cost of its socialist policies, loss in productivity, unwise international debt burden, global oil shocks, and falling commodity prices bankrupted the country. As a result, Tanzania narrowly avoided becoming the first country to default on World Bank loans. McNamara himself had become disillusioned by Tanzania's efforts when he visited the country's northern provinces and discovered that roads had deteriorated so badly that they were almost impassable. Nyerere's failures were by no means unique, and the 1970s and 1980s came to be referred to as the "lost decades" of African development.

To remedy out-of-control third-world debt caused in part by the World Bank's policies, in September 1979 McNamara and the **International Monetary Fund** (IMF) created "structural adjustment programs" (SAPs). SAPs refinanced government loans with interest-free loans over 40 years in exchange for government promises to liberalize foreign **trade** and domestic markets. They often failed because the ensuing rise in prices for basic commodities and cuts in government jobs created political instability, which led governments to stop the reforms. The World Bank did not punish the governments for reneging on the SAP agreements, and new SAPs often were issued. Even when a SAP succeeded, national standards of living fell. In Tanzania, a SAP undid many of Nyerere's social successes.

Under McNamara's leadership, Bank lending increased from $953 million per year to $12.4 billion, and professional staff increased from 1,600 to 5,200 employees from all over the world instead of primarily from the West. He retired at age 65.

MELES ZENAWI (1955–). Ethiopian guerilla leader, prime minister (1991–95), and president (1995–), who was recognized by President **Bill Clinton** as a leader of the African Renaissance just months before he fought a disastrous war against **Eritrea**. Meles was a Communist university student who rebelled in 1975 against **Mengistu Haile Mariam**'s Communist dictatorship, which was backed by the **Soviet Union**. After the **Ogaden War** against **Somalia**, as Soviet power was turned against internal guerilla movements, Meles and his party turned from Soviet- to Albanian-style communism. His brilliance and resourcefulness helped lead to the overthrow of Mengistu in 1991, after which he was selected prime minister and later president. As leader of Ethiopia, Meles gave up Marxism and became an important U.S. ally. On 24 May 1993 he allowed Eritrea to become independent, but war broke out in 1998, which Ethiopia won in 2000 at the cost of perhaps 100,000 soldiers and resources taken from famine relief in 1999–2000. Hundreds of thousands of soldiers remained under arms thereafter and Ethiopia suffered another famine in 2002–03.

Although Meles may have stolen elections in 2000 and 2005 and brutally cracked down on opponents after the latter election, he remained a strong U.S. ally due to his support for the **Global War on**

Terror (GWOT). Ethiopia worked with the U.S. to defeat Somalia's **al Qaeda**–supported Islamist Islamic Courts Union (ICU) in 2006–07, a war launched with Washington's tacit encouragement and military support, including air- and ship-to-shore bombing of suspected al Qaeda forces. *See also* AFWERKI, ISAIAS.

MENGISTU HAILE MARIAM (1936?–). Ethiopian army officer and ruler (1977–91), who communized Ethiopia, purged and ordered the murder of hundreds of thousands of opponents, real and imagined, and used famine as a weapon against regions fighting for autonomy or independence. Mengistu was the dark-skinned, illegitimate son of an army laundress, whom his opponents claimed to have been a prostitute. Mengistu's color led to racist treatment by the overwhelmingly light-skinned Ethiopian officer corps. He also was the victim of racism during military training in the southern United States, which was the alleged root of his intense dislike of the U.S.

In June 1974, Mengistu was appointed to the ruling Dergue (Amharic, "Committee"), which had recently overthrown Emperor **Haile Selassie**, whom Mengistu himself subsequently reputedly killed. Mengistu quickly and ruthlessly worked his way to become vice chairman, then killed the chairman and anyone else who demonstrated less than complete loyalty. As a member of the Dergue, Mengistu fell under the sway of the Ethiopian People's Revolutionary Party (EPRP), a Communist party, but disagreed with them over how best to implement his National Democratic Revolution, which would communize Ethiopian urban and rural life. He launched the "Red Terror" against them and any other potential dissidents, killing as many as 100,000 people. Despite Mengistu's move to the Left, U.S. Secretary of State **Henry Kissinger** believed he could keep Mengistu allied with Washington by dramatically increasing military assistance. Nonetheless, Mengistu continued to gravitate into the **cold war** orbit of the **Soviet Union**, and on 14 December 1976 secretly signed a massive arms deal with them. President **Jimmy Carter** significantly cut U.S. aid on 24 February 1977, and Mengistu ordered virtually all Americans out of Ethiopia.

Mengistu's brutal policies led to regional rebellions, the most significant of which occurred in the Ogaden Desert, which was populated with ethnic Somalis who were assisted by the Soviet-backed

Muhammad Siad Barré, president of **Somalia**. When Somalia launched the **Ogaden War** in July 1977, **Cuba**'s Fidel Castro strongly urged the Soviet Union to change sides and support Mengistu, which it did, providing Ethiopia with a massive amount of armaments. In November 1977, the Soviets began airlifting approximately 15,000 **Cuban** troops along with East German and Soviet specialists. The Soviets and Cubans insisted on taking total control of the war effort, and Mengistu agreed. Because Somalia had violated Ethiopia's territorial integrity, the Carter administration refused to provide Siad with assistance.

From 1983 to 1985, Mengistu oversaw a famine that killed hundreds of thousands. It was exacerbated by forced agricultural collectivization and his refusal to allow food into rebellious provinces. In 1989, Ethiopia's various rebellious ethnic guerilla forces united, and the Soviets under Mikhail Gorbachev abandoned Ethiopia, forcing the Cubans to withdraw their forces on 26 July 1990. Mengistu renounced communism and offered to improve relations with Washington, which refused. As his army collapsed, Mengistu quietly bought property in **Zimbabwe**, and fled to there from Ethiopia on 21 May 1991. Guerilla leader **Meles Zenawi** succeeded him as president. In exile, Mengistu told people that while Soviet premier Leonid Brezhnev was "like a father to me," Gorbachev's abandonment of Ethiopia had made him into a victim of the **cold war**. He reportedly advises his friend, Zimbabwe's President **Robert Mugabe**. On 26 May 2008, the Ethiopian Supreme Court sentenced Mengistu in absentia to death for genocide. *See also* AFWERKI, ISAIAS; BRZEZINSKI, ZBIGNIEW; ERITREA; FOREIGN AID; ISRAEL; MUSIC; NON-GOVERNMENTAL ORGANIZATIONS (NGOs); VANCE, CYRUS; YOUNG, ANDREW.

MILLENNIUM CHALLENGE CORPORATION (MCC). Signature **foreign aid** program of President **George W. Bush**, which provides economic and technical assistance to impoverished countries if they reach 18 benchmarks on economic reform, foreign **trade** liberalization, educational funding, civil rights, democratization, and fighting corruption.

Created in January 2004, the MCC focuses spending on third-world countries' infrastructure and education in order to help create sustainable economic growth. For countries that have not reached the 18 benchmarks but have shown substantial effort and progress, the MCC provides Millennium Challenge Threshold Grants to help them reach these goals. For countries that have met the benchmarks, the MCC negotiates with their government to create Millennium Challenge Compacts for specific projects. African countries that had negotiated compacts by mid-2008 were Benin, Cape Verde, **Ghana**, Lesotho, Madagascar, Mali, **Morocco**, **Mozambique**, and **Tanzania**, for a total of $3.8 billion. Eight other countries received Threshold Grants to expand their anti-corruption efforts and improve governance. The MCC's stringent criteria resulted in reforms such as Lesotho's government passing a law to give women equal legal standing with their husbands, and led to Gambia's suspension from eligibility after having initially qualified, due to evidence of worsening human and civil rights and increased corruption.

MOBUTU SESE SEKO (BORN MOBUTU, JOSEPH-DÉSIRÉ) (1930–1997). Congolese/Zaïrian army officer and ruler (1960–61, 1965–97). Throughout the **cold war**, the United States supported Mobutu, considering him a strongman who provided stability, protected **Congo/Zaïre**'s tremendous wealth in vital and precious natural resources, kept the **Soviet Union** out of the center of Africa, and actively supported U.S. foreign policy goals, especially in **Angola**. Mobutu was an avid reader and admirer of Machiavelli's *The Prince*, and he made ample use of Machiavelli's principles during the 37 years he dominated Congo/Zaïre.

Mobutu was born to a poor country family and enlisted in the army as a journalist. In 1958, nationalist leader **Patrice Lumumba** appointed him as his personal secretary and, following independence and selection as prime minister, Lumumba appointed Mobutu army chief of staff. Mobutu lost faith in his boss due to Lumumba's increasingly dictatorial ways, especially in late August 1960, when Lumumba allowed Soviet military advisers to indoctrinate soldiers in the army camp outside Léopoldville, the capital. When President **Joseph Kasavubu** fired Lumumba and Lumumba fired Kasavubu, the disgusted Mobutu overthrew both men, installed a government of technocrats, closed Eastern Bloc embassies, expelled all their citizens, and personally staged a mock execution of the Soviet KGB station chief.

Days before the coup, **Central Intelligence Agency** (CIA) station chief **Larry Devlin** promised Mobutu in the name of the U.S. government that the U.S. would recognize his government and give him $5,000 for the families of the coup leaders in the event of its failure. Devlin, who had only briefly met Mobutu twice before (contrary to legend that he had recruited Mobutu in Brussels in 1959) agreed to do so without consulting Washington because Mobutu demanded an immediate answer under threat of calling off the coup. The CIA validated Devlin's decision but the State Department subsequently demanded that Mobutu restore Kasavubu as figurehead president to avoid sub-Saharan Africa's first military overthrow of a government. Mobutu unhappily agreed. He returned to the barracks on 9 February 1961, but a similar deadlock between Kasavubu and Prime Minister **Moïse Tshombe** prompted Mobutu once more to overthrow the government in November 1965, this time for good. Although he had not warned the U.S. about the second coup because of Washington's strong support for Kasavubu, he met with Devlin the day after to compare notes on possible cabinet members. The U.S. National Security Council was not optimistic about Mobutu's staying power, concluding in an 8 June 1966 memorandum that he was "the latest in a series of disastrous Congolese leaders," whose "days are numbered."

Throughout his tenure as military chief and president, Mobutu's army was brutal, corrupt, and rapacious against unarmed civilians, which made it a mirror image of the numerous rebel armies that vied for control of Congo/Zaïre or attempted to secede. The difference was that Mobutu's army usually ran from its opponents at the first sign of resistance except when foreign mercenary soldiers acted as a vanguard. The army's corruption helped keep Mobutu in power because he bought off his military elite in an extreme patron–client relationship, just as corruption kept political and tribal elites dependent on Mobutu. But the army's brutality helped fuel the rebellions that periodically threatened his rule, and its incompetence meant that Mobutu constantly needed military advisers, training, and assistance by troops from the **United Nations** (UN), the U.S., **Belgium, France, China, Morocco**, or **Egypt** to defeat his opponents in, among other areas, **Katanga**/Shaba in 1960–63, 1967, 1977, and 1978; eastern Congo in 1960–61 and 1964–65; and Kwilu in 1963–65.

Mobutu's excellent relations with the U.S. soured in 1973 when, flush with huge profits from historically high copper prices, he began to move closer to China and adopted Cultural Revolution–style policies following a January visit; broke relations with **Israel** during a vitriolic 1973 speech at the UN just as the **Arab–Israeli War of 1973** was beginning, outraging Secretary of State **Henry Kissinger**; and announced his Zaïrianization program that nationalized, often without compensation, over 2,000 foreign and domestic businesses and farms. Without rules or policy for distributing Zaïrianized businesses, Mobutu kept most for himself or gave them to cronies, marking a dramatic expansion of already endemic corruption that would continue to the end of his reign and beyond, leading political scientists to coin the term "kleptocracy"—government by thieves—to describe his rule. U.S. relations improved in 1974 when Mobutu began allowing the U.S. and China to provide massive support to Holden Roberto's *Frente Nacional de Libertação de Angola*/National Liberation Front of Angola (FNLA) in the civil war against the Communist-led and -supported *Movimento Popular de Libertação de Angola*/Popular Movement for the Liberation of Angola (MPLA). In November 1975, Mobutu sent 1,200 troops to assist Roberto's unsuccessful drive to capture Luanda, the capital of Angola, days before **Portugal** granted independence. Most of the Zaïrians fled during their first skirmish with the enemy. That same year, Mobutu was pushed into much greater dependency upon the U.S. by the collapse of copper prices.

President **Jimmy Carter** made the strongest effort to force Mobutu into reform and democratization, and Carter provided only minimal nonlethal supplies during the March 1977 Shaba Invasion. By 1978, Carter began to adopt a more nuanced cold war policy, and when rebels invaded Shaba again in May 1978, he ordered military logistical support that saved Mobutu's government. U.S. relations dramatically improved under President **Ronald W. Reagan**. In the mid-1980s, Mobutu allowed U.S. arms to be channeled to the Zaïrian bases of another Angolan guerilla chieftain, **Jonas Savimbi** of the *União Nacional para a Independência Total de Angola*/National Union for the Total Liberation of Angola (UNITA), and he sent troops to **Chad** in 1981 and 1983 to stop attempts by **Libya**'s **Muammar Qaddafi** to annex the country. Mobutu visited Reagan at the White House three times and was the first African head of state to meet with President **George H.W. Bush**.

Despite these excellent relations, he created many difficulties for U.S. ambassadors, sometimes demanding that they be expelled. This behavior mirrored his constant reshuffling, firing, jailing, sometimes torturing, and then restoring to power members of his own cabinet. One of Reagan's ambassadors, Brandon Grove, concluded that Mobutu was resentful of his dependence on the U.S., resigned to the fact that the collapse in copper prices meant that Zaïre would never prosper, and bored by total domestic power with little ability to shape affairs beyond Zaïre's borders.

With the end of the cold war, the U.S. Congress stopped economic aid to Zaïre in 1992, and neither Bush nor President **Bill Clinton** replaced the U.S. ambassador from March 1992–November 1995 in order to show U.S. pique following Mobutu's order of her expulsion after nine months. Clinton also encouraged international lending agencies to demand economic reforms and pressure Mobutu toward democratization and greater respect for human rights, causing Mobutu to lament that he was another cold war victim. When the Tutsi-dominated government of **Rwanda** demanded that Mobutu control refugee camps from which the recently defeated radical Hutu government was raiding the country, Mobutu refused, allegedly because of bribes from Hutu leaders, despite having received warnings from CIA Director George Tenet in April 1996. Rwanda attacked Zaïre to create a buffer zone on the Rwandan border. At the time, Mobutu was in Switzerland undergoing treatment for prostate cancer. Mobutu's army collapsed, leading the Rwandans to conclude that they could conquer Zaïre and overthrow his government. Mobutu returned to Zaïre in December, but his army was defeated, he fled into exile on 17 May 1997, and was replaced by **Laurent-Désiré Kabila**.

Mobutu died in Morocco on 7 September 1997. Following his death, the Zaïrian government sought to repatriate $7 billion from his Swiss bank accounts, a figure at the high end of sums commonly bandied about as Mobutu's net worth, but it was discovered that he had barely $4 million in the bank along with properties around the world worth approximately $50 million. His portfolio had collapsed due to the worldwide fall in copper prices, constant bribery of military and political leaders, huge expenditures to turn his home town, Gbadolite, into a city of marble, and exorbitant payments to Serbian mercenaries hired in the last days of his rule in a desperate effort to keep power. *See also* ADOULA, CYRILLE; CONGO CRISIS; CONGO, CENTRAL INTELLIGENCE AGENCY INVOLVEMENT IN; KATANGA; MULELE, PIERRE; SHABA, INVASIONS OF; SIMBAS; STANLEYVILLE (KISANGANI) HOSTAGE RESCUE.

MODERNIZATION THEORY. Approach to economic and political development created by economic historian W.W. Rostow and others, which used the rise of the West as a model for assisting third-world countries to become wealthy, democratic, and economically egalitarian. Rostow and his colleagues concluded that all nations follow similar paths to development, a continuum from mass poverty to modernity, but the process can be accelerated to "economic takeoff" through economic and technical assistance based on centralized national planning within a capitalist economic system. **Foreign aid** and military assistance to provide for social spending would help countries avoid political unrest during the sometimes tumultuous transition from traditional society to modernity. The result would be a rapidly improving standard of living, decreased possibility of revolution by desperate people, and democracy, whether of a liberal or socialist sort. Rostow laid out the theory in an influential book, *The Stages of Economic Growth: A Non-Communist Manifesto*. President **John F. Kennedy** embraced modernization theory. He appointed Rostow to a senior position with the National Security Council and made modernization theory central to his vision of relations with the third world. The **Agency for International Development** (AID) was created to implement this policy.

Conservative critics have focused on modernization theory's one-size-fits-all approach to economic development and democratization, which ignores local history, culture, and politics. The Left countered modernization theory with dependency theory, which argues that modernization keeps underdeveloped countries in poverty by tying them into the international capitalist system. The resulting neo-colonialism forces them to provide raw materials in exchange for finished goods, thus ensuring their poverty and dependence.

MOI, DANIEL ARAP (1924–). Second president of **Kenya** (1978–2002). Although Moi was from a small tribe, was not charismatic, and was not considered exceptionally bright, President **Jomo**

Kenyatta appointed him as a compromise vice president because he was a hard worker and loyal member of the ruling Kenya African National Union (KANU). He ascended to the presidency when Kenyatta died in 1978. Moi was considered to be a caretaker while powerful Kikuyu politicians fought for control. Instead, Moi gave the army and police huge raises, winning their support, and pushed aside the Kikuyu leaders.

Moi became an ally of the United States out of fear that the Horn of Africa wars could spill over into Kenya and that the **Soviet Union** might seek to subvert his country. In February 1980, he signed an agreement with Washington giving the U.S. Central Command the right to use the port and airfield at Mombassa. Following an attempted coup by air force enlisted men on 1 August 1982, Moi moved even closer to the U.S., allowing American interests to supplant those held by **Great Britain**. Moi's rule saw corruption mushroom while the economy went into serious decline. The situation grew so bad that in July 1997, the **International Monetary Fund (IMF)** refused to provide any further loans until the government began effectively fighting corruption.

With the end of the **cold war**, President **George H.W. Bush** moved away from Moi, encouraged by U.S. Ambassador Smith Hempstone, a noted conservative journalist and Africa specialist. Hempstone used U.S. power to bludgeon Moi into accepting multiparty democracy, but he was unable to get opposition parties to unite, allowing Moi to win the 1992 elections with 32 percent of the vote. President **Bill Clinton** removed Hempstone despite Hempstone's plea to stay on for six months to monitor Moi's actions, and Moi then backed out of his agreements, winning himself another decade in power. He retired in 2002 and, despite his best efforts to fix the election, saw his KANU party defeated. In July 2007, Moi's successor Mwai Kibaki appointed Moi special peace envoy to **Sudan**. The following month, Moi endorsed Kibaki's reelection.

MOROCCO. Northwest African nation that was the world's first to grant the United States recognition and today is partner in the longest unbroken treaty relationship with the U.S. Since 1953, Washington has provided Morocco with over $2 billion in **foreign aid**, more than any African or Arab country except **Egypt**.

During the American Revolution, the U.S. government sought recognition from Moroccan Sultan Muhammad III to keep **Barbary Pirates** from attacking U.S. ships, which were no longer under the protection of **Great Britain**. Muhammad granted protection to U.S. merchant ships, and thus *de facto* recognition of the U.S. government on 20 December 1777. Capture of the U.S. warship *Betsy* in 1783 by Moroccan pirates led to negotiations that resulted in the crew's release in 1785 and a treaty of peace and friendship on 18 July 1787 that continues today. The U.S. supported Morocco during the Madrid and Algeciras Conferences of 1880 and 1906, which nonetheless whittled down Moroccan sovereignty and presaged **France**'s creation of a Moroccan protectorate in 1912. In 1904, President **Theodore Roosevelt** successfully threatened the Moroccan sultan to force him to negotiate with a guerilla who was holding hostage a man believed to be a U.S. citizen.

The U.S. invaded Morocco on 8 November 1942 as one prong of **Operation Torch**, the World War II campaign to retake North Africa from the Germans and Italians. The following year, Morocco joined the Free French and President **Franklin Delano Roosevelt** met with Sultan **Muhammad V** during the Casablanca Conference on 22 January 1943. Thereafter, Muhammad was a strong supporter of the U.S. and constantly sought Washington's support for independence. While the U.S. frequently antagonized the French with its support for Moroccan aspirations, **cold war** considerations kept Washington from pushing too hard, as in 1951, when France agreed to allow the U.S. Air Force to create five Moroccan airbases for its Strategic Air Command (SAC) bombers. Continuous but quiet U.S. support helped lead to independence in 1956. Muhammad thereafter worked with the U.S., which reportedly employed the **Central Intelligence Agency** (CIA) to reorganize his intelligence service, but he antagonized Washington by sponsoring the Casablanca Conference of radical African states.

The foreign policy of his successor, **Hassan II**, was anti-Communist, anti-radical, and generally in accord with U.S. goals. He sent troops to assist the government of **Zaïre** against Communist-backed rebels in 1977 and 1978; allegedly was prepared to funnel U.S. aid to **Muhammad Siad Barré** of **Somalia** in his war against **Ethiopia** until President **Jimmy Carter** stopped the operation in 1977; took in the ailing Shah of Iran for several months in early 1979; served as go-between for the Israelis and Arabs including for Egyptian President **Anwar Sadat** prior to his flight to Jerusalem; met with **Israel**'s Prime Minister Shimon Peres in 1986; was the first Arab leader to condemn Iraq's 1990 invasion of Kuwait and then provided troops for Operation Desert Shield and Operation Desert Storm; and provided troops and observers during the 1992–93 U.S.-organized famine relief and state-building missions in Somalia. The U.S. did not support Hassan's "Green March" that took Spanish Sahara in 1975, and Washington has supported **United Nations** (UN) mediation efforts between Morocco and the region's Polisario Front rebels.

Hassan's son and successor, Muhammad VI, was among the first Arab leaders to condemn **al Qaeda**'s 11 September 2001 terrorist attacks in the U.S. and has been a strong supporter of the **Global War on Terror** (GWOT), so much so that in June 2004 President **George W. Bush** declared Morocco a "major non-NATO ally." The U.S. provided significant intelligence and military assistance following major al Qaeda terrorist attacks in Casablanca on 16 May 2003. The close relationship is also seen in the U.S. Senate's overwhelming passage of a U.S.–Moroccan free **trade** agreement on 22 July 2004. *See also* AGENCY FOR INTERNATIONAL DEVELOPMENT (AID); ALGERIA.

MOZAMBIQUE. Southeast African nation that won its independence from **Portugal** under the leadership of the *Frente de Libertação de Moçambique*/Front for the Liberation of Mozambique (FRELIMO), a Communist-led political party backed by the **Soviet Union.** FRELIMO was founded in 1962 and initially led by Eduardo Mondlane, a U.S-educated moderate socialist, who launched armed struggle against the Portuguese in late 1964. He was assassinated in 1969, probably by the Portuguese and dissident elements within FRELIMO although accusations have also been made against **South Africa** and the Soviets, who never trusted him. After a bloody internal struggle, Mondlane was succeeded by FRELIMO's military commander **Samora Machel**, a hardline Marxist who moved the party sharply to the Left.

FRELIMO was incapable of winning independence through force of arms, but it did create a "liberated zone" along the border with

Rhodesia where **Robert Mugabe**'s Zimbabwe African National Union (ZANU) set up guerilla camps. The cost to Portugal in men and wealth to hold its empire together precipitated the coup that resulted in a September 1974 treaty and the granting of Mozamibique's independence as a one-party state under FRELIMO in June 1975. Portuguese policy of educating only the tiniest minority of blacks meant that FRELIMO and black Mozambique lacked skilled managers and technicians to run the government and economy. Machel's government created economic catastrophe when it gave white Mozambicans the infamous "24/24 order"—leave in 24 hours with 24 kilos of belongings—and nationalized most large private and church holdings. As the whites left, many destroyed whatever they were not allowed to carry. The Soviets and East Germans tried to fill the gap by providing military assistance and technicians, as well as security specialists who set up a secret police, which especially persecuted northern tribes, the Catholic Church, and traditional leaders. This was responsible for deaths variously estimated to number between 10,000 and 100,000.

To counter Machel's support for ZANU, Rhodesia helped to create the *Resistência Nacional Moçambicana*/Mozambican National Resistance (RENAMO), which launched a guerilla war. After Rhodesia became independent as **Zimbabwe**, RENAMO moved to **South Africa** to counter Mozambican support for the African National Congress (ANC). RENAMO was infamous for kidnapping children to serve as soldiers and for amputating the limbs of opponents, although a few U.S. analysts claim that this was done by agents working secretly for FRELIMO to create an international backlash against RENAMO. If true, it was a successful operation because the administration of President **Ronald W. Reagan** would not follow the **Reagan Doctrine** and supply RENAMO to overthrow FRELIMO because the State Department considered RENAMO a pariah.

On 16 March 1984, Washington persuaded Machel and pressured South African President **P.W. Botha** into signing the Nkomati Accord peace agreement in which Mozambique agreed to throw out the ANC and South Africa agreed to stop supporting RENAMO. Neither party lived up to the letter of the agreement but support by each was substantially cut. Machel, who did not trust the Soviets—he had earlier told South African Communist Party leader Oliver Tambo that they sought to dominate Africa (Tambo then told the Soviets what he had said), did not warn the Soviets about the accord.

Relations with the U.S. continued to improve. The U.S. began to provide Mozamibique with economic assistance in January 1985, and Reagan had a friendly meeting with Machel at the White House on 19 September 1985 after which the State Department pushed for military assistance against RENAMO. That year Machel also began liberalizing the economy. He died in an airplane crash on 19 October 1986, probably due to pilot error although the South Africans and the Soviets have been accused of having been behind it. Machel's successor, Joaquim Chissano, slowed down Machel's reforms, but in 1990, under heavy U.S. and **International Monetary Fund** (IMF) pressure, he sped up the liberalization and announced the end of the Marxist system.

Just as with the leaders of **Angola, Namibia**, and South Africa, Chissano was forced to negotiate with his opponents following the collapse of the Soviet Empire. With the U.S. acting as a neutral broker that was not formally part of the peace process, FRELIMO and RENAMO agreed on 4 October 1992 to the Rome General Peace Accords that ended one-party rule and, under **United Nations** (UN) supervision, slowly but methodically integrated RENAMO into the political system and the armed forces, culminating in 28 October 1994 elections that Chissano and FRELIMO won by small margins. Estimates of the number killed in the civil war range from 100,000 to 200,000 and much of the national infrastructure was destroyed.

President **Bill Clinton** recognized Chissano as a leader of the "African Renaissance" because of Mozambique's democracy and rapidly growing economy, but overlooked rapidly growing political and economic corruption. Chissano did not run for reelection in 2004 and the elections saw a great drop in RENAMO's vote followed by charges from outside observers of electoral fraud and lack of transparency.

MUBARAK, HOSNI (1928–). Military officer, vice president, president of **Egypt** since the 1981 assassination of **Anwar Sadat**, and close ally of the United States. Mubarak was an air force officer who became Sadat's close adviser and vice president. As president, he has followed a moderate and anti-Islamist foreign policy that has earned

Egypt billions of dollars in U.S. **foreign aid**. His dictatorial politics were generally overlooked, although he received mild criticism from the administration of **George W. Bush** because of his repression against political opponents. Mubarak joined the U.S. in the 1991 Gulf War, reportedly being compensated by the U.S. with $20 billion in economic aid and $20 billion in debt forgiveness. He opposed the second Gulf War that began in March 2003 but has worked closely with the U.S. in the **Global War on Terror** (GWOT). In 2004, Mubarak began an economic liberalization program overseen by his son, Gamal, which has led to impressive economic growth. Mubarak is popularly known to Egyptians as "the Pharaoh," and analysts believe that he is grooming Gamal to succeed him as president.

MUGABE, ROBERT (1924–). Rebel leader, prime minister of **Zimbabwe** (1980–87), and president (1987–). Before his election as prime minister, Mugabe was known within Zimbabwe as cold, austere, and ruthless, but public perception changed about what this meant, transforming his public image in Zimbabwe from revolutionary Marxist to conciliator and then, within two years, to tribal warlord, and ultimately dictator.

Mugabe was a teacher who, in 1960 joined what became the Zimbabwe African People's Union (ZAPU), a black party in opposition to the illegal government of **Rhodesia**. Mugabe and the Reverend Ndabaningi Sithole broke with ZAPU on 9 August 1963, accusing party leader **Joshua Nkomo** of being too opportunistic and moderate in his methods and willingness to work with whites. They established the Zimbabwe African National Union (ZANU) with Mugabe as secretary-general and second in command. All three were jailed by Prime Minister **Ian Smith** in 1964.

The April 1974 overthrow of the government of **Portugal** and its subsequent withdrawal from **Mozambique** provided ZANU with an opportunity because the Leftist government of President **Samora Machel** allowed it to infiltrate guerillas at any point on Rhodesia's border. Later that year, **South Africa** pressured Smith to release Mugabe and the other black nationalist leaders in a failed bid for a peace settlement, and Mugabe escaped to Mozambique to join the guerillas rather than attend December 1974 peace talks with Smith. Seeing opportunity and concluding that Sithole did not share his Maoist politics and was ready to compromise with the government instead of carrying on the war, Mugabe overthrew him and may have had a hand in the March 1975 murder of ZANU's interim leader, Herbert Chitepo, although it may have been the work of the Rhodesian army. Another death that benefited Mugabe came days after signing the December 1979 agreement that would bring him to power, when the commander of ZANU's guerilla forces, Josiah Tongogara, died in a mysterious automobile accident.

Mugabe rejected the late 1976 effort by Secretary of State **Henry Kissinger** to reach a Rhodesia settlement, although the leaders of the surrounding African states forced him to join a coalition with Nkomo called the Patriotic Front (PF). Neither Mugabe nor Nkomo played a part in Smith's Internal Settlement with Sithole, Methodist Bishop **Abel Muzorewa,** and Chief Jeremiah Chirau that created the short-lived and internationally unrecognized Zimbabwe–Rhodesia. As government power waned in 1979, Mugabe prepared to launch a new offensive, but was stopped by Mozambique's Machel, who demanded that Mugabe join negotiations in London with Muzorewa and Nkomo or face being thrown out of Mozambique. The furious Mugabe was forced to join despite believing he was at the brink of winning total power. He signed the 21 December 1979 agreement that returned Zimbabwe–Rhodesia to the control of **Great Britain** followed by elections that would give **Zimbabwe** its independence but reserve some legislative seats for whites for 10 years.

Mugabe insisted that the PF split for the election, giving his newly christened ZANU-PF the advantage due to its large tribal base among the Shona, who made up over 70 percent of the country's population. Mugabe used his guerillas to terrorize opposition voters, and largely ignored his agreement to move them to camps where they would be disarmed and integrated into a national army along with Nkomo's forces and the Rhodesian army. He and his military leaders also publicly said that they would not accept defeat. The result was a huge ZANU-PF victory, 63 percent of the vote against Nkomo's 24 percent, which was based among the minority Ndebele tribe, and Muzorewa's 8 percent. Mugabe became prime minister on 4 March 1980 and Zimbabwe was given *de jure* independence on 18 April 1980. Twenty thousand people had died in the war for majority rule.

As prime minister, Mugabe impressed skeptical whites with his intelligence and reasonableness, which came after he heeded the warning from Machel not to lose Zimbabwe's whites and suffer the economic collapse that Mozambique had suffered when its Portuguese skilled workers and farmers were driven out of the country at independence. Mugabe understood that white commercial farmers were vital to Zimbabwe's economy and that reneging on promises to protect them could imperil the huge amount of **foreign aid** that he was receiving (£900 million was pledged for the first years of independence and the British government alone provided £500 million by 1992 including £47 million specifically designated to purchase white-owned land). He also realized that whites were no longer a political threat; instead he focused on the Ndebele.

After Nkomo refused to disband ZAPU to join ZANU-PF in June 1982, Mugabe proceeded to crush Ndebele power in their Matabeleland home, using the newly created 5 Brigade, which was specially trained by North Korea for this purpose. The U.S. and British governments did little beyond a sort of constructive engagement with Mugabe because both were committed to keeping Zimbabwe out of the Soviet camp, although he had been militarily supported by **China** during the war for independence. Most of the Western press portrayed Matabeleland as a rebellion rather than near genocide, and continued to portray Mugabe as a racial reconciler because he had left whites alone. By the time the *Gukurahundi* (chiShona, "separating wheat from chaff") ended with Nkomo agreeing to a virtual one-party state on 27 December 1987, as many as 25,000 Ndebele were dead. Four days later, Mugabe ordered parliament to proclaim him executive president, formalizing his dictatorship.

When former President **Jimmy Carter** visited Zimbabwe in 1986, he attended a Fourth of July celebration with Mugabe, who proceeded to attack the U.S. and **Ronald W. Reagan**'s foreign policy. Carter walked out of the dinner and the Reagan administration cut off foreign aid to Zimbabwe after Mugabe refused to apologize.

From the start of Mugabe's rule, corruption was significant. He and his cohorts took for themselves white-owned land and businesses paid for by international assistance and looted a fund for impoverished war veterans. By the 1990s, corruption was endemic. In the 1990 election, Mugabe turned against whites, blaming them for the collapsing economy, and in 1992 he began taking over white farms, first through acts of parliament, then, after failing to pass a referendum that would have expanded his power and legalized uncompensated takeovers in February 2000, through armed invasions by "war veterans" too young to have served, which continued through 2008. The operation was chaotic and brutal, with hundreds dying, thousands of black employees driven off the land, the economy destroyed, hundreds of thousands going hungry due to lost jobs and collapsed food production, and Mugabe and his clique stealing the best land.

From August 1998 to October 2002, Mugabe sent an estimated 12,000 troops to **Congo** to support Congolese President **Laurent-Désiré Kabila**, who in return gave Mugabe and his friends concessions on mining and timber land. The Zimbabwean government claimed that at its height the cost was $3 million per month, but internal documents indicated that it cost Zimbabwe more than $25 million per month.

Responding to these events, trade union leader **Morgan Tsvangirai** organized the Movement for Democratic Change (MDC), a political party that led the successful campaign against Mugabe's 12–13 February 2000 referendum. Tsvangirai and the MDC became Mugabe's chief opponents and were kept from office in subsequent elections through massive corruption, use of food as a weapon, intimidation, violence, and murder.

When the predominantly Shona people of the shantytowns around Harare, the capital, also turned against Mugabe, he ordered Operation *Murambatsvina* (chiShona: "cleaning up the shit") from May to July 2005, in which the army bulldozed 100,000 homes and businesses and dumped 700,000 people in the countryside without food or shelter. Perhaps 350,000 died and the **United Nations** (UN) estimated that 2.4 million people were affected. The plan was reportedly urged upon Mugabe by his friend **Mengistu Haile Mariam**, the exiled Communist ruler of **Ethiopia**.

By the 29 March 2008 elections, Zimbabwe suffered 80 percent unemployment, inflation was estimated as high as 4 million percent, and one-third of the population became economic or political **refugees**. On 30 March, Secretary of State **Condoleezza Rice** called Mugabe a "disgrace" to Zimbabwe and all of Africa. Mugabe reportedly lost the election when Tsvangirai received over 50 percent of the vote as indicated by the aggregate of totals posted on every voting precinct across the country, but his government released no official total for over a month. In April, South African labor unions blocked Chinese weapons from being shipped to Zimbabwe across South Africa, and the **George W. Bush** administration pressured neighboring governments not to allow the ship to land in their ports. When the vote totals were officially reported on 2 May, Tsvangirai had a plurality but not a majority, requiring a runoff. Mugabe's forces killed over 100 MDC officials and activists and Tsvangirai fled to the Dutch embassy and withdrew from the runoff to stop the violence. On 22 June, the Bush administration demanded, "The government of Zimbabwe and its thugs must stop the violence now." Bush sought UN sanctions against Zimbabwe's leaders, but they were vetoed by Russia and China on 11 July. On 17 July, Zimbabwe responded to inflation by introducing the $100 billion note. By this point, Zimbabwean money already included a date of expiration. On 21 July, Mugabe and Tsvangirai met and laid out preconditions for negotiations to create a government of national unity.

Mugabe has publicly described himself as having "a degree in violence" and has called himself the "black Hitler." Because of the repression and corruption, the U.S. imposed travel sanctions on Zimbabwean leaders and froze their U.S. assets in 2002, 2003, and 2008. *See also* COLD WAR; MANDELA, NELSON ROLIHLAHLA; MBEKI, THABO; YOUNG, ANDREW.

MUHAMMAD, MURTALA (1938–1976). Army officer and military ruler (1975–76) of **Nigeria**. Muhammad came to prominence as one of the chief instigators behind the 29 July 1966 coup that overthrew the Ibo-dominated military government of Johnson Aguiyi-Ironsi, but he was passed over for the presidency by his fellow officers, who selected Lieutenant Colonel **Yakubu Gowon**, a compromise choice who had not participated in the coup. Murtala later overthrew Gowon on 29 July 1975 in a nonviolent coup. As president, Murtala quickly became extremely popular by beginning a vigorous anti-corruption crusade and moving from Gowon's neutralist foreign policy that worked through regional and international institutions, to a Nigeria-first policy that tilted toward Leftist causes and directly confronted the United States. This was most clearly seen in his **Angola** policy.

Following the military intervention in the civil war by troops from **Cuba** and **South Africa**, Muhammad reversed Gowon's U.S.-supported effort to bring Angola's three rebel groups together, instead launching an active campaign among African states to back the Communist-led *Movimento Popular de Libertação de Angola*/Popular Front for the Liberation of Angola (MPLA) and providing it with $20 million and the promise of $100 million. Publicly, Muhammad said the U.S. was Nigeria's principal enemy along with **Great Britain** and Gowon, but six days before his assassination, his foreign minister met with Secretary of State **Henry Kissinger**, after which the Nigerians criticized U.S. policy but also agreed that the countries had begun to work out their differences. Murtala was killed in an unsuccessful coup attempt, and he was succeeded by his deputy, **Olusegun Obasanjo**.

MUHAMMAD V (1909–1961). Sultan of **Morocco** who became king when he won independence from **France**. Muhammad, like all Moroccan sultans, was both a political and religious leader by dint of the Moroccan belief that he was a direct descendant of the Prophet Muhammad and was thus the Prince of the Faithful.

Under the rule of the pro-Nazi Vichy government of France, Muhammad refused to impose its anti-Jewish laws. When the U.S.-led Allies invaded North Africa in November 1942, Muhammad called on Moroccans to support them. During the January 1943 Casablanca Conference meeting of President **Franklin Delano Roosevelt**, Prime Minister Winston Churchill of **Great Britain**, and Free French leader Charles de Gaulle, Roosevelt had a private dinner with Muhammad on 22 January 1943. Although the president probably did not tell Muhammad that he supported independence for Morocco, as was widely rumored, the mere fact that he dined with Muhammad showed the U.S. belief that Morocco was a sovereign entity as well as a French protectorate. Muhammad publicly proclaimed his support for independence at a Tangier Conference in April 1947, and the French forced him to abdicate and sent him into exile on 20 August 1953 to halt the push for independence. Moroccans responded with a civil war that the French could not contain because of the civil war in neighboring **Algeria**, and Secretary of State **John Foster Dulles**, concerned that public U.S. pressure to restore the sultan could worsen

France's precarious **cold war** position (harmed by massive strikes at home and impending failure in Vietnam) worked behind the scenes to push the French to give domestic self-rule to Morocco and **Tunisia**. In 1955, the French restored Muhammad to the throne and on 2 March 1956, granted independence with Muhammad elevating himself to king the following year.

As king, Muhammad acted as an intermediary between the Arab states and **Israel**. Relations with the U.S. suffered beginning in 1958 when Muhammad began to establish relations with the **Soviet Union**, the Eastern Bloc, and radical Arab governments. In January 1961, he hosted his own Casablanca Conference at which radical African states formed a common purpose. Included at the conference were Leftist rulers **Gamal Abdel Nasser** of **Egypt**, **Kwame Nkrumah** of **Ghana**, and **Ahmed Sékou Touré** of **Guinea**, which outraged Washington. Muhammad mollified the U.S. by allowing the **Central Intelligence Agency** (CIA) to reorganize his intelligence service in 1960, and he encouraged a phased rather than immediate withdrawal of U.S. bomber airbases on Moroccan soil while suggesting that communications facilities could remain. Negotiations were ongoing when he died on 26 February 1961 and they were successfully concluded by his son and successor, **Hassan II**.

MULELE, PIERRE (1929–1968). **Congo**'s first education minister and rebel leader after his dismissal for being a follower of Prime Minister **Patrice Lumumba**. Mulele had received military training in the Eastern Bloc, and the U.S. government believed he was an agent of the **Soviet Union**. President **Joseph Kasavubu** fired Mulele along with Lumumba on 5 September 1960. In late September, **Central Intelligence Agency** (CIA) station chief **Larry Devlin** stopped a Mulele agent from killing General Joseph-Désiré Mobutu (**Mobutu Sese Seko**). Mulele left Congo for **China**, where he received training in urban and rural guerilla warfare. He returned to Congo espousing Maoist agrarian-based communism, began guerilla operations in western Kwilu province in August 1963, and his urban guerillas commenced terrorist bombings in Léopoldville, the capital. His rebellion proved so effective that the government declared a state of emergency in Kwilu on 21 January 1964. Unlike the other Congolese rebels, Mulele spent most of his time in the bush with his soldiers, and his guerilla forces were the best disciplined. He was the only rebel leader who was not criticized by Che Guevara, the revolutionary from **Cuba** who had come to Congo to assist the revolution, although the two men never made contact. His rebellion was put down in late 1965 and Mulele went into exile. He returned to Congo when Mobutu proclaimed an amnesty in 1968. Within a span of 10 days, Mulele was feted by the government, arrested, tried, and executed, with some reports alleging that he was drawn and quartered.

MUSEVENI, YOWERI (1944?–). Guerilla leader and president of **Uganda**, who rescued the country from the rule of Milton Obote, but grew increasingly dictatorial during his second 10 years in power. Museveni helped to overthrow dictator **Idi Amin** in 1979, then went back to the bush after Obote stole the 1980 election. He overthrew Obote and took power on 29 January 1986.

Museveni ruled as a benevolent despot, providing stability, liberalizing the economy, and maintaining human rights while refusing the return of political parties, which he argued were the engine of ethnic conflict. Museveni also spearheaded an anti-**AIDS** campaign that became a model for third-world countries. The United States and other Western countries responded with massive amounts of foreign assistance, and Uganda's economy grew at a rapid rate. Museveni returned Uganda to democratic rule in 1996, winning election for president, but continued to ban political parties. In 1997, Museveni assisted President **Paul Kagame** of **Rwanda** with his invasion of **Zaïre** and overthrow of President **Mobutu Sese Seko** to install **Laurent-Désiré Kabila**.

Museveni's record earned him a visit by President **Bill Clinton** during his March 1998 African tour and Clinton's plaudits as one of a "new generation of African leaders," who was bringing an "African Renaissance." By that time, corruption had grown rampant in Uganda. The following year, Museveni assisted Rwanda a second time, invading the renamed **Congo** to overthrow Kabila and thus launching what has become known as "Africa's World War," with nine African countries fighting in Congo. Rwandan and Ugandan forces were repulsed and the U.S. cut off Ugandan military aid in protest. The following year, Rwanda was fighting Uganda over Congolese spoils, but they rejoined forces to prevent **United Nations**

(UN) investigators from entering Ugandan-held Congolese territory to follow up reports of human rights violations. In December 2005, the International Court of Justice ruled that Uganda must pay Congo compensation for human rights violations. That same year, Museveni changed the constitution to allow himself to run for a third term as president despite pleas from President **George W. Bush** that he retire. To allay protests, Museveni also amended the constitution to allow the return of political parties. He used the power of the state, including jailing his chief opponent, to win reelection on 23 February 2006. In 2007, Human Rights Watch claimed that Museveni's government had abandoned its former AIDS policy and was now discriminating against HIV-infected adults. In July 2008, the Ugandan government indicted a leading general for theft of millions of dollars in foreign aid that had been earmarked for the anti-AIDS campaign.

Despite Museveni's dictatorial practices, he has been a strong U.S. ally due to his support for the **Global War on Terror** (GWOT) and Uganda's strategic location near **Sudan** and **Somalia**, both of which have been closely tied to **al Qaeda**. At U.S. urging, Museveni sent Ugandan troops to Somalia in 2007 as part of an **African Union** (AU) peacekeeping force to prevent the Islamist Islamic Courts Union (ICU) from regaining power. By mid-2008, they were the only AU troops in the field with a token force from Burundi. President Bush met with Museveni at the White House on 7 October 2007 and afterwards neither of them mentioned having discussed human rights.

MUSIC. African music played a crucial role in the development and shaping of American popular music thanks to the influence of Africans brought to America as slaves and their descendants. In the 20th century, the movement of musical influence was reversed, and American music strongly influences African popular music.

While the origins of the American blues lie in several sources, it was African slaves and their descendants who first sang the blues as we know it. Recent research has shown that the African roots of the blues and black gospel music are indirect and not linear, but it is clear that the use of call and response, multi-layered rhythms, and instruments such as the banjo, guitar, and drum and bell (now cymbal) all have distinct and direct origins in West Africa. The Caribbean, especially Cuba, and New Orleans also must be noted in tracing the music of the slaves and their descendants. As for the music of North Africa, such instruments as the shawm, tar, and rebab are ancestors of Western European instruments.

As the blues began to develop in the U.S. South into its standardized 12-bar form of three lines of rhyming iambic pentameter, ragtime and brass bands were flourishing in New Orleans. It was not long until the **African Americans** living there, with access to a variety of African dances and drum rhythms at Congo Square (now named **Louis Armstrong** Park), would take the lead in creating jazz. Almost every pioneer of American jazz was African American. As soon as jazz was commercially available on wax cylinders, it found its way to the African continent, particularly **South Africa** in the early 1900s. Jazz's influence led Southern African musicians to adopt the guitar, homemade guitar, and banjo-like instruments as their primary vehicle of music-making because they can synthesize traditional African bow playing with the modern jazz and blues sounds, and because they are versatile, portable, and easy to maintain.

Other forms of American music began to develop along with the blues, and they in turn influenced African music. Most notable were the black gospel style still found in churches, and the minstrel show, in which white performers blacked their faces and acted as stereotypical black characters. African Americans copied the format and produced live comedy shows complete with banjo, tambourine, and bones, all instruments with African origins. This musical style came to South Africa during the U.S. Civil War (1861–65), when the *Alabama*, a warship from the rebelling Confederate States of America, docked in Cape Town, and the ships' African slaves put on impromptu minstrel shows, which were copied by South African blacks.

Black gospel music in the U.S. was first put into concert form by the Fisk University Jubilee Singers of Nashville, Tennessee. This group was copied across the U.S., and in the late 1800s an American gospel group went to South Africa, where it performed in Cape Town. Black South Africans subsequently adopted the style. In 1956, jazz singer and trumpeter Louis Armstrong toured the Gold Coast (**Ghana**) to huge crowds, prompting the U.S. Information Agency (USIA) to send Armstrong on an African tour in 1960–61 and to send other "jazz ambassadors" to Africa.

Jazz in the U.S. morphed into rhythm and blues, which was copied by white singers and combined with country musical styles to become rock and roll. This infectious music of rebellious youth found its way worldwide thanks to improvements in musical transmission technology from wax cylinder to 45 records, which were sold or played on radio stations. All of the popular American musical styles were also played on Voice of America (VOA), an arm of the U.S. government that sought to bring American culture to the world. In the 1980s, African Americans took another bold musical step with the creation of hip hop and rap. Since each of these musical styles grew out of the blues or gospel, each has a common African ancestor.

In Africa, the acceptance of hip hop and rap was immediate and influential. This form of music, with its steady and driving backbeats, lyrics that closely resemble chanting, rhyme scheme, and use as a tool for social commentary, spoke to young Africans, especially the poor of South Africa, newly freed from **apartheid**, but angry over the lack of opportunity that freedom and democracy had brought them.

Several U.S. artists have had a significant impact in bringing popular African music to the U.S. musical scene. Pete Seeger's "A Wimoweh," based on South African singer Solomon Linda's song, "Mbube," was one of the first African songs to become a hit in the U.S. Walt Disney purchased the rights to the song for use in its blockbuster **film**, *The Lion King*, as "The Lion Sleeps Tonight," which led to a lawsuit by Linda's family that was settled out of court. Controversy also surrounded singer Paul Simon's effort to bring South African music to the U.S. with his Emmy Award–winning *Graceland* album. Simon went to South Africa to perform with black South African musicians during the international cultural boycott against apartheid. Although he had approval from the Anti-Apartheid Committee of the **United Nations** (UN), some accused him of breaking the boycott for his own personal gain, although Simon made it clear that only black South Africans profited. The album introduced South African musical styles and artists to the U.S., but only Ladysmith Black Mambazo was able to follow up on the album's success with U.S. audiences.

U.S. musicians have come together on several occasions to offer their support to raise money for Africa-related causes. Most famously, in 1985 a group of some 40 performers formed a group called USA for Africa to sing "We Are the World," produced and conducted by Quincy Jones, to raise money for famine victims in **Ethiopia**. The song became the center of simultaneous worldwide "Live Aid" concerts on 13 July 1985 organized by rock and roll figures Bob Geldof and Midge Ure. An estimated 1.5 billion people in over 100 countries watched the concerts live or on satellite and USA for Africa raised $67 million for Ethiopia. Unknown to the performers, the country's hunger was largely the product of a terror famine purposely created by the Communist government of **Mengistu Haile Mariam** to crush a civil war. Mengistu's government used the food assistance to feed his army, freeing up resources to pay for weapons, and to force people in the rebellious regions into government-controlled villages. A second 1985 charity album, *Sun City*, also featured leading U.S. artists in protest against South Africa's apartheid government. The album, produced and largely funded by rock and roll singer Steve Van Zandt, raised over $1 million for anti-apartheid organizations.

Twenty years later, Geldof and Ure organized the worldwide Live 8 concerts in nine countries including the U.S. and South Africa on 2 July and 6 July 2005. Over 1,000 musicians performed and the concerts were seen or heard around the world. Live 8's purpose was to pressure the Group of 8 (G8) leaders who were meeting 6–8 July, to persuade them to increase economic assistance for third-world countries, cancel the foreign debts of the poorest countries, and liberalize international **trade**. The G8 leaders pledged to double economic aid from $25 billion to $50 billion by 2010 with $25 billion for Africa, and agreed to cancel the debts of 18 of the world's poorest countries, estimated at the time to be $40 billion. The leaders also agreed to liberalize trade, but little was done subsequently to achieve this goal. In 2007, Yoko Ono donated the rights to John Lennon's songs to Amnesty International and an album called *Instant Karma* was compiled with leading singers performing Lennon's songs. The money raised was used to pay for Amnesty's publicity campaign to mobilize people to join human rights activists in support of the people of **Darfur** province in **Sudan** who are victims of the government's genocidal policies, and to assist victims of other human rights catastrophes.

Only a small number of African musicians have become stars in the U.S. South African jazz musicians Hugh Masekela and Miriam

Makeba ("Mama Africa") broke through during the 1960s, thanks in part to the assistance of American singer Harry Belafonte. Both became leading anti-apartheid activists. Masekela had a number one hit with his light-instrumental "Grazin in the Grass" (1968) and his "The Coal Train" (1973) powerfully attacks apartheid. Makeba, who had a coquettish and sexy persona reminiscent of Eartha Kitt, introduced U.S. audiences to her native Xhosa, a "click" language, with her hit song "Pata Pata" (1967). She and Belafonte together earned an Emmy for their anti-apartheid album, *An Evening with Belafonte/Makeba*. Makeba married U.S. radical civil rights activist Stokely Carmichael (who changed his name to Kwame Touré), which ruined her U.S. career, and they moved to **Guinea** where Makeba became a strong supporter of its president, **Ahmed Sékou Touré**, who was responsible for the death or exile of 40 percent of Guinea's population.

Since the decline of jazz as a popular musical style in the U.S., few African musicians have become part of the mainstream U.S. market, with Sade Adu the most prominent. Such important African stars as Brenda Fassie, Fela Kuti, Salif Keita, Papa Wemba, and Sam Mangwana failed to break into the U.S. market. Their musical styles such as highlife, Afrobeat, kwaito, kwazaa-kwazaa, and soukous all seem antiquated compared with the current fast-changing and technically advanced U.S. market.

MUTOMBO, DIKEMBE (1966–). Congolese American basketball player and philanthropist considered to be one of the greatest defensive players in National Basketball Association (NBA) history. Mutombo created the Dikembe Mutombo Foundation in 1997 to do charitable works in his native **Congo**, starting with a $29 million hospital in Kinshasa, the capital, for which he personally donated $18.5 million. The hospital was not completed until 2006 due to the country's continuing political and economic turmoil. Mutombo is a spokesman for CARE and works with the **United Nations** (UN) Development Program.

MUZOREWA, ABEL (1925–). United Methodist Church bishop, nationalist leader, and prime minister of the illegal government of Zimbabwe–Rhodesia (1979). Muzorewa was a Methodist minister who attended college at religious seminaries in the United States. He was elected as the first indigenous black bishop of the Central African Episcopacy on 28 August 1968. Known for his charisma and speaking ability, Muzorewa became a prominent advocate for nonviolent resistance to the illegal white-ruled government of **Rhodesia**. When the government of **Great Britain** negotiated a December 1971 constitution with Prime Minister **Ian Smith** that would have maintained white rule for decades, Muzorewa founded the African National Council (ANC), which mobilized Rhodesian blacks against the plan and persuaded a British fact-finding commission to recommend withdrawing the proposal, which it did.

Muzorewa was appointed titular leader of all the black nationalist parties under the ANC umbrella during the unsuccessful December 1974 negotiations with Smith. Guerilla leaders **Joshua Nkomo** and Ndabiningi Sithole subsequently tried to take over the ANC in September 1975. Muzorewa's home was bombed and he fled into exile for 14 months. He returned to Rhodesia to negotiate the transfer to majority rule with Smith. The Internal Settlement, signed on 3 March 1978, gave blacks majority rule but continued white command of the military and secret police during a two-year transition. Muzorewa was appointed prime minister of the newly named Zimbabwe–Rhodesia after winning a landslide election on 29 May 1979. U.S. election observers called the election free and fair and Bayard Rustin, a black civil rights leader, called it the freest African election that he had ever seen. Nonetheless, no country recognized Muzorewa's government, President **Jimmy Carter** was actively hostile, and the guerilla war worsened. Muzorewa was such an international outcast that after guerilla leaders Nkomo and **Robert Mugabe** spoke to the **United Nations** (UN), he was denied the podium.

Pressured by the guerillas, the Front Line States (countries mostly bordering Zimbabwe–Rhodesia), the British, and the U.S., Muzorewa agreed to lengthy talks at Lancaster House in London, which produced an 11 December 1979 peace settlement that included a new name for the country, **Zimbabwe** (which Muzorewa had pushed for during his brief rule), confinement of all guerilla fighters to camps where they would be disarmed and integrated with the Rhodesian army into a new Zimbabwean army, and restoration of British rule until elections. Mugabe reneged on the agreement, keeping many of

his guerillas out of the camps, and they terrorized much of Mashona-
land, the tribal homeland he shared with Muzorewa. Muzorewa and
Nkomo protested to British authorities to no avail. Combined with
the failure of Muzorewa's government to bring peace and fears that
Mugabe would make good threats to go back into the bush if he lost
the election, Muzorewa's forces received only 8 percent of the vote.
In 1983, Mugabe jailed Muzorewa for 10 months, alleging that he
was plotting with **South Africa** and **Israel** to overthrow his government. In 1995, Muzorewa ran for president against Mugabe and was
defeated by an overwhelming margin.

– N –

NAGUIB, MUHAMMAD (1901–1984). General, prime minister
(1952–54), and president (1953–54) of **Egypt**. Humiliation played a
significant role in General Naguib's decision to join the **Gamal Abdel Nasser**–led nationalist Free Officers Movement. King **Farouk**'s
inability to stop **Great Britain** from surrounding his palace and forcing him to accept an anti-Nazi premier on 4 February 1942 led then-
Colonel Naguib to offer his resignation from the army, which Farouk
refused. Egypt's dismal performance in the **Arab–Israeli War of
1948–49**, in which General Naguib was one of the few heroes, convinced him that Egypt needed change. When Lieutenant Colonel
Nasser asked Naguib to become the figurehead leader of the Free Officers, Naguib agreed. Naguib apparently was the commander of the
soldiers who took control of Cairo on 22–23 July 1952. On 26 July,
Farouk was forced to abdicate and the Free Officers' leaders, who
called themselves the Revolutionary Command Council (RCC),
chose Naguib to be prime minister and then president, although
Nasser is believed to have been the power behind the throne.

To strengthen the Free Officers' rule, entice them into joining the
U.S.-backed Middle East Defense Organization (MEDO), and
strengthen Naguib himself against radicals in the RCC, U.S. Secretary of State **Dean Acheson** negotiated a large-scale military assistance program with the Egyptians, but President **Harry S. Truman**
vetoed the deal, apparently due to protests from American supporters
of **Israel** and the Israeli and British governments. Whether or not this

failure to assist the coup leaders would have made any difference is unknown, but the Free Officers subsequently rejected joining any Western defense pact and Naguib, who considered himself more than a figurehead, saw his position and his more moderate stand toward the United States and Israel diminished. President **Dwight D. Eisenhower** remained optimistic that Naguib could be convinced to join an alliance against the **Soviet Union**, so he did not pressure Naguib to make peace with Israel in order to avoid undercutting his position with the RCC and the Egyptian people. He also pressured the British to negotiate withdrawal from their Suez Canal Zone military bases. Domestic issues led Nasser and the RCC to force Naguib's resignation on 25 February 1954, but following 10 days of protests, he was restored to the presidency. Nasser spent the next month and a half making more thorough preparations and removed Naguib on 17 April, taking for himself the position of prime minister. Nasser used the October 1954 attempt on his life by members of the Muslim Brotherhood, a radical Islamist party, as a pretext for ousting Naguib from the RCC and placed him under house arrest where he remained until released by President **Hosni Mubarak** 28 years later.

NAMIBIA. Southwestern African nation that, while known as Southwest Africa, was the last African colony. Namibia's struggle for independence from **South Africa** led to extensive U.S. diplomatic efforts as leader of the **Western Five Contact Group** of nations. Southwest Africa had been a German colony but South Africa occupied the territory in 1915 and, following Germany's defeat in World War I, it was granted to South Africa under a League of Nations mandate of unspecified duration in 1920, with the proviso that South Africa was prohibited from annexing it. South Africa continued to rule the territory even after its mandate was revoked by the **United Nations** (UN) General Assembly on 26 August 1966.

In 1958, black Southwest Africans founded two political organizations that evolved into the South West Africa People's Organization (SWAPO), which became the primary anti-colonial movement under its president, **Sam Nujoma**. SWAPO lobbied the UN to revoke South Africa's mandate and by 1962, Nujoma and the leadership had concluded that guerilla warfare was the only way to achieve independence, so the party began to send young men to radical African nations, the

Soviet Union, and **China** for military training. Guerilla warfare began in 1966 but the South African military drove the guerilla camps out of the country. The guerillas only regained some effectiveness when the Communist-led *Movimento Popular de Libertação de Angola/* Popular Movement for the Liberation of Angola (MPLA) took over **Angola** in 1975 (initially, SWAPO had supported **Jonas Savimbi**, whose *União Nacional para a Independência Total de Angola/*National Union for the Total Independence of Angola [UNITA] shared its Ovambo tribal base with SWAPO). Nonetheless, South Africa quickly drove the guerillas off the border.

SWAPO's official political positions included multiracialism and agnosticism on the question of whether to socialize the nation, but its leaders' rhetoric was violent and Marxist, which made the South Africans more intransigent. President **Jimmy Carter** made Namibian independence a priority because of his foreign policy's regionalist rather than global **cold war** orientation. He supported U.S. creation of the Western Five Contact Group (the United States, **Great Britain**, Canada, **France**, and West Germany), which worked together to negotiate peace in Namibia, reflecting his determination to demonstrate the value of multilateral efforts in international affairs. The Contact Group pressured South Africa to negotiate and in 1978 created a plan for elections that became the foundation for Namibian independence in 1990.

Namibia's first decade of independence under Nujoma was democratic and relatively prosperous, but corruption grew significantly and the government strongly favored the Ovambo at the expense of smaller tribes. Nujoma's third term, granted to him via a controversial constitutional amendment, proved more problematic as his government grew more repressive, he launched foreign policy adventures, including intervention in **Congo**, and confiscated white-owned property for distribution to the masses that often went to Nujoma and his clique. Nonetheless, Nujoma voluntarily retired at the end of his third term, and was replaced by Hifikepunye Pohamba, whom Nujoma personally selected. Pohamba unexpectedly launched an anti-corruption drive, which has won him popularity. *See also* YOUNG, ANDREW.

NASSER, GAMAL ABDEL (1918–1970). Egyptian army officer, prime minister (1954–56), and president (1956–70). Following King

Farouk's humiliation by **Great Britain** on 4 February 1942 when the British forced him to remove all Axis power influence, Second Lieutenant Nasser concluded that the only way to rid **Egypt** of corruption and foreign domination was to rid Egypt of Farouk. To accomplish this, he organized the nationalist Free Officers Movement. The disastrous **Arab–Israeli War of 1948–49**, in which Nasser preformed heroically, strengthened the Free Officers. Nasser moved against Farouk on 23 July 1952 when he learned that the king had uncovered the Free Officers' plot against him. After Farouk abdicated, the Free Officers, who called their government the Revolutionary Command Council (RCC), selected General **Muhammad Naguib** to be Egypt's president, but Lieutenant Colonel Nasser was the power behind the throne.

The United States was initially friendly toward the government because the **Central Intelligence Agency** (CIA) had assisted it in coming to power and its leadership was anti-Communist, called for modernization, cleaned up corruption, and professed willingness to work with the British over the question of whether **Sudan** would remain tied to Egypt or become independent, but the RCC also demanded British military withdrawal from its Suez Canal base. Nasser orchestrated Naguib's removal in 1954 and disbanded the RCC. Shortly thereafter, the U.S. detected that he was moving toward a neutralist position, and rumors spread that the **Soviet Union** planned to offer Egypt a large economic assistance package. Although he was more radical than Naguib, Nasser worked out a compromise with the British to withdraw their troops from the Canal Zone while allowing British technicians to continue operating the canal.

The administration of President **Dwight D. Eisenhower** tried to work with Nasser and chilled relations with **Israel** in an effort at even-handedness, but Secretary of State **John Foster Dulles'** push for a Middle Eastern anti-Soviet alliance that ultimately centered on Nasser's enemy, Iraq, with creation of the **Baghdad Pact**, and U.S. refusal to sell Egypt weapons in order to avoid a Middle East arms race caused Nasser to go to the Soviets, who sold him $200 million in arms through Czechoslovakia in September 1955. His rhetoric also turned virulently anti-Western. The U.S. responded on 19 July 1956 by backing out of an agreement to help fund the **Aswan High Dam**, Nasser's most coveted economic objective. The Soviets later took over the project. Nasser illegally nationalized the Suez Canal on 26 July 1956. Great Britain, **France**, and Israel ignored U.S. counsel to negotiate and jointly attacked Egypt on 29 October. Eisenhower used economic and diplomatic pressure to force them into a cease-fire eight days later and subsequently to withdraw. Nasser's popularity among Egyptians and all Arabs grew mightily after the **Suez Crisis** and he strove to unite the Arabs into one powerful nation, which he believed European colonialists had artificially divided. Despite diplomacy, subversion, and armed intervention in Yemen, his effort failed.

Nasser's decision to order the **United Nations** (UN) to remove its **peacekeeping** force on Egypt's border with Israel, stationed following the Suez Crisis, caused Israel to launch the **Arab–Israeli War of 1967**, which proved disastrous for Nasser and Pan-Arabism. Accusing the U.S. of having assisted Israel in launching the war, Nasser severed diplomatic relations and moved closer to the Soviet Union to rebuild his army. He died of a heart attack on 28 September 1970, sparking mass hysteria across the Middle East. *See also* BUNCHE, RALPH; JOHNSON, LYNDON B.; KENNEDY, JOHN F.; RUSK, DEAN; SADAT, ANWAR AL-.

NATIONAL SECURITY COUNCIL (NSC) MEMORANDUM 5719/1. The first official document that laid out U.S. policy toward sub-Saharan Africa, largely the result of lobbying by Vice President **Richard M. Nixon** within the administration of President **Dwight D. Eisenhower**. Issued on 23 August 1957, NSC Memorandum 5719/1 established that the U.S. would encourage orderly decolonization to foster good relations with newly independent African nations while maintaining close ties with European allies. The document itself explained that the U.S. had not previously had a guiding policy on Africa because the continent was seen as having "limited military and strategic value." Growing fears about communism and eastern Africa's proximity to the Middle East caused the Eisenhower administration to revise NSC 5719/1 within the year, superseding it with NSC 5818, which called for greater diplomatic focus on sub-Saharan Africa.

NATIONAL SECURITY STUDY MEMORANDUM 39 (NSSM 39). U.S. policy document that laid out the Southern Africa policy of the **Richard M. Nixon** administration. The document was premised on the stated belief of Secretary of State **Henry Kissinger**: "The whites are here to stay and the only way that constructive change can come about is through them." NSSM 39 reflected the National Security Council's (NSC) consensus that industrialization and economic development would cause **South Africa** to liberalize, while criticism and coercion would make each of the region's governments more obdurate in resisting change. Washington also feared that pushing too hard could put U.S. investment at risk. The result was a compromise in which the administration continued relatively *pro forma* public criticism of the governments' racism but behind the scenes eased economic restrictions and worked to end the regime's political isolation. In this it was similar to President **Ronald W. Reagan**'s policy of "**Constructive Engagement**." Opponents called NSSM 39 the "**Tar Baby Option**," arguing that once it was begun, the administration was stuck to the policy and could not abandon it, and black African governments would see the U.S. as attached to the region's racist governments. *See also* ANGOLA; MOZAMBIQUE; PORTUGAL; ZIMBABWE.

NETO, AGOSTINHO (1922–1979). Doctor, poet, and rebel leader, who won the presidency of **Angola** (1975–79) following a civil war and independence from **Portugal**. Neto was a Communist who was a founder of the *Movimento Popular de Libertação de Angola*/Popular Movement for the Liberation of Angola (MPLA). In 1961, he launched a brief and unsuccessful guerilla war against Portugal. Although he was a Communist, the **Soviet Union** always considered him a maverick and too weak and scholarly a character to lead a revolution. Likewise, **Cuba** at first saw him as an armchair revolutionary although Fidel Castro became a strong supporter by the mid-1970s.

The fall of the Portuguese empire in April 1974 caused the Soviets to renew support for Neto, who was competing for power with two other rebel movements that claimed to be anti-Communist. Moscow ordered its representatives in Angola to "repair" the MPLA and provide it with weapons. The Portuguese set up talks for power sharing among the MPLA, the *Frente Nacional de Libertação de Angola*/National Front for the Liberation of Angola (FNLA), and the *União Nacional para a Independência Total de Angola*/National Union for the Total Independence of Angola (UNITA), to prepare for independence in November 1975, but all sides continued to fight. That fall, Castro pressured the Soviets to support an all-out push for victory, arguing that winning in Angola could spark the African socialist revolution. After defeating the FNLA in November, by mid-December Cuba had sent over 12,000 Cuban troops to back the MPLA and defeated UNITA, which was supported by 3,000 troops from **South Africa**. South Africa withdrew from Angola by year's end. Following a February 1976 vote by the **Organization of African Unity** (OAU), Neto was recognized as Angola's ruler. Despite the Soviets' view that he was weak, Neto imposed a rigorous socialist rule backed by East German–trained secret police, although he left Gulf Oil alone to pump **oil** in Cabinda province. He died while receiving medical care in Moscow during 1979. *See also* OPERATION IAFEATURE.

NEW YORK ACCORDS. Agreement signed 22 December 1988 by **South Africa**, **Angola**, and **Cuba** that brought **Namibia** its independence from South Africa and set a successful timetable for the removal of Cuban troops from Angola. The accords were signed at the **United Nations** (UN) as the result of pressure by the United States and the **Soviet Union** on their respective allies in their effort to bring the **cold war** to an end. They also set the stage for an unsuccessful effort to end the Angolan civil war. *See also* BOTHA, PETER WILLEM (P.W.); NUJOMA, SHAFILSHONA SAMUEL ("SAM"); REAGAN, RONALD W.; SAVIMBI, JONAS.

NIGER. Landlocked west-central African country that became important in U.S. domestic politics because of 16 words about Niger in President **George W. Bush**'s 2003 State of the Union address. U.S. relations with Niger, as with most of France's former colonies in Equatorial Africa, were distant but friendly until Bush said, "The British Government has learned that Saddam Hussein recently sought significant quantities of uranium from Africa." It was quickly revealed that Niger was the country in question. Subsequent information emerged that disputed Bush's claim and thus his justification for invading Iraq when it was learned that forged documents obtained by the **Central Intelligence Agency** (CIA) claimed Iraq sought uranium from Niger, and former Ambassador to Niger Joseph Wilson said that he found no evidence of a Nigerien–Iraqi tie. The CIA subsequently revealed that its analysts believed that Wilson's report that a former Iraqi nuclear energy official had gone to Niger on a **trade** mission tended to confirm the British intelligence. The Senate Select Committee on Intelligence issued a report on 7 July 2004 that reached the same conclusion as the CIA about Wilson's evidence, and the Butler Report issued by the Parliament of **Great Britain** on 14 July 2004 called Bush's words "well founded." Bush's press secretary, Ari Fleischer, retracted the 16 words on 7 July 2004.

NIGERIA. West African nation that is Africa's most populous, one of the world's largest **oil** producers, and an important source of U.S. oil. Despite Nigeria's great potential—it has sub-Saharan Africa's largest population and the potential to be its wealthiest country—the diplomatic relationship between Nigeria and the United States has rarely been important for either country. Nigeria's record of internal instability in the form of ethnic and religious conflict (the number of tribes is variously reported at 200 to over 300), corruption, a boom-and-bust oil-based economy, and military coups and countercoups launched ostensibly to solve these problems has caused the country to turn inward. Successive Nigerian governments have squandered their huge oil revenues on corruption and ineptly designed and executed development projects, themselves larded with vast quantities of corruption, reported by the Nigerian Corruption Commission in 2005 at over £220 billion stolen or squandered from independence to 2005.

President **John F. Kennedy** believed that Nigeria would be a key regional power and made it the largest sub-Saharan African recipient of U.S. assistance in the belief that it would serve as a model for stable and democratic African government as well as a counterweight to the radical West African governments in **Ghana** and **Guinea**. By 1964, conflict among Nigeria's three major tribes—the Hausa, Yoruba, and Ibo—made Nigeria neither powerful nor activist in foreign policy. By 1966, military coups and ethnic massacres destroyed democracy. The Ibos of eastern Nigeria concluded that they were no longer safe and seceded in 1967, creating the nation of **Biafra**. A brutal two-and-a-half–year war followed. President **Lyndon B. Johnson** tried to remain neutral, refusing to sell arms to either side, and began an aid program for Biafra, all of which angered Nigerian ruler **Yakubu Gowon**. Johnson's successor, **Richard M. Nixon**, concerned about the humanitarian disaster enveloping Biafra and hoping to score points with liberals as a humanitarian, proposed recognizing the Biafran government, but was dissuaded by his advisers, who believed that doing so would alienate most sub-Saharan African governments, for whom colonial borders were almost sacred. His advisers also argued that Nigeria was destined to win, so it would be foolish to antagonize its government. Nonetheless, Nixon further antagonized Gowon by ordering a significant increase in humanitarian assistance for Biafra, where perhaps 10 percent of the population (over one million people) died from starvation and battle.

When Nixon resigned in August 1974, his successor, **Gerald R. Ford**, relied upon Secretary of State **Henry Kissinger** to oversee Africa policy. As the U.S. Congress took greater control of foreign policy from the president, Kissinger tried to make Nigeria part of the "**Nixon Doctrine**," which sought to create a system of friendly regional powers that would contain communism. Kissinger hoped that Nigeria would be the West African bulwark, but that was short-circuited by a coup by General **Murtala Muhammad**, which removed Gowon, a failed countercoup six months later that killed Muhammad and brought to power his deputy, General **Olusegun Obasanjo**, and Obasanjo's decision to move away from international affairs to focus on returning Nigeria to democratic civilian rule.

President **Jimmy Carter**, like Kennedy, sought to make the Nigerian relationship central to U.S.–Africa policy. Less than two months after taking office, in March 1977, he sent UN Ambassador **Andrew Young** to meet with the skeptical Obasanjo, winning him over. Obasanjo visited Carter in Washington during October 1977, offering his support for a joint plan by Washington and **Great Britain** to shepherd **Rhodesia** to majority rule. He reaffirmed the offer when Carter went to Nigeria from 29 March to 2 April 1978. The relationship dramatically deteriorated as the **cold war** returned to Africa when Fidel Castro sent 12,000 of his soldiers from Angola to Ethiopia. Carter criticized Cuba and the **Soviet Union** in a 7 June 1978 speech, warning that détente with the Soviets was at stake, and the Nigerian government responded by bitterly attacking Carter, accusing him of having sought good relations solely to protect U.S. investments.

The primary relationship between Washington and Nigeria has been commercial. The Arab oil embargo in 1973 dramatically raised oil prices and created an opening for newly producing oil fields. By year's end, Nigeria was the third most important U.S. oil supplier and it has remained among the most important. In 1979, the second oil crisis led to even greater Nigerian oil revenue, $20 billion the first year, and the amount continued to rise thereafter. Nigeria's newly elected civilian president, Shehu Shagari, proved to be the leading advocate in the Organization of the Petroleum Exporting Countries (OPEC) for high prices. Carter met with Shagari in 1980 and urged him to increase production beyond limits set by OPEC and to agree to long-term sales contracts with the United States, but Shagari refused. During this period of supreme self-confidence, Nigeria's government spoke of acquiring nuclear weapons (the "African bomb") and began to push for a permanent seat on the **United Nations** (UN) Security Council.

When Saudi Arabia drove down prices through massive production in 1981, Shagari's government was left with little money to lubricate the patronage system that he had created as a political alternative to actual programmatic accomplishment. As the country slid into bankruptcy, the military again intervened, overthrowing Shagari on 31 December 1983 and replacing him with General Muhammadu Buhari. There followed a succession of brutal and corrupt military governments that culminated in the regime of Sani Abacha, who took power in 1993. Abacha and his cronies stole billions of dollars while jailing for life political opponents such as former President Obasanjo and executing others including writer and environmental activist **Ken Saro-Wiwa**. Despite this record, U.S. investment in Nigeria during the Abacha years rose from $3 billion to $7 billion. The administration of **Bill Clinton** rarely criticized Abacha and took no significant action against his regime beyond refusing to allow members of his regime to come to the U.S. and cutting off most military aid for its peacekeeping intervention in **Sierra Leone**. Following Abacha's death, the Clinton and **George W. Bush** administrations had strong relations with his elected successor, the newly freed Obasanjo, even as Obasanjo's government grew politically corrupt and ineffectual. Obasanjo did make the central government more transparent and curbed economic corruption to such an extent that Nigeria received some international debt relief in 2005. The Bush administration actively discouraged Obasanjo from undertaking his failed effort to change Nigeria's constitution so that he could run for a third term. In 2007, he was succeeded by his handpicked successor, little known Governor Umaru Yar'Adua, who won an election almost universally derided as fraudulent. Yar'Adua surprised his countrymen by launching a vigorous and effective anti-corruption drive.

NIMEIRI, GAAFAR (1930–). Military ruler and president of **Sudan** (1969–85). Nimeiri came to power with Communist backing on 25 May 1969 and created a Pan-Arab, socialist government based on the example of **Gamal Abdel Nasser** in **Egypt**. An attempted Communist coup in 1971 moved him into the Western camp. Nimeiri's primary goal was to end a civil war that started in 1955 between the Arab Muslim north and the south, which was black and Christian or animist. Through negotiation, he created a federal government that brought peace in 1972.

Poor economic performance caused Nimeiri to begin flirting with Islamist politicians as a means to counter growing opposition, especially following 6 October 1981 when he was in the grandstand near his friend, Egyptian President **Anwar Sadat**, when he was assassinated by Egyptian Islamic Jihad. Thereafter, Nimeiri began a firm move toward Islamist government that culminated in September 1983 when he introduced sharia law for the entire country and redrew the border between north and south to put newly discovered oil fields in the northern half of the country while taking other steps to weaken southern power. Mass defections by southern soldiers restarted the civil war by the end of the year. The administration of President **Ronald W. Reagan** provided Nimeiri with a massive amount of arms to serve as a counterweight to **Muammar Qaddafi** of **Libya** and **Mengistu Haile Mariam** of **Ethiopia**, both of whom supported the southerners; instead Nimeiri used the weapons against the south and to encourage tribal warfare by arming southern ethnic militias, a precursor to the **Janjaweed** militia used for genocide in **Darfur** by the government of **Omar Bashir**. Nimeiri was overthrown and exiled following street demonstrations in Khartoum in April 1985.

NIXON, RICHARD M. (1913–1994). U.S. vice president (1953–61), president (1969–74), and elder statesman. As vice president under

President **Dwight D. Eisenhower**, Nixon became the leading administration spokesman for an activist Africa policy, arguing that neglect would lead to the **Soviet Union** making gains on the continent that could rob the West of vital strategic materials. During the 1960 presidential election campaign against **John F. Kennedy**, Nixon went so far as to claim that "in the struggle with the Russians, Africa is the most critical area in the world." By the time Nixon was elected president, his foreign policy focus was the interrelated problems of détente with the Soviets, ending the Vietnam War, and reshaping the international order by creating a *de facto* strategic alliance with China against the Soviets.

Nixon's presidential interest in Africa was to prevent crises that would force it to his attention. He sought to accomplish this with the **Nixon Doctrine**, which turned over responsibility for African stability to regional powers, and with **National Security Study Memorandum 39** (NSSM 39), known to opponents as the "**Tar Baby Option**," which concluded that white-ruled Southern African governments were "here to stay" and therefore the best policy approach was to re-engage them in order to move them gently toward equitable treatment for their black majorities. Nixon allegedly told National Security Adviser **Henry Kissinger** that he should leave "the niggers" in Africa to Secretary of State William P. Rogers while they would "take care of the rest of the world."

The one instance where Nixon showed personal interest in sub-Saharan Africa was the **Biafra** crisis in **Nigeria**. Nixon monitored the situation and briefly pushed within his administration for recognition of the breakaway state. The State Department was horrified by the idea that he would violate the Africans' core belief in the sanctity of colonial borders, and was also unhappy when he dramatically expanded Biafran relief aid, which angered the Nigerian government. Kissinger later suggested that Nixon was motivated as much by a desire to score points off morally preening liberals, who almost uniformly opposed Nixon's foreign policy proposals, as he was by his genuine horror at the starvation in Biafra.

Nixon showed somewhat greater interest in the Middle East than in sub-Saharan Africa, but was convinced that **Egypt** was a spent force following the **Arab–Israeli War of 1967** and thus there was no need to pressure **Israel** into negotiations. Egypt's October 1973 invasion, precipitating the **Arab–Israeli War of 1973**, changed this calculus, but Nixon was so caught up in the Watergate scandal that he was forced to delegate much of his responsibility to Kissinger and the White House chief of staff, General Alexander Haig. Nixon did order an elevated state of military alert as a means to show the Soviets the seriousness of the situation when they threatened to intervene on the side of Egypt. To avoid impeachment, Nixon resigned on 9 August 1974, the first president to do so, and spent the rest of his life as a foreign policy sage, advising presidents and world leaders, and writing numerous books, none of which made more than cursory mention of sub-Saharan Africa.

NIXON DOCTRINE. Policy by President **Richard M. Nixon** to support regional powers such as **Zaïre**, **Ethiopia**, and, possibly **Nigeria** and **South Africa**, as local "policemen" against Communist incursions. The Nixon Doctrine would allow Nixon and National Security Adviser **Henry Kissinger** to shed some international responsibilities so that they could focus their energy on ending the Vietnam War, creating a new international order based on détente between the U.S. and the **Soviet Union**, and creating a *de facto* strategic alliance between Washington and **China**.

NKOMO, JOSHUA (1917–1999). Zimbabwean rebel leader and cabinet minister. In the struggle for black majority rule that transformed the illegal **Rhodesia** colony into independent **Zimbabwe**, Nkomo was pragmatic and at times ruthless, preferred over **Robert Mugabe** by Rhodesian whites and President **Kenneth Kaunda** of **Zambia**, but held in suspicion by the United States and **Great Britain** because of his ties to the **Soviet Union**. Nkomo was also a member of the minority Ndebele tribe, which probably made moot the machinations of the Rhodesians, the Zambians, the Soviets, and the West.

Nkomo was a labor leader and lay preacher appointed to lead several successive Rhodesian black nationalist organizations culminating in the Zimbabwe African People's Union (ZAPU), founded in December 1961. Known as a political moderate who supported a multiracial society, Nkomo negotiated a much-criticized constitution in 1961 that gave blacks only 15 of 65 seats in the national legislature. He subsequently repudiated the agreement and, to reestablish his nationalist credentials, oversaw a campaign of violence that quickly grew out of control against blacks who registered to vote in elections under the new constitution. The following year, he expanded the attacks to include whites and economic targets. Nkomo apparently had no real plan beyond the hope that escalating violence would force the British to intervene and grant Rhodesia independence under black rule.

Nkomo spent most of his time outside Rhodesia to collect money and support, but many of his colleagues saw him as jet-setting rather than working, an image enhanced by his huge size and appetites. Members of the Shona majority also resented being led by an Ndebele. In August 1963, Ndabiningi Sithole and Mugabe, both Shona, broke away and founded the Zimbabwe African National Union (ZANU), which followed a more militant anti-white policy and came to be seen as a Shona party. All three leaders were jailed in 1964 and released in December 1974 to participate in unsuccessful negotiations with Rhodesian Prime Minister **Ian Smith** under the auspices of Bishop **Abel Muzorewa**'s African National Council (ANC). Nkomo unsuccessfully tried to take over the ANC the following year, creating a rift with the bishop. Nkomo secretly and unsuccessfully negotiated with Smith from December 1975 to March 1976, U.S Secretary of State **Henry Kissinger** in 1976, then with all parties at a British- and U.S.-backed Geneva, Switzerland, conference in October 1976. Prior to the conference, on 9 October, leaders of the nations bordering Rhodesia, known as the Front Line States, forced Nkomo to create a joint party with Mugabe called the Patriotic Front (PF), although in reality ZAPU and ZANU remained independent of one another. The PF rejected the March 1978 Internal Settlement by Smith, Muzorewa, Sithole, and Chief Jeremiah Chirau that created black-majority ruled Zimbabwe–Rhodesia, but on 14 August, Nkomo secretly met with Smith, Zambia's Kaunda, and **Nigeria**'s former foreign minister, Joseph Garba, to discuss joining the government. The participants did not inform Mugabe, Muzorewa, or the other Front Line heads of state. Smith offered Nkomo leadership of the government until elections could be held, which Nkomo rejected, demanding immediate power for the PF. Despite Nkomo's hard line, Mugabe was furious when he learned about the meeting. To regain his standing as a radical nationalist, in a move reminiscent of 1961–62, Nkomo's forces shot down Rhodesian passenger airliners in September 1978 and February 1979 and slaughtered the survivors, which he chortled about to the press.

Zambia-based and strongly supported by the Soviets, Nkomo's forces were the stronger of the two guerilla movements until **Portugal**'s military withdrew from **Mozambique** in late 1974. The guerilla *Frente de Libertação de Moçambique*/Front for the Liberation of Mozambique (FRELIMO) filled the Mozambican power vacuum and gave ZANU total access to the 760-mile border with Rhodesia. With easy guerilla infiltration and a Shona tribal base that was more than three times larger than Nkomo's Ndebele, ZANU's fighters quickly supplanted ZAPU's as the more important guerilla movement, a position strengthened by Nkomo's following Soviet and North Vietnamese advice to avoid dissipating his forces through guerilla war, instead building up for a final offensive. Mugabe accused him of sparing his forces while ZANU's guerilla forces suffered the brunt of Rhodesia's firepower. The final offensive was aborted by the late 1978 Lancaster House Conference, an all-party constitutional conference that briefly returned Zimbabwe–Rhodesia to British rule, set up elections for early the next year, and changed the country's name to Zimbabwe. Shortly thereafter, Mugabe surprised Nkomo by announcing that ZANU, renamed ZANU-PF, would run independently. Mugabe's violent rhetoric and threats to continue the civil war if ZANU-PF lost, combined with intimidation and murderous violence by ZANU's guerillas against Muzorewa's supporters, led Nkomo to join Muzorewa in demanding that the British disqualify Mugabe and ZANU-PF, but the British refused. Mugabe won the election with an overwhelming Shona-based majority while Nkomo swept the Ndebele, taking a quarter of the total vote.

Nkomo had supported a one-party state prior to Lancaster House, but the prospect of the one party being ZANU-PF and not ZAPU gave him a new appreciation for multiparty democracy. When Mugabe invited him to bring ZAPU into ZANU-PF, Nkomo refused. Mugabe virtually banned Nkomo in 1981 by taking his passport and restricting him to the city of Bulawayo. The following year, Nkomo secretly fled the country following a government-backed assassination attempt, ZAPU's leadership team was jailed where many died, and Mugabe sent a North Korean–trained unit of the army into Matabeleland, the Ndebele's homeland, which killed as many as 25,000.

Nkomo returned to Zimbabwe in 1985 for parliamentary elections in which ZAPU again carried Matabeleland but little else, and ended the violence by letting ZANU-PF swallow ZAPU on 22 December 1987. Mugabe appointed him second vice president of Zimbabwe, which he remained for the rest of his life, but his primary role was to cajole the Ndebele not to make trouble.

NKRUMAH, KWAME (1909–1972). Charismatic West African states-man, Pan-Africanist, prime minister (1951–60), and president (1960–66) of **Ghana**. Nkrumah sought to industrialize and socialize Ghana by building a dam that would provide electricity and make use of Ghana's vast bauxite reserves by powering a domestic aluminum-smelting industry, and he tried to bring the African peoples together into a United States of Africa under his leadership. Nkrumah attended college in the U.S. at Lincoln University, a **historically black college and university** (HBCU) located outside Philadelphia, where he was heavily influenced by socialist and Pan-Africanist ideas. In 1951, he was elected prime minister of the Gold Coast, Ghana's colonial name, and led the British colony to independence in 1957. Ghana was the first sub-Saharan African country granted independence. An extremely charismatic figure who adopted for himself the title *Osagyefo* — the "redeemer" — Nkrumah immediately sought to unite Africa by peaceful union with **Guinea**, Mali, and **Congo**, and by subversion, providing ideological and military training to guerillas from **Nigeria**, Cameroon, Ivory Coast, **Niger**, Togo, and Upper Volta. Both methods proved unsuccessful.

Nkrumah's other goal was to modernize and socialize Ghana. Al-though his socialist policies and belief that the U.S. was a neo-colonial power that sought to keep Ghana and Africa subordinate and weak militated toward working with the **Soviet Union**, Nkrumah moder-ated his rhetoric and policies in order to win U.S. government back-ing for a **Volta River Dam** that he hoped would provide electricity for massive industrialization. The administration of President **Dwight D. Eisenhower** funded a technical study of the proposal, and President **John F. Kennedy** approved the project following a March 1961 meeting with Nkrumah at the White House, the first sub-Saha-ran African leader with whom the president met. Once approved, Nkrumah grew increasingly bold in his anti-Americanism and moved progressively closer to the Soviets, leading to repeated U.S. threats to abandon the project and causing Kennedy and his successor, **Lyndon B. Johnson**, to rue the decision. Despite his attacks on the U.S., Nkrumah had been much impressed with Kennedy, and agreed not to allow the Soviets to use Ghana to refuel airplanes bound for **Cuba** during the missile crisis, thus reinforcing the sea blockade of the island.

Domestically, on 1 July 1960, Nkrumah changed Ghana to a republic and he was elected president with almost total power. Shortly thereafter he had himself chosen president for life, subverted the judiciary and purged the chief justice, promulgated a more draconian detention law than **South Africa**'s, and jailed hundreds of opponents. What remained of the opposition was banned by making Ghana a one-party state. Even ordinary people who gossiped about Nkrumah's or Ghana's problems were jailed. Ghanaians were indoctrinated in "Nkrumahism," a personality cult that was a somewhat amorphous melding of scientific socialism with African culture and demands for African unity. Nkrumah also began to follow the Soviet line in foreign policy and, by 1964, Soviets and East Germans were heavily involved in the security services. Corruption became endemic and Nkrumah himself stole $5 million, almost every state-run enterprise failed, and Ghana's foreign exchange reserves of $500 million at independence were exhausted, leaving a national debt of $1 billion.

Following an August 1962 assassination attempt, Nkrumah became increasingly paranoid about his personal safety. He said that the **Central Intelligence Agency** (CIA) was trying to kill him and was behind all that went wrong in Ghana, including manipulation of international cocoa prices. In 1963, Kennedy reportedly wrote a personal letter assuring Nkrumah that there were no CIA operations in Ghana, but following a second assassination attempt in January 1964, Nkrumah grew far more anti-American, culminating in the October 1965 publication of his book, *Neo-Colonialism: The Last Stage of Imperialism*, which accused the CIA, the **Peace Corps**, and the U.S. Information Agency (USIA) of seeking to bring down his government. Days later, the U.S. turned down his request for $100 million in food aid, instructing the ambassador to Ghana to leave Nkrumah with the impression that the refusal was retaliation. On 21 February

1966, Nkrumah flew to Beijing and Hanoi to try to settle the Vietnam War although Ho Chi Minh had told him that he was uninterested in negotiation, and the U.S., not wanting to enhance his prestige, had told him not to fly on to Washington. He landed in Beijing on 24 February and learned that he had been overthrown by the army and police. Public celebration was greater than it had been on independence day. Nkrumah emigrated to Guinea, where his friend **Ahmed Sékou Touré** appointed him co-president until his death, although he had no power.

NON-GOVERMENTAL ORGANIZATIONS (NGOs). International organizations created through national or international legal processes by private individuals or organizations. Normally the term NGO refers to nonprofit corporations, which have as their purpose the improvement of society, rather than for-profit corporations. Therefore, NGOs are morally obligated to place their organizational mission over profit. NGOs may receive government assistance as long as government representatives do not run the organization.

U.S. NGOs that work with Africa date back to the **American Colonization Society** (ACS), which assisted **African Americans** in moving to **Liberia**. In the 21st century, the missions of NGOs that work in Africa include monitoring and reporting on democracy and economic freedom, such as Freedom House; buying and freeing slaves in Sudan, such as Christian Solidarity International; providing teachers and teacher education, such as the Oprah Winfrey Leadership Academy; assisting trade unions, such as the **American Federation of Labor–Congress of Industrial Organizations** (AFL-CIO); spreading Christianity, such as church missionary organizations of every denomination; fighting disease, such as the Bill & Melinda Gates Foundation; assisting with economic development, such as the Ford Foundation; providing disaster relief and assisting political **refugees**, such as CARE; and intervening to negotiate peace settlements or transitions to democracy, such as the Carter Center.

NGOs historically have had a positive reputation because of their good works. Many NGOs came under strong international criticism during the U.S. and **United Nations** (UN) intervention to stop the famine in **Somalia** (1992–95), and following the Rwandan Genocide (1994). Even the most famous and well managed such as CARE and

Feed the Children were seen as being part of a "disaster industry" that profited from civil wars and government repression. In Somalia, warlords prevented the humanitarian NGOs from providing assistance unless they were paid bribes, strengthening the warlords' hold on power. In **Rwanda**, all but a handful of NGOs abandoned the country during the Hutu-extremist genocide against the Tutsi. The NGOs returned after the defeat of the "Hutu power" government and the end of the genocide, but focused their efforts on refugee camps in neighboring countries where they provided assistance to the now-defeated Hutus. Exacerbating the anger of Rwanda's new Tutsi-led government was that the NGOs did not stop former "Hutu power" government leaders from organizing the camps and distributing the food, thus allowing the *génocidaires* to maintain complete control over the camps and use them as guerilla bases to invade Rwanda.

Since the Rwandan Genocide, NGOs have acknowledged that they are much better suited for assisting after a natural disaster than following a politically created humanitarian crisis, and have sought ways to minimize the benefits that their intervention brings to the repressive governments that precipitate the crises. *See also* RWANDA, GENOCIDE IN.

NUJOMA, SHAFILSHONA SAMUEL ("SAM") (1929–). Namibian rebel leader and president (1990–2005), who brought his country to independence. Nujoma received primary education plus some night school and worked at various times as a shepherd, a custodian, and a clerk. He had a persuasive way with people and was an outstanding public speaker, which led him into union organizing and politics. In 1959, he founded a branch of an ethnic organization that supported Ovambo rights that later morphed into the South West Africa People's Organization (SWAPO), becoming its president in April 1960. In February 1960 he was sent to the **United Nations** (UN) to plead Southwest Africa's case for independence, traveling surreptitiously through seven African countries before he was finally able to cross the ocean. In March 1961 he set up SWAPO's headquarters in **Tanzania** and began touring the world to generate support. In 1966, Nujoma ordered guerilla warfare in northern Namibia, supported by Tanzania, **Egypt**, and **Algeria**, although he remained outside the country and continued to travel the world. In 1976, Nujoma launched the first in a series of purges ostensibly directed at South African spies, but which focused on those considered too educated or critical of the leadership. Thousands were imprisoned in the camps and tortured, and many disappeared. Ten of the top dissident leaders were detained on his behalf by the government of **Zambia** and later imprisoned in Tanzania.

President **Jimmy Carter** worked with four other Western powers in the **Western Five Contact Group** to exert strong pressure on **South Africa** to free Namibia, but the South Africans and Nujoma proved intransigent on key issues. Independence came largely on Namibian terms as South African morale flagged in the face of increasing losses to troops from **Cuba** based in **Angola** and as the Communist threat rapidly diminished because Mikhail Gorbachev pared back the **Soviet Union**'s overseas commitments. Nujoma was elected and took office as Namibian president on 21 March 1990. Without the possibility of Soviet support, he moved to the center and governed with a mixed economy. After his constitutionally allotted two terms, Nujoma followed in the footsteps of his hero, **Zimbabwe**'s President **Robert Mugabe**, and had himself elected to a third term, with a victory margin inflated by government intimidation and use of the levers of power. Nujoma became more authoritarian, sending the army into **Congo** to assist **Laurent-Désiré Kabila** without consulting the legislature and then never reporting the number of troops sent, the cost, or casualties. He also allowed the Angolan government to enter Namibian territory to hunt down **Jonas Savimbi** and his *União Nacional para a Independência Total de Angola*/National Union for the Total Liberation of Angola (UNITA), again without consulting parliament. Nujoma began to speak out against whites who owned large and prosperous farms, although the farms that the government had purchased for redistribution had often gone to the president and his cronies, and by the end of his rule the government began confiscating white-owned farms. Nujoma unexpectedly and voluntarily retired at the end of his third term, replaced by Hifikepunye Pohamba, whom he personally selected. In 2007, Namibia's National Society for Human Rights petitioned the International Criminal Court in The Hague to investigate Nujoma for the disappearance of 4,200 Namibians during the civil war and his presidency.

NYERERE, JULIUS (1922–1999). Prime minister (1961–64) and president (1964–85) of **Tanzania**. In retirement, he was an international statesman. Nyerere was known for his humanity, decency, and virtuousness, as well as his deep commitment to socialist principles and ending white rule in Southern Africa. Less well known were his authoritarian practices and the economic disaster that his policies brought to Tanzania. Nyerere was a teacher who came to power as a strongly anti-colonial socialist on 9 December 1961, but he was forced to call in British troops to save his government from a 20 January 1964 military coup while he humiliatingly hid in a grass hut in the bush. On 15 December of the following year, Nyerere broke relations with the **Great Britain** to protest its failure to crush the rogue government of **Rhodesia**, at an overall cost to his country of £7 million in lost foreign assistance.

Although himself a Fabian socialist who believed in a uniquely African socialism of uplifting peasants through teaching them to use more sophisticated tools and modern agricultural practices, which he called *Ujamaa* (Swahili, "familyhood"), Nyerere's views evolved during a 1965 visit to China when he visited communes and was persuaded by the Maoist argument that peasants are the most conservative element in any society and therefore government must force them to adapt to socialist policies for their own good. He publicly laid out his views of agrarian socialism from the bottom up in which the state would control all means of production and exchange when he issued the Arusha Declaration on 7 February 1967, which he followed with pell-mell nationalization of the economy's commanding heights. In September, he called for voluntary creation of consolidated socialist *Ujamaa* villages, but when the peasants failed to heed his call in significant numbers, in November 1973 he began to use the army to destroy their homes and drive them into villages, which were often nothing more than piles of lumber on the side of a road. To enforce his political and economic policies, Nyerere made liberal use of a preventive detention law he pushed through in 1962, throwing approximately 1,000 opponents in jail during the late 1970s without having to reveal their names, making his government one of Africa's most repressive. Approximately 11 million people were removed to *Ujamaa* villages by 1978 although many moved back to their old homes as quickly as they could get away with it.

The government completed *Ujamaa* by taking over every small store throughout the country. As a result, the productive economy collapsed, but the West, especially Scandinavian countries and **Robert McNamara**, who led the **World Bank**, loved *Ujamaa* and from 1970 to 1995 assisted Tanzania with approximately $20 billion (unadjusted for inflation) to make it work, which was the highest per capita aid in Africa. The West's "Tanzaphilia" could not make Tanzania productive or government officials less corrupt. The 1978–79 war with **Uganda** combined with the Organization of the Petroleum Exporting Countries (OPEC) **oil** price spike of 1979 caused collapse that even outsiders could not halt. Nyerere resigned on 5 November 1985. In his farewell speech, he said of his economic policies, "I failed. Let's admit it."

Nyerere's foreign policy was more effective. He became an international leader because of his strong support for central and southern Africa's independence and for anti-**apartheid** movements. Nyerere served as chairman of the five Front Line States that supported the guerilla movements and he allowed the guerilla leaderships to locate headquarters and training camps in Tanzania. He used the Tanzanian army to remove **Idi Amin** as president of Uganda at great cost to Tanzania, but then worked successfully behind the scenes to place his friend, the brutal Milton Obote, in the presidency. Nyerere was also the leading advocate in an unsuccessful drive for a New International Economic Order of resource redistribution from Global North to South through international law. In retirement, he continued to be a leading African statesman, speaking out repeatedly for the poor and mediating Burundi's civil war in 1996 until his death in 1999.

– O –

OBAMA, BARACK H. (1961–). African American politician and the first African American president. Obama's father was a native of **Kenya** who left his son's white mother when Barack was two years old and died in 1982. Obama visited Kenya for the first time in 1988 and met many family members. Obama was elected to the U.S. Senate in 2004, received the Democratic Party's nomination for president in August 2008, and was elected on 4 November 2008.

As senator, Obama made African affairs a focus, travelling to **Kenya, Chad**, Djibouti, **South Africa**, and **Ethiopia** as a member of the Senate Foreign Relations Committee in August–September 2006. In Kenya, he rebuked the government of Mwali Kibaki for corruption and tribalism. Obama worked closely with Republican Senator Sam Brownback of Kansas on African issues, successfully co-sponsoring legislation in 2006 to encourage U.S. support for peace in **Congo**, and the **Darfur** Peace and Accountability Act, also in 2006, which calls for greater U.S. assistance to end the genocide in the Darfur region of **Sudan**. Obama urged divestment from Sudan and divested from his own portfolio $180,000 worth of shares in companies that do business with the government of Sudan.

Obama said little about Africa in his campaign for president, but joined opponents Hillary Clinton and John McCain in a 28 May 2008 joint statement demanding that the government of Sudan end the genocide in Darfur before the U.S. presidential inauguration on 20 January 2009 or face "unstinting resolve" from the U.S. government to bring peace and security to Darfur.

OBASANJO, OLUSEGUN (1937–). Military ruler (1976–79) of **Nigeria** who restored democratic rule in 1979, and democratically elected president (1999–2007) following a second democratic transition. Obasanjo became military ruler following the assassination of **Murtala Muhammad** on 13 February 1976. He continued Muhammad's policy of returning Nigeria to civilian rule, but in foreign policy he canceled a scheduled meeting with Secretary of State **Henry Kissinger** after learning of apparently baseless rumors of U.S. involvement in Muhammad's assassination. Obasanjo's relations with President **Jimmy Carter** were much better, and they worked together to bring majority rule to **Rhodesia**. Following the election of Margaret Thatcher as prime minister of **Great Britain**, Obasanjo quietly halted negotiations on **oil** contracts to pressure Thatcher into continuing to oppose the transitional government of Zimbabwe–Rhodesia. He turned power over to democratically elected president Shehu Shagari on 1 October 1979 and retired from the military.

Obasanjo became an important critic of the military leaders who overthrew Shagari and then one another, especially General Sani Abacha. Abacha had Obasanjo convicted of treason and sentenced to life in prison, but international outcry led Abacha to cut the sentence to 15 years. After Abacha's death, Obasanjo was elected president and he became a close ally of Presidents **Bill Clinton** and **George W. Bush**. Despite Obasanjo's promise to clean up corruption, massive corruption continued, as did increasingly widespread and brutal ethnic and religious violence, all while the Nigerian economy continued to implode despite huge increases in oil revenues starting in 2000. Obasanjo failed in an attempt to change Nigeria's constitution to run for a third term in 2007. He turned over power to Umaru Yar'Adua on 21 April 2007 following elections that international observers believed were fraudulent. In 2008, the government investigated Obasanjo for corruption.

ODINGA, OGINGA (1911–1994). Kenyan businessman and Communist politician who served briefly as vice president under **Jomo Kenyatta** in the 1960s, and in the early 1990s led opposition against President **Daniel arap Moi**. Odinga's business skill and wealth led him into politics, where he was a leading anti-colonialist and supporter of socialism. Odinga was also a Luo chief, which gave him a natural constituency, although tribal tradition required that he give up his title to enter politics. He received secret financial backing from the **Soviet Union** and **China** and allowed them to infiltrate Communists into teaching positions at a government school created for training government bureaucrats. Odinga's ambition put him into conflict with **Tom Mboya**, another ambitious Luo, who also hoped to succeed Kenyatta, a Kikuyu, as president. U.S. Ambassador William Attwood informed Kenyatta about the Communist role in the government school, and Mboya was able to use it to forestall a party takeover by Odinga's people and then to maneuver him out of the party.

Kenyatta jailed Odinga for two years in 1969, the year of Mboya's assassination, and Odinga did not make a political comeback until the early 1990s when he became the leader of the political opposition to President Moi. With the fall of the Soviet Union, the **George H.W. Bush** administration no longer feared Odinga's Communist past, and U.S. Ambassador Smith Hempstone strongly supported him, forcing Moi to accept multiparty democracy and earning Moi's hatred. In December 1992, Hempstone asked newly elected President **Bill Clinton** to extend his tour for six months to help shepherd the democratic system, but Clinton refused. Moi took advantage of the transition period to eviscerate the democratic reforms. Despite increasing senility, Odinga refused to give up leadership of the opposition. Since his death, his son Ralia led the opposition forces and came to power as prime minister as part of a power-sharing agreement with President Mwai Kibaki following elections acknowledged to have been fraudulent.

OGADEN WAR. War fought 1977–78 between **Ethiopia** and **Somalia** over Ethiopia's Ogaden region, a desert that is almost exclusively populated by Somalis. With the assistance of 15,000 troops provided by **Cuba**, Ethiopia defeated and repelled the invaders. *See also* BRZEZINSKI, ZBIGNIEW; CARTER, JAMES E. (JIMMY); MENGISTU HAILE MARIAM; SIAD BARRÉ, MUHAMMAD; SOVIET UNION; YOUNG, ANDREW.

OIL. In 2006, Africa supplied the United States with 22 percent of its petroleum imports, increasing rapidly from 15 percent in 2004. The leading African countries from which the U.S. imports oil include **Nigeria**, the fourth most important source of U.S. oil, **Angola** (seventh), **Algeria** (eighth), **Chad** (thirteenth), **Libya** (fifteenth), and **Equatorial Guinea** (twenty-fifth). Commercially significant amounts of oil are also found in Gabon, the Republic of Congo (Congo–Brazzaville), and **Sudan**. In 2006, the U.S. bought 33 percent of Africa's oil exports. Oil is found in economically viable quantities off the coast of West Africa and on the mainland in West and Central Africa. In 2008, Africa had 10 percent of the world's proven oil reserves, and the U.S. Department of Energy estimates that African oil production could increase by 91 percent from 2002–25. Africa has many as yet unexplored regions that may prove to be significant oil sources, and since 2000 one-third of the world's new oil discoveries have been found in Africa.

West African oil is especially prized on the world market because it is "sweet," an oil industry expression that means the oil is low in sulfur and therefore needs less refining than Middle East oil, which is "sour." West African oil is usually located near natural harbors or offshore, especially in the Gulf of Guinea, which makes it easy and inexpensive to ship to the U.S. and Western Europe. Also making African oil attractive is that only Nigeria, Algeria, and Angola belonged to the Organization of the Petroleum Exporting Countries (OPEC) in mid-2008.

Every African oil producer had suffered from the "resource curse," endemic and massive corruption accompanied by dictatorship or political instability, with little of the oil wealth trickling down to the people. Nigeria is the most famous example, having suffered through an estimated $380 billion in losses from corruption since independence to 2005 and from revolving door military dictatorships, with the result that in 2007, 57 percent of Nigerians lived on $1 per day or less despite being the world's seventh-largest oil producer. In the country's oil-producing region, the Niger Delta, 70 percent of the people live on $1 or less per day, powerful and politically connected gangs tap into oil pipelines and kidnap oil company employees for ransom, and approximately 1,000 people per year die in ethnic violence.

Angola suffered 25 years of civil war following independence, fueled by the **cold war**, oil, and **blood diamonds** mined by **Jonas Savimbi**'s rebel *União Nacional para a Independência Total de Angola*/ National Union for the Total Independence of Angola (UNITA). At several points during the civil war, troops from **Cuba** were protecting oil fields owned by Gulf Oil, a U.S. oil company, which were under threat from Savimbi's U.S.-backed troops. Angola has been a dictatorship since independence, even after Savimbi's death and the collapse of his movement in 2002.

Many analysts regard Equatorial Guinea's government as Africa's most repressive, and U.S. oil companies have invested $10 billion in its oil industry. Chad's government agreed to invest 95 percent of its oil earnings for the betterment of the masses in return for the U.S. and **World Bank** underwriting the cost of development and building a pipeline to the coast. Chad's government has reneged and used much of the money for weapons and corruption. In 2006 it announced the nationalization of ChevronTexaco's share of the business and has threatened to break agreements with Exxon Mobil. Reportedly the government would like to replace these U.S. firms with oil companies from **China**, which ignores corruption and human rights violations. Gabon is ruled by a repressive and corrupt dictatorship, Algeria has been a dictatorship since independence and suffered a brutal civil war and Islamist terror throughout most of the 1990s, Libya has been ruled for 40 years by **Muammar Qaddafi,** Sudan's government brought back slavery and has fought brutal civil wars against minority tribes including the genocide in **Darfur,** and the Republic of Congo has suffered throughout its history from corrupt, repressive government and civil war.

OLAJUWON, HAKEEM (1963–). Nigerian American basketball player who led the Houston Rockets basketball team to consecutive National Basketball Association (NBA) championships (1994–95). Olajuwon emigrated from **Nigeria** to play basketball for the University of Houston. He became a superstar on a team known as "Phi Slama Jama," which went to the Final Four in three National Collegiate Athletic Association (NCAA) championship tournaments. In the NBA, Olajuwon was known as "The Dream," and in 1996 he was chosen as one of the 50 greatest players of all time.

Outside of basketball, Olajuwon is known for his philanthropic work. He endorsed a $35 basketball shoe, which is a retail price more than $100 cheaper than competing brands, because of the theft and violence by young predominantly black men in pursuit of the styles endorsed by other NBA players. Olajuwon also helped to found a mosque that was closed by the U.S. government because it had provided assistance to terrorist-affiliated charities, although Olajuwon denied having known about the tie.

OPERATION DRAGON ROUGE. *See* STANLEYVILLE (KISANGANI) HOSTAGE RESCUE.

OPERATION ENDURING FREEDOM–HORN OF AFRICA (OEF-HOA). The Horn of Africa sector of Operation Enduring Freedom, the worldwide U.S. anti-terror operation begun by President **George W. Bush** as part of the **Global War on Terror** (GWOT) following the 11 September 2001 attacks. Included in it are the land-based Combined Joint Task Force–Horn of Africa (CJTF-HOA), which began operations in October 2002, and the multinational naval Combined Task Force 150 (CTF-150), which began operations in December 2002. OEF-HOA was originally under the U.S. Central Command, which was responsible for East Africa, the Middle East, and Central Asia, but is now under the **United States Africa Command**

(AFRICOM), which was created in October 2007 and covers all of Africa except **Egypt**. Both task forces operate out of a forward operations base at Camp Le Monier in Djibouti. Approximately 2,000 U.S. and coalition military personnel are based at the camp. The task forces have been used to interdict weapons and drugs shipped to the area; to stop piracy; to train anti-terror forces for Djibouti, **Kenya**, and **Ethiopia**; to provide air support for the Ethiopian invasion of southern **Somalia** that destroyed the **al Qaeda**–supported Islamic Courts Union (ICU); and to prevent ICU and al Qaeda forces from escaping the Ethiopian invasion. *See also* OPERATION ENDURING FREEDOM–TRANS SAHARA (OEF-TS); TERRORISM.

OPERATION ENDURING FREEDOM–TRANS SAHARA (OEF-TS). The North African and Sahelian sector of Operation Enduring Freedom, the worldwide U.S. anti-terror operation begun by President **George W. Bush** as part of the **Global War on Terror** (GWOT) following the 11 September 2001 attacks. It is also the military component of the **Trans-Sahara Counterterrorism Initiative** (TSCTI). The OEF-TS mission of training regional rapid deployment forces, performing reconnaissance, and assisting in killing or capturing terrorists is carried out by Joint Task Force Aztec Silence (JTF Aztec Silence), which was originally under the command of the U.S. European Command but since October 2007 has been under the **U.S. Africa Command** (AFRICOM), which covers all of Africa except **Egypt**. *See also* OPERATION ENDURING FREEDOM–HORN OF AFRICA (OEF-HOA); TERRORISM.

OPERATION IAFEATURE. Central Intelligence Agency (CIA) operation launched on 18 July 1975 to intervene in the civil war in **Angola** by providing $48 million in economic and military aid, military training, and mercenaries to the *Frente Nacional de Libertação de Angola*/National Front for the Liberation of Angola (FNLA), led by **Holden Roberto**, and **Jonas Savimbi**'s *União Nacional para a Independência Total de Angola*/National Union for the Total Liberation of Angola (UNITA). Secretary of State **Henry Kissinger** was the leading force behind IAFEATURE, whose goal was to prevent from coming to power the Communist-led *Movimento Popular de Libertação de Angola*/Popular Movement for the Liberation of Angola

(MPLA), which was backed by the **Soviet Union** and **Cuba**. Strong circumstantial evidence indicates that IAFEATURE was in conjunction with the government of **South Africa**, which launched an almost simultaneous covert operation in Angola. When December 1975 newspaper reports revealed both IAFEATURE and the South African intervention, Congress aborted the operation on 19 December 1975 by passing the **Tunney Amendment**, which cut off all U.S. operations in Angola, and the **Clark Amendment**, which made the ban permanent. President **Ronald W. Reagan** won repeal of the Clark Amendment on 8 August 1985 in order to aid Savimbi as part of his **Reagan Doctrine**. *See also* FORD, GERALD R.; KAUNDA, KENNETH; MOBUTU SESE SEKO; NETO, AGOSTINHO.

OPERATION RESTORE HOPE. Also known as the Unified Task Force (UNITAF), was a U.S.-led operation sanctioned by the **United Nations** (UN) in which approximately 30,000 U.S. troops and military forces from 24 other countries occupied much of southern **Somalia** in order to feed **refugees** and local people starving from a civil war–created famine. The operation was authorized under UN Security Council Resolution 794, began 9 December 1992, and was scheduled to end on 20 January 1993, but the main body of U.S. forces remained until 4 May 1993.

Prior to the intervention, an estimated 300,000 people had died from the civil war and famine, and 1.5 million were considered at risk because the food supply system provided by **foreign aid**–supplying **non-governmental organizations** had broken down. President **George H.W. Bush** received reports from aid agencies that as much as 80 percent of the food was being stolen by militias and gangs as the price for providing protection, which UN peacekeepers, operating as the UN Operation in Somalia (UNOSOM I), were too weak and jurisdictionally unable to provide. Subsequent analysis showed that the amount stolen was closer to 20 percent. The operation's genesis was the horror felt by President Bush and the American people at televised scenes of the famine. Bush's resolve to act was solidified by letters from a coalition of U.S. aid agencies known as InterAid, which requested U.S. action under the UN umbrella, and pressure from UN Secretary-General **Boutros Boutros-Ghali**, who requested intervention on the grounds that Somalia's anarchy was a threat to peace in the Horn of Africa. Operation Restore Hope halted the famine and stopped the fighting. Estimates vary widely as to the number of lives saved by the mission, with a minimum of 10,000 and maximum of "hundreds of thousands."

Boutros-Ghali and Bush's successor, **Bill Clinton**, warned that when the peacekeepers left, the civil war would resume since the combatants still had their weapons. To prevent this, both pushed successfully to expand the mandate to make the UN operation a **peacekeeping** force that would disarm the combatants and rebuild the national polticial structure. This was done by passage of UN Security Council Resolution 814 on 26 March 1993, which created UN Operation in Somalia II (UNOSOM II), a more powerful force than UNOSOM I but much less powerful than UNITAF since the U.S. would provide only 4,500 troops. The operation was under the direction of former U.S. Admiral Jonathan Howe. UNOSOM II's mission was expanded to include actively disarming competing militias and building a new Somali government.

OPERATION TORCH. The Allied invasion of French North Africa during World War II. Overseen by U.S. General **Dwight D. Eisenhower**, the purpose was to protect Middle Eastern **oil** from German Field Marshall Erwin Rommel's Afrika Korps, which was operating in **Egypt** and **Libya**, while laying the groundwork for the invasion of Italy. It was also a response to demands by the **Soviet Union**'s ruler, Josef Stalin, that the Allies create a Western front, which would force the Germans to take troops out of Eastern Europe.

Torch was launched on 8 November 1942 with landings in **Algeria** and **Morocco**. Eisenhower hoped that the government of Axis-allied Vichy **France**, which controlled North Africa, would join the Allies. Instead, there was fierce fighting in some sectors and Eisenhower was compelled to make an agreement with Admiral Jean-François Darlan, the anti-Semitic and fascistic commander of Vichy's armed forces, to terminate the fighting and ensure that the French continued to keep the peace among the Arab tribes. The ensuing uproar in the United States and **Great Britain** almost cost Eisenhower his job, but the Allied rear was protected. Darlan's assassination by a French monarchist on 24 December also eased the political situation for Eisenhower. Allied pressure gradually forced the Vichyists to liberalize, and Free French leader Charles de Gaulle took control of North Africa in mid-1943. Torch was followed by the **Tunisia Campaign**, which defeated the Axis powers in North Africa on 13 May 1943.

Torch and the subsequent fighting had been the first wartime command of Eisenhower's career, and it marked the first European battles for U.S. troops. Neither did well at first, but the experience proved invaluable in preparing Eisenhower and the U.S. Army for the invasions of Europe.

OPERATION WIZARD. Central Intelligence Agency (CIA) operation launched in **Congo** in August 1960 to destabilize and bring down Prime Minister **Patrice Lumumba**, whom the CIA had concluded was either a Communist or, more likely, an unstable dupe whom the **Soviet Union** would use to take control of Congo. CIA Director **Allen Dulles** ordered station chief **Larry Devlin** to bribe government officials to oppose Lumumba, pay reporters to write articles defaming him, and pay others to organize demonstrations against him. Operation Wizard was suspended by Dulles' order to Devlin to kill Lumumba, which Devlin did not carry out, and by Lumumba's removal from power following a coup by Joseph-Désiré Mobutu (**Mobutu Sese Seko**). *See also* CONGO CRISIS.

ORGANIZATION OF AFRICAN UNITY (OAU). Organization that was the culmination of the Pan-Africanist dream of a United States of Africa. The OAU was made reality on 25 May 1963 thanks in significant part to the efforts of **Kwame Nkrumah** of **Ghana**, who envisioned himself as its president, but concern over his ambition led to the selection of **Ethiopia**'s Emperor **Haile Selassie** as first chairman, because of his international renown as an advocate for international collective action in the years leading up to World War II. The OAU's headquarters were also located in the Ethiopian capital, Addis Ababa, instead of Ghana. Despite the hopes of Pan-Africanists, the OAU quickly transformed itself into a regional interest group. Fifty-two of Africa's 53 nations were members when it was disbanded and reconstituted as the **African Union** (AU) in 2002: **Morocco** withdrew in 1983 following the 1982 admission of the Sahrawi Arab Democratic Republic, both of which claim to be the legitimate government of the former Spanish Sahara.

The OAU created numerous committees and agencies charged with improving the continent's economic, social, and cultural life. It also created the African Development Bank to augment and extend the African work of the **World Bank**. The OAU's most important and successful goal was bringing together the continent's governments to drive out the European colonial powers and end **apartheid** in **South Africa** through moral suasion, economic and political sanctions, recognition of liberation movements and, if necessary, material support for guerilla forces. The OAU also settled border disputes as nations decolonized, mediated intra-African conflicts, and kept nations talking with one another through annual meetings of heads of state and biannual foreign ministers' meetings.

As Africa decolonized, the OAU's most sacrosanct principles became the inviability of arbitrarily drawn colonial borders and the sovereignty of member states. Scholars have debated whether an opportunity was missed when African nations did not redraw their boundaries to bring together divided tribes, separate peoples with historical rivalries or animosities, and make nations more economically viable, but the problems of how sweeping the changes should have been and the possibility of war by countries that lost territory, resources, or population has led most scholars to conclude that African leaders were correct not to tamper with their borders. The principle of state sovereignty (noninterference in national domestic behavior) sometimes degenerated into allowing despots to treat their subjects as prey rather than citizens, leading to economic disaster, dictatorship, and mass murder. The OAU's nadir came when **Idi Amin** of **Uganda** and **Mengistu Haile Mariam** of **Ethiopia**, two of Africa's most brutal dictators, took the helm as chairman in 1975–76 and 1983–84 respectively. Amin's elevation was made even worse in the eyes of the United States and much of the rest of the world when he received a rousing welcome at the 1977 OAU Summit in Gabon. President **Ronald W. Reagan** personally interceded with President Shehu Shagari of **Nigeria** to ask for help in stoping Mengistu's elevation, but Shagari said it was impossible, causing a dramatic worsening in relations between the two countries. This failure to act against dictators at such a basic and seemingly simple level led many to dismiss the OAU as the "dictators' club." **Julius Nyerere** of **Tanzania** denounced what he considered to be the OAU's pandering to Amin in

1978 when Uganda invaded Tanzania, saying that for African leaders, "Blackness has become a certificate to kill with impunity." Competition to hold OAU heads of state meetings led countries to spend hundreds of millions of dollars for conference facilities that were unnecessary once the conference had ended.

With the rise of a new generation of African leaders in the new millennium many of whom considered the OAU a vestige of an African past marred by dictatorship, poverty, and ineffectuality, the OAU itself issued a report in October 2001 that accepted the criticism that its key purpose had become to protect the interests of African heads of state and that the principle of non-interference had prevented African states from taking action against mass killing, kleptocracy, economic disaster, and the fight against diseases such as HIV/**AIDS**. To address these problems, the OAU was dissolved on 9 July 2002 and replaced that day with the AU. Its final chairman was President **Thabo Mbeki** of South Africa. *See also* DIVESTMENT (DISINVESTMENT) FROM SOUTH AFRICA MOVEMENT.

– P –

PACT OF MUTUAL COOPERATION. *See* BAGHDAD PACT.

PATON, ALAN (1903–1988). South African writer whose novel, *Cry, the Beloved Country* (1948), introduced many Americans to South African racism. Paton was a founder of the Liberal Party in 1953 and was its leader until the party was banned in 1968.

PEACE CORPS. Quasi-missionary, voluntary organization created by President **John F. Kennedy** to provide developmental assistance to underdeveloped countries. People and governments in the third world were inspired by the enthusiastic idealism of the organization's young participants, by the way that they lived among and under the same living conditions as the people they were assisting, and by the organization's rigorously apolitical stance. The program's success pushed and pulled most developed countries into creating similar organizations, and helped make Kennedy a hero throughout the third world.

The genesis of the Peace Corps was a late-night, off-the-cuff promise that Kennedy made in November 1960, days before the presidential election. The idea received immediate favorable press coverage and a still more favorable response from young people. Kennedy made the Peace Corps a foreign policy priority and pushed it through Congress on 22 September 1961. Its goals were to provide trained manpower to the third world, promote understanding of Americans among people in the third world, and promote understanding of the third world among Americans. In its first year, 1961–62, 2,940 mostly young people were sent out to the field, with the number growing every year until its peak in 1966 with 15,556 volunteers. Of these, between one-quarter and one-third were sent to Africa every year. Despite efforts to recruit people with technical skills that would assist in development, most volunteers in the early years were teachers and most African governments requested teachers.

Vice President **Lyndon B. Johnson** and Secretary of State **Dean Rusk** played significant roles in keeping the Peace Corps independent of the foreign policy and **foreign aid** bureaus, and its first director, Kennedy's brother-in-law Sargent Shriver, fought all efforts by the State Department and the **Central Intelligence Agency** (CIA) to co-opt volunteers.

Although rigidly apolitical, the Peace Corps was used by President Kennedy to improve international perceptions of the U.S. He used it as a tool to improve relations with the Leftist government of **Kwame Nkrumah** in **Ghana**, and to wean **Ahmed Sékou Touré** of **Guinea** away from the **Soviet Union** to a U.S.-friendly neutralist position in the **cold war**.

By the 1970s, the Peace Corps was no longer an important component of U.S. foreign policy, and youthful enthusiasm for the organization waned. Volunteers in the field dropped below 10,000 in 1970, and never again rose to that level. Its composition also changed, as older people with technical and engineering skills joined. In his 2002 State of the Union Address, President **George W. Bush** called for increasing the number of volunteers in the field to 14,000, but was unable to gain congressional support. In 2008, there were 8,079 volunteers and the budget was approximately $335 million. By 2008, over 187,000 volunteers had been sent throughout the world, with one-third having worked in Africa.

PEACEKEEPING. The United States has played a significant role in supporting Middle East peacekeeping, but has played a comparatively minimal and even negative role in sub-Saharan African peacekeeping. Following the **Suez Crisis** of 1956, **United Nations** (UN) special envoy **Ralph Bunche**, an **African American**, created what became the classic notion of peacekeeping, under which UN forces would be posted along a border, separating the belligerents.

In sub-Saharan Africa during the **Congo Crisis**, approximately 20,000 UN troops were sent with an expanded mission to keep the peace. Prime Minister **Patrice Lumumba** of **Congo** and the **Soviet Union** demanded that the *Opération des Nations Unies au Congo*/UN Operation in the Congo (ONUC) expand its mission to use military force against illegal secessionist governments in **Katanga** and South Kasai, but UN Secretary-General **Dag Hammarskjöld** refused because the Security Council did not expand ONUC's mandate. When Lumumba was overthrown in September 1960, ONUC found itself protecting him from his opponents until he snuck past Congolese army lines in a failed attempt to join a rebellion, which ultimately led to his execution. Following Hammarskjöld's September 1961 death while on a Congolese peacekeeping mission, the Security Council expanded ONUC's mission in late 1962 and UN officials took an even broader construction of the mandate in order to justify attacking Katanga and forcing its reintegration with Congo. The U.S. government of **John F. Kennedy** was unhappy about the expanded mission but felt compelled to support it.

Bitter **cold war** differences between the West and the Soviet Bloc over the Congo mission kept the UN from launching further peacekeeping missions in sub-Saharan Africa until the cold war's end. African regional organizations such as the **Organization of African Unity** (OAU) likewise were usually unable to act because of ideological differences. The post–cold war years saw a renewal of commitment to peacekeeping operations around the world and particularly in Africa. U.S. support, strong at first with the 1992 U.S.-led UN intervention in **Somalia**, all but disappeared after the Battle of Mogadishu in which 18 U.S. soldiers were killed. The administration of President **Bill Clinton** responded with **Presidential Decision Directive 25** (PDD-25), which dramatically limited U.S. participation in peacekeeping. This policy was carried out in **Rwanda** during the genocide, when the U.S. sought to remove all peacekeepers as it began, but settled for cutting the mission's size by 90 percent. The Clinton administration also offered only minimal support for the Economic Community of West African States Monitoring Group (ECOMOG) peacekeeping missions led by **Nigeria** in **Liberia** and **Sierra Leone**, instead impelling the Sierra Leonean government to accept the terrorist Revolutionary United Front (RUF) in its government.

In February 2000, the UN intervened in the latest Congo crisis by sending the *Mission de l'Organisation des Nations Unies en République démocratique du Congo*/UN Mission in the Democratic Republic of Congo (MONUC) to keep the peace. It became the UN's largest mission, with 17,000 troops in April 2008. MONUC reportedly brought stability to some parts of Congo, helped disarm warring factions, ran democratic elections, and assisted with reconnaissance, but UN Secretary General **Kofi Annan** admitted in December 2006, shortly before leaving office, that peacekeepers from **Morocco** had been involved in widespread sexual abuse. In April 2008, an 18-month British Broadcasting Corporation (BBC) investigation revealed that Pakistani and Indian peacekeepers had provided arms to rebel fighters in Congo and engaged in illicit gold, ivory, and drug trades with often brutal local militias including the "Hutu power" **Interahamwe** militia, which had committed the Rwandan Genocide. UN insiders told the BBC that the UN prevented them from continuing its investigations for political reasons having to do with fear of alienating two of the organization's largest providers of peacekeepers. Investigators with the Save the Children United Kingdom **nongovernmental organization** (NGO) found that peacekeepers had raped children and forced them into prostitution and pornography in exchange for food or protection in Ivory Coast and southern **Sudan**. Other abuses have occurred in **Kenya**, Liberia, and Burundi. A 2008 UN investigation of its $5 billion peacekeeping contracts found fraud involved in contracts worth $310 million of the $1.6 billion that it vetted. *See also* AFRICAN UNION (AU); MOBUTU SESE SEKO; RWANDA, GENOCIDE IN; TSHOMBE, MOÏSE.

PLAYER, GARY (1935–). Golfer and philanthropist from **South Africa**. Player won 24 Professional Golfers' Association (PGA) tournaments, 25th best of all time, including the PGA's "Grand Slam" tournaments a total of nine times. Player has been a sometimes controversial figure in South Africa and internationally. His 1966 autobiography quotes him as saying that he supported his country's racist **apartheid** system, although he claimed to have been misquoted by his ghostwriter. Thereafter, he publicly criticized the apartheid regime and threatened to withdraw from South African golf tournaments if blacks were not allowed to play. His Player Foundation has raised over $25 million since 1983 for the education of underprivileged children in South Africa and around the world. In 2007 Player was criticized by former President **Nelson Mandela** and Archbishop **Desmond Tutu** for building a golf course in Myanmar (Burma), and Player defended himself by claiming that work had begun during 2002 when it appeared that the government was easing its repressive rule.

POINT FOUR. Technical assistance program for the third world recommended by President **Harry S. Truman** in his 20 January 1949 Inaugural Address. The name Point Four comes from Truman calling technical assistance the fourth major focus of U.S. foreign policy. Point Four launched the idea that U.S. assistance to the third world was a moral imperative and that the U.S had the technical ability and social, economic, and political understanding of how to make poor nations stable, prosperous, and democratic.

Truman accompanied Point Four with a push toward encouraging Western European powers to decolonize. These efforts were derailed the following year by the Korean War, in which the U.S. needed the strong support of its Western European allies in the **United Nations** (UN), and by the U.S. Congress, which refused to fund most of Point Four. Truman privately admitted that the program was dead on 6 July 1950, 11 days after the war's outbreak.

PORTUGAL. Western European colonial power that refused to decolonize in the face of armed resistance movements until a military coup in August 1974. Portuguese ruler Antonió Salazar and his successor, Marcello Caetano, refused to give up their African colonies, Guinea–Bissau, **Angola**, and **Mozambique**, because they considered colonies prestigious sources of national pride and reminders of Portugal's historical role as the first colonial power in the 15th century.

Mozambique and Angola were each also home to several hundred thousand Portuguese colonists, and the Portuguese feared that the **Soviet Union** would fill the vacuum if they left.

President **Dwight D. Eisenhower** had maintained strong relations with the Portuguese because the U.S. military required access to Portugal's Azores Islands sea and airbases, but **John F. Kennedy** began his administration by voting against Portugal in the **United Nations** (UN) on a resolution dealing with its colonial policy. He could not maintain his support for decolonization because the Portuguese used the Azores as leverage, and in 1963, Kennedy told the Portuguese ambassador that the early UN vote had been a mistake. Relations with Portugal improved under President **Richard M. Nixon**, who had concluded that Portuguese rule over Mozambique and Angola was assured for the long term, so the U.S. should make the best of it by working in desultory fashion behind the scenes to encourage Portuguese decolonization. Instead of stability, the huge number of troops that Portugal was forced to send to Mozambique, Angola, and Guinea–Bissau, the steady death toll, the tremendous expense, and the seeming impossibility of victory finally led the Portuguese army to overthrow the government on 25 April 1974 and announce that it would cease hostilities in Africa preparatory to granting its colonies independence. Secretary of State **Henry Kissinger** was stunned by the coup and its consequences and strove to ensure that Communists did not take over Portugal. Seeing the possibility that the U.S. could stop the Communist-led and Soviet-backed *Movimento Popular de Libertação de Angola*/Popular Movement for the Liberation of Angola (MPLA) from taking power, Kissinger ordered the **Central Intelligence Agency** (CIA) to work with **Zaïre** and **Zambia** in support of two competing non-Communist guerilla movements, the *Frente Nacional de Libertação de Angola*/National Liberation Front of Angola (FNLA) and the *União Nacional para a Independência Total de Angola*/National Union for the Total Independence of Angola (UNITA), apparently in concert with **South Africa**. *See also* MACHEL, SAMORA; NETO, AGUSTINHO; OPERATION IAFEATURE; ROBERTO, HOLDEN; SAVIMBI, JONAS.

POWELL, COLIN (1937–). U.S. soldier and statesman who was the first **African American** to serve as national security adviser

(1987–89, under **Ronald W. Reagan**), chairman of the joint chiefs of staff (1989–93, under **George H.W. Bush** and **Bill Clinton**), and secretary of state (2001–05, under **George W. Bush**). Although Africa was not a top priority, Powell had greater personal interest in the continent than any prior secretary of state. He admitted that his interest in Africa stemmed in part from his heritage, but always added that U.S. interest was his responsibility.

During George W. Bush's campaign for president, he said that Africa was not a personal or national priority, but once elected, Powell encouraged the president to become engaged in Africa. As secretary of state-designate, Powell signaled his interest in Africa by holding his first State Department meeting with foreign service officers from the Bureau of African Affairs. As secretary, he pushed for greater foreign aid for Africa and assistance in fighting HIV/**AIDS**, and he also took interest in local issues, using U.S. government resources to help **Rwanda** find officials who had overseen that country's 1994 genocide, taking the lead among world political figures on 9 September 2004 by being the first to call **Sudan**'s **Darfur** policy genocide, supporting U.S. engagement with Sudan that led to the 2005 treaty ending the civil war against southern Sudan, and unsuccessfully pressuring President **Thabo Mbeki** of **South Africa** to sanction President **Robert Mugabe** of **Zimbabwe** for his anti-democratic and economically disastrous policies. *See also* AFRICAN AFFAIRS, STATE DEPARTMENT BUREAU OF; RWANDA, GENOCIDE IN; TERRORISM.

PRESIDENTIAL DECISION DIRECTIVE 25 (PDD-25). Revised U.S. policy for multilateral peace operations ordered by President **Bill Clinton** in the wake of the 3 October 1993 Battle of Mogadishu fiasco in which 18 U.S. soldiers died during a **United Nations** (UN) operation to impose peace on **Somalia**. PDD-25 limited U.S. participation in multilateral **peacekeeping** missions by requiring that policy makers first answer if U.S. interests were at stake, if the situation was a true threat to international peace, if means other than intervention could solve the crisis, and if there was a substantive answer to what specific objective the intervention would achieve. PDD-25 also directed the UN to be more selective in launching peacekeeping missions. Although not officially implemented until May 1994, the Clinton administration followed PDD-25's guidelines during the Rwandan Genocide, which began in April 1994. Thereafter, the United States followed PDD-25 when it refused to intervene during mass murders in Burundi, civil wars in **Sudan** and **Zaïre/Congo**, and a much wider war that grew out of the latter. *See also* AIDEED, MUHAMMAD FARAH; RWANDA, GENOCIDE IN.

– Q –

QADDAFI, MUAMMAR AL- (1942–). Libyan ruler (1969–), whose support for **terrorism** made him the most targeted U.S. enemy in the 1980s and made **Libya** an international pariah state during the 1990s. Qaddafi was a young army officer when he and a band of young followers of **Egypt**'s **Gamal Abdel Nasser** overthrew King Idris I on 1 September 1969. Qaddafi quickly emerged as the leader. When his effort to fulfill Nasser's vision of a Pan-Arab state failed, Qaddafi turned his attention to support for international terror and creating a Pan-African state. He purchased massive amounts of modern arms from the **Soviet Union** for his 55,000-man army, with estimates of his expenditures as high as $20 billion, but failed in attempts to acquire nuclear-weapons technology from the Soviets, who had concluded that he was dangerously unstable. Qaddafi responded by refusing to allow the Soviets to base their military on Libyan soil. Throughout the 1980s and 1990s, Qaddafi sought to purchase nuclear weapons, but settled for buying a chemical weapons plant from West German businessmen. Among the weapons of mass destruction (WMD) that Libya obtained were large quantities of mustard gas and the precursor chemicals for nerve gas.

In 1979, President **Jimmy Carter**'s State Department put Libya on its first State Sponsors of Terror list, and **Ronald W. Reagan** repeatedly confronted Qaddafi with military force, once reportedly killing his adopted daughter and almost killing him. In sub-Saharan Africa, the Reagan administration provided assistance to the government of **Sudan** against a Libyan-backed invasion in February 1983 and supported **Chad**'s ruler, **Hissene Habré**, to stop Qaddafi's repeated efforts to take control of his country. In August 1987, Qaddafi launched a final Chadian offensive, which Habré repelled with U.S. military assistance, driving the Libyans out of most Chadian territory while capturing thousands of Libyan soldiers and over $1 billion in Soviet armaments.

Many analysts have concluded that Qaddafi responded to U.S. attacks with increased **terrorism** against U.S. and Western targets, culminating in the downing of a passenger airliner over Lockerbie, Scotland, on 21 December 1988, which killed 270. Other analysts argue that Qaddafi and the groups he supported, including Abu Nidal's organization and the Irish Republican Army, were capable of launching such attacks regardless of Reagan's actions. Worldwide sanctions against Libya followed the Lockerbie bombing. Internationally isolated and threatened by Islamist groups that consider his *Green Book* apostasy, Qaddafi turned over for trial two intelligence agents allegedly involved in Lockerbie on 5 April 1999, and one of them was found guilty on 31 January 2001. The world eased sanctions and, following the 11 September attacks, Qaddafi expressed sympathy to the U.S. and began secretly providing Washington with information on Islamist terrorists.

In March 2003, days before the invasion of Iraq, Libyan officials met with officials in the **George W. Bush** administration to discuss dismantling Libya's WMD program. In August, Qaddafi agreed to pay $2.7 billion to the families of the Lockerbie victims and, on 12 September, the **United Nations** (UN) lifted all sanctions. On 19 December, five days after the announcement that U.S. forces had captured Iraq's Saddam Hussein, Libya announced that it was giving up all WMD. The government turned over all weapons, parts, and documents to the U.S. and **Great Britain**, which used the materials to uncover the illegal A.Q. Khan international nuclear weapons supply network. In May 2006, Washington restored full diplomatic relations with Libya and removed it from the State Sponsors of Terrorism list. In March 2008, Qaddafi complained to Bush that the U.S. was not following through with promised economic and political incentives and that the U.S. Congress had passed a January 2008 law that added new economic sanctions against Libya in reaction to additional acts of terrorism. On 31 October, $1.5 billion was added to the fund to compensate all victims.

QUTB, SAYYID (1903?–1966). Philosopher from **Egypt** whose collegiate studies in the United States turned him into a radical Islamist. After studying at Colorado State College of Education (University of Northern Colorado), Sayyid wrote that while attending a student dance, the licentious atmosphere turned him against all things Western and brought him back to the Qur'an, eventually converting him to radical Islam. Author Lawrence Wright researched Sayyid's time in the U.S. and found that the party he attended was put on by a local church and that it was a no alcohol event in a "dry" town.

Qutb joined the Muslim Brotherhood after his return to Egypt and became the editor of its newspaper and its propaganda chief. Qutb supported the coup against King **Farouk** but turned against the secular government of **Gamal Abdel Nasser**. He was imprisoned from 1954–64, arrested again in 1965, and executed 29 August 1966 for leading a movement that sought to assassinate Nasser and other Egyptian leaders. Qutb's teaching about the injustice of Muslim governments that are insufficiently Islamic in orientation and the unending hatred that non-Muslims have for Muslims significantly shaped the Islamist movement and play a key role in **al Qaeda**'s philosophy. Qutb also taught that an Islamic revolutionary vanguard would lead Islam to worldwide victory, another idea adopted by al Qaeda. **Osama bin Laden** attended lectures by Qutb's brother and follower, Muhammad, and al Qaeda second-in-command Ayman al-Zawahiri studied under him. *See also* TERRORISM.

– R –

RAWLINGS, JERRY (1947–). Military ruler (1979, 1981–93) and elected president (1993–2001) of **Ghana**. Rawlings, who is half Scottish, was a charismatic 31-year-old pilot known for his polo-playing skills when he unsuccessfully tried to overthrow the corrupt military government of General Fred Akuffo on 15 May 1979. Although the U.S. government concluded that he was a mentally unstable adventurer, a popular revolution followed that freed Rawlings from prison and made him military ruler. Rawlings ordered the execution of Akuffo and two predecessors, the public whipping of market women accused of price gouging, and the destruction of Accra's market. He then returned to the barracks. Neither the violence nor democratic elections improved Ghana's public morality or economy, leading Rawlings to overthrow the government again in 1981 and keep power. He ruled as an austere socialist acolyte of former President **Kwame Nkrumah**, but continued economic crisis forced Rawlings to follow **International Monetary Fund** (IMF) liberalization policies. The ensuing economic boom transformed Rawlings into a committed capitalist but created a backlash that led him to jail former allies, put down attempted coups and follow them with executions, and perhaps play a role in the unsolved murder of three supreme court justices who opposed the changes. In 1993, Rawlings allowed elections, which he won, and President **Bill Clinton** proclaimed him a leader of the "African Renaissance." He retired in 2001 and opposition leader John Kufuor defeated Rawlings' hand-chosen heir. Rawlings allowed the result to stand, one of the first instances of a democratically elected opposition coming to power in Africa. Rawlings has at times bridled in retirement, periodically hinting that he might launch a third coup.

REAGAN, RONALD W. (1911–2004). U.S. actor, politician, and president (1981–89), whose hawkish foreign policy played a significant role in precipitating the collapse of the **Soviet Union**. Reagan's Africa policy was a part of a multi-pronged assault on Soviet power including tough moralistic rhetoric, a massive military buildup, and support for efforts to defeat far-flung outposts of the Soviet Empire that came to be known as the **Reagan Doctrine**. Reagan applied his doctrine to Africa, successfully pushing Congress to repeal the **Clark Amendment**, which outlawed U.S. support for guerillas in **Angola**, and by putting economic and military pressure on the ruler of **Libya**, **Muammar Qaddafi**. To counter Qaddafi's ambitions, Reagan provided military support to **Sudan** and **Chad** and border reconnaissance information to **Egypt**, conducted military exercises off the Libyan coast that prompted armed confrontations with Libyan warplanes and warships, and bombed Libya in retaliation for a Libyan-backed terrorist attack on a nightclub frequented by U.S. soldiers. The conflict with Libya took on a personal aspect as Reagan and Qaddafi developed a deep hatred for one another. The **Central Intel-**

ligence Agency (CIA) reported that Qaddafi sent an assassination team to the U.S. to kill Reagan, and Reagan almost killed Qaddafi when U.S. warplanes bombed his tent during the retaliatory strike.

Reagan's Southern Africa policy, formulated by Assistant Secretary of State for African Affairs Chester Crocker, was meant to piggyback on his anti-Soviet strategy. The policy called for pressure on the Communist government of Angola to force it to negotiate a power-sharing agreement with rebel leader **Jonas Savimbi**'s *União Nacional para a Independência Total de Angola*/National Union for the Total Independence of Angola (UNITA) or even to overthrow the government, and to force it to withdraw soldiers from **Cuba** that propped it up. In exchange, the U.S. would pressure **South Africa** to grant Southwest Africa (**Namibia**) its independence. The last part of the policy called for what Crocker called "**Constructive Engagement**" with South Africa, treating it as a valued anti-Communist ally rather than a pariah state while working behind the scenes with quiet diplomacy to express U.S. abhorrence for **apartheid** and to persuade the government to end repression and grant its black population civil rights. The policy bore some fruit, as South Africa dismantled so-called petty apartheid, the sort of segregation used in the Jim Crow American South, and the South Africans ended pass laws, which required blacks to carry internal passports. Nonetheless, the central apartheid policy of "separate development" through the creation of autonomous or independent *Bantustans* (so-called tribal homelands) was strengthened.

U.S. public opinion began to turn against Constructive Engagement beginning on the day before Thanksgiving in 1984 when protesters led by **TransAfrica** held a sit-in at the South African embassy to protest apartheid. The sit-in movement spread to colleges across the U.S. and was augmented by student demands that their colleges divest from their portfolios stock in corporations doing business with South Africa. The pressure hit its peak with passage over Reagan's veto of the **Comprehensive Anti-Apartheid Act** (CAAA) on 2 October 1986.

On 22 December 1988, the U.S. helped conclude the **New York Accords**, which created the roadmap to Namibia's independence in 1990 and removal of Cuban troops from Angola the following year. Historians debate whether primary credit should go to a combination of Reagan's policies and South African intervention, or to Cuba's role in supporting the Angolan government against South Africa's intervention, with most giving credit to Cuba.

REAGAN DOCTRINE. Name given by newspaper columnist Charles Krauthammer to President **Ronald W. Reagan**'s policy of stopping and rolling back the worldwide advance of the **Soviet Union.** In Africa, the doctrine was applied in **Angola**, where assistance was given to **Jonas Savimbi**'s *União Nacional para a Independência Total de Angola*/National Union for the Total Independence of Angola (UNITA), which forced the Soviets to provide billions of dollars in military assistance and **Cuba** to assist with 57,000 combat troops. Conservative Washington leaders such as Senator **Jesse Helms** pushed to expand the doctrine to include support for **Mozambique**'s *Resistência Nacional Moçambicana*/Mozambican National Resistance (RENAMO), but Assistant Secretary of State for African Affairs Chester Crocker persuaded Reagan to ignore Helms because of RENAMO's unsavory reputation and Mozambican President **Samora Machel**'s movement away from communism in the face of economic disaster brought on by his economic policies and RENAMO's attacks on the nation's infrastructure. *See also* AFRICAN AFFAIRS, STATE DEPARTMENT BUREAU OF.

REFUGEES. The United States allows the admission of political refugees, who have fled their home country because they fear persecution on the grounds of race, nationality, religion, sex, political opinions, membership or participation in social groups, or for social activities. In 1996, a Togolese woman, Fauziya Kassindja, was accepted for asylum to protect her from undergoing forced female circumcision. Since passage of the Refugee Act of 1980, more than 200,000 African refugees have been admitted to the U.S. for permanent resettlement. The largest groups are from **Somalia** (over 65,000) and **Ethiopia** (over 43,000), with significant numbers also coming from **Sudan, Liberia, Congo (Zaïre), Eritrea, Rwanda, Sierra Leone,** and **Angola**. In recent years, the program has grown more diverse, with refugees from 29 African nations admitted to the U.S. In 2008, a limit of 16,000 refugees may be admitted from Africa, with relatives of previous refugees receiving priority.

RESOLUTION 242, UNITED NATIONS SECURITY COUNCIL. A broad-based plan for peace in the Middle East that was passed on 22 November 1967 following the **Arab–Israeli War of 1967**. The Resolution calls for a peace treaty and concessions from each side. Arab states would recognize **Israel**, its right to exist within internationally recognized borders, and its freedom of navigation on international waterways controlled by Arab states. Israel would withdraw from "territories" (purposely ambiguous as to whether this meant all territories) occupied during the war. Both sides would agree to just treatment of **refugees**. Resolution 242 was the cornerstone for many of the comprehensive Middle East peace plans that followed.

RESTORE HOPE, OPERATION. *See* OPERATION RESTORE HOPE.

RHODESIA. Colonial name for **Zimbabwe** (Southern Rhodesia) and **Zambia** (Northern Rhodesia). Rhodesia was also Zimbabwe's name during the illegal white-ruled government of 1965–78.

RICE, CONDOLEEZZA (1954–). First **African American** woman to serve as national security adviser (2001–05 under **George W. Bush**) and first African American woman to serve as secretary of state (2005–2009, also under Bush). As Bush's national security adviser, Rice's role in U.S. Africa policy seems to have been minimal except for Rice's reported role with **Darfur** in 2004 after the government of **Sudan** launched genocide against its black populace. Bush, who had written "Not on my watch" on a report dealing with President **Bill Clinton**'s failed handling of the Rwandan Genocide, was reportedly prepared to intervene militarily in Sudan when Rice persuaded him not to, arguing that Muslims' reaction to a U.S. attack against another Muslim country following the invasions of Afghanistan and Iraq could be disastrous. Instead of invasion, the administration spoke out against Sudan with Secretary of State **Colin Powell** and Bush publicly accusing Sudan of committing genocide, and the U.S. leading diplomatic efforts to sanction Sudan.

As secretary of state, Rice appeared to leave Africa to the State Department's African Affairs Bureau until her final year in office. In February 2008, Rice forcefully and successfully pressured President

Mwai Kibaki of **Kenya** to make a "genuine" power-sharing agreement with opposition leader Raila Odinga following the disputed December 2007 election. After presidential elections in **Zimbabwe** that were allegedly stolen by President **Robert Mugabe**, Rice called Mugabe a "disgrace" to Zimbabwe and all of Africa, and said that the July 2008 runoff was a "sham." She unsuccessfully called on the **African Union** (AU) and the **United Nations** (UN) to issue sanctions against his government. *See also* AFRICAN AFFAIRS, STATE DEPARTMENT BUREAU OF; RWANDA, GENOCIDE IN.

ROBERTO, HOLDEN (1923–2007). Guerilla leader who sought the liberation of **Angola** from **Portugal**, but spent most of his life in **Congo (Zaïre)**. Roberto founded Angola's first black–nationalist movement, which became the *Frente Nacional de Libertação de Angola/* National Front for the Liberation of Angola (FNLA) in 1956. It was dominated by Roberto's Bakongo tribe. On 15 March 1961, Roberto sent his forces into Angola for the first time, attacking farm settlements on the northern frontier and killing every person, black or white, that they encountered. Over 1,000 whites died and thousands of blacks. The Portuguese responded with a brutal counterinsurgency that killed perhaps 20,000 suspected supporters and others who were in the way. Roberto became a significant figure in Congo, and to solidify his position, he divorced his wife and married the sister-in-law of Congolese ruler Joseph-Désiré Mobutu (**Mobutu Sese Seko**). The **Central Intelligence Agency** (CIA) began to provide Roberto with limited funding, $50,000 per year, starting in 1961.

Competing with Roberto in the war against the Portuguese were **Agostinho Neto**'s *Movimento Popular de Libertação de Angola/*Popular Movement for the Liberation of Angola (MPLA), a Communist-led party, and **Jonas Savimbi**'s *União Nacional para a Independência Total de Angola/*National Union for the Total Independence of Angola (UNITA), which broke away from the FNLA in 1966 due to its tribal bias and Roberto's refusal to join his men in the field. In June 1974, following the collapse of the Portuguese empire, Roberto's forces began to receive training and weapons in Zaïre from **China** while the CIA raised the FNLA's funding to $10,000 per month and provided it with mercenaries and training assistance. In January 1975, the Portuguese announced that they would grant Angola independence on 11 November. A scramble for power ensued and outside intervention increased dramatically. The United States funneled millions of dollars in assistance to Roberto as part of the CIA's **Operation IAFEATURE** as did **South Africa**. The aid was sent through Mobutu, who appropriated much of it for his own army and sold another share on the black market. The CIA noted that Roberto was racist, ethnocentric, venal, and incompetent, and had last set foot in Angola in 1956. By November, Roberto had returned to Angola. He proclaimed on 5 November that his forces would fight their way into Luanda, the capital, by 10 November, and take control of independent Angola the next day. On 10 November, less than 20 miles from Luanda, Roberto refused to listen to his South African and CIA advisers, ordering his men and 1,200 Zaïrian paratroopers into an obvious trap in Quifangondo Valley. Cannons that were located on hills above the valley and manned by troops from **Cuba** slaughtered Roberto's men while Mobutu's fled at the sound of the first shots. Roberto's army was annihilated and he returned to Congo. Thereafter, Roberto showed no inclination to leave his Zaïrian villa and the FNLA was a negligible force. In 1991, Roberto ran for president of Angola and received 2.1 percent of the vote.

ROOSEVELT, FRANKLIN DELANO (1882–1945). U.S. politician and president (1933–45). Roosevelt was a strong anti-colonialist who believed that colonizers exploited colonies while giving little back. Roosevelt opposed the Italian invasion of **Ethiopia** in 1935–36, but supported a ban on arms sales to both belligerents, which harmed the poorly supplied Ethiopians while having minimal impact on the Italians. After the Italian victory, he lifted the embargo in hope that doing so would induce Benito Mussolini not to join Germany's Adolf Hitler. Roosevelt also hoped that the colony could be a home for displaced German Jews.

Before the U.S. entered World War II, Roosevelt met with Prime Minister Winston Churchill of **Great Britain** from 9–12 August 1941 to discuss the postwar world order, the outline for which was published on 14 August and known as the **Atlantic Charter**. Roosevelt worried that postwar disputes over colonies could lead to war among Western European nations. To avoid this, he pressured Churchill into accepting Article 3 of the Charter, under which the U.S. and Great

Britain agreed to "respect the right of all people to choose the form of government under which they will live; and they wish to see sovereign rights and self-government restored to those who have been forcibly deprived of them." Churchill later reneged, claming that it referred only to those nations conquered by the Axis powers. To fulfill the Charter's colonial sections, Roosevelt created the Advisory Committee on Post-War Foreign Policy. Its members concluded that Africans did not want independence; instead, they proposed that a world body take over the world's colonies in a system similar to the League of Nations' mandate system but with set dates for independence as the U.S. had done in the Philippines. To push **Great Britain** toward such a system, he quietly urged **African American** newspaper publishers to direct "pitiless publicity" against the British Empire. Roosevelt considered **France** to be even more exploitive than the British, and he tried to use France's weak position from its defeat by the Germans to force it to give up its colonies.

At the Casablanca Conference in **Morocco** during 1943, Roosevelt met with Sultan **Muhammad V**, outraging French leaders, and he may have implied to Muhammad that he would support Moroccan independence after the war. He also met with President Edwin Barclay of **Liberia**. Shortly before he died, Roosevelt told Prime Minister **Jan Smuts** of **South Africa** that he opposed all permanent mandates such as South Africa had been granted by the League of Nations over Southwest Africa (**Namibia**), but international pressure forced him to back down on his colonial policy, and he sought to apply it only to colonies held by defeated Italy and Japan.

In international economic affairs, Roosevelt sought to avoid the disastrous worldwide depression that followed World War I. The mechanisms he proposed at a July 1944 international conference in Bretton Woods, New Hampshire were the **World Bank** and the **International Monetary Fund** (IMF). Both were established after his death, on 27 December 1945.

ROOSEVELT, THEODORE (1858–1919). U.S. politician, vice president (1901), and president (1901–09). In 1904, Roosevelt threatened to invade **Morocco** to compel its government to turn over Ion Perdicaris, who had been kidnapped by guerilla chieftain Mulai Ahmed er Raisuli (Perdicaris was believed to be a Greek American citizen but was subsequently found to have forfeited his citizenship). Roosevelt sent seven warships to the coast of Morocco and had Secretary of State John Hay announce that U.S. policy was "Perdicaris alive or Raisuli dead." The Moroccan government obtained his release.

In 1908, **African American** leader **Booker T. Washington** persuaded Roosevelt to meet with a delegation from **Liberia** to discuss the country's economic crisis, which threatened its continued independence. Afterward, Roosevelt sent a delegation to Liberia to assess what could be done to restore the country to solvency. In order to keep the Europeans at bay, Roosevelt ordered three warships to accompany the delegation and to remain until the group had finished.

After his retirement as president, Roosevelt led a huge safari accompanied by many newspapermen into the heart of Africa. Breathless stories about Roosevelt's exploits, the prodigious number of animals that he killed for museums, and the customs of the African peoples he encountered excited Americans' interest in Africa.

RUSK, DEAN (1909–1994). American diplomat, president of the Rockefeller Foundation, and secretary of state (1961–69). Rusk grew up in impoverished and segregated Cherokee County, Georgia, which he believed provided him insight into life in the third world. Rusk's experience at the Rockefeller Foundation gave him intimate knowledge of **modernization theory** and broad-based development planning. As secretary of state, Rusk believed that the U.S. should defer to the former colonial powers in Africa because of their more intimate knowledge and better contacts with African governments, and because he wanted to avoid overextending Washington's power. Rusk's perspective on sub-Saharan Africa came through clearly during the 1960–65 **Congo Crisis** when he chided the ambassador from **Belgium** for Western Europe's refusal to send troops to put down the rebellion, calling the situation "above all their responsibility." Nonetheless, he was instrumental in encouraging President **John F. Kennedy** to vote against **Portugal** in a March 1961 **United Nations** (UN) resolution calling for independence for **Angola**. Rusk also played a significant role in persuading President Kennedy to promise **Ghana's** President **Kwame Nkrumah** that Washington would assist in funding the **Volta River Dam** project and then, on 5 December 1961, to go forward with this assistance despite Nkrumah's subsequent attacks against Kennedy and the U.S. as Ghana moved much closer to the **Soviet Union**. Rusk argued that the impact from aborting the dam would be a disaster for U.S.–Africa relations akin to what followed President **Dwight D. Eisenhower**'s refusal to fund **Egypt**'s **Aswan High Dam** under similar circumstances. Rusk was criticized for never visiting Africa during his eight-year tenure as secretary of state, but explained that he could find no formula for visiting a few countries that would not antagonize the rest of the continent.

In the Middle East, Rusk sought closer ties to **Gamal Abdel Nasser**'s Egypt through provision of **foreign aid**, and in June 1962, the U.S. government's Food for Peace program began providing massive amounts of assistance, spending tens of millions of dollars and feeding approximately 40 percent of the population. Nasser accepted the largesse but announced to the Egyptian people that the U.S. could "throw your aid into the Red Sea!" Congress responded by dramatically cutting assistance to Egypt, ignoring Rusk's testimony in support. Despite his hope of working with Nasser, Rusk deeply resented his often brutal anti-American rhetoric and considered him unstable because of his constant desire to play to the emotions of Arab crowds. In May 1967, when Nasser illegally blocked the Strait of Tiran from use by **Israel**, Rusk sought to put together an international coalition that would force open the blockade, but received almost no support. He also conferred with regional actors and the Soviets, counseling restraint, and believed that he had such assurance from the Israelis, which he transmitted to the Soviets. When Israel attacked Egypt on 5 June, beginning the **Arab–Israeli War of 1967**, the Soviets activated the Hot Line with Washington for the first time and Nasser broke relations with the U.S. Rusk successfully convinced the Soviets that the U.S. had no foreknowledge of the invasion. Rusk played an important role in drafting UN Security Council Resolution 242, a broad framework for Middle East peace that was approved on 22 November 1967 with the concurrence of Egypt and Israel.

Domestically, Rusk came to the assistance of African diplomats who could not find a barber in the segregated greater Washington, D.C., area by allowing them to have their hair cut in his office by State Department barbers. He was the first Kennedy administration official to testify for the administration's 1963 civil rights bill, which was supported and welcomed by African leaders. *See also* RESOLUTION

242, UNITED NATIONS SECURITY COUNCIL; WILLIAMS, G. MENNEN "SOAPY."

RWANDA. Central African nation, whose "Hutu Power" government tried to exterminate its Tutsi population beginning in April 1994. Rwanda is now a leading U.S. ally following the July 1994 overthrow of the "Hutu Power" government *génocidaires* by the Tutsi-dominated *Front Patriotique Rwandaise*/Rwandan Patriotic Front (RPF). Although a colony of **Belgium**, Rwanda had fallen into **France**'s sphere of influence following independence, and the U.S. had minimal interest there, as in most of Francophone Africa. This changed with the genocide, although the administration of President **Bill Clinton** did its best not to become involved, even trying to kill a **United Nations** (UN) **peacekeeping** mission that was protecting Tutsi and moderate Hutus. After the RPF overthrew the government following the deaths of 947,000, the U.S. sent millions of dollars of assistance to help **refugees**, ironically assisting Hutus who remained under the control of *génocidaires* who had taken over camps from international relief agencies. When **Mobutu Sese Seko** of **Zaïre** (**Congo**) refused or was unable to stop Hutu attacks on Rwanda from the refugee camps, Rwanda's President **Paul Kagame** along with President **Yoweri Museveni** of **Uganda** combined forces to overthrow him. They installed **Laurent-Désiré Kabila** as president, but when he turned on them, the Congolese war turned into a much wider war, with nine nations sending troops and even former allies Rwanda and Uganda fighting against one another.

The U.S. ultimately began to provide significant **foreign aid** and investment to the Rwandan government, and supplanted both France and Belgium as the dominant foreign interests in Rwanda's economy. Kagame became a strong U.S. ally, whom Clinton called a leader of the "African Renaissance," because of his efforts to reconcile ethnic division in Rwanda and turn it into a regional banking and high tech center. Kagame has said that his goal is to turn Rwanda into the "Singapore of Africa." *See also* INTERAHAMWE; RWANDA, GENOCIDE IN.

RWANDA, GENOCIDE IN. Government-sponsored genocide of **Rwanda**'s Tutsi population in 1994. Ethnic cleansing by the "Hutu

Power" government, especially by its **Interahamwe** militia, and civil war with the Tutsi-dominated *Front Patriotique Rwandaise*/Rwandan Patriotic Front (RPF) led to **United Nations** (UN) intervention with a **peacekeeping** force in 1993.

In January 1994, a high-ranking Rwandan official told the UN commander, General Roméo Dallaire, that the government was planning to commit genocide and it would begin with the massacre of peacekeepers from **Belgium**. Dallaire informed his superior at the UN, **Kofi Annan**, whose staff ordered Dallaire to maintain his neutrality and inform Rwanda's President Juvénal Habyarimana, whom Dallaire believed was implicated in the plan. Following a power-sharing meeting with the RPF, Habyarimana and the president of Burundi were assassinated when their plane was shot down over Rwanda's airport. Genocide commenced and the Rwandan army butchered 10 Belgian peacekeepers. Belgium immediately decided to withdraw from Rwanda and asked the United States to support their decision by calling on the UN to remove the peacekeeping mission. Secretary of State Warren Christopher ordered UN Ambassador **Madeleine Albright** to do so on 15 April, but Albright persuaded Christopher and the UN to allow 270 soldiers to remain.

Neither President **Bill Clinton**, nor Christopher, nor National Security Adviser Anthony Lake met with their advisers about Rwanda, leaving National Security Council staff member Richard Clarke to manage the U.S. response. Clarke was responsible for drafting **Presidential Decision Directive 25** (PDD-25), written in the wake of the failed U.S.-led UN intervention in **Somalia**. PDD-25 severely circumscribed U.S. participation in international peacekeeping missions, and Clarke followed its guidelines although it was not formally issued until 6 May 1994. Clarke later explained that his chief concerns were that low-level U.S. participation in Rwanda could create a slippery slope ending in intervention; fear that a failed mission could diminish congressional support for peacekeeping; and the political consideration that intervention in Rwanda could hurt Clinton's standing with Congress and the public, both of which opposed intervention.

Because genocides are violations of international law that require the international community to intervene to stop, Christopher ordered U.S. officials not to use the word even though the pope, the Red

Cross, Human Rights Watch, Oxfam, and Dallaire were calling it a genocide by the end of the first week. Clinton himself finally allowed the use of the word on 15 June under pressure from the Senate Foreign Relations Committee.

The genocide ended in July 1994 when the RPF overthrew the government. There were 947,000 dead, most of them Tutsi. Although Clinton later apologized for his inaction, Annan said he would have done nothing differently if given the chance. *See also* KAGAME, PAUL.

– S –

SADAT, ANWAR AL- (1918–1981). Egyptian military man, vice president, and president (1970–81). Sadat was a member of the Free Officers Movement that overthrew King **Farouk**, and became vice president under **Gamal Abdel Nasser**, gaining the nickname "Nasser's poodle." Sadat moved quickly and ruthlessly to consolidate power after Nasser's death on 28 September 1970. He reportedly despised the Russians and, after signing a Treaty of Friendship and Cooperation in 1971 that allowed him to increase the amount of armaments that they provided him, in 1972 he expelled 20,000 of the military and economic specialists the **Soviet Union** had provided him, abrogated the treaty, and ended military basing rights that had been granted by Nasser. Sadat also worked behind the scenes to begin a peace process with **Israel**, but when the United States proved slow to take the opening and the Israelis refused to negotiate, he successfully launched the **Arab–Israeli War of 1973** on 6 October, which restored Egyptian and Arab military credibility even though in the end he had to rely on intercession by the U.S. to save his army from destruction. With the war over, Sadat worked closely with U.S. National Security Adviser **Henry Kissinger**'s "**shuttle diplomacy**" to win cease-fires and supported Washington's effort to keep the Soviets from returning to a central role in the region. On 19 November 1977, Sadat flew to Jerusalem, in part because of growing restiveness by Egyptians, who were demanding a better life that could only come from ending hostilities, and to preclude Soviet reentry in the Middle East through President **Jimmy Carter**'s proposed Geneva Peace Conference.

Negotiations that followed with Israeli Prime Minister Menachem Begin stopped, so Carter intervened by inviting both men to the Camp David presidential retreat in October 1978 where they agreed to a framework for peace that produced a peace treaty and mutual recognition on 26 March 1979. Although extremely popular in the U.S., Sadat grew increasingly unpopular in Egypt because of his failure to improve the economy and his increasingly brutal repression of political dissent. On 6 October 1981, Islamist extremists assassinated him. *See also* TERRORISM.

SARO-WIWA, KENULE "KEN" (1941–95). Nigerian playwright and advocate for the Ogoni people, who was executed by the military government of Sani Abacha. Saro-wiwa's writing and organization of protest rallies in his Ogoniland homeland, which suffered great environmental damage without compensation by the Nigerian **oil** extraction industry, brought unwelcome pressure on Shell Oil and the Nigerian government to clean up the pollution and give the region a share of the profits. Saro-Wiwa and six colleagues were accused of inciting the killing of six tribal chiefs, were convicted, sentenced to death, and secretly hanged despite international outcry. Saro-Wiwa's execution and the imprisonment of former President **Olusegun Obasanjo** led to international sanctions against Nigeria, including President **Bill Clinton** refusing to provide more than nonlethal assistance to the Nigerian-led **peacekeeping** mission in **Sierra Leone**.

SAVIMBI, JONAS (1934–2002). Charismatic guerilla leader, who fought an almost 40-year war against **Portugal** for **Angola**'s independence and then against the Communist-led post-colonial government of Angola. Savimbi was the quintessential guerilla: courageous, smart, cunning, dashing, and physically powerful. He had a doctorate from Lausanne University in Switzerland, spoke seven languages, and was trained in **China** for guerilla warfare. Savimbi led the *União Nacional para a Independência Total de Angola*/National Union for the Total Independence of Angola (UNITA) and received support at various times from China, Portugal, **South Africa**, **Zambia**, **Zaïre (Congo)**, and the United States, often justifying his contact with racist and Communist governments by citing the World War II example of the U.S. allying with Soviet dictator Josef Stalin to defeat

Adolf Hitler, and explaining that he would take assistance from anybody to win Angola's freedom from colonialism and communism. Although he was the only leader of an Angolan liberation movement to lead his men in the field, Savimbi received little outside assistance prior to 1975 because he led the smallest guerilla army.

The November 1975 defeat of **Holden Roberto**'s *Frente Nacional de Libertação de Angola*/National Liberation Front of Angola (FNLA), which was heavily backed by Zaïre, South Africa, and the United States, at the hands of **Agostinho Neto**'s *Movimento Popular de Libertação de Angola*/Popular Movement for the Liberation of Angola (MPLA), backed by **Cuba**, the **Soviet Union**, and the Eastern Bloc, focused West and East on UNITA, which was backed by U.S. weapons and advisers, mercenaries, and 3,000 South African troops. Cuba poured over 12,000 troops into the fight, driving the South Africans home and Savimbi into the bush. The MPLA's repression, corruption, and economic mismanagement saved Savimbi's movement. He reemerged in the mid-1980s with control of much of southern Angola. Conservative U.S. politicians and intellectuals were entranced by Savimbi's larger-than-life personality, and the administration of **Ronald W. Reagan** began to provide him with significant support in its effort to roll back communism in the third world, popularly known as the **Reagan Doctrine**. President **George H.W. Bush** continued the support. Again backed by South African troops and assistance, Savimbi ultimately forced the Cubans to send 57,000 troops into Angola. Cuba and the South Africans reached a stalemate in 1988, and South Africa agreed to withdraw from Angola and Southwest Africa (**Namibia**) in exchange for Cuban withdrawal from Angola.

Savimbi spoke eloquently about democracy and free enterprise, telling U.S. government officials and journalists that he had seen the failures of dictatorship and socialism in Africa and would not repeat them. At some point though, Savimbi turned totalitarian himself. He reportedly used witchcraft trials against his own cadres because they were becoming too popular among his followers and abroad. Whole families were wiped out in the purges. Other UNITA sources said that the killings were the brutal result of an affair with Savimbi's wife.

The collapse of the Soviet Union's empire forced change upon the Angolan government. In April 1991, the MPLA announced that Angola was no longer Communist. In May, they signed a peace treaty with Savimbi and elections were set for the following year. Savimbi was expected to win the presidency and parliament, but he campaigned arrogantly and belligerently, frightening many erstwhile supporters. Voting was held on 29–30 September under **United Nations** (UN) auspices, which allowed the MPLA to count the ballots. The UN declared that the MPLA won the first round of voting, but U.S. election observers declared that the tally was a fraud. Internal UN documents were later leaked, which showed election rigging and a UN cover-up. The genesis of what followed is unclear, but the MPLA began systematically killing thousands of UNITA officials and cadres in the cities, and UNITA killed hundreds of MPLA figures in the countryside. Savimbi returned to the bush and the war resumed, funded by the government's **oil** and mining of **blood diamonds** by UNITA. The administration of President **Bill Clinton** supported the MPLA government, cutting off aid to Savimbi. Negotiations continued and Savimbi joined a national unity government that was formed in April 1997. The MPLA began buying off UNITA legislators and in September 1998 announced that it would no longer work with Savimbi, and Savimbi again returned to the bush. Without allies because of South Africa's transition to majority rule in 1994 and the 1997 fall of **Mobutu Sese Seko** of Zaïre, and now leading a splintered movement, Savimbi's area of operations grew smaller and smaller until he was ambushed by a former ally and killed on 22 February 2002.

SHABA, INVASIONS OF. Unsuccessful invasions on 3 March 1977 and 3 May 1978 of **Zaïre**'s Shaba province (formerly and, since 1997, known as **Katanga**; scheduled to be divided into four provinces in 2010) by rebels based in **Angola**. The attacks, known as Shaba I and Shaba II, had the goal of overthrowing President **Mobutu Sese Seko** rather than seceding from Zaïre. The invasions were launched by the *Front pour la Libération National du Congo*/Front for the National Liberation of the Congo (FNLC), which consisted of former members of **Moïse Tshombe**'s Katangan *gendarmerie* and a younger generation of exiles, who had been trained by military instructors from **Cuba** and Angola.

Shaba I saw the immediate collapse of Zaïre's army during the first skirmish and Mobutu's call for international military assistance. Mobutu blamed the attack on Cuba, which had approximately 15,000 soldiers in Angola, although the evidence remains unclear whether or not they were behind it. U.S. President **Jimmy Carter** had been inaugurated only two months before and, under the sway of **United Nations** (UN) Ambassador **Andrew Young** and other regionalists in his administration who tried to separate Africa from the **cold war**, was reluctant to become involved. Mobutu was rescued after 80 days thanks to joint assistance by **France** and **Morocco** while Washington provided minimal nonlethal assistance, most of which Mobutu and his generals sold on the black market.

In Shaba II, the FLNC immediately took Kolwezi, an important mining city that was a primary source of income for Mobutu's government. The rebels may have lost control of their men, who went on a rampage of looting and murder, killing 1,000 Zaïrians and 200 Europeans, although the killings may have had the purpose of terrorizing Europeans into leaving the country and thereby causing economic collapse. This time the U.S. took decisive action. Intelligence reports indicated that Cuba was behind the attack (although Secretary of State **Cyrus Vance** later concluded that the reports were unreliable) and Carter, under pressure from cold warriors such as National Security Adviser **Zbigniew Brzezinski**, who believed that the Soviets were on the march in Africa and the Middle East, ordered the Air Force to fly military aid and paratroopers from France and **Belgium** to Kolwezi and the strategically important city of Kamina. Within two weeks, the rebels had been driven back into Angola. In July, Zaïre and Angola established diplomatic relations and the following month Mobutu met with Angolan President **Agostinho Neto**, who agreed to stop support for the FLNC in exchange for Mobutu ending support for **Holden Roberto**'s *Frente Nacional de Libertação de Angola*/Front for the National Liberation of Angola (FNLA), **Jonas Savimbi**'s *União Nacional para a Independência Total de Angola*/ National Union for the Total Independence of Angola (UNITA), and the *Frente para a Libertação do Enclave de Cabinda*/Front for the Liberation of the Enclave of Cabinda, a separatist group in the oil-rich Cabinda province.

SHUTTLE DIPLOMACY. Name given to the peripatetic capital-to-capital negotiation conducted by U.S. Secretary of State **Henry Kissinger** to end the **Arab–Israeli War of 1973**. Kissinger's shuttle diplomacy restarted peace talks between **Israel** and the Arab states led by **Egypt**, and froze the **Soviet Union** out of the peace negotiations. Kissinger's effort helped to give Egyptian President **Anwar Sadat** confidence to make a complete break with the Soviet Union. The term has since been applied to any such effort, such as Kissinger's 1976 attempt to negotiate the transition to black-majority rule in **Rhodesia (Zimbabwe)**.

SIAD BARRÉ, MUHAMMAD (1919–1995). **Somali** general and dictator (1969–91), who led his country into a disastrous war with **Ethiopia** followed by national dissolution, anarchy, and mass famine. Siad was the Somali army chief of staff when he overthrew the government on 21 October 1969, proclaimed a Communist government, and dramatically expanded his army to become Africa's fourth largest by 1975. Despite minimal education, Siad quickly learned the language of scientific socialism, pleasing the **Soviet Union**, which became his patron, giving him hundreds of millions of dollars worth of weapons and providing East German security personnel to create a secret police. In return, Siad signed a Treaty of Friendship and Cooperation in 1974 and the Soviets built huge naval and air bases on the Red Sea. Despite Siad's claim to be a Marxist–Leninist, the Soviets learned that he was really a Somali nationalist whose true goal was to use their weapons to conquer neighboring Somali-majority territories in **Kenya**, Djibouti, and **Ethiopia**.

Siad's strongest effort was against Ethiopia, where he funded separatist guerillas in the Ogaden Desert (where his mother had been born) and then, in July 1977, sent approximately 40,000 Somali soldiers, which began the **Ogaden War**. His Soviet friends abandoned him because the Ethiopian government had made a sudden and definitive turn to Marxism–Leninism in early 1977, and President Fidel Castro of **Cuba** concluded that the new Ethiopian ruler, **Mengistu Haile Mariam**, was a true Communist while Siad was not. The Soviets airlifted 15,000 Cuban troops to the Ogaden, and they drove out the Somalis in March 1978. Siad abandoned Marxism–Leninism and tried to switch sides in the **cold war** by turning to the United States for assistance, but his attempt to alter national borders by force and his dismal human rights record prevented Washington from providing assistance until 1980 and this, compared to the Soviet effort, was minimal.

Siad's fortunes declined as Somalia's clans turned on one another and Washington cut off military aid in 1989 because of his human rights record. In January 1991, he was driven out of the capital, Mogadishu, by forces under **Muhammad Farah Aideed**, and briefly became a regional clan warlord, but shortly thereafter fled to **Nigeria**, where he died. Siad's scorched earth policies and the civil war his policies created forced over a million Somalis to flee as **refugees**, led to famine that killed hundreds of thousands, and began a continuous cycle of violence that killed an estimated one million people by mid-2008.

SIERRA LEONE. West African nation that saw the rise of a new type of guerilla movement that randomly and savagely mutilated and murdered in order to force its way into the government for the purpose of turning it into a criminal enterprise. Sierra Leone broke into the world's consciousness because of a civil war led by Foday Sankoh, a Sierra Leonean who had trained as a guerilla in **Libya** where he met **Charles Taylor** of **Liberia**. Sankoh accompanied Taylor to Liberia in the late 1980s, fought for Taylor in that country's civil war, and in 1991 the Liberian gave him his own guerilla force, the Revolutionary United Front (RUF), which invaded Sierra Leone from Liberia on 23 March 1991, taking control of Sierra Leone's diamond mines. The RUF became the most notorious of the **blood diamond** suppliers. Taylor's guerillas had begun the practice of turning children into murderers by forcing them to kill village elders or even family members then keeping them high on drugs and performing ritual cannibalism. Sankoh took the brutality to a new level by ordering his child soldiers to amputate civilians' arms and legs. In 1996, disaffected army officers overthrew the Sierra Leonean government and held elections won by Ahmad Tajan Kabbah, who was overthrown by the army the next year.

In 1998, **Nigeria** organized a military intervention by the Economic Community of West African States Monitoring Group (ECOMOG) to stop that country's civil war. The ECOMOG removed the military government, restored President Kabbah to power, and began fighting the RUF. Although the United States had strongly supported

Sierra Leone's transition to democracy, it refused to provide logistical assistance to the Nigerians because President **Bill Clinton** did not approve of Nigerian military ruler Sani Abacha's often brutal government. In November 1998, the Nigerians, who had captured Sankoh, turned him over to Sierra Leone, which sentenced him to death. To free him, the RUF launched a vicious attack on Freetown, the capital, killing over 6,000, disfiguring by amputation children as young as 18 months, and capturing thousands of children to serve as soldiers and sex slaves. In the wake of the attack, Clinton sent his special envoy to Africa, **Jesse Jackson**, to help negotiate a peace agreement, although lower level State Department officials warned Clinton and Jackson about the RUF's violence and ties to international criminal syndicates.

Jackson pressured Kabbah into agreeing to pardon Sankoh and appoint him vice president, grant a blanket amnesty to RUF fighters, and give control of Sierra Leone's diamond mines to Sankoh in exchange for Sankoh's promise to disarm the RUF and renounce violence. The **United Nations** (UN) sent a 6,000-man **peacekeeping** force to replace the ECOMOG, which left in April 2000. The RUF immediately resumed the civil war and, starting on 1 May 2000, captured approximately 500 UN soldiers, who had tried to disarm the RUF as part of the peace agreement. Soldiers from **Great Britain** under UN auspices were rushed in, rescued the troops, and crushed the rebellion. On 8 May, RUF fighters shot protestors demonstrating in front of Sankoh's home, killing a score. Sankoh was arrested and stripped of his vice presidency. Following the civil war, a war crimes commission was established in Sierra Leone, but in 2003 Sankoh died in jail awaiting trial. After Sankoh's defeat, a newspaper reporter learned that Sankoh and Taylor had been major suppliers of cut-rate diamonds to **al Qaeda** for resale in Europe. *See also* TERRORISM.

SIMBAS. Rebel army from eastern **Congo** that fought in the civil war of 1964–65. Simbas (Swahili, "lions") were generally teenagers who spent most of their time drugged. Disorganized, undisciplined, badly led, murderous, and sometimes ritualistically cannibalistic, they nonetheless fought ferociously because *féticheurs* (persons with a magical power) had blessed them with liquids that they were told made them invulnerable to bullets, which turned to water when fired at them (a common trope in Eastern and Central Africa that dated back to early European colonization and is believed by some rebel groups today). The Congolese army soldiers would frequently flee at the mere sight of an unarmed *féticheur* leading boys into battle. The Simbas were defeated by the Congolese army in 1964 and mopped up in 1965 following the July 1964 appointment of **Moïse Tshombe** as prime minister, ending the **Congo Crisis**. Tshombe hired mercenary forward units, the **Central Intelligence Agency** (CIA) created a tiny Congolese air force of Cuban contract pilots that gave the government air superiority, and on 24 November 1964 the U.S. Air Force dropped Belgian paratroopers on the rebel capital, **Stanleyville**, crushing the main body of resistance. *See also* GIZENGA, ANTOINE; KASAVUBU, JOSEPH; MOBUTU SESE SEKO; STANLEYVILLE (KISANGANI) HOSTAGE RESCUE.

SMITH, IAN (1919–2007). Prime minister of **Rhodesia**, 1964–79, who illegally announced the colony's unilateral declaration of independence (UDI) from **Great Britain** and then oversaw a war to maintain white power. Tough, crafty, but without vision, Smith passed up opportunities to work with black moderates until it was too late, paving the way for rule by **Robert Mugabe**.

Smith was a farmer and Royal Air Force veteran who came to power on 13 April 1964 with the slogan "no majority rule in my lifetime." Two months later, he ordered the imprisonment of several hundred leading black nationalists, including **Joshua Nkomo** of the Zimbabwe African People's Union (ZAPU) and the Zimbabwe African National Union's (ZANU) Ndabiningi Sithole and Robert Mugabe, and banned both parties. Smith argued that Rhodesia should be independent under white rule because it was Christian, reliably anti-Communist, well run, and prosperous, in stark contrast to the often abysmal governments to the north in black Africa. The British refused to countenance such an eventuality so, despite whites only making up 5 percent of the population, Smith announced the UDI on 11 November 1965. **United Nations** (UN) sanctions followed, which were enforced by the United States until the **Byrd Amendment** allowed an exception for the purchase of Rhodesian chrome, ferrochrome, and nickel.

Surrounded by **Portugal**'s **Mozambique** to the east, the **apartheid** government of **South Africa** to the south, weak and sparsely populated **Botswana** and South African–controlled Southwest Africa (**Namibia**) on the west, and black-ruled but economically dependent **Zambia** in the north, Smith's Rhodesia faced little challenge from the guerillas until the collapse of Portuguese colonialism following the April 1974 coup. Independent Mozambique allowed Mugabe's ZANU to infiltrate guerillas all along the 760-mile border and Zambia provided bases for Nkomo's ZAPU. Despite daring and imaginative attacks by the Rhodesian army on guerilla bases and leaders in the surrounding black-led countries as well as punishing attacks on Zambian and Mozambican people and infrastructure, Rhodesia's position crumbled as the eastern countryside became unsafe for whites and their black employees. South Africa's government concluded that Rhodesia was doomed, so it pressured Smith to release the rebel leaders in December 1974 for negotiations that proved unsuccessful. Mugabe escaped to Mozambique to lead the guerilla war.

As the situation worsened in 1976, the U.S. government pressured Smith to negotiate, with Secretary of State **Henry Kissinger** leading an unsuccessful effort at "**shuttle diplomacy**." An end-of-year British-backed Geneva conference based on Kissinger's work also failed. Smith began to negotiate an internal settlement with Methodist Bishop **Abel Muzorewa**, a nationalist leader and member of the majority Shona tribe, and other moderate leaders. The final agreement of 3 March 1978 gave universal adult suffrage, allotted whites one-third of parliament and one-quarter of the cabinet seats including justice and defense for two years, and changed the country's name to Zimbabwe–Rhodesia. At the invitation of U.S. Senator **Jesse Helms**, a conservative Republican, Smith and Sithole visited the U.S. on 7 October to make their case for U.S. support. Although the **Jimmy Carter** administration initially blocked the visit, Secretary of State **Cyrus Vance** met with the two men, telling them that the U.S. would only accept a government that emerged from an all-parties conference. Five days later, Smith told members of the Senate Foreign Relations Committee that he was willing to attend such a meeting.

Smith turned power over to Muzorewa on 31 May 1979, but the guerilla war continued and the rest of the world rejected the new government. President Carter joined British efforts to force a settlement and, under intense pressure, Smith and Muzorewa negotiated an agreement with the guerilas at Lancaster House in England between September and December 1979. Smith won constitutional guarantees for whites to receive 20 percent of parliamentary seats for 10 years and for their property to be protected in perpetuity. The war had cost 20,000 people their lives, although the period of the Internal Settlement had the highest number of casualties.

Mugabe won a huge majority, but Smith was re-elected to a white seat. Until 1981, Smith and Mugabe got along well. Smith was impressed by what he considered to be his opponent's good sense for taking no retaliatory measures against whites, but after Smith warned Mugabe about the danger to Zimbabwe's international standing if Mugabe went forward with his plan to create a one-party state, Mugabe turned against him and began pointing to him as the leader of economic wreckers who were responsible for the regime's economic troubles. Smith responded by calling Mugabe a typical African dictator. Zimbabwe's white voters angered Mugabe by continuing to re-elect Smith until their constitutionally reserved parliamentary seats ended in 1990. Smith continued to live in Zimbabwe with relatively few government-sponsored problems. He died in South Africa although most of his land in Zimbabwe was not confiscated by the government during his lifetime.

SMUTS, JAN (1870–1950). Military man and prime minister of **South Africa** (1919–24, 1939–48), who worked closely with the United States to create both the League of Nations—formulating the mandate system for colonies of the defeated Central Powers under which South African took control of Southwest Africa (**Namibia**)—and the **United Nations** (UN), for which he wrote the preamble.

SOMALIA. East African country on the Horn of Africa, which is one of only four African nations that is overwhelmingly populated by a single tribe (the Somalis). Somalia is nonetheless today a state only in name, torn apart by clan violence.

Modern Somalia was created by the union of Somaliland colonies ruled by **Great Britain** and Italy. Even before independence on 1 July 1960, the Somali government demanded that kinsmen in **France**'s Djibouti colony, **Great Britain**'s **Kenya**, and independent

Ethiopia be amalgamated into a Greater Somalia, by force if necessary. These ambitions were stifled to the south when Kenya repressed its Somalis in the Northern Frontier District during the Shifta Rebellion (1963–67) with often brutal villigization tactics based on British policies during the Mau-Mau rebellion. To the north in Djibouti, 95 percent of the population voted for independence rather than union with Somalia (1977) and it was clear that the French would protect Djibouti from Somali ambitions. Ethiopia was a close ally of the United States, which provided weaponry and kept Somalia from doing more than assisting guerillas in Ethiopia's Somali-populated Ogaden region.

Somali strongman **Muhammad Siad Barré**, who took power in a 21 October 1969 coup, declared Somalia a Marxist–Leninist state and formally allied it with the **Soviet Union** in its **cold war** struggle against the U.S. and its allies. The Soviets traded immense quantities of arms for naval and air bases on the Red Sea at Mogadishu and Berbera. In 1974, the Soviets signed a treaty of friendship with Siad, although by now they realized that his Somali nationalism trumped his communism. Following the overthrow of Emperor **Haile Selassie** of Ethiopia in September 1974, Ethiopia began to unravel as the revolutionary government of **Mengistu Haile Mariam** destroyed the old order and began to create a Communist state. The Soviets recognized Mengistu as a true believer and began to ship Ethiopia weapons and advisers, dramatically increasing the amount in December 1976 although rebellions and civil wars increased around the country. Siad saw his chance and clandestinely sent weapons and regular army troops to the Ogaden to resuscitate the Western Somali Liberation Front, a separatist guerilla organization that had been defeated by the Ethiopian government in 1964. Seeing that his allies were abandoning him, Siad secretly turned to Washington for aid, despite having himself thrown out the **Peace Corps** and dramatically reduced the U.S. embassy staff when he took power.

In late May 1977, following Siad's urgent request, President **Jimmy Carter** ordered Secretary of State **Cyrus Vance** and National Security Adviser **Zbigniew Brzezinski** to do whatever they could to make Somalia a U.S. friend, but Vance warned Carter that no military aid should be forthcoming until the **Ogaden War** was settled. Ignoring the secretary's advice, on 26 July Carter publicly announced that the U.S. would give Somalia military assistance to protect itself against Ethiopia. Three days before, the Somalis had themselves invaded the Ogaden with 40,000 troops. Behind the scenes, Secretary Vance demanded that the president void the arms deal because of Somalia's aggression, which he did on 4 August.

Even without U.S. help, Somali forces quickly won 90 percent of the territory, but Siad was stopped by the Soviet Bloc, which had tried but failed to work out a peace settlement between the old and new allies. Convinced that Mengistu's communism was authentic and that populous and potentially powerful Ethiopia could lead an African socialist revolution, **Cuba** and the Soviets abandoned Somalia and airlifted approximately 15,000 Cuban troops and 1,000 Soviet military advisers to Ethiopia, driving the last Somalis out of the Ogaden on 9 March 1978. The U.S. finally agreed to assist Siad in 1980, providing him with $53 million in economic and development foreign aid and $40 million in military aid in exchange for the former Soviet naval and air bases on the Red Sea at Mogadishu and Berbera.

Thereafter, as other clans grew restive under his rule, which favored his own clan, Siad embraced a scorched earth policy against his opponents, precipitating civil war. Congress pressured the **George H.W. Bush** administration to suspend military aid, which it did in late 1989. Siad was overthrown in January 1991 and the Somali state collapsed. On 18 May 1991, the former British Somaliland seceded, calling itself Somaliland, but by mid-2008 it had received no international recognition. Several parts of the breakaway state subsequently declared their independence from Somaliland as well. In the rest of the country, chaos reigned and warlords emerged from Somalia's clans leading militias of thugs that were often child soldiers. Fighting destroyed Somalia's infrastructure and, combined with drought and confiscation of food by militias, killed hundreds of thousands and threatened the life of a million **refugees**. Starting 14 August 1992, the Bush administration quietly launched Operation Provide Comfort, a massive food assistance **foreign aid** program. As news media interest in the humanitarian disaster grew during the fall, international pressure grew to do more, so Bush launched **Operation Restore Hope**, a U.S.-led mission to feed starving Somalis. The **United Nations** (UN) joined the effort to feed the starving as did several thousand **non-governmental organizations** (NGOs). The foreign aid bureaucracy grew so vast that U.S. soldiers derisively called it a "self-licking ice cream cone." An estimated 240,000 people were killed by the famine while estimates on the number saved by foreign assistance, primarily from the US, range from 100,000 to one million.

The leading Somali warlord, **Muhammad Farah Aideed**, tolerated the food assistance, but he was threatened by the efforts of Bush's successor, **Bill Clinton**, to expand the mission by working with the UN to use soldiers to disarm the militias. Aideed retaliated, leading to open warfare between his forces and the U.S.-led UN troops. The UN commander, retired U.S. Admiral Jonathan Howe, put a price on Aideed's head, and the result was the 3 October 1993 Battle of Mogadishu in which 18 U.S. soldiers were killed. Clinton removed U.S. forces from combat on 7 October, and withdrew all U.S. forces from Somalia on 26 March 1994. The last remaining UN forces followed on 2 March 1995. Aideed conquered most of Somalia by September 1995, but his success bred resentment among his allies and he died after being wounded in an August 1996 battle.

Following Aideed's death, warlords formed a provisional government and divided up Somalia until the Islamist Islamic Courts Union (ICU) defeated them, taking Mogadishu and much of southern Somalia. The ICU imposed sharia law and ended violence where it held sway, but its ties to **al Qaeda** and **Eritrea**, the latter of which reportedly sent weapons and 2,000 fully equipped soldiers to support the ICU, led Ethiopia to invade with tacit U.S. support on 8 December 2006. Between 5,000 and 10,000 Ethiopian troops attacked Somalia and defeated the ICU, whose leadership fled to Eritrea. Ethiopia restored the warlord-led government and continued to occupy the country by July 2008. The U.S. provided logistical support and several times launched sea and air attacks on suspected al Qaeda **terrorism** targets, killing the top al Qaeda leader in Somalia on 1 May 2008.

The **African Union** (AU) pledged to send a peacekeeping force on 19 January 2007, but by mid-2008 the African Union Mission to Somalia (AMISOM) consisted of 2,450 soldiers from **Uganda** and Burundi. In June 2008, the Somali combatants met in the 15th peace conference in 17 years. By mid-2008, an estimated one million people had died since the civil war to overthrow Siad Barré began in the late 1980s, and the UN estimated that the invasion by Ethiopia had displaced one million Somalis who faced imminent danger of hunger because emergency food shipments had been halted due to the danger from pirates. Across the Horn of Africa in mid-2008, the UN estimated that 14.5 million people required humanitarian assistance. *See also* BIN LADEN, OSAMA; BOUTROS GHALI, BOUTROS; YOUNG, ANDREW.

SOUTH AFRICA. The most industrialized and powerful country in Africa, whose white minority ruled until May 1994. South Africa's relations with the United States became important following World War I at the Paris Peace Conference in 1919 when South African military man and politician **Jan Smuts** formally proposed the creation of a powerful international organization, which became the League of Nations. Prime Minister Smuts put forth a revised proposal for such an organization at the founding meeting of the **United Nations** (UN) in San Francisco in 1945. Following World War II, South Africa's mineral wealth, including uranium for atomic bombs, and its geographic position, controlling sea lanes used by **oil** tankers bound for Western Europe, made its stability and pro-Western foreign policy vital to U.S. interests, but its racist **apartheid** system, begun in 1948 following the election of the Afrikaner-dominated National Party, made it progressively more difficult for the U.S. to remain an ally.

The 21 March 1960 Sharpeville Massacre, when South African police shot and killed 69 nonviolent demonstrators who were emulating the tactics of the U.S. Civil Rights Movement, ended exclusively nonviolent resistance by the African National Congress (ANC), the primary black resistance group. In Sharpeville's wake, the ANC formed a guerilla force, *Umkhonto we Sizwe* (translated as "Spear of the Nation"; abbreviated MK), led by **Nelson Mandela** and with the participation of the South African Communist Party (SACP). Following Mandela's August 1962 arrest, Joe Slovo, an SACP leader and staunch supporter of the **Soviet Union**, became MK's leader. Slovo's accession saw the Soviets expand their financial support network, which had annually provided funds to the SACP since the 1920s, to include hundreds of thousands of dollars per year to the ANC. The Soviets also began training MK leaders in the Soviet Union. The ANC and SACP created a formal relationship in 1969.

The Sharpeville Massacre made U.S. relations with South Africa still more difficult. President **John F. Kennedy** supported a UN

Security Council nonmandatory arms embargo against South Africa in 1963, but otherwise he did little to damage relations. Poor treatment of black U.S. sailors on shore leave led President **Lyndon B. Johnson** to act in 1967 when he banned U.S. Navy ships from docking in South African ports and suspended intelligence sharing and coordination with the South African navy. President **Richard M. Nixon** ended Johnson's restrictions on intelligence and naval coordination policy because his administration had concluded in **National Security Study Memorandum 39** (NSSM 39) that white governments would survive in Southern Africa for the indefinite future and the best way to move them to more equitable treatment of their black populations was to work and **trade** with them. Closer relations with South Africa were also in keeping with the **Nixon Doctrine**, which sought to use regional hegemons to keep the peace without the need for U.S. intervention or even attention.

Soviet interest in South Africa began in the summer of 1970 following a KGB estimate that black Southern Africans despaired that the U.S. would help them and had become much more radicalized than the first generation of African leaders. Soviet leader Leonid Brezhnev wanted to exploit the potential strategic benefit that would come from a Communist takeover in **Angola**, a colony of **Portugal**. Soviet interest in Southern Africa was solidified with independence in **Mozambique** under the Communist-led *Frente de Libertação de Moçambique*/Front for the Liberation of Mozambique (FRELIMO) following the 1974 Portuguese coup, which dramatically escalated the guerilla war in Rhodesia and increased pressure on South Africa. South African Prime Minister **John Vorster** responded with a détente policy that sought better relations with black Africa, intervention in Angola to bring to power a friendly black government, and a crackdown on blacks at home.

The Angola intervention, which escalated from money and trainers to combat forces on the front line, was formally launched on 14 July 1975, just four days before the U.S. began **Operation IAFEATURE**, a covert operation to aid anti-Communist forces there. Strong circumstantial evidence and statements by South African leaders indicate a coordinated effort with the U.S., although Secretary of State **Henry Kissinger** denies it. Following revelations about the U.S. and South African interventions, Congress passed the **Tunney Amend-**

ment, which forced President **Gerald R. Ford** to end the intervention. The lack of U.S. support combined with defeat at the hands of troops sent from **Cuba** in support of the Communist-led *Movimento Popular de Libertação de Angola*/Popular Movement for the Liberation of Angola (MPLA) drove South Africa out of the war by the end of 1975. The following year, Secretary of State Henry Kissinger worked with South Africa to force **Ian Smith**, the prime minister of the illegal government of **Rhodesia**, to reach a power-sharing agreement with the black opposition, but Kissinger's effort and South African détente were broken by the 16 June 1976 Soweto riots, which spread across the country, killing over 500 people. Soweto was black South Africans' response to anger over Vorster's harsh enforcement of apartheid, which included the forced removal and attendant social dislocation of over three million blacks to economically destitute tribal homelands known as *Bantustans*.

South Africa's troubles prompted the Reverend Leon Sullivan, a member of General Motors' (GM) board of directors, to push the board in 1977 to adopt what came to be known as the **Sullivan Principles**, which required GM to treat all South African employees equally and in an integrated environment. As South Africa's leading employer of black workers, GM forced many other businesses to adopt the Sullivan Principles as a requirement for doing business with GM. The U.S. government endorsed the principles and President **Ronald W. Reagan** made them central to his "**Constructive Engagement**" policy, although he opposed congressional legislation that sought to make them U.S. law. Sullivan himself had by then concluded that they did not go far enough. Reagan's predecessor, **Jimmy Carter**, increased the pressure on South Africa. Vice President Walter Mondale met with Vorster and demanded that he end apartheid, and UN Ambassador **Andrew Young** told an audience of South African blacks that Carter would defeat South African apartheid just as he had beaten white racists during the struggle for civil rights when he was governor of Georgia. Although Carter kept rhetorical pressure on South Africa, especially following Black Consciousness leader **Stephen Biko**'s murder, little discernible progress followed.

Reagan's Constructive Engagement eased pressure on South Africa, with African Affairs Assistant Secretary Chester Crocker arguing that working with South Africa was the best way to influence it. Early in his administration, Reagan said that in light of South Africa's vital mineral wealth and support for the West, the U.S. could not abandon it to possible Communist takeover. Although Vorster's successor, **P.W. Botha**, made many changes that ended the worst aspects of South African discrimination such as the 1986 repeal of the pass laws (that required blacks to carry internal passports), Reagan's position began to collapse because of the violent black reaction to Botha's attempt to rationalize apartheid through changing South Africa's constitution to give separate parliaments to whites, Asians (East Indians), and Coloreds (mixed race) while giving *Bantustans* their independence. The world saw on television the brutal response by South African police to the black riots and the ANC's brutal but largely successful effort to make ungovernable the black townships that surround major cities, all of which galvanized Americans' opposition to South Africa's government.

Significant U.S. protests had begun on the day before Thanksgiving in 1984 when **TransAfrica** began sit-ins at the South African embassy. The anti-apartheid movement reached its peak with the 1986 passage of the **Comprehensive Anti-Apartheid Act** (CAAA) over Reagan's veto, despite the president's arguments that black African nations traded with South Africa, and black South African leaders like **Mangosuthu "Gatsha" Buthelezi** said that sanctions would hurt South African blacks. The CAAA banned U.S. investment or loans for South Africa, sales of goods to the police and military, and imports of most South African products. It also imposed the Sullivan Principles on U.S. multinational corporations in South Africa. The European Community and Japan followed the U.S. lead.

The confluence of economic retrenchment brought by worldwide sanctions against the South African economy, the collapse of the Soviet Empire in November 1989 and with it the loss of the ANC's chief patron and white South Africans' greatest fear, low public morale in the face of soldiers' deaths during a second Angolan intervention, and general public malaise over living in an international pariah state led Botha's cabinet colleagues to force him out of office on 13 February 1989, replacing him with **F.W. de Klerk**, a liberal reformer. De Klerk ended apartheid. On 2 February 1990, he made a nationally televised speech announcing that all political prisoners including Mandela would be freed and that the banning order against the ANC and SACP along with other opposition groups was now lifted. He freed Mandela in February 1990 and ended the legal underpinnings of the

Bantustan system on 5 June 1991. In August 1991 at the suggestion of Slovo, Mandela announced that the ANC was ending the armed struggle. De Klerk's effort to reform the system by negotiating power sharing with Mandela and the ANC failed amid continuing ethnic violence, and majority rule came with Mandela's April 1994 election as president and the ANC's overwhelming victory in parliamentary elections. The U.S. strongly supported Mandela and his efforts at racial reconciliation, which carried over into the rule of his successor, **Thabo Mbeki**, whom Clinton called one of the "new breed of African leaders." U.S. relations with South Africa soured due to Mbeki's opposition to the use of AZT and other drugs to treat HIV/**AIDS**, which had become an epidemic, and because of his coddling of **Zimbabwe**'s President **Robert Mugabe**. Mbeki became the **African Union** (AU) mediator for Zimbabwe in 2007, but intraparty rivalry and Mbeki's failure to take action to stop May 2008 riots against foreigners, primarily Zimbabweans, resulted in 42 dead and thousands homeless. Despite his 21 July oversight of the signing of a preliminary agreement between Mugabe and opposition leader **Morgan Tsvangirai**, which laid out terms for negotiations to end Zimbabwe's political crisis, Mbeki's mishandling of the situation in May 2008 led to the ANC forcing him to resign on 24 September.

U.S. and worldwide pressure on South Africa also changed South African nuclear weapons policy, forcing Botha in 1987 to begin bringing South Africa into compliance with the 1968 Nuclear Non-Proliferation Treaty (NPT). South Africa had begun nuclear weapons research in 1969, working with **Israel**. Joint U.S. and Soviet pressure prevented the government from conducting nuclear tests in August 1977, but South Africa may have exploded a nuclear bomb in September 1979. By the time Botha began discussions with the International Atomic Energy Agency (IAEA), South Africa had six nuclear weapons. De Klerk signed the NPT on 10 July 1991, gave up South Africa's nuclear bombs, and shut down its nuclear program, the world's first country to give up its nuclear weapons capability voluntarily. *See also* AFRICAN AFFAIRS, STATE DEPARTMENT BUREAU OF.

SOUTHWEST AFRICA. *See* NAMIBIA.

SOVIET UNION. Former name of the empire that encompassed Russia and its neighboring European and Asian states that Russians now call the "Near Abroad." The Soviet Union took the **cold war** to Africa in the hope of breaking the dependence of African states on their neo-colonial masters, which Leninist theory said would hasten the economic collapse of the West. Soviet intervention in sub-Saharan Africa came in two waves: the initial independence period, when it provided economic, military, and secret police assistance to Leftist governments such as **Kwame Nkrumah**'s **Ghana**, **Sékou Touré**'s **Guinea**, Mobido Keita's Mali, and **Patrice Lumumba**'s **Congo**; and in the wake of the collapse of the racist Southern African governments, which provided opportunity in **Angola**, **Mozambique**, **Zimbabwe**, **Namibia**, Guinea–Bissau, **South Africa**, and indirectly, **Ethiopia**.

The Soviets' initial foray failed due to the inherent instability of impoverished states and, the Soviets concluded, because these regimes were "African socialist" rather than scientific socialist (i.e., Communist) and came to power with the consent of their colonizers, thus maintaining the neo-colonial relationship despite the regimes' rhetoric. The second wave was led by true Marxist–Leninists, the Soviets concluded, and the violent revolutions that they commanded could provide the necessary break with the world imperialist system and spread across Africa. This analysis also proved faulty, as these countries had mono-crop or extractive industry economies that relied upon Western buyers for survival. Instead, the heavy expense paid by the Soviets in propping up these governments helped to create the crisis that destroyed the Soviet Empire and the Soviet Union itself.

In North Africa, the result was similar. Assistance to **Ahmed Ben Bella**'s **Algeria** proved of fleeting value when he was overthrown by radical but independent Houari Boumédienne, and billions of dollars in assistance, a treaty of friendship and cooperation, and use of ports and military bases proved of ephemeral value when **Anwar Sadat** of **Egypt** evicted the Soviets and allied with the United States following the death of Soviet ally **Gamal Abdel Nasser**. The Soviets sold vast amounts of arms to **Libya**, using it as a source of cash and a means of profiting from the distribution of weapons to liberation and **terrorism** movements, but they concluded that its dictator, **Muammar Qaddafi**, was dangerously unstable, and refused to assist in his efforts to obtain nuclear weapons.

After Mikhail Gorbachev took power at the Kremlin in 1985, he began to question his government's massive spending in Africa and concluded that the Soviet Union's African allies were bankrupting it without benefit. Beginning in 1988, Gorbachev worked with President **Ronald W. Reagan** to end the cold war in Africa. The U.S. pressured South Africa to grant independence to Southwest Africa (Namibia), and the Soviets pressured Angola and **Cuba** to withdraw Cuban troops, resulting in the New York Accords, signed 22 December 1988, which brought Namibia its independence from South Africa and set a successful timetable for the removal of Cuban troops from Angola. There followed successful and peaceful settlements in Mozambique and South Africa, the fall of the **Mengistu Haile Mariam** regime in Ethiopia, and an unsuccessful settlement in Angola, all of them largely the result of pressure from the Soviets and the U.S. *See also* CHINA; CONGO CRISIS; ODINGA, OGINGA.

SPORTS. The interchange of sports between Africa and the United States has been small. Africa's most popular sports, soccer and rugby, have found minimal footholds in the U.S., and neither baseball nor American football has been popular in Africa. Individual sports such as track and golf have seen much more interchange, while boxing has seen minimal, but basketball has grown in popularity in Africa since the 1980s.

Marathon runners from **Ethiopia** such as the barefoot Abebe Bikila who won the 1960 and 1964 Olympics and middle distance runners from **Kenya**, such as two-time Gold Medal–winner Kipchoge "Kip" Keino, have been among the most prominent sources of American interest in Africa. In 2008, these events continued to have strong performances by runners from Ethiopia and Kenya, as well as from **Morocco**.

Golf has seen several white players from **South Africa** become international stars. The most famous is **Gary Player**, who won numerous tournaments worldwide including each of the Professional Golfers' Association's (PGA) "Grand Slam" tournaments. Player has been controversial at home and abroad for contradictory positions on the racist **apartheid** system imposed by the former white South African government.

Boxer Dick Tiger of **Nigeria** (born Richard Ihetu) won the World Middleweight and Light Heavyweight titles and was voted one of the 80 greatest in the history of the sport. His efforts to raise money and support for his secessionist **Biafra** homeland helped create U.S. awareness of the civil war in Nigeria. Africa's most famous connection with boxing was the "Rumble in the Jungle," sponsored by President **Mobutu Sese Seko** of **Zaïre** (**Congo**), in which **Muhammad Ali** regained the World Heavyweight Championship from George Foreman.

Basketball has proven to be the only U.S. team sport with popularity in Africa, and star players from Africa in the National Basketball Association (NBA) have included **Hakeem Olajuwon** from Nigeria, **Dikembe Mutombo** from Congo, Manute Bol from **Sudan**, and Steve Nash from South Africa. Mutombo, Bol, and Nash are also well known for their philanthropic work. Since 2003, the NBA has worked with two organizations to build basketball in Africa. In Senegal, the NBA joined the government and a Senegalese telecommunications company to create Sports for Education and Economic Development, an intensive 10-month athletic and educational clinic. The NBA also sends players to South Africa every year to conduct clinics for the Basketball without Borders Africa program in conjunction with the International Basketball Federation and Basketball South Africa. Along with basketball, the four-day clinic emphasizes education and life skills. Primarily as a result of these efforts and the fame of the handful of past stars, by 2008 a growing number of Africans were attending U.S. colleges on basketball scholarships.

STANLEY, HENRY M. (BORN JOHN ROWLANDS) (1841–1904). Welsh-born American newspaperman and explorer of Africa made famous in the United States for his search for missionary David Livingstone, which culminated in his immortal but perhaps apocryphal question, "Dr. Livingstone, I presume?" Stanley, who led other exploration safaris into the African interior, was known to Africans as Bula Matari (Kikongo, "crusher of rocks") for both his brutal treatment and his ability to accomplish his objectives against all obstacles. Stanley joined the payroll of King Léopold II of **Belgium** in 1877, helping him to lay claim to much of Central Africa, then supported his claims to the **Congo** at the Berlin Conference of 1884–85. Stanley returned to **Great Britain**, was elected to Parliament, and was knighted for his African work.

STANLEYVILLE (KISANGANI) HOSTAGE RESCUE. City in **Congo** where on 24 November 1964, a U.S.-led military operation rescued over 3,000 foreign hostages. Following the rescue, conducted with troops from **Belgium**, the mercenary-led Congolese army defeated the rebels. Stanleyville immediately became a symbol of U.S. support for mercenary racism and Belgian neo-colonialism despite the prior failure of negotiations, the Congolese government having granted permission for the rescue, and the imminent danger facing the hostages.

Stanleyville was the former base of Prime Minister **Patrice Lumumba**, and it became an anti-government center throughout the **Congo Crisis** following his overthrow and execution. Rebel soldiers, known as **Simba** warriors, took the city on 11 August 1964 and imposed a brutal rule that included massacres, murders, and ritual cannibalism. The conquest of Stanleyville was the high point of Simba fortunes because militarily effective foreign mercenaries, hired by newly appointed Congolese Prime Minister **Moïse Tshombe**, were put in the vanguard of the inept Congolese army and began to make steady progress eastward. The rebels countered by taking hostage 3,000 foreigners, most of them Belgians but including approximately 40 Americans of which five were U.S. consular employees (two of whom were undercover **Central Intelligence Agency** [CIA] agents), with the apparent intention of using them as human shields in the event of attack on Stanleyville, or to massacre them in a revenge killing. Negotiations by the **Lyndon B. Johnson** administration, working with **Tanzania** and **Kenya**, proved ineffective and, as the situation deteriorated, the U.S. and Belgian governments decided that only armed liberation could save the hostages. On 24 November 1964, U.S. airplanes dropped Belgian paratroopers on Stanleyville in Operation Dragon Rouge. A total of between 120 to 300 hostages, including two Americans, died in the period before the rescue, during the rescue itself, and in massacres in the countryside that followed. Simba resistance collapsed thereafter and by the end of 1965, the Congolese army had mopped up the remaining pockets of rebels.

SUDAN. Central African nation that has had a half-century history of civil wars that began shortly before independence on 1 January 1956 because Sudan straddles Arabized, Muslim north Africa and black, Christian and animist Southern Africa. Prior to colonization by **Great Britain**, tribes in what is modern northern Sudan frequently raided southern Sudanese villages for slaves. The legacy of northern arrogance and southern grievance has played a vital role in fostering the country's north–south division. The civil war was finally ended in 1972 by Colonel **Gaafar Nimeiri**, who had overthrown the government in order to end the war. Nimeiri created a federal government that gave the south great autonomy. Although he had been a Communist-backed Leftist, Nimeiri became a close ally of the United States following an unsuccessful Communist coup. Poor economic performance caused Nimeiri to flirt with Islamist politicians, and following the assassination of his close ally **Anwar Sadat** of **Egypt**, Nimeiri ordered the adoption of Islamic-based sharia law over the entire country, which caused the southerners to recommence the civil war in 1983. Nimeiri began providing arms to southern ethnic militias to create disunity among his opponents. He was overthrown in April 1985.

Nimeiri was eventually succeeded by General **Omar Bashir**, who overthrew a civilian government in 1989 because of its lack of progress in the war. Bashir vigorously prosecuted the war and was responsible for a significant share of its two million deaths before it ended in January 2005. Black slavery played a significant role in the war—Bashir himself allegedly owned slaves—and it continues to be practiced, complete with active slave markets. During the first decade of his rule, Bashir was under the sway of Islamist scholar **Hassan Turabi**, who made Sudan a center of **terrorism**, inviting many terrorists and terrorist organizations to base in Sudan including **Osama bin Laden**, who created **al Qaeda** there. International pressure led Bashir to fire Turabi and expel bin Laden after first offering him to Saudi Arabia and the U.S.

Bashir was among the first Muslim leaders to denounce the 11 September 2001 attacks and he provided the U.S. with valuable intelligence in the **Global War on Terror** (GWOT). Under strong political pressure from the U.S., Bashir negotiated peace with southern Sudan, granting remarkable autonomy to the region and the option to secede in 2015. Concurrently, in 2003 Bashir launched what became genocide against black Muslims in **Darfur** province. The **George W.**

Bush administration has been the leading government in speaking out against Sudan's use of its military and **Janjaweed** militia for ethnic cleansing, rape, and murder, and Secretary of State **Colin Powell** was the first world leader to call it genocide, which the president quickly affirmed. Bush reportedly considered military intervention in Sudan to stop the genocide, but was convinced not to do so by National Security Adviser **Condoleezza Rice**, who worried about the reaction by Muslims across the world if the U.S. attacked a third Muslim country after Afghanistan and Iraq. Subsequently, Bush has not pushed Bashir as hard as his rhetoric would suggest because of fear that it would cause Bashir to stop providing assistance in the GWOT and could cause the peace with southern Sudan to collapse. From 2004 to 2008, the U.S. contributed over $3 billion for aid programs in Sudan and refugees and displaced people in eastern **Chad**, including $600 million appropriated for fiscal year 2008. The U.S. had also spent $500 million to assist the **African Union** (AU) Mission in Sudan (AMIS) and its successor, the **United Nations** (UN)–AU Mission in Sudan (UNAMID). Based on figures from 2007 and 2008, the UN estimated that over 5.82 million Sudanese from across the country were either internally displaced or **refugees**.

In 2007, Congress passed the Sudan Accountability and Divestment Act, which authorizes state and local governments to divest from businesses with operations in Sudan and prohibits the U.S. government from contracting with them. On 28 May 2008, the three major U.S. candidates for president released a joint statement that said each would take immediate action against the government of Sudan if "peace and security" were not restored to Darfur by the time one of them took office. The chief prosecutor of the International Criminal Court, Luis Moreno-Ocampo, asked judges to issue an arrest warrant for Bashir on 14 July for crimes against humanity in Darfur, and Sudanese officials warned that it could not guarantee the safety of UN and AU **peacekeeping** forces if Bashir is indicted. *See also* AGENCY FOR INTERNATIONAL DEVELOPMENT (AID); CHINA; FOREIGN AID; IMMIGRATION; OIL.

SUEZ CRISIS (1956). Joint invasion of **Egypt** by **Great Britain**, **France**, and **Israel** beginning on 29 October 1956, intended to bring down Egyptian President **Gamal Abdel Nasser** and regain control of the Suez Canal, which he had nationalized on 26 July 1956. Foiled by U.S. political and economic pressure, Nasser had nationalized the canal in retaliation for Washington's announcement the week before that a consortium it was leading with the British and the World Bank would not fulfill its agreement to provide significant funding for the **Aswan High Dam**.

By nationalizing the canal, Nasser had violated a treaty with the British and the French, who jointly operated it. Seventy percent of British **oil** was shipped from the Arab Gulf states through the canal, giving Nasser the power to choke the British economy, a danger the British considered very real in light of Nasser's anti-colonialism, their conclusion that he had a Hitlerian drive to rule all the Arabs, and his soaring prestige among the Arab people across the Middle East and North Africa for having essentially defeated the colonial powers by taking the canal from them. The Western Europeans had blamed Nasser for the March 1954 overthrow of the Syrian government and for a series of attempted coups and riots in 1956 by Arab nationalists against conservative pro-Western governments. The French also believed that Nasser was the funding and weapons source for **Algeria**'s *Front de Libération Nationale*/National Liberation Front (FLN) rebels. The U.S. reserved judgment on all these issues and advised calm.

With their national security endangered and believing that Washington was following a path of appeasement, the French and British began to conspire against Nasser. They were joined by the Israelis, who had had enough of attacks by Fedayeen guerillas from Egyptian terrorist camps over whom Nasser claimed to have no control. The Israelis also believed that Nasser would continue to deny them access to the Suez Canal which, combined with his illegal blockade of the Gulf of Aqaba, left Israel with no outlet to Asia or East Africa. The conspirators hoped that the November U.S. presidential elections would distract Eisenhower and prevent him from stopping them.

On 29 October, Israel launched Operation Kadesh, invading the Sinai and moving quickly toward the canal. The next day, the British and French demanded that both the Israelis and the Egyptians withdraw 10 miles away from the canal or they would occupy the canal zone to protect the canal. As expected, Nasser refused the ultimatum, so the Europeans bombed Egyptian positions on 31 October. That same day, in Central Europe, Hungary announced that it was withdrawing from the **Soviet Union**'s Warsaw Pact. U.S. Secretary of State **John Foster Dulles** believed this was the start of the Soviet Empire's internal collapse. He was furious that U.S. allies were giving the Soviets the cover they needed to intervene and stop it, which they did with brutal force on 4 November. On 5 November, the British and French finally began their invasion, called Operation Musketeer, which did not go smoothly or well. In the interim, Washington proposed a resolution in the **United Nations** (UN) Security Council condemning the Israelis, British, and French, which the Soviets supported but the British vetoed. Washington responded by pushing a harshly worded cease-fire resolution through the UN General Assembly, where there is no veto, and began to apply tremendous political and economic pressure on its allies, including doing nothing to stop a dramatic depreciation of the British pound sterling; threatening to intervene in money markets to cause further damage to the British currency; and refusing to provide the Europeans with oil to compensate for a rapidly worsening shortage caused by Nasser blocking the canal by sinking several dozen ships, Syria cutting an oil pipeline that ran through its territory, and the Gulf Arab states imposing an oil embargo.

The pressure was so great that the same day they launched the invasion, the British and French announced that they would withdraw the moment UN peacekeepers arrived. That evening, when it became clear that the British and French had given up, Soviet Premier Nikolai Bulganin publicly announced that the Soviet Union would rain missiles upon London and Paris if the British and French did not withdraw. To ensure that it was only a bluff, the next day Eisenhower ordered the U.S. military on alert and warned that the U.S. would resist Soviet intervention. The same day, 6 November, Eisenhower was reelected president and British Prime Minister Anthony Eden announced that the invasion had been halted. The invaders stopped fighting on 7 November without regaining control of the canal. Eisenhower later admitted that had the allied forces quickly taken the canal and overthrown Nasser, he would have been forced to accept the *fait accompli*, but the Europeans' tardiness allowed Arab and world opinion to build up against the West intolerably, creating an opening for the Soviets in the Middle East. He told colleagues that he would not support the British and French if it meant losing the Arabs.

Nasser's prestige was now transcendent among Arabs and the third world, reinforcing his efforts to foment rebellion among conservative Arab monarchies and forcing them to move closer to Egypt. The Arabs and much of the third world also credited the Soviets' rocket-rattling with having forced the Europeans to give up, tremendously boosting the Communists' image as anti-colonialists. Soviet relations with Nasser became very close and they supplied him with millions of dollars in military and economic aid, culminating in their agreement to finance and build the **Aswan High Dam**. Among the now-divided North Atlantic Treaty Organization (NATO) allies, Prime Minister Eden was forced to resign in January 1957, British and French prestige in the Middle East was irreparably damaged, the British began to disengage from the Middle East, and decolonization in sub-Saharan Africa and the Caribbean rapidly accelerated. The Israelis managed to benefit from the fiasco, refusing to leave Egyptian territory until Nasser agreed to allow a UN **peacekeeping** force, called the UN Emergency Force (UNEF), to serve as a buffer between the two nations. The U.S. briefly won plaudits in the UN for its stance against its friends, but Eisenhower was forced to supplant the British in the Middle East, leading him to announce the **Eisenhower Doctrine** on 5 January 1957, which put Middle Eastern countries under Washington's protection from Soviet invasion. He was immediately denounced by Nasser and Arab nationalists as planning a new colonialism.

SULLIVAN PRINCIPLES. Code of corporate conduct for doing business in **South Africa** that was created by the Reverend Leon Sullivan, a member of General Motors' (GM) board of directors, which GM adopted in 1977. The Sullivan Principles required GM to treat all South African employees equally and in an integrated environment. GM made adoption of the Sullivan Principles a requirement for businesses that sought to work with GM. The U.S. government endorsed the principles and President **Ronald W. Reagan** made them central to his "**Constructive Engagement**" policy, although he opposed congressional legislation that sought to make them U.S. law. On 2 October 1986, Congress passed the **Comprehensive Anti-Apartheid Act** (CAAA) over Reagan's veto, which forced U.S.-based multinational corporations with branches in South Africa to follow the Sullivan Principles. Reagan's veto came because of the CAAA's ban of further U.S. investment or loans for South Africa and **trade** for most South African products, not because it made the Sullivan Principles a legal requirement for doing business in South Africa. Four days later, under heavy public pressure, GM reluctantly voted to divest itself from South Africa.

– T –

TANZANIA. Tanzania is the product of the 26 April 1964 union between Tanganyika and the island nation of **Zanzibar**. The founding president, **Julius Nyerere**, was much admired internationally for his policies of agrarian socialism and strong support for anti-colonial and anti-**apartheid** movements in Southern Africa, turning Tanzania into a far more important state in Africa and internationally than its sparse population, poverty, and lack of important natural resources would imply.

For U.S. policy makers, Nyerere's support for Southern African liberation movements was frequently an irritant, so much so that in the summer of 1964, **Central Intelligence Agency** (CIA) officials proposed but apparently were denied permission to supply weapons to unspecified Tanzanian opposition groups because they had concluded that Nyerere's policy of supporting **Congo**'s **Simba** guerillas and allowing them to operate from Tanzania had become a genuine danger. In November, Nyerere was the most vociferous African critic of the **Stanleyville (Kisangani) rescue** of hostages by the U.S. and **Belgium**. He continued to allow weapons to be shipped through Tanzania to Congo until the end of 1965, and allowed **Cuba**'s guerilla leader Ernesto "Che" Guevara to use Tanzania as a base before and after his failed intervention in the Congolese civil war. Along with providing sanctuary for Guevara's Cubans, Tanzania's capital, Dar es Salaam, became a center for African liberation movements, including a row of storefront offices used by independence and liberation movements from Congo, **South Africa, Rhodesia (Zimbabwe), Mozambique**, Southwest Africa (**Namibia**), and **Angola**. Nyerere even agreed to train as many as 30 **African Americans** led by Stokeley Carmichael to fight in Portuguese Guinea (Guinea–Bissau), but

Carmichael did not follow through on the offer. Nyerere also allowed Cuba to set up its largest African embassy. A National Security Council (NSC) report in June 1966 called Tanzania the center of radicalism in East Africa and noted strong Communist influence from the **Soviet Union** and **China**, especially on Zanzibar. It called Nyerere "mercurial and fiercely independent."

Tanzania became important to U.S. policy again in 1976 when Secretary of State **Henry Kissinger** met with Nyerere in the first step of his unsuccessful effort to reach a settlement in Rhodesia that would lead to black-majority rule. The administration of President **Jimmy Carter** emphasized that he did not see Africa through the **cold war** prism of his predecessors when he inviting Nyerere to be the first African leader to meet with him at the White House. Carter stunned Nyerere when the president publicly agreed with his tough demands for majority rule in Rhodesia. Thereafter, UN Ambassador **Andrew Young** worked closely with Nyerere and often used him as a sounding board for ideas on Washington's Africa policy. The **Ronald W. Reagan** administration was not enamored of Nyerere, and when Tanzania failed to pay even the interest on money owed to the U.S. in 1984, Reagan cut off all **foreign aid** except emergency food aid assistance. Nyerere retired in 1985. On 7 August 1998, **al Qaeda** attacked the U.S. embassy, killing 11 Tanzanians.

Since Nyerere's retirement and especially since his death in 1999, Tanzania has moved in a progressively capitalist direction and opened up free **trade**, so much so that Tanzania received the largest **Millennium Challenge Corporation** (MCC) grant, $698 million for improving transportation, energy, and water quality and delivery. MCC grants are provided by the U.S. to countries that meet benchmarks in democratization, capitalism, social progress, and good government. President **George W. Bush** recognized Tanzania's progress by visiting the country during his February 2008 Africa tour.

TAR BABY OPTION. Nickname given by opponents to the conciliatory U.S. Southern Africa policy of President **Richard M. Nixon**, embodied in **National Security Study Memorandum 39** (NSSM 39). Nixon's National Security Council (NSC) staff concluded that white rule in **South Africa**, the illegal white government of **Rhode-**

sia, and **Portugal**'s **Angola** and **Mozambique** colonies would continue for the indefinite future. Because each played an important strategic role by dint of their vital mineral resources, location along important sea lanes, strong anti-communism, and Portuguese control of the Azores Islands (important fueling stops for U.S. Air Force cargo airplanes), the NSC concluded that the U.S. should try to work with these governments rather than publicly chastise them, should ease President **Lyndon B. Johnson**'s strict interpretation of **United Nations** (UN) sanctions against South Africa, for example, and should quietly persuade them to improve the civil rights of their black majorities. At the core of the policy was the economic determinist argument that prosperity and economic development would inevitably lead to better conditions for the black majority.

Opponents called the policy the "Tar Baby Option" because they argued that black African governments would see the U.S. as being stuck to the white racist governments just as Br'er Rabbit became stuck to the Tar Baby in the Joel Chandler Harris "Uncle Remus" tale. Likewise, they argued that once the policy was begun, the administration was stuck to it and could not abandon it. The result, argued critics, would be to hurt U.S. prestige in Africa, aid in penetration of the region by the **Soviet Union**, and turn African nations against the U.S. in the UN.

TAYLOR, CHARLES (1948–). Warlord and president of **Liberia** (1997–2003), who perfected the creation of the state as criminal enterprise. A member of the nation's **Americo-Liberian** elite through his father, Taylor had been an officer in President **Samuel Doe**'s government but fled to the United States after being accused of stealing $1 million. He became friends with Donald Payne of New Jersey, who later led the Congressional Black Caucus, and spent time in a Massachusetts prison from which he escaped allegedly by bribing the guards. After fleeing the United States, Taylor went to **Libya** and participated in **terrorism** training. On 24 December 1989, Taylor launched a civil war at the head of a ragtag militia of Gio, Dan, and Mano tribesmen, all of which had been brutally oppressed by Doe and his Krahn tribe. Taylor revolutionized African civil wars by making use of child soldiers, who called him "Pappy" and were bound to him through forced participation in drugs, torture, terror, and other shared atrocities. The most brutal of these child soldiers made up a special force called the Small Boys Unit.

Taylor quickly took control of the Liberian countryside, which prompted intervention by **Nigeria** and a nominal few troops from other West African nations in 1990 under the auspices of the Economic Community of West African States (ECOWAS). The intervention, 3,000 soldiers called the Economic Community of West African States Monitoring Group (ECOMOG), was a failure thanks in part to Nigeria's opposition to both Doe and Taylor. The force also was badly led, underfunded, and lacked support from developed nations—the first soldiers to arrive had no uniforms and were forced to buy them from the militia of Taylor's former ally turned enemy, Prince Johnson. The **United Nations** (UN) sent 368 observers who proved of little assistance except to Taylor, whose forces gained local credibility by kidnapping them.

From 1990–96, 150,000 people were killed—7 percent of Liberia's population—hundreds of thousands more were driven into exile, and half the remaining people were left homeless. Gang rapes, slitting the bellies of pregnant women, ritualistic cannibalism, and the use of enemy body parts as talismans were everyday parts of the civil war. Skulls decorated militia checkpoints and were used as turf markers between warring militias. Taylor himself was protected by his Small Boys Unit and a praetorian guard of Libyan-trained soldiers.

In 1996, Taylor attacked and destroyed much of Monrovia, Liberia's capital. ECOMOG's resistance was disorganized and often inept. It failed to protect civilians when fighting broke out, many of its Nigerian military commanders dealt drugs, and sometimes Nigerian soldiers joined the looting, raping, and killing. Nigerian President Sani Abacha sought increased U.S. assistance, but President **Bill Clinton** refused because of Abacha's myriad human rights violations. Nonetheless, the force managed to bring a semblance of order that allowed former President **Jimmy Carter** to negotiate a peace settlement that brought elections on 19 July 1997. Taylor won through a combination of intimidation and corruption. His young supporters' slogan was, "He killed my ma, he killed my pa, I'll vote for him." International observers allowed the results to stand out of fear that preventing Taylor from taking power would restart the war.

As president, Taylor sought to spread his "Revolution" throughout the region, supporting the even more brutal Revolutionary United Front (RUF) in **Sierra Leone**, and rebels in **Guinea** and Ivory Coast. His goal was a "Greater Liberia," and he carried with him a map that showed Liberia's borders to include parts of Guinea and Sierra Leone's diamond fields. The RUF smuggled diamonds through Liberia, which were smuggled out of the country for international sale by **al Qaeda**. Taylor also used Liberia as a center for smuggling and illegal drugs distribution, reportedly earning $250 million per year. Diplomats called Liberia "Charles Taylor Incorporated."

Carter, whom Taylor had earlier fooled by praying with him as a fellow Baptist, protested Taylor's human rights violations, but relations with the Clinton administration were generally good thanks in large part to Taylor's relationship with Congressman Payne and **Jesse Jackson**, Clinton's special envoy for Africa. At Jackson's behest, Clinton telephoned Taylor from Air Force One during his Africa tour, and the State Department even played down its report of a 19 September 1998 attack by Taylor's police on the U.S. embassy that wounded one American while in pursuit of a rival warlord who had fled into the embassy. Jackson used Taylor as a go-between in his effort to integrate the RUF into the government of Sierra Leone. Taylor also received support from evangelist Pat Robertson, who invested $8 million in a Liberian gold mining venture.

Taylor's effort to create Greater Liberia led to his neighbors backing guerilla wars against him beginning in 1999. In early 2003 Taylor's army was defeated, and on 27 June 2003, President **George W. Bush** called on him to resign. Bush sent a U.S. Navy task force to patrol off the Liberian coast to reinforce his point. He was instrumental in persuading Nigeria to reenter Liberia as a peacekeeping force on 4 August, and in exerting the pressure that forced Taylor to go into exile to Nigeria on 11 August 2003. Taylor's last words before leaving Liberia were, "God willing, I will be back." He left a destroyed country with half the population displaced or **refugees**, no services, rampant disease, and 300,000 dead across West Africa. On 29 August 2006, Nigeria acceded to Liberian and U.S. pressure and extradited Taylor to Sierra Leone to be tried for crimes against humanity. He was transferred to the International Criminal Court at The Hague in 2006 and the trial began the following year.

TERRORISM. U.S. Statute 22 U.S.C. sec. 2656f(d)(2) defines terrorism as "premeditated, politically motivated violence perpetrated against noncombatant targets by subnational groups or clandestine agents." This definition is narrower than the common perception of terrorism in the U.S., which would include religiously motivated violence as well as violence perpetrated against combatants.

The difficulty with defining terrorism has proven to be embodied in the cliché that one man's terrorist is another man's freedom fighter. This is especially true in the African context in which **France, Portugal, South Africa**, and **Rhodesia** accused guerillas fighting for independence or black-majority rule as being "terrorists" because of such terroristic actions as massacring civilians; likewise, African governments called the guerillas "freedom fighters" and accused the white-dominated governments of being terrorists for attacking liberation movements' headquarters in urban areas, targeted assassinations of opponents, use of torture, and search and destroy missions in the bush with rules of engagement that often led to civilians being killed in the cross fire.

Leftist governments in **Angola, Ethiopia**, and **Mozambique** accused anti-Communist guerillas of being terrorists and accused the U.S. government of facilitating terrorism through the **Reagan Doctrine**, which provided support for **Jonas Savimbi**'s *União Nacional para a Independência Total de Angola*/National Union for the Total Independence of Angola (UNITA). Of these accusations, the most widely accepted case was against Mozambique's *Resistência Nacional Moçambicana*/Mozambican National Resistance (RENAMO), which most analysts agree abducted child soldiers and massacred or mutilated friend and foe alike in an effort to destroy the government's legitimacy. The administrations of **Ronald W. Reagan** and **George H.W. Bush** accepted this argument and refused to provide support for RENAMO despite the pro-RENAMO efforts of conservatives such as Senator **Jesse Helms**. A decided minority of experts claim that the massacres and mutilations were done by the Mozambican government to discredit RENAMO, and point to RENAMO's electoral success after the civil war had ended in regions that it allegedly terrorized as evidence thereof.

More clear-cut were the terrorist guerilla movements in **Liberia, Charles Taylor**'s National Patriotic Front of Liberia (NPFL), and in

Sierra Leone, Foday Sankoh's Revolutionary United Front (RUF). These movements attacked villages and abducted boys to create armies of child soldiers and girls to supply them with prostitutes and camp labor. Taylor forced boys to kill their families or village elders, kept them high on drugs and alcohol, and ordered them to massacre tens of thousands. In addition, the RUF forced child soldiers to amputate the limbs of friends and foes alike and enslaved people to work in diamond fields. Taylor also secretly worked with **al Qaeda**, using its operatives as a conduit through which he sold Sierra Leone's diamonds, known as **blood diamonds**, to fund his regime and the RUF.

During the 1970s and 1980s, **Muammar Qaddafi** of **Libya** was Africa's leading supporter of terrorism, backed by the **Soviet Union**. Qaddafi's training camps taught terrorists and guerillas from over 70 organizations from around the world, most with ostensibly Marxist orientations, including Taylor and Sankoh, but also guerillas from South Africa's African National Congress (ANC). The rise of Islamic terrorism in the 1990s led to the supplanting of Libya as the most important terrorist center because of Islamist revulsion for Qaddafi's idiosyncratic blend of Islam and socialism. Libya was replaced by **Sudan** under the ideological leadership of **Hassan Turabi**. Although a Sunni, Turabi sought to follow the example of the Ayatollah Ruhollah Khomeini in Shiite Iran as an exporter of revolutionary fundamentalist Islam, and reportedly worked with Iran in an effort to unite radical Islam. Turabi brought **Osama bin Laden** to Sudan where he created al Qaeda, which became the key organization in the movement by providing ideology and inspiration, leadership, money, and training for guerillas and terrorists. Important al Qaeda operations in Africa have included support for **Somalia**'s warlord **Muhammad Farah Aideed** in his fight with U.S. forces in 1993, and the terrorists behind the 1998 bombing of the U.S. embassies in **Kenya** and **Tanzania**.

Turabi's defeat in a power struggle with President **Omar Bashir** in 1999 resulted in bin Laden's expulsion and the loss of radical Islam's African base. Al Qaeda has subsequently taken advantage of East African turmoil, garnering a foothold in Somalia with the Islamist Islamic Courts Union (ICU), which briefly held power in 2006–07, and reportedly receives protection from the government of **Eritrea**. Al Qaeda has also sought to use unpopulated areas of the Sahara Desert as bases from which it has inspired and supported terrorist Islamist organizations in **Algeria** and **Morocco**.

The Bush administration has responded to Islamist terror in Africa with the **Global War on Terror** (GWOT). Its military response includes **Operation Enduring Freedom–Horn of Africa** (OEF-HOA), **Operation Enduring Freedom–Trans Sahara** (OEF-TS), and the **Trans-Sahara Counterterrorism Initiative** (TSCTI). To coordinate its military in Africa, the U.S. launched the **U.S. Africa Command** (AFRICOM) in 2007. The U.S. has also supported Ethiopia in its war against Somalia's ICU, including intelligence and military strikes against concentrations of al Qaeda fighters, and in its rivalry with Eritrea by working behind the scenes to reopen a **United Nations** (UN) commission's ruling that granted Eritrea disputed border territory over which the two sides had fought a bloody war from 1998–2000.

TOLBERT, WILLIAM, JR. (1913–1980). President of **Liberia** (1971–80) and close ally of the United States, which relied upon him for use of an important **Central Intelligence Agency** (CIA) transmission center. Tolbert was a member of the **Americo-Liberian** elite who assumed the presidency after the death of President **William Tubman**. Tolbert inherited an economic system heavily dependent on foreign investment. As a result, the international recession that followed the Organization of the Petroleum Exporting Countries (OPEC) price increases of 1973 and 1979 combined with drops in the prices of rubber and iron ore hit Liberia particularly hard. Revenue shortfalls made it impossible for Tolbert to maintain the vast patronage state that Tubman had built. Particularly hard hit were revenues for the indigenous tribes that Tubman had brought into the political system as his allies, although Tolbert did build roads into the interior to help integrate them into national life.

Forced to find new revenues, in April 1979 Tolbert ordered a 50 percent price increase in the price of rice, the country's dietary staple, providing a windfall to his brother-in-law, who controlled rice imports. Soldiers attacked a peaceful protest in Monrovia, Liberia's capital, leaving over 200 dead. For the next year, Tolbert tenuously held onto power as discontent grew among the overwhelmingly indigenous ranks of the enlisted corps of the armed forces. Tolbert was murdered in his bed on 12 April 1980, allegedly disemboweled by the coup's leader, Master Sergeant **Samuel Doe**. Public celebrations followed and most of Tolbert's top advisers, including his brother and son, were brutally executed by drunken soldiers before raucous mobs within days of the coup.

TORCH, OPERATION. *See* OPERATION TORCH.

TOURÉ, AHMED SÉKOU (1922–1984). Charismatic West African labor leader, Pan-Africanist, and president of **Guinea** (1958–84). Touré vaulted to international fame in 1958 during a joint appearance with President Charles de Gaulle of **France** in which he insulted the French by calling on Guineans to vote for independence rather than semi-autonomous association with France, proclaiming, "We prefer poverty in liberty to riches in slavery." Outraged, de Gaulle refused Touré's subsequent private imploring effort to heal the breach and, when 95 percent of Guineans voted for independence, the French granted it on 2 October 1958 and did all they could to derail the Guinean economy by removing everything that could be taken, including tearing telephones from the walls. As a radical socialist with few diplomatic options, Touré gravitated toward the **Soviet Union**, accepting massive amounts of aid and imposing a brutal and repressive regime on Guineans. In 1961 he won the Lenin Peace Prize, beating his West African socialist allies **Kwame Nkrumah** of **Ghana** and Modibo Keita of Mali.

Senator **John F. Kennedy** had met with Touré at Disneyland in 1959 while Touré was visiting the United States and had been very impressed. Following Kennedy's election as president, Touré continued rhetorical attacks against the U.S., but the president believed that Touré's nationalism could be used to overcome his commitment to Moscow. Kennedy spearheaded the effort with the **Peace Corps**. The Soviets responded by trying to stir unrest against Touré, who expelled their ambassador but maintained close economic ties. In October 1962, Kennedy met with Touré at the White House and won him over. Days later, during the Cuban missile crisis, Touré refused to allow the Soviets to refuel their airplanes in Guinea at an airstrip they had just upgraded, a major setback for the Soviets' effort to break the U.S. Navy's blockade of **Cuba**.

In 1966, Touré again turned against the U.S., blaming it for the overthrow of his friend, Nkrumah, whom Touré appointed co-president of Guinea. To protest against the coup and detention of a Guinean delegation by Ghana's military government (which Touré also blamed on Washington), Touré ordered the Peace Corps out of the country within 12 hours, had the U.S. ambassador placed under house arrest, and apparently told Guinea's youth corps to attack and destroy the U.S. Cultural Center. Touré grew increasingly paranoid and ordered tens of thousands jailed, many of whom were tortured, shot, or starved to death, which Touré mordantly called the "black diet." In 1974, Touré allowed Fidel Castro to use Conakry's airport as a refueling stop for airplanes transporting Cuban troops to fight in **Angola**'s civil war. Four years later, he cut ties with the Soviets and reestablished good relations with Washington and Paris. These on-again, off-again relations would continue until his 26 March 1984 death in a Cleveland, Ohio, hospital where he was being treated for a heart ailment.

Touré was proud of his performance as president, despite the economic disaster he had caused, because he had been one of the few African rulers who had broken the neo-colonial bonds that he said the U.S. and the West had used to tie Africans into economic, cultural, and political dependency. Within days of his death, the military overthrew and killed his half-brother, Ismael, and announced that it would dismantle Touré's Pan-Africanist socialist system and open up to the West.

TRADE. U.S. trade with sub-Saharan Africa is tiny compared to trade with the rest of the world, but is growing rapidly thanks in large part to the rising cost of **oil**. Exports to the region increased by 17 percent between 2005 and 2006 to $12.1 billion, mostly in machinery, aircraft, vehicles, and refined oil. Imports also rose significantly, 15 percent, from $50.3 billion to $59.175 billion, focused primarily on crude oil and minerals. Most U.S. trade was with oil-producing countries: **Nigeria**, **Angola**, **Algeria**, **Libya**, the Republic of Congo (Congo–Brazzaville), Gabon, **Chad**, and **Equatorial Guinea**. American oil purchases from Africa in 2006 almost equaled U.S. oil bought from the Middle East. U.S. purchases from **South Africa** for minerals and such "smoke-stack" industries as iron, steel, and aluminum were also significant.

The **African Growth and Opportunity Act** (AGOA), passed in 2000 to remove some textile quotas and make products duty free when they are imported for consumption, accounted for $44.26 billion in exports to the U.S., up 16 percent from 2005. Most of these exports, 93 percent, were petroleum products. Almost half of the remaining $3.2 billion (up 7 percent) was minerals and metals, transportation equipment from South Africa, and agricultural products. Textiles and clothing sales were down 11 percent to $1.3 billion. Oil producers and South Africa were the leading beneficiaries of AGOA. Illegal trade in Africa includes **blood diamonds**, drugs, and even slaves.

TRANSAFRICA. African American–led civil rights organization that played a leading role in the movement to make the U.S. government align itself against the **apartheid** government of **South Africa**. TransAfrica was founded in 1975 as the Black Forum on Foreign Policy. In September 1976, Randall Robinson was appointed executive director and the organization was renamed TransAfrica. TransAfrica initially focused without success on lobbying Congress to make mandatory the **Sullivan Principles**, which would force U.S.-based multinational corporations with branches in South Africa to treat black workers equally.

Following the reelection of President **Ronald W. Reagan**, Robinson decided to use direct action protest tactics he had learned in college. On 21 November 1984, the day before Thanksgiving, he and two colleagues met with the South African ambassador, then refused to leave his office, launching the anti-apartheid sit-in movement. They were arrested and spent the night in jail. Extensive press coverage led thousands of people to join the movement, including political and religious leaders, marching in front of the embassy or entering and being arrested. The campaign became known as the "Free South Africa Movement." Robinson even set up a schedule for sit-in participants to be arrested in order to ensure that there was a continuous flow of people and arrests. The movement spread to South Africa's consulates across the U.S. and to college campuses, where protesters demanded that trustees divest from businesses with branches in South Africa.

Within days of TransAfrica's first sit-in, congressional leaders of Reagan's Republican Party began to pressure the president to take action against South Africa, and Republican congressmen, including Newt Gingrich, the future speaker of the House of Representatives, wrote a letter to the South African government, telling its leaders that it had to act. By 10 December 1984, Reagan himself criticized the South African government for the first time although he continued to oppose sanctions. TransAfrica's pressure played a leading role in the **divestment (disinvestment) from South Africa movement**, which successfully pressured major universities and businesses to divest from South Africa and culminated in congressional passage of the December 1986 **Comprehensive Anti-Apartheid Act** (CAAA) over Reagan's veto. *See also* NON-GOVERMENTAL ORGANIZATIONS (NGOs); TUTU, DESMOND.

TRANSATLANTIC SLAVE TRADE. Slave **trade** between Africa and the Western Hemisphere. The most definitive estimates are that 10,247,500 people reached the Americas and 13.1 percent of those who left Africa died while making the voyage. Of the millions who left Africa, 559,800 reached what is now the United States between the 17th century and 1865. *See also* AFRICAN AMERICANS; IMMIGRATION.

TRANS-SAHARA COUNTERTERRORISM INITIATIVE (TSCTI). Joint interagency initiative consisting of U.S. military, diplomatic, and developmental agencies. They are working together to assist North African and Sahelian governments to take control of largely unpopulated regions of their countries that have served as bases for **terrorism** or routes for infiltration by terrorists. U.S. officials believe this area could become **al Qaeda**'s primary base of operations. The TSCTI was created by Congress in December 2004 with an appropriation of $500 million over six years to expand and supersede the Pan Sahel Initiative, which had been created in November 2002 to train rapid deployment forces in **Chad**, Mali, Mauritania, and **Niger**. The new program, part of **Operation Enduring Freedom–Trans Sahara** (OEF-TS), would assist **Algeria**, Chad, Mali, Mauritania, **Morocco**, Niger, **Nigeria**, Senegal, and **Tunisia** to build up their anti-terrorism capabilities, including creation and training of rapid deployment forces. In 2007, 480 U.S. special forces were stationed across the region for this purpose. Reconnaissance operations and military forces trained under the initiative have assisted in the capture or killing of al Qaeda–associated guerillas in Chad. The TSCTI also includes communications and development assistance through the State Department and the **Agency for International Development (AID)**.

The TSCTI has been controversial, as some analysts have argued that al Qaeda could not make the Trans-Sahara region into a base, the presence of U.S. forces could serve to inflame Muslim sensibilities and convert people to radical Islam, and governments could use the newly trained special forces to repress their own people.

TRIPOLITANIA. Northwest region of **Libya**. Tripolitania was an Italian colony until Italy's defeat in World War II. The **Soviet Union** sought control of the region in order to acquire a Mediterranean naval base, but was blocked by the Western powers. The colony was turned over to the **United Nations** (UN) in 1947. The following year, in an unsuccessful attempt to help the Italian Communist Party win national elections, the Soviets demanded that Italy be allowed to retain the colony. After the Communists lost the election, the Soviets lost interest in Tripolitania. Tripolitania received its independence as part of Libya in 1951.

TRUMAN, HARRY S. (1893–1971). U.S. vice president (1945) and president (1945–53). Truman's strong support for **Israel** and against arms sales to the Middle Eastern belligerents made U.S. relations with **Egypt** difficult, and relations with African nationalist leaders were harmed by Truman's policies that usually supported Western European colonialists.

Truman granted immediate recognition to Israel when it declared independence on 14 May 1948, despite the obviously imminent attack by the surrounding Arab states and despite opposition from his top foreign policy advisers and the bureaucracies of the departments of State and Defense. His motives were both personal conviction and the need for strong Jewish–American support in the 1948 presidential election. After the January 1949 cease-fire ended the **Arab–Israeli War of 1948–49**, Truman sought unsuccessfully to create a permanent peace settlement. Making the U.S. relationship with Egypt more difficult was the determination of **Great Britain** and **France** to maintain control of the Suez Canal Zone, the U.S. need for the airbases in the

Canal Zone that could strike petrochemical sites in the **Soviet Union**, and the strategic military reserve provided by 81,000 British troops stationed there.

In an attempt to overcome these difficulties with Egypt, the Truman administration joined a 1950 British effort to unite the Arab states in a military alliance against the Soviets called the Middle East Command (MEC). The Egyptian government of King **Farouk** rejected the offer and demanded that the British withdraw their military forces from Suez. Following Farouk's 1952 overthrow, the Egyptian Revolutionary Command Council (RCC) government of General **Muhammad Naguib** and Colonel **Gamal Abdel Nasser**, which had come to power with **Central Intelligence Agency** (CIA) assistance, rejected a new version of the alliance called the Middle East Defense Organization (MEDO). Along with these attempts to unite the Arab states, Truman joined the British and French in an effort to keep the peace in the region by issuing the Tripartite Declaration on 25 May 1950 in support of which they agreed to provide weapons only to Middle Eastern countries that pledged nonaggression against their neighbors and to use the weapons exclusively for national or regional defense or to maintain internal order. The three powers in turn pledged that they would take action within the **United Nations** (UN) or unilaterally as a group to repel any state that violated the pledge and attacked another.

In sub-Saharan Africa, Truman's personal opposition to colonialism was circumscribed by concern about the future of Western European colonial powers. The threat posed by Soviet power, the colonial powers' economic weakness following World War II, and the loss of confidence and national pride in France, **Belgium**, and the Netherlands after defeat by Germany led Truman and his advisers to conclude that maintaining the colonial empires would provide the West with raw material and markets necessary for a return to economic stability while restoring a sense of national greatness in the colonialists. The economic and political stability brought by the Marshall Plan for rebuilding Western Europe, which began in July 1947, and political victories over Communist parties in France in 1947 and Italy in 1948 led the State Department and the **Central Intelligence Agency** (CIA) to create the first comprehensive U.S. foreign policy on colonialism, although its focus was Asia. The proposal called for greater economic assistance, greater expressions of public sympathy for the colonial world, and diplomatic efforts to push the Europeans toward decolonization. Truman began to put this into practice with his 20 January 1949 Inaugural Address, when he announced his **Point Four** program to assist with the economic development of the third world.

The effort to win European support for the North Atlantic Treaty Organization (NATO) in early 1949 forced the Truman administration to backtrack on colonialism because of pressure from France and **Portugal**. The U.S. agreed to include protection of French **Algeria** and Portuguese overseas territories as part of the defense agreement. The administration returned to a more anti-colonial policy with a May 1950 speech by the State Department's George McGhee, which outraged the colonial powers when he called for eventual independence for the world's colonies. This approach was finally abandoned following the North Korean invasion of South Korea on 25 June 1950 because of the need for united Western support. Eleven days later, Truman told advisers that congressional opposition had killed Point Four. By 1951, McGhee was lecturing **Kwame Nkrumah** of the Gold Coast (**Ghana**) about the benevolence of British rule. The Korean War did assist **Ethiopia**, which strongly supported South Korea and provided troops for the war effort. The Truman administration successfully pushed the UN to give **Eritrea** to Ethiopia instead of Italy, its former colonial ruler, or placing it under a UN trusteeship to prepare it for eventual independence. *See also* ACHESON, DEAN G.; DULLES, ALLEN W.; EGYPT, CENTRAL INTELLIGENCE AGENCY INVOLVEMENT IN.

TSHOMBE, MOÏSE (1919–1969). Secessionist leader (1960–63) and national prime minister (1964–65) of **Congo**. Tshombe was ruthless and opportunistic, but also fearless, a tremendous leader and organizer, and second only to **Patrice Lumumba** in charisma among Congolese leaders. Tshombe's breakaway **Katanga** republic was a stable, prosperous, and multiracial state, but he garnered the undying hatred of much of the world because he introduced white mercenaries to Africa, maintained close relations with the white-dominated governments in Southern **Rhodesia**, **South Africa**, and **Portugal**'s colonies, and presided over Lumumba's assassination. Tshombe was the son of one of Congo's wealthiest black businessmen, was related to the king of the Lunda people, and was the king's son-in-law, although they often acted as rivals rather than allies. After failing at business, he entered politics and immediately became a Katangan leader, founding the *Confédérations des Associations Tribales du Katanga*/National Confederation of Tribal Associations of Katanga (CONAKAT) political party.

Tshombe worked closely with a white-dominated settler party and swept most of Katanga in the May 1960 national elections prior to independence. Because no party received more than one-quarter of the national vote, a coalition government emerged dominated by President **Joseph Kasavubu** and Prime Minister Lumumba, but southerners such as Tshombe received few and unimportant cabinet posts. Tshombe tried to meet with the leaders to discuss Katanga's place in the government during the period leading up to 30 June 1960 and independence from **Belgium**, but they rebuffed him. When the Congolese army rebelled on 5 July and Belgian troops intervened on 10 July, Tshombe declared Katanga's independence, claiming to have acted to protect his territory from the spreading mayhem. In this, he was encouraged by the Belgian government and the *Union Minière du Haut-Katanga* (UMHK), a huge copper-mining consortium that was Congo's largest business. Tshombe recruited a force of white mercenaries to lead his armed forces and continued to use whites to run Congolese ministries and big business since only a handful of black Congolese had the requisite education or training. Although Washington officially decried Katanga's secession, behind the scenes it was sometimes supportive.

In response to pleas from Kasavubu and Lumumba, the **United Nations** (UN) sent a **peacekeeping** force to Congo that was mandated to restore order but not to interfere in Congolese internal politics, which meant that it could not be used against Katanga despite Lumumba's continuous and ultimately violent demands. When Lumumba invited the **Soviet Union** to assist him in attacking Katanga, Kasavubu, army chief of staff Joseph-Désiré Mobutu (**Mobutu Sese Seko**), and other Congolese leaders overthrew and ultimately delivered Lumumba to Tshombe on 17 January 1961. Tshombe and his cabinet drunkenly took part in a horrific beating of Lumumba and two of his allies, and were present at Lumumba's execution. Tshombe lamely tried to cover up the assassination, but nobody believed his protestations of innocence.

In March 1961, Tshombe met with all the Congolese factions except for the Leftist **Antoine Gizenga**, and they agreed to reform Congo as a confederation. Pressure from the U.S. and especially the UN aborted this effort and, at a subsequent meeting in April, the Congolese government decided to continue with a unitary government. Government officials had Tshombe arrested on 26 April and threatened to try him for killing Lumumba, but when Tshombe's government did not collapse, Mobutu made a deal releasing him in exchange for his agreement to reintegrate with Congo, which he promptly ignored.

In late 1961, Mobutu attacked Katanga but failed to retake it. The UN failed a month later, but a December 1962 UN offensive crushed Katangan resistance. Tshombe was arrested on 14 January 1963 and sent into exile in Spain. When the Congolese government was on the verge of collapse from rebellions throughout the country in June 1964, the leadership brought Tshombe back and shocked the world when Kasavubu appointed him prime minister on 6 July 1964. Tshombe immediately hired his mercenary friends to serve in the Congolese army, requested assistance from **South Africa**, which turned him down, authorized the U.S.-organized November 1964 **Stanleyville (Kisangani) rescue** mission to save foreign hostages and retake the city, and crushed the rebellions. His success was so great that his CONAKAT Party scored impressive electoral gains in 1965 national elections. On 13 October 1965, Kasavubu fired Tshombe as prime minister, but the legislature refused to approve the dismissal. The political stalemate led Mobutu to overthrow the government on 24 November 1965 as he had done in September 1960, but this time he did not relinquish power.

Tshombe was again exiled to Spain and was sentenced in absentia to death for treason on 13 March 1967. On 30 June 1967, as Congolese mercenaries prepared to rebel, Tshombe flew to meet with prospective supporters in Malta, but the United States tipped off Mobutu about his plans. The flight was a trap and Tshombe was kidnapped and flown to **Algeria** where he was imprisoned at Mobutu's behest. He died in an Algerian jail on 30 June 1969, ostensibly from a heart attack, but commonly assumed to have been by poison.

TSVANGIRAI, MORGAN (1952–). Miner who became a labor union leader in **Zimbabwe**, founder of the Movement for Democratic Change (MDC) political party, and unsuccessful presidential candidate. Tsvangirai left school early to find work and ultimately became a miner. A charismatic speaker, he became involved in union affairs and was elected secretary-general of the Zimbabwe Congress of Trade Unions (ZCTU) in 1988. The ZCTU was a branch of President **Robert Mugabe**'s Zimbabwe African National Union–Patriotic Front (ZANU-PF) political party, but Tsvangirai concluded that it would be more effective for its members as an independent trade union, so he broke away in 1989 and was sentenced to jail for six weeks as a spy for **South Africa**. Tsvangirai organized a 1997 general strike that prevented Mugabe from raising taxes to pay hundreds of millions of dollars to veterans of Zimbabwe's war for independence, which would replace millions of dollars stolen by Mugabe and his friends. War veterans responded with a brutal but unsuccessful attempt to kill Tsvangirai.

In September 1999, Tsvangirai led the effort to create the MDC, Zimbabwe's first powerful opposition party since Mugabe had created a virtual one-party state in December 1987. MDC organizing prevented Mugabe from passing a February 2000 referendum that would have increased his power and allowed the government to confiscate without compensation land owned by white Zimbabweans, but Mugabe responded with fraud, intimidation, and violence, which allowed him to hold onto a parliamentary majority in the June 2000 elections. Mugabe increased the fraud and violence in 2002 to win reelection against Tsvangirai. The **George W. Bush** administration joined the European Union (EU) in sanctioning Zimbabwe by freezing the overseas assets of Mugabe and other leaders in his government, banning their travel to the sanctioning countries, and halting the sale of military equipment to Zimbabwe. The U.S. extended the sanctions the following year to end all **foreign aid** except for humanitarian assistance.

In May 2001, Tsvangirai was charged with treason and was twice accused of plotting to kill Mugabe, but was found not guilty on all charges. On 11 March 2007, he was arrested with 49 other MDC members while on his way to an illegal prayer rally. Government forces beat and tortured him, fracturing his skull and causing internal bleeding. The U.S. protested and in January 2008 further expanded the sanctions to include Zimbabwean intelligence officials and government-operated businesses.

Tsvangirai's MDC won a narrow majority of legislative seats in 29 March 2008 elections, although ZANU-PF soon began to go to court to challenge enough districts' electoral results to prepare for a legislative majority. In the presidential election, Tsvangirai received over 50 percent of the vote as indicated by the aggregate of totals posted on every voting precinct across the country, but the government released no official figures for over a month. During the interim, South Africa's Transport and Allied Workers Union refused to unload or transport a containership loaded with weapons for Mugabe from the government of **China**. Unions across Southern Africa followed the South African unions' lead and the U.S. government also pressured Southern African governments not to allow the ship to land, and it was finally forced to return to China.

When vote totals were finally officially reported on 2 May, Tsvangirai had a plurality but not a majority, which required a runoff. During the campaign, despite pressure from the U.S., the EU, and many African states, Mugabe's forces unleashed extreme violence on MDC officials and activists, killing over 100. Tsvangirai fled to the Dutch embassy and finally withdrew from the election. After Mugabe's victory, the two men met on 21 July and laid out preconditions for negotiations to create a government of national unity. *See also* MANDELA, NELSON ROLIHLAHLA; MBEKI, THABO; SOUTH AFRICA.

TUBMAN, WILLIAM (1895–1971). Longtime president of **Liberia** (1944–71), and ally of the United States. Although Tubman was an **Americo-Liberian**, he was not born into the Monrovia elite, instead growing up in rural Maryland County where his ancestors had settled from Georgia in the 1830s. In 1943, Liberian president Edwin Barclay chose the little-known Tubman as his successor in the mistaken belief that he could control him from behind the scenes. Instead, Tubman proved himself to be a political magician who quickly took control of Liberia's political and economic patronage and with them, control of Liberian politics. Tubman opened the economy to international investment and foreign **trade**, using the revenue to expand the bureaucracy, fund internal improvements, and provide development assistance for the indigenous peoples. As a result, Tubman garnered immense popularity with this heretofore marginal group. Nonetheless, the indigenous people remained cut off from the rest of the country, with the only paved road from Monrovia to the interior going 78 miles inland to one of Tubman's farms.

Tubman played a vital role in the early period of African independence as an anti-colonial leader and supporter of U.S. foreign policy. During World War II, he had allowed Washington to build an airfield for military aircraft that continued to be used after the war. Thereafter, he permitted construction of a forest of communications equipment that was publicly explained as Voice of America (VOA) transmitters and an emergency shipping navigation station, but was primarily used by the **Central Intelligence Agency** (CIA) as its African transmission center.

To maintain his control, Tubman employed five different security forces. Elections were farces and any attempt at real opposition led directly to jail. Despite his reforms, Liberia continued to be dominated by the Americo-Liberians at the time of his death in 1971. *See also* TOLBERT, WILLIAM.

TUNISIA. North African nation that has been a moderate presence in the Middle East and a friend of the United States since independence in 1956. The first U.S. contact with Tunisia began in the 1780s as **Barbary Pirates** (privateers) preyed on U.S. shipping. A 1797 treaty protected U.S. ships, but at a price of over $100,000 with continued tribute payments thereafter until the U.S. Navy destroyed the Barbary Pirates' bases in 1815. Tunisia next entered U.S. strategic thinking with **Operation Torch**, the U.S. invasion of North Africa in 1942. Under the command of General **Dwight D. Eisenhower**, Torch had the purpose of securing **Morocco** and **Algeria** in order to launch the **Tunisia Campaign**. Following a bloody U.S. defeat at the **Battle of Kasserine Pass** on 19 February 1943, the U.S. finally took Tunisia on 13 May. Tunisia then served as the launching point for the invasion of Fascist Italy.

Following independence on 20 March 1956, Tunisian leader **Habib Bourguiba** strove to secularize Tunisian life. He ordered his government to take over Islamic schools, dissolve Islamic sharia courts, pass laws to guarantee the rights of women and end polygamy, and personally and publicly broke the Ramadan fast. Although Bourguiba supported the *Front de Libération Nationale*/National Liberation Front (FLN) rebels in Algeria, his foreign policy was moderate and he opposed the radical revolutionary policies followed by **Gamal Abdel Nasser** of **Egypt**. Bourguiba was especially close to President **John F. Kennedy**, who also approved of Bourguiba's efforts at modernization under a moderate socialist domestic policy. Relations between the two countries cooled in July 1961 when **France** bloodily broke a Tunisian blockade of its naval base at Bizerte, the last French military presence in Tunisia. Kennedy ordered the U.S. delegation to abstain on a 26 August 1961 **United Nations** (UN) General Assembly vote condemning France, explaining to his advisers that he was willing to risk the criticism of Bourguiba and the Afro-Asian bloc because "their cause won't be helped by the overthrow of [French President Charles] de Gaulle." Relations with Tunisia quickly recovered and Kennedy made Tunisia the highest per capita recipient of U.S. **foreign aid** in Africa.

Tunisia moved to a rigid socialist system in 1964, which ruined the economy by 1969. During this period, the U.S. and the **World Bank** significantly cut support, which was restored as Tunisia moved to economic liberalization in 1970. Economic liberalization and a World Bank structural adjustment program (SAP) led to significantly higher prices, periodic violent unrest, and the growth of Islamic radicalism. **Muammar Qaddafi** of **Libya** encouraged unrest starting in the late 1970s, which prompted the U.S. to shift much of its aid from economic to military. Bourguiba's successor, Prime Minister Zine al-Abidine Ben Ali, improved relations with Libya and tried unsuccessfully to mediate between Qadafi and the U.S. Ben Ali had removed Bourguiba from power, due to senility, on 7 November 1987. Ben Ali believed that Bourguiba had become obsessed with radical Islamists and that the president's effort to crush the movement was causing it to spread. As president, Ben Ali freed hundreds of Islamists from jail but refused to legalize their political party, which led to violent unrest. He crushed the movement in 1992, prompting international human rights organizations to protest.

Beginning in 1982, Middle Eastern politics became a periodic source of contention between Tunisia and the U.S. after the administration of

President **Ronald W. Reagan** successfully pressured Bourguiba to accept relocation of the Palestine Liberation Organization (PLO) from Lebanon to Tunis after **Israel** drove it out of Beirut. Israel's 1 October 1985 air raid on a PLO compound, which killed some Tunisians, led to anti-U.S. protests when the U.S. failed to condemn Israel at the UN. Anti-U.S. protests also followed the Israeli assassination of Palestinian terrorist leader Abu Jihad (Khalil al-Wazir) near Tunis in 1988. By 1990, the U.S. had provided Tunisia with $1 billion in aid, but Tunisian support for Iraq's invasion of Kuwait in 1990 caused President **George H.W. Bush** to order a 70 percent cut in U.S. aid in 1991, and the following year it was reduced to $1 million. Despite human rights organizations' criticisms of Tunisia for its crackdown on the Islamist opposition, the administration of **Bill Clinton** provided foreign aid of $32 million in 1993, exceeding pre–Persian Gulf War levels, because of U.S. government concern that Algeria's civil war against radical Islamists would spread to Tunisia. The PLO's move from Tunis to Gaza in 1994 also removed a potential source of disagreement. Tunisia exchanged an "interest section" with Israel in 1996, making it the second Arab country to formalize relations. The Tunisian economy has grown rapidly since the early 1990s under Ben Ali's rule, which continued into 2008.

TUNISIA CAMPAIGN. Military campaign to drive the Axis powers out of North Africa during World War II, which followed **Operation Torch**, the bungled yet successful Allied invasion of French North Africa. Allied commander **Dwight D. Eisenhower** launched the campaign on 17 November 1942. Although troops from **Great Britain** fought well, the badly led and trained U.S. Army did not. Despite strong superiority in numbers and weapons, and having the Germans and Italians under Field Marshall Erwin Rommel outflanked, the "Desert Fox" managed to hold off the Allies with several defensive engagements, and defeated U.S. forces at the **Battle of the Kasserine Pass**. These fights proved invaluable as training for the U.S. forces and for Eisenhower, who replaced incompetent officers and ordered significant changes in how American soldiers were prepared for battle. The result was a transformed army that performed credibly by campaign's end. The Germans surrendered on 13 May 1943, and 275,000 soldiers were taken prisoner. In July, Eisenhower oversaw the invasion of Sicily from North Africa, which was the first step in the invasion of Southern Europe.

TUNNEY AMENDMENT. Amendment to the 1975 Defense Department Appropriations Bill signed on 9 February 1976, which forced the administration of President **Gerald R. Ford** to stop overt and covert U.S. funding of anti-government guerillas in **Angola**. Secretary of State **Henry Kissinger** had hoped to use U.S. intervention in Angola to show the **Soviet Union** and the world that Washington was still capable of responding to Soviet advances in the third world despite setbacks in southeast Asia. The Tunney Amendment, proposed by California Senator John Tunney, put an end to the **Central Intelligence Agency**'s (CIA) **Operation IAFEATURE**, which had secretly provided **Jonas Savimbi**'s *União Nacional para a Independência Total de Angola*/National Union for the Total Independence of Angola (UNITA) with arms shipped from **Zaïre**. Newspaper revelations about the operation combined with reporting on **South Africa**'s intervention in support of Savimbi antagonized Democrats in Congress, who constituted overwhelming majorities in both the House and Senate but had not been consulted about the operation. Congress was determined to pull back from international conflict, a policy later derided by Republicans as the "Vietnam Syndrome." The Tunney Amendment was the first time that Congress passed a law preventing the president from using the CIA in a covert operation. *See also* CLARK AMENDMENT.

TURABI, HASSAN AL- (c. 1932–). Sudanese Islamist professor of law, politician, and de facto ruler of **Sudan**, who made it the center of Islamist terrorism during the 1990s. Turabi had earned a doctorate in law from the Sorbonne and was a longtime Sudanese politician. He came to power as the government's chief ideologist following a 1 July 1989 military coup led by Colonel **Omar Bashir**. Although sometimes a liberal and sometimes a conservative prior to the coup, Turabi governed as a hardcore Islamist. He oversaw the re-introduction of sharia law in northern Sudan (in 1983 as attorney general for a previous government, he had imposed it nationwide), advocated the use of torture, supported slaving by Arab northerners in the black south, and called on the army to use whatever tactics were necessary to crush the south in the ongoing civil war.

Turabi made Sudan of particular interest to the United States because of his support for Islamist **terrorism** movements. He invited such leading terrorists and organizations as Abu Nidal, Carlos "the Jackal" Ramirez, **Osama bin Laden**, who created his **al Qaeda** network there, and Hezbollah to relocate in Sudan. In April 1991, Turabi began hosting a yearly meeting of Islamists, the Islamic Arab Popular Conference. His purpose was to use opposition to the U.S. and the West as a means to overcome divisions between Shiite and Sunni Muslims while moving nationalists toward Islamist thought. Washington added Sudan to its "State Sponsors of Terrorism" list following the 1993 World Trade Center bombing that killed six and wounded over 1,000. Turabi supported Sudanese participation in terrorist activities in **Egypt**, **Uganda**, **Eritrea**, and **Ethiopia**, most notably an unsuccessful attempt on the life of Egyptian President **Hosni Mubarak** in 1995, which led to **United Nations** (UN) sanctions against Sudan. In response, the military side of the Sudanese government offered to extradite bin Laden to Saudi Arabia or the U.S., but was turned down by both, so it forced him and his organization to leave for Afghanistan. Turabi also served as a link between Iraq and al Qaeda, negotiating a non-aggression pact between Saddam Hussein and bin Laden along with agreements to work together on projects of mutual interest. The relationship continued until Turabi's ouster from power on 12 December 1999. He was jailed by Bashir in March 2004 and released on 28 June 2005.

TUTU, DESMOND (1931–). Anglican archbishop, who won the Nobel Peace Prize in 1984 for his work against **apartheid** in **South Africa**. Tutu's often courageous opposition to apartheid grew out of his belief in the social gospel and the Black Consciousness ideas of **Stephen Biko**. His charismatic leadership of the South African Council of Churches beginning in 1978 gave him international standing, and his support for both nonviolent change and economic sanctions against South Africa made him a unique figure whose message resonated with the Left while assuaging the worst fears of the Right. Tutu's selection as winner of the Nobel Peace Prize gave him an international pulpit that had a huge impact on U.S. foreign policy as Tutu became the sometimes ubiquitous face of black South

Africa on television and the all-purpose source of quotations for newspaper stories.

Following the transition to majority rule, President **Nelson Mandela** appointed Tutu chairman of the Truth and Reconciliation Commission in 1995. Tutu insisted that investigation had to be impartial, and the Commission revealed horrific atrocities committed by numerous groups, including the apartheid government and Mandela's African National Congress (ANC) although Mandela himself was not implicated in any crimes. Tutu has been very critical of President **Thabo Mbeki**'s constructive engagement–style policy with **Robert Mugabe** of **Zimbabwe**, and of Mbeki's economic policies, which Tutu claimed were ignoring the needs of South Africa's impoverished majority.

– U –

UGANDA. East African nation well endowed with agricultural resources but victimized by brutal despots. Uganda entered U.S. consciousness in the mid-1970s because of the buffoonish antics and mass murder by military ruler **Idi Amin**, particularly following his elevation to the chair of the **Organization of African Unity** (OAU) in 1975–76. U.S. commentators were shocked when Amin received a hero's welcome from the other heads of state thanks to his anti-Western rhetoric and expulsion of East Indians from Uganda. As the Ugandan economy collapsed and reports emerged that Amin had killed over 200,000 of his people, the U.S. Congress passed a **trade** embargo in 1978. In October, rebellious Ugandan troops invaded **Tanzania**. Tanzanian President **Julius Nyerere** ordered a counterinvasion that overthrew Amin on 11 April 1979. Amin's final toll was estimated to be over 250,000 dead Ugandans.

Nyerere maneuvered to put back into power his friend, former President Milton Obote, despite Obote's harsh rule and economically ruinous socialism having set the stage for Amin's military coup. Obote won rigged elections in December 1980 and ruled as brutally but far more systematically than Amin, killing over 300,000 Ugandans through repression and civil war. Obote was overthrown by a guerilla army led by **Yoweri Museveni** on 29 January 1986, one of the first times that guerillas had overthrown an independent African government. Museveni restored stability, human rights, and economic prosperity, and in 1990 began an anti-**AIDS** program in which the government worked with churches and **non-governmental organizations** to get Ugandans to talk about HIV/AIDS and change their sexual practices. Washington and the developed world responded with **foreign aid** that made up 40 percent of Uganda's national budget.

In 1999, the continuing crisis between **Congo** and **Rwanda** led Museveni to enter the war on the side of Rwanda, whose leader, **Paul Kagame**, with 3,000 Rwandan soldiers had served in Museveni's guerilla army. Ugandan army officers, including Museveni's half-brother, turned corrupt from the myriad opportunities that Congo offered for illicit trade, and corruption led to fighting with the Rwandans over the spoils. Corruption in Uganda itself became so bad that donors began cutting off aid while the **George W. Bush** administration refused to provide infrastructure funding from the **Millennium Challenge Corporation** (MCC), despite close relations with Uganda because of its support for the **Global War on Terror** (GWOT). The administration did give Uganda $10.4 million for programs to fight corruption that could make Uganda eligible for future infrastructure grants. Museveni changed Uganda's constitution in 2005 to allow himself to run for a third term in 2006, which he won in an election that may have been stolen. Museveni's growing dictatorial practices have not seriously harmed his relationship with Washington because of Uganda's strategic location near **Sudan** and **Somalia**, both of which have been closely tied to **al Qaeda**. With U.S. support, Museveni sent Ugandan troops to Somalia in 2007 as part of an **African Union** (AU) **peacekeeping** force to prevent the Islamist Islamic Courts Union (ICU) from regaining power. By mid-2008, the Ugandans and a token force from Burundi were the only AU troops in the field. Bush met with Museveni at the White House on 7 October 2007. Afterwards, neither man mentioned having discussed human rights.

UNITED NATIONS (UN). World government body created at a San Francisco, California, conference that began 25 April 1945 as World War II was coming to an end. Conceived to replace the failed League of Nations, the UN's multiple purposes include maintaining international order through discussion and negotiation, implementing and facilitating the creation of international law, assisting in economic development, fostering social progress, and protecting human rights. It is a universal organization including virtually every nation in the world and all 53 African countries, excluding only the Sahrwai Democratic Republic, which is in a dispute with **Morocco** over competing claims to be the legitimate government of former Spanish Sahara. The UN has a two-tier governing system divided between the Security Council, which itself has two tiers—five permanent members (the United States, **France**, **Great Britain**, Russia, and **China**) with the power of veto, and elected members from each world region that do not have veto power—and the General Assembly, in which each state has an equal vote and there is no veto. There is also a Secretariat that serves as the UN's bureaucracy, an Economic and Social Council, and the International Court of Justice.

Africa's potential 53-vote bloc enhanced the continent's importance during the **cold war** as the U.S. and the **Soviet Union** vied for its support. This influence was further strengthened when African states joined former colonies in Asia (the Afro-Asian bloc), with so-called neutralist nations from around the world in the Non-Aligned Movement, or with Asia and Latin America (the third-world bloc). African states' numbers have also made them influential in UN specialized agencies, which give each member state a vote. Among the specialized agencies are the UN Educational, Scientific, and Cultural Organization (UNESCO), the World Health Organization (WHO), the **World Bank**, and the **International Monetary Fund** (IMF).

UN involvement in Africa began in 1946 when India protested treatment of East Indian citizens and expatriates by the government of **South Africa** for violating the UN Charter's provisions on human rights; when South Africa, which had a League of Nations mandate over Southwest Africa (**Namibia**), refused to turn the territory over to a UN trusteeship and asked to annex it, which the UN refused in December 1946; and when residents of what would become **Somalia** and **Eritrea** used the UN to persuade the Great Powers and the world to prevent their recolonization by Italy. Each of these early efforts was precedent-setting by involving the UN in member nations' domestic practices, by putting the UN on the side of the colonized versus colonizers, and by allowing colonial peoples to speak directly to the UN rather than exclusively through their colonial masters. The South African case was especially significant because Prime Minister **Jan Smuts** had been the most important author of the UN Charter. The ultimate result of these precedents was vigorous UN opposition to racist regimes in Southern Africa, with voluntary sanctions against selling military equipment to South Africa announced on 8 August 1963, mandatory sanctions against **trade** with **Rhodesia**, and creation of the Committee of Twenty-four, a third world–dominated committee that pushed for immediate decolonization. U.S. presidents had assumed that the U.S. and the West would dominate the UN, and Washington quickly grew ambivalent about each of these streams, weighing the price of opposing colonialism and supporting civil rights and black-majority rule in Southern Africa against strategic dangers such as conflict with colonizers that were cold war allies and the risk of losing access to critical minerals from Southern Africa.

By the late 1960s, the third-world bloc had emerged in the UN and often allied itself with the Soviet Union and its bloc. Third-world countries engaged in intensive criticism of Western powers, especially the U.S., and sought to impose major changes in world economic and information systems through creation of a "New International Economic Order," which would bring a massive redistribution of wealth from Western nations to the third world, and a "New International Information Order," which would correct perceived Western media bias against third-world countries by creating a UN-led mechanism for regulating news coverage and reportage. The administration of **Ronald W. Reagan** effectively killed both measures and he ordered the U.S. to quit UNESCO in large part because of its leadership in these campaigns.

The UN's mandate was extended further at the end of the **Arab–Israeli War of 1948–49** when it sent a **peacekeeping** force, the UN Emergency Force (UNEF), to separate **Egypt** and **Israel**. Since then, 18 UN peacekeeping missions have been sent to separate combatants in 14 different conflicts in Africa. Peacekeeping was transformed into peacemaking during the **Congo Crisis**, when the UN again extended its mandate by including invasion and reintegration of the rebel **Katanga** province. Such a transformation of goals was subsequently made in Somalia in 1992–93, but the disastrous Battle of Mogadishu turned U.S. and world opinion against peacemaking missions. As a result, only minimal and ineffectual UN peacekeeping missions were sent to try to stop genocides in **Rwanda** and **Darfur** province in **Sudan**, and to stop the continent-wide war in Congo. UN peacekeepers have been accused of human rights violations, including allegations of systemic brutality and indiscipline, extortion, corruption, sexual slavery, and use of child prostitutes in Congo, southern Sudan, **Kenya**, Ivory Coast, **Liberia**, and Burundi.

Presidents **Gerald R. Ford**, Reagan, and **George W. Bush** used UN Ambassadors Daniel Patrick Moynihan, Jeanne Kirkpatrick, and John Bolton to provide vociferous opposition to anti-U.S. rhetoric and actions by the Soviet and third-world blocs, while President **Jimmy Carter** tried to work with Africans through UN Ambassadors **Andrew Young** and Donald McHenry. President **George H.W. Bush** tried to use the UN to create a largely undefined "New World Order," with the Somalia intervention as a first effort in the third world. His successor, **Bill Clinton**, continued the Bush policy until the Battle of Mogadishu, after which he issued **Presidential Decision Directive 25** (PDD-25), dramatically limiting U.S. participation in peacekeeping and providing the intellectual basis for the U.S. working to abort the peacekeeping mission in Rwanda. George W. Bush proved notoriously reluctant to work through the UN in Iraq and on issues relating to the **Global War on Terror** (GWOT), but sought to work with it on global efforts to fight disease. *See also* AIDEED, MUHAMMAD FARAH; KASAVUBU, JOSEPH; LUMUMBA, PATRICE; RESOLUTION 242, UNITED NATIONS SECURITY COUNCIL; RWANDA, GENOCIDE IN; TSHOMBE, MOÏSE.

UNITED STATES AFRICA COMMAND (AFRICOM). U.S. military command created to coordinate U.S. defense policy in Africa. AFRICOM was established in response to the **Global War on Terror** (GWOT) as a way to centralize U.S. defense policy in Africa, which was spread among the European (EUCOM), Central (CENTCOM), and Pacific (PACOM) Commands. AFRICOM's responsibilities include 52 of Africa's 53 nations, with **Egypt** remaining the responsibility of CENTCOM. It will be the sixth U.S. regional command.

AFRICOM was created by President **George W. Bush** on 6 February 2007. It was established as a sub-unified command to EUCOM and based in Stuttgart, Germany, on 1 October 2007, and is scheduled to become an independent command on 1 October 2008. AFRICOM was originally slated to move its headquarters and forward base to a sub-Saharan African nation, but the U.S. first revised these plans to have several regional bases throughout the continent in **Liberia**, **Botswana**, and **Rwanda**, and it finally indefinitely postponed plans to move from Stuttgart, reportedly because of protests from African nations. Instead it will work through military personnel already assigned to U.S. embassies.

AFRICOM's purpose is to assist African nations to maintain stability through U.S. military participation with nation-building projects as well as military training and assistance. AFRICOM is unique among U.S. military commands because it integrates military and civilian personnel from such bureaucracies as the State Department and the **Agency for International Development** (AID). AFRICOM's second-in-command denied reports that the command's purpose is to counter the growing influence of **China** on the continent. *See also* OPERATION ENDURING FREEDOM–HORN OF AFRICA (OEF-HOA); OPERATION ENDURING FREEDOM–TRANS SAHARA (OEF-TS); TERRORISM; TRANS-SAHARA COUNTERTERRORISM INITIATIVE (TSCTI).

– V –

VANCE, CYRUS (1917–2002). U.S. public official and secretary of state (1977–80) under President **Jimmy Carter**. Along with **United Nations** (UN) Ambassador **Andrew Young**, Vance supported assisting the development efforts of African nations, pushed hard to prevent U.S. recognition of the Internal Settlement government in Zimbabwe–Rhodesia, and played a significant role in bringing about the Lancaster House Conference that ended the civil war in **Rhodesia** and brought Zimbabwe–Rhodesia to legal recognition as **Zimbabwe**.

While Vance was interested in working with Africans to solve African problems, he considered African interventions by the **Soviet Union** and **Cuba** to be inconsequential sideshows that threatened détente. This policy was seen in **Zaïre** in March 1977 when Washington refused to provide more than token non-lethal assistance to President **Mobutu Sese Seko** during an invasion by rebels based in Communist-ruled **Angola**. That summer, Vance successfully pushed for a hands-off policy in the Horn of Africa following **Somalia**'s invasion of **Ethiopia**'s Somali-dominated Ogaden Desert, and Carter continued to follow his counsel even after Cuban troops entered the fray in January 1978. The Horn of Africa began Vance's split with National Security Adviser **Zbigniew Brzezinski**, who argued that the Soviet intervention put at risk U.S. interests on the Arabian peninsula. Failure to respond, he said, signaled to the Soviets that they could act with impunity throughout the third world. The split between the men contributed to an at-times incoherent Carter administration foreign policy.

Vance's role in the Middle East was circumscribed by Carter's direct and intense role in bringing together **Anwar Sadat** of **Egypt** and **Israel**'s Menachem Begin, and Vance and the State Department played a decidedly secondary role in the resulting peace treaty. The Soviet invasion of Afghanistan and the Iranian hostage crisis effectively ended Vance's interest in sub-Saharan Africa and derailed any chance to broaden Middle East peace. He resigned as secretary of state on 28 April 1980 over his adamant opposition to the Iranian hostage rescue mission, a rare instance in U.S. history of a cabinet official resigning over policy differences with the president.

VOLTA RIVER DAM. Ghanaian dam known locally as the Akosombo Dam that was part of an industrial complex that included hydroelectric power and aluminum smelting. It was built with funding by the United States, **Great Britain**, and the **World Bank** at a cost of approximately $370 million of which over $200 million came from Washington in loans and grants, making it the largest U.S. investment in Africa. Ghanaian Prime Minister **Kwame Nkrumah** began seeking U.S. support for the dam soon after **Ghana** became independent in 1957, sending Finance Minister Komla Gbedemah to the U.S. in hopes of gaining backing for the project. The administration of President **Dwight D. Eisenhower** showed no interest in meeting with Gbedemah until he was refused service at a Dover, Delaware, restaurant because he was black. The embarrassing newspaper headlines that followed prompted Eisenhower to arrange an immediate meeting, after which he told Vice President **Richard M. Nixon** to arrange funding for a technical study. The following year, Nkrumah toured the U.S. and, to help win funding for the project, publicly said that stories about racism and discrimination in the United States were often exaggerated by U.S. enemies, although he himself had experienced both while he was a college student at Lincoln University near Philadelphia. Nkrumah also won substantial **African American** support following a tour of Harlem, and he met Edgar Kaiser of Henry J. Kaiser Aluminum, who became a strong supporter.

To make the project economically viable, Kaiser agreed to build an aluminum smelter that would use the dam's excess electric capacity, but because of worldwide overproduction of aluminum, the Ghanaian government agreed to a long-term contract with Kaiser that guaranteed low prices for the power. As originally envisioned, Kaiser would smelt locally mined bauxite, but the cost of mining and refining it into alumina for smelting was such that it was agreed to import alumina until the dam was profitable enough to use excess revenue to build the necessary refining infrastructure. President **John F. Kennedy** agreed to provide significant funding for the project following a March 1961 meeting with Nkrumah, but Nkrumah's increasing support for the **Soviet Union** and his anti-American rhetoric caused Kennedy to reassess the commitment. Under pressure from the British and with concerns about another fiasco like that which followed the Eisenhower administration's decision not to fund the **Aswan High Dam** in **Egypt**, Kennedy agreed to give the go-ahead on 16 December 1961. Construction began on 22 January 1962 and, following threats to abort the aluminum smelter because of Nkrumah's increasingly virulent anti-Americanism, the administration of **Lyndon B. Johnson** allowed work to go forward in December 1964. Nkrumah and Kaiser officially opened the dam and smelter on 22 January 1966.

VORSTER, BALTHAZAR JOHANNES (JOHN) (1915–1983). Prime minister (1966–78) and president (1978–79) of **South Africa** who played a significant role in building the **apartheid** state as justice minister in the 1960s and then in trying to preserve it as prime minister with his unsuccessful détente toward South Africa's black-ruled neighbors. Vorster was interned during World War II for his leadership of a pro-Nazi organization, but became more mainstream in his politics thereafter, quickly rising in the National Party, which set about constructing apartheid after winning power in 1948. Vorster was appointed justice minister in 1961, charged with crushing black opposition, which he did using mass arrests and torture.

As prime minister, Vorster increased repression at home but in the near abroad he executed an audacious policy that did not fit his image of embodying dour Afrikaner stolidity and conservatism. Vorster created a policy of economic incentives and coercion to compel his neighbors to soften their anti–South African rhetoric and behavior. He also began to lessen petty apartheid to create an international atmosphere of goodwill. The next step, Vorster hoped, would be official recognition of South Africa by the surrounding states. The policy grew more urgent with the collapse of **Portugal**'s empire in April 1974 and impending freedom for **Angola** and **Mozambique**. With urging from the United States (as revealed by South African documents), **Zambia**'s President **Kenneth Kaunda, Mobutu Sese Seko** of **Zaïre**, and at least four other African leaders, Vorster ordered South African troops into **Angola** to join the civil war in support of **Holden Roberto**'s *Frente Nacional de Libertação de Angola*/National Front for the Liberation of Angola (FNLA) and **Jonas Savimbi**'s *União Nacional para a Independência Total de Angola*/National Union for the Total Independence of Angola (UNITA) in September 1975. Roberto's incompetence knocked the FNLA out of the war and massive intervention by **Cuba** after Fidel Castro learned about the South African intervention defeated UNITA and drove the South Africans out of the country.

Vorster made a second try for détente in 1976, working with U.S. Secretary of State **Henry Kissinger** to force the white government of **Rhodesia** to accept majority rule, but failed because the Rhodesian guerilla leaders believed they could win on the battlefield. The Soweto riots that began in June 1976 and lasted into early 1977 showed that real reform was not on Vorster's agenda, and the election of President **Jimmy Carte**r completely changed the international dynamic. Alcoholic and in ill health, Vorster resigned as prime minister in 1978, accepting the ceremonial role as president, but was forced to resign in the wake of a scandal that revealed the South African government had used millions of dollars to influence foreign journalists and to create the only English-language South African newspaper that supported the government.

– W –

WASHINGTON, BOOKER T. (1856–1915). African American teacher and civil rights leader known as the "Wizard of Tuskegee" who founded Tuskegee University (Tuskegee Normal and Industrial Institute in Alabama), at the time a college exclusively for blacks, and popularized "industrial education." Washington's idea of industrial education, teaching African Americans to be better farmers and craftsmen as a way to uplift the race from the bottom up while eschewing demands for social equality, became the primary focus of most **historically black colleges and universities** (HBCUs) across the southern United States. Under his leadership, Tuskegee became a world leader in scientific agriculture and agricultural education. Washington's ideas made him the enemy of those who supported traditional liberal arts education for blacks, most famously **W.E.B. Du Bois**.

Washington's ideas proved very popular in **Great Britain**'s African colonies with both the colonizer and colonized. Colonial governments and missionaries saw industrial education as a way to make Africans more productive without widening their political horizons. A handful of colleges in **South Africa**, **Rhodesia**, the Gold Coast (**Ghana**), **Kenya**, and Tanganyika (**Tanzania**) successfully adopted the model, but most schools that attempted it lacked teachers skilled in modern agricultural techniques, limiting their success. Washington understood that colonial officials wanted to use industrial education as a means of control, but he believed that working with colonial governments to create industrial education would ultimately benefit blacks, serving as a way to build or protect blacks' self-reliance and self-respect. African intellectuals were inspired by Washington's message in his autobiography, *Up from Slavery*, which was translated into numerous languages, including Zulu. His work inspired many African students to attend Tuskegee. Occasionally he publicly aired his views about the treatment of blacks in Africa, for example, when the education commissioner of South Africa asked him for educational advice, Washington recommended industrial education modified for the region to include mining education. Going beyond what the commissioner expected, Washington also wrote that the South African government should give educated blacks civic equality, and should pay a fair wage for free labor, thus implying that the government should end forced labor. His suggestions were ignored.

Along with his work on colonial education, Washington advised colonial governments and businesses on agriculture. At the request of the German government, he sent an American agricultural team from Tuskegee to Togo in a successful effort to grow commercially viable cotton. He also recommended graduates for cotton growing schemes in **Sudan** and **Nigeria** although records do not indicate if they played significant roles in these colonies' successful cotton production.

In the U.S., Washington worked within the political process to protect black Africans' rights. He personally lobbied President **Theodore Roosevelt** and the Senate Foreign Affairs Committee to pressure the government of **Belgium** to end abuses in the Congo Free State (**Congo**), and made a speaking tour with author Mark Twain against the misrule of King Léopold II. An American agent of Léopold's wrote to the king, "Dr. Washington is no small enemy to overcome." In 1912, at Tuskegee, he organized the International Conference on the Negro, which was attended by many Americans and a few blacks from 18 countries. Working behind the scenes, Washington ensured that the conference report accused colonial governments of discrimination against black missionaries.

Washington's most sustained work on Africa was with **Liberia**. In the early 1900s, as Great Britain, **France**, and Germany threatened to annex Liberian territory and take control of its finances, Washington personally escorted a Liberian government delegation to meet with President Theodore Roosevelt to explain their plight. Shortly before leaving office, Roosevelt created an investigative commission to go to Liberia and asked Washington to lead it. Instead, Washington selected his personal secretary to take his place and helped choose the other commissioners. After the commission's report was issued, calling for the U.S. to lend Liberia enough money to cover its foreign debts, Washington worked to interest international bankers to invest in Liberia. Despite his strong support for Liberia, Washington could be critical of its government, writing to President Arthur Barclay to request better treatment for indigenous people by the **Americo-Liberian** elite, and he helped create scholarships to Tuskegee that went specifically to indigenous peoples. At the end of his life, Washington worked with several charitable groups, including the **American Colonization Society** (ACS), to create an industrial education center in Liberia. Completed after his death, it was named the Booker T. Washington Industrial Institute.

WESTERN FIVE CONTACT GROUP. Created by the United States in 1977 to oversee peace and decolonization negotiations for **Namibia**. U.S. Deputy **United Nations** (UN) Ambassador Donald McHenry emerged as its leader. The Contact Group consisted of **South Africa**'s five largest trading partners (the U.S., Canada, **Great Britain**, **France**, and West Germany), which sought to force the South African government to grant independence to a majority-ruled government in **Namibia** (known to the South Africans as Southwest Africa), a colony that was illegally controlled by South Africa under a revoked League of Nations mandate. McHenry was highly regarded by his colleagues Secretary of State **Cyrus Vance** and UN Ambassador **Andrew Young** as well as by African national and guerilla leaders, which gave him much influence over the negotiations. The Contact Group acted as a mediating buffer between the Front Line States (**Angola**, **Botswana**, **Mozambique**, **Tanzania**, **Zambia**, and, following its independence, **Zimbabwe**) and South Africa, and between the South West Africa People's Organization (SWAPO) and South Africa. From April 1978 until late 1979 the South Africans and SWAPO alternated acts of bad faith that prevented a settlement. McHenry's added responsibilities as the new UN ambassador following his promotion in September 1979 followed by the November Iranian hostage crisis and the invasion of Afghanistan by the **Soviet Union** in December caused U.S. interest in Namibia to flag.

The Contact Group was revived under the administration of **Ronald W. Reagan**. Assistant Secretary of State for African Affairs Chester Crocker followed up on South African demands that **Cuba** leave Angola concurrently with South Africa leaving Namibia, a position that only Great Britain accepted. As a result, Crocker worked almost alone on bringing the parties together. In 1988, South Africa suffered battlefield reversals against the Cubans that threatened a gigantic hydroelectric power station and eroded popular support for the war. The Soviet Union had also begun dramatic cuts in funding its overseas allies, removing the fear of communism that had prompted South African intransigence. In August, all parties agreed to a cease-fire and elections in 1989, and South Africa withdrew from Namibia shortly thereafter, concluding the Contact Group's mission. *See also* BUSH, GEORGE H.W.; NEW YORK ACCORDS.

WILLIAMS, G. MENNEN "SOAPY" (1911–1988). Former governor of Michigan who served as Assistant Secretary of State for African Affairs under Presidents **John F. Kennedy** and **Lyndon B. Johnson** (1961–66). Williams was Kennedy's first State Department appointment, proceeding even Secretary of State **Dean Rusk**, which in conjunction with Williams' high profile for such a low-level post signaled the president's interest in African affairs. In an early 1961 speech, Williams said that the chaos that came from the unmet revolution of higher expectations that followed African independence was a greater threat to African peace than was intervention by the **Soviet Union**, and the way to deter the Soviets was by fostering economic growth. To improve relations with Africa, Williams said that the U.S. needed more students studying about Africa and more cultural exchange programs, and Washington needed to solve its own Civil Rights crisis, which was having a terrible impact on Africans' opinion of the U.S. Most famously, he called for "Africa for the Africans," which created a furor among European colonial powers and Europeanists in the State Department that only calmed down when Kennedy replied to reporters' questions, "I don't know who else Africa should be for." Williams had much less influence with President Johnson, who did not share Kennedy's interest in Africa, and he resigned to resume his political career in Michigan. AFRICAN AFFAIRS, STATE DEPARTMENT BUREAU OF.

WILSON, THOMAS WOODROW (1856–1924). U.S. president (1913–21), whose Fourteen Points proposal to end World War I called for colonial adjustment based on the interests of the native peoples and for creation of a League of Nations to guarantee "political independence and integrity to great and small alike." Nonetheless, Wilson agreed with the Europeans that African colonies were not ready for independence, but he opposed the Allies taking Germany's colonies. A compromise was reached in which the Allies divided the colonies, most of which were governed under League of Nations "Class B" mandates that required the colonizer to prepare the colony for eventual independence at an undetermined future date. Southwest Africa (**Namibia**) was the exception, given to **South Africa** under a "Class C" mandate that did not countenance future independence due to its unviable population base. Each mandate laid out extensive protections for the civil rights of the native peoples, which were generally ignored. Wilson's ideas of national determination played a significant role in the rise of third-world nationalism although he did not consider them appropriate for Africa.

WIZARD, OPERATION. *See* OPERATION WIZARD.

WOODS, DONALD (1933–2001). Crusading liberal **South African** newspaper editor, whose coverage of **Stephen Biko** and the Black Consciousness movement helped to make them household names in South Africa. Following Biko's beating and death by police in September 1977, Woods was arrested at the airport on his way to the United States for a series of speeches about Biko, and was banned (restricted in speech and movement) for five years. The South African Security Police injured his daughter by sending her an acid-covered t-shirt, and five shots were fired into his house, so Woods and his family snuck out of South Africa on 29 December 1977. He went on a world speaking tour to keep alive Biko's memory and work, and wrote his biography, which became a best seller. A speech before the executive committee of the **American Federation of Labor–Congress of Industrial Organizations** (AFL-CIO) immediately prompted U.S. labor to pass a resolution calling for corporate withdrawal from South Africa. Woods' work was made into the **film** *Cry, Freedom*, released in November 1987.

WORLD BANK. Officially known as the International Bank for Reconstruction and Development, the World Bank was proposed along with the **International Monetary Fund** (IMF) in July 1944 at an international conference in Bretton Woods, New Hampshire, that was planning the post–World War II international economic order. It was established on 27 December 1945. The Bank was part of President **Franklin Delano Roosevelt**'s postwar vision for preventing a second Great Depression and the international instability and warfare that had come in the Depression's wake.

The Bank's official mission is "to fight poverty with passion and professionalism." From its inception, it has insisted that borrowers be allowed to spend loan money in any country, so-called untied loans, and that the money be spent only after competitive bids had been made in order to ensure that the borrower received maximum value from the money. Although the Bank itself is a financial cooperative owned by most of the world's governments, the United States has played the significant role because of U.S. world economic dominance and its role as the largest contributor. Every chairman has been an American. The Bank has a staff of 13,000, with over 1,400 working on Africa-related issues or projects, and it loans $25 billion per year to poor and "middle-income" countries. The Bank initially focused on raising money to rebuild Western Europe through project-specific lending. After Europe had recovered from World War II, the Bank promoted continued expansion of world **trade**, encouraged the free flow of capital, and pushed for market-centered domestic policies in countries that received its assistance. In this, it largely served the interest of U.S. and Western capital, prompting many critics to claim that the Bank was a tool of Wall Street. Its first African loan was to **Ethiopia** in 1950, and the Bank shifted its focus from Western Europe to the third world by the mid-1950s. Its loans centered on infrastructure to improve international trade, which was in keeping with the "trade, not aid" policies of President **Dwight D. Eisenhower**. While most third-world countries' gross national products increased during the 1960s, there was minimal commensurate rise in standards of living.

World Bank President **Robert Strange McNamara**, appointed in 1967 after serving as U.S. secretary of defense, sought to continue the Bank's economic growth policies while adding efforts to improve global standards of living. To do this, McNamara successfully pushed for the Bank to create a five-year plan that would double the total amount of money provided in loans ("loan volume") to the third world than had been given from 1964–68. During 1969–73, McNamara expanded Bank activities to include social programs such as birth control, income redistribution, education, public health, and urban squatter settlement programs. In his second five-year plan, the goal was to improve agriculture, particularly for impoverished farmers, and the plan included land and tenancy reform. For these goals, he virtually turned **Tanzania** into a national demonstration project, sharing with many other lenders great enthusiasm for the humane socialist vision of President **Julius Nyerere** embodied in his *Ujamaa* policy of villagization. McNamara ensured that grants and loans totaling in the billions of dollars were provided to Tanzania in support of this vision. McNamara also overturned previous policy by moving the Bank to provide assistance for gigantic state-owned industrial plants. Almost all of these policies failed and came to be known as "black elephants," an African play on the term "white elephant." Although standards of living improved in some African nations, the cost of socialist policies, loss in productivity, unwise international debt burden, and global **oil** shocks and falling commodity prices bankrupted many World Bank aid recipients, including Tanzania, and the 1970s and 1980s came to be referred to as the "lost decades" of African development.

To remedy out-of-control third-world debt caused in part by the World Bank's policies, in September 1979 McNamara and the IMF created "structural adjustment programs" (SAPs). SAPs gave governments the opportunity to refinance their loans without interest over 40 years in exchange for government promises to make comprehensive reforms, including reduction in the size of government, selling off state-owned industries such as those the Bank had financed and encouraged, weeding out corruption, ending subsidies for food, fuel, and other necessities, and generally liberalizing international trade and domestic markets. SAPs often failed because the instability they created led governments to pull back from reform, or even caused their overthrow. Even when SAPs succeeded, national standards of living fell. Many governments ignored their promises, continued their previous policies, did not repay their loans, and received new SAPs. From 1981–91, 29 African countries received $25 billion in SAPs, but the Bank concluded that only six of these countries had performed well. By 2002, only Burkina Faso was judged to have made lasting reforms. In 1989, the Bank concluded that half its

African development projects had failed, and during the 1990s, Africa had the most Bank projects but the lowest performance in project sustainability, bank performance, and borrower performance. The situation in Africa and the third world was so bad that the Bank began to manipulate economic statistics about countries that had received its assistance, or withheld them. During this period, the Bank expanded its mission to include loan requirements that governments implement policies to empower women and to protect the environment.

The Bank's charter does not allow it to involve itself in domestic politics, so its loan policy has historically taken little account of whether or not a country was democratic or dictatorial or if it suffered from government corruption. On a per capita basis since the end of the **cold war**, it has provided equal funding to democratic and undemocratic nations. Critics have argued that the Bank's technocrats have preferred dictatorships to ensure that their often unpopular top-down reforms are implemented. World Bank President James Wolfensohn (1995–2005) introduced reforms aimed at limiting loans to corrupt governments, a policy that was much expanded by his successor, Paul Wolfowitz (2005–07), who suspended loans to **Kenya** and **Chad** and was overruled by the Bank's board from doing so to the Republic of Congo (Congo–Brazzaville). In addition, 58 corporations and firms, several prominent, were banned from competing for World Bank contracts because of corruption. Wolfowitz also worked to change the Bank's emphasis from loan volume to analysis of the impact of its projects. He quickly lost his job in part because of institutional resistance to these reforms. Many Bank officials opposed Wolfowitz's emphasis on corruption, arguing that it was wrong to sanction impoverished people for the actions of their leaders.

By the turn of the Millennium, SAPs and the sort of gigantic programs that the Bank had supported were out of favor internationally. The Bank and other supra-national organizations began to be supplanted by international capital flows into Africa through private investment, and by the work of **non-governmental organizations** (NGOs) that would intervene during crises or attack illnesses like HIV/**AIDS**. International debt forgiveness by industrialized nations, the Bank, the IMF, and the African Development Bank (all primarily funded by Western nations) in exchange for opening up markets and fighting corruption likewise made the World Bank and IMF of much less importance. The focus on trade and investment by the administrations of Presidents **Bill Clinton** and **George W. Bush**, which pointed to the successful economic performance of East Asian economies that followed similar policies, ironically brought the world back to the Eisenhower policy of "trade, not aid" and revived criticism that the purpose of **foreign aid** is to serve Western capital. To retain its relevance, the Bank has also encouraged such polices and has sought to work around governments by creating advisory focus groups of local non-governmental actors to determine where loans should go rather than consulting with governments, and it has sought to provide assistance to "community-driven" programs rather than to governments. From 2002–07, the Bank shifted its lending profile, with 90 percent of its loans going to 27 "middle-income" nations rather than the most impoverished.

– Y –

YOUNG, ANDREW (1932–). U.S. civil rights leader, **United Nations** (UN) ambassador under President **Jimmy Carter** (1977–79), and politician. Young's service as the first **African American** UN ambassador symbolized Carter's reorientation of foreign policy from Kissingerian realism and focus on the global **cold war** to a softer foreign policy that emphasized human rights and regional solutions to ostensibly regional problems. It also saw a change in tone for U.S. foreign policy, especially Africa policy. Within weeks of taking office, Young said that **Cuba**'s army in **Angola** provided "a certain stability and order" and later said much the same thing about Cuban troops in **Ethiopia**, chastised former presidents **Gerald R. Ford** and **Richard M. Nixon** as "racists," called people in **Great Britain** and Sweden "racists," told blacks in **South Africa** that their government was like the racists that Carter had beaten while governor of Georgia, told the French newspaper *Le Matin* that he did not believe that **Rhodesia**'s Patriotic Front (PF) guerillas were capable of the atrocities that they were shown to have committed, told *Le Matin* that while there were political prisoners in the **Soviet Union**, there were also "hundreds, perhaps thousands of political prisoners in the United

States," and told reporters in early 1979 that Americans would soon consider Iran's Ayatollah Ruhollah Khomeini "somewhat of a saint."

Despite the new tone he brought to diplomacy, Young strongly influenced the first two years of Carter's foreign policy, putting new focus on sub-Saharan Africa and persuading Carter to detach African conflicts from the cold war. Young's influence was quickly seen when Cuban-trained rebels invaded **Zaïre** from Angola in March 1977 and Carter announced that the United States would not intervene militarily. Likewise, backed by Young and Secretary of State **Cyrus Vance**, Carter refused to support **Somalia** in the war against Soviet-backed Ethiopia because Somalia had violated Ethiopia's borders when it invaded the heavily Somali Ogaden Desert, and he took no action beyond public complaints about the Soviets' adventurism when they flew 15,000 Cuban troops to assist Ethiopia in late 1977. Young also persuaded Carter to refuse to support Bishop **Abel Muzorewa**'s transitional government in Zimbabwe–Rhodesia (**Zimbabwe**) following April 1979 elections, rejecting strong congressional pressure to send observers to monitor the election that brought Muzorewa's government to power and to end sanctions against the country. Carter repeated Young's argument that Muzorewa's government was illegitimate because it did not include Patriotic Front (PF) rebels, which were backed by the Soviet Union and **China**. The first sign that Young's influence was eroding came during a second invasion of Zaïre in May 1978. This time Carter ordered significant U.S. assistance. The president also began to accept National Security Adviser **Zbigniew Brzezinski**'s argument that the Soviets were creating an "arc of crisis" from Afghanistan to the Horn of Africa that was creating a pincer around Saudi **oil**. Young was fired in August 1979 for getting caught violating administration policy by secretly meeting with a Palestinian Liberation Organization (PLO) representative.

– Z –

ZAÏRE. Name given to **Congo** by President **Mobutu Sese Seko** as part of his "Authenticity" movement. Zaïre's name is believed to be a mispronunciation of the Kongo word *nzere* or *nzadi*, which means "the river that swallows all rivers." The country's name was changed back to the **Democratic Republic of Congo** by **Laurent-Désiré Kabila** after he overthrew Mobutu in 1997.

ZAMBIA. Copper-producing Southern African nation that was a Front Line State in the struggle for **Rhodesia** to achieve majority rule as **Zimbabwe**. Zambia's founding president, **Kenneth Kaunda**, was much admired for his opposition to colonialism and racist rule and for his Zambian Humanism socialist policies at home. Even before Southern Rhodesia proclaimed its Unilateral Declaration of Independence (UDI) as **Rhodesia** in November 1965, Kaunda had offered to **Great Britain** the use of a Zambian airbase for British troops to retake the colony, but the British declined. Once independence came, Zambia became a strong opponent of Rhodesia despite its railway system connecting to Rhodesia's so that 95 percent of its imports and all of its copper exports used Rhodesian railroads, its electric power being produced in Rhodesia, and its civil service consisting largely of white Rhodesians. When the British embargoed Rhodesian petroleum products in hopes that this would cause the government's collapse, Zambia suffered much more in consequence because the Rhodesians could rely upon **South Africa** for fuel supplies. Great Britain, the United States, and Canada responded in mid-December with a massive and expensive airlift of petroleum products to Zambia that lasted until mid-1966. Thereafter, deliveries continued by road until an **oil** pipeline was completed to **Tanzania** in August 1968.

Although Kaunda allowed **Joshua Nkomo**'s Zimbabwe African People's Union (ZAPU) to conduct guerilla operations out of Zambia and he maintained a strong public stance against the Rhodesians and South Africans, Kaunda was also pragmatic in his dealings with the racist governments, working behind the scenes including meetings with Rhodesian representatives and South African Prime Minister **John Vorster** for a peaceful resolution to the Rhodesian crisis. On 25 August 1975, Kaunda and other African leaders pressured Nkomo and Zimbabwe African National Union (ZANU) leader **Robert Mugabe**, among other black Rhodesians, to meet with Rhodesian Prime Minister **Ian Smith** at Victoria Falls, but the meeting was not a success.

Kaunda was also close to guerilla leader **Jonas Savimbi**, who led the *União Nacional para a Independência Total de Angola*/National

Union for the Total Independence of Angola (UNITA) in **Angola**'s civil war, and helped to convince U.S. Secretary of State **Henry Kissinger** to intervene in the war. Only when it was publicly revealed that Savimbi had covertly received South African and U.S. assistance, a fact that Kaunda well knew, did he renounce the relationship. Following the disastrous U.S. policy in Angola, Kissinger began to work with Kaunda and Nkomo to try to bring peace to Rhodesia. Although the plan ended in failure, Kissinger had laid the groundwork for President **Jimmy Carter**'s successful joint effort with the British, although the Carter administration tended to work more closely with Tanzania's President **Julius Nyerere** instead of Kaunda. Majority rule in Zimbabwe dramatically lessened Zambia's international role, and a precipitous drop in copper prices beginning in 1974 combined with disastrous socialist policies and attendant corruption led the government to turn inward. Following food riots and political protests, Kaunda allowed multiparty elections on 31 October 1991 and lost to labor union leader Frederick Chiluba, receiving less than 20 percent of the vote. After two terms in office, Chiluba's efforts to amend the constitution to allow himself a third term were rejected, and he and his wife were subsequently tried for corruption. A British court on 4 May 2007 found him guilty of having stolen $46 million and some charges were pending as of mid-2008.

ZANZIBAR. Archipelago off the coast of Tanganyika, which was an independent nation from 10 December 1963 until it joined Tanganyika to form **Tanzania** on 26 April 1964. At independence, Zanzibar was ruled by its Arab minority, but on 12 January 1964, a mass uprising of blacks overthrew the government and killed thousands, perhaps tens of thousands, primarily Arabs and Indians. From the chaos emerged the black-led government of Abeid Kumare, which had two Communist ministers and followed a bizarre amalgam of communism and strict Muslim cultural policy. Officials in the administration of President **Lyndon B. Johnson** worried that a revolutionary Zanzibari government could serve as an example for other African states. They believed that it was under the control of **Cuba**, although this apparently was not the case, and Eastern Bloc officials and technicians began to arrive including East Germans, who created the country's secret police. Every U.S. official with African responsibilities unsuccessfully urged the British to send troops, and behind the scenes, the U.S. encouraged Tanganyika's **Julius Nyerere** to intervene, which he ultimately did by uniting his country with Zanzibar.

ZIMBABWE. The last European-held African colony to be granted independence and, as **Rhodesia**, the only African colony to declare independence unilaterally, although neither the British colonizer nor any other nation recognized its Unilateral Declaration of Independence (UDI). At the time of the UDI, approximately 5 percent of the population was white, who early in the 20th century had pushed indigenous Shona and Ndebele into overcrowded lands with poor soils, thus forcing many to become wage laborers on plantations and in mines. A system similar to Jim Crow in the United States evolved, with racial discrimination, petty indignities, and exceedingly high property and literacy requirements for black suffrage.

In the early 1960s, it became clear that **Great Britain** wanted at least a fig leaf of black-majority rule, so Rhodesian whites turned away from even minimal attempts at racial accommodation and overwhelmingly elected the newly formed Rhodesian Front (RF) in December 1962. The RF began moving toward UDI with the accession to power of **Ian Smith** as prime minister in April 1964. In June, Smith imprisoned African nationalist leaders including **Joshua Nkomo** of the Zimbabwe African People's Union (ZAPU), and Ndabiningi Sithole and **Robert Mugabe** of the Zimbabwe African National Union (ZANU). Smith declared Rhodesian independence on 11 November 1965.

During the presidencies of **John F. Kennedy** and **Lyndon B. Johnson**, Washington consistently worked with the British to crush Smith's government through economic and weapons sanctions but, like the British, both men rejected military intervention. The **United Nations** (UN) issued mandatory sanctions against Rhodesia in 1966 and 1968, unprecedented actions that were adhered to by the U.S. When these failed, the British offered Smith three transitional constitutions, each allowing whites to maintain their rule for progressively longer periods. Smith rejected the first two but accepted the last in 1971, which could have kept whites in power for over 60 years, but blacks led by Methodist Bishop **Abel Muzorewa** organized and protested, calling for immediate black rule. The British revoked the offer.

Just as the black population began to organize, **Portugal** began to lose its hold on neighboring **Mozambique**. In 1972, Mozambique's *Frente de Libertação de Moçambique*/Front for the Liberation of Mozambique (FRELIMO) created a "liberated zone" along its northeastern border with Rhodesia, which allowed ZANU's guerillas to set up bases and infiltrate the colony. When the Portuguese government was overthrown in 1974 and Mozambique was granted independence, Mugabe's guerillas, supported by **China**, began to enter along the entire 760-mile border. Nkomo's forces ran a less vigorous Soviet-supported guerilla operation from **Zambia**. The war turned against the Rhodesian government, and **South Africa** and the U.S. pressured Smith to allow majority rule out of fear that continued resistance would destabilize Southern Africa and give the **Soviet Union** an opening.

A British- and U.S.-backed Geneva, Switzerland, conference met from 28 October to 14 December 1976 but failed because Smith demanded a two-year transition to majority rule including control over the army and secret police, while guerilla leaders Mugabe and Nkomo, now in a paper coalition called the Patriotic Front (PF), demanded total power for themselves. Smith responded by negotiating an internal settlement with Muzorewa, Sithole, and Chief Jeremiah Chirau, which they signed 3 March 1978. Muzorewa was elected prime minister on 21 April 1979. The **Jimmy Carter** administration and the British refused to recognize the new government or to end sanctions. The following month, Secretary of State **Cyrus Vance** and British Foreign Secretary David Owen met with the PF and the leaders of the African countries surrounding Rhodesia, known as the Front Line States. The PF was pressured into accepting all-party constitutional negotiations at Lancaster House in Great Britain. The international community pledged £900 million in **foreign aid** for the first years of independence, and the British government alone provided £500 million by 1992, including £47 million specifically designated to purchase white-owned land. Mugabe won the ensuing elections, assisted by violence and intimidation throughout the eastern half of the country, and took office as prime minister on 18 April

1980. An estimated 20,000 people died during the civil war with almost half killed following the internal settlement.

Because Mugabe left whites alone, he won international plaudits, but he launched brutal attacks on the Ndebele minority, killing as many as 25,000 people. The U.S. did little because it was afraid of driving Mugabe into the Soviet camp. In the 1990 election, he turned against whites, blaming them for the moribund economy, and in 2000 he began confiscating white-owned farms without compensation. By the 1990s, corruption was endemic and Mugabe and his cronies took many of the confiscated farms for themselves. The medical system collapsed and Zimbabwe suffers one of the world's worst HIV/**AIDS** epidemics, with an average lifespan for women estimated at 30 years, the lowest in the world, and the world's highest percentage of AIDS orphans. When the predominantly Shona people of the shantytowns around Harare, the capital, turned against Mugabe, he ordered Operation *Murambatsvina* (chiShona: "cleaning up the shit") in June 2005. The army attacked the shantytowns, bulldozing 100,000 homes and businesses. The UN estimated that 2.4 million people were affected, 700,000 were made homeless and dumped in the countryside without food or shelter, and some human rights organizations posit that half of them died.

A new opposition political party, the Movement for Democratic Change (MDC), led by labor leader **Morgan Tsvangirai**, was created in 1999 because of the worsening conditions and proved to be a significant threat to Mugabe's rule on 12–13 February 2000 when it led voters to reject the president's national referendum to expand his power and legalize uncompensated expropriation of white-owned farms. Mugabe responded with repression—within days, organized groups of "guerilla war veterans," many too young to have served, began expropriating white-owned farms, sometimes killing the owners and their black employees and driving them all off the land—and with electoral fraud, allegedly stealing elections in 2000, 2002, 2005, and 2008. The U.S. responded by imposing progressively greater sanctions against Zimbabwean leaders in 2002, 2003, and 2008, and the **George W. Bush** administration labeled Zimbabwe one of the world's six "outposts of tyranny."

In the 29 March 2008 election, with 80 percent unemployment, inflation estimated as high as four million percent, and one-third of the population economic or political **refugees**, Mugabe reportedly lost when Tsvangirai received over 50 percent of the vote as indicated by the aggregate of totals posted on every voting precinct across the country, but the government released no figures for over a month. In April, Southern African labor unions and governments blocked shipment of Chinese weapons from a Chinese cargo ship, which was forced to return to China. When vote totals were finally officially reported on 2 May, Tsvangirai had a plurality but not a majority, which required a runoff.

Despite protests from the U.S., the European Community (EU), and many African governments, and calls from the **African Union** (AU) for a government of national unity based on the example from **Kenya** earlier in 2008, over 100 MDC officials and activists were killed by the army, police, and paramilitaries, and Tsvangirai fled to the Dutch embassy and finally withdrew from the runoff to stop the violence. President Bush called Mugabe's government "illegimate" and sought UN sanctions against it, but they were vetoed by Russia and China on 11 July. On 17 July, Zimbabwe introduced the $100 billion note. By this point, Zimbabwean money already included a date of expiration. On 21 July, Mugabe and Tsvangirai met and laid out preconditions for negotiations to create a government of national unity. In the months that followed, government violence continued against the MDC, and Mugabe appointed ZANU-PF officials to the most important ministries. *See also* BYRD AMENDMENT; COLD WAR; FORD, GERALD R.; KISSINGER, HENRY A.; MACHEL, SAMORA; MANDELA, NELSON ROLIHLAHLA; MBEKI, THABO; VORSTER, BALTHAZAR JOHANNES (JOHN); YOUNG, ANDREW.

Bibliography

CONTENTS

INTRODUCTION

This bibliography provides a representative sample of English-language books on U.S. relations with Africa. It is not comprehensive because of the breadth of the subject: 53 countries (54 if the Sahrawi Arab Democratic Republic is included), the transatlantic slave trade, African Americans, decolonization and the role of Western Europe, the cold war, intervention by the Soviet Bloc and China, conflict in the Middle East, economic and political development, international terrorism, and the post–cold war transition to democracy and neo-liberalism.

Primary sources on U.S. relations with Africa can be found in the *Foreign Relations of the United States* (*FRUS*) series. By mid-2008, volumes dealing with Africa through the end of the Gerald R. Ford administration had been published with the exceptions of the Congo Crisis (1960–1968), Southern Africa (1969–1976), North Africa (1973–1976), and the Middle East (1969–1976). Beginning with the administration of John F. Kennedy, all of the African volumes can be found online at http://www.state.gov/r/pa/ho/frus/ with the exception of a microfiche supplement to the Kennedy administration. The Central Intelligence Agency (CIA) website, www.cia.gov, has a search engine for finding recently released declassified documents. The *9/11 Commission Report*, which includes material on al Qaeda in Africa, is available online at http://govinfo.library .unt.edu/911/report/index.htm or in several hardbound editions with or without commentary.

A huge trove of documents on U.S. relations with South Africa, *South Africa: The Making of US Policy, 1962–1989*, is available on microfiche from the National Security Archive, a non-government source located at George Washington University in Washington, D.C., that has taken the lead in seeking the declassification of U.S. government documents through Freedom of Information Act (FOIA) requests and legal cases. The Archive also has a printed document collection by Kenneth Mokoena, *South Africa and the United States: The Declassified History*, and online collections at its website, www.gwu.edu/~nsarchiv, dealing with the Rwandan genocide, U.S. policy during the Arab–Israeli War of 1973, a 2000 report on lessons learned from humanitarian intervention that includes a section on Sudan, the United States and South African nuclear policy, and the U.S. response to reports that Algeria was developing a nuclear program. Copies of the documents as well as those declassified since these publications can be found at the Archive.

Colin Legum's *Africa Contemporary Record*, published from 1968–2002, is a yearly compendium of primary documents and essays. Translations of fascinating documents from Eastern and Central European files dealing with Soviet Bloc intervention in Africa are available in the *Cold War International History Project Bulletin*, issue 8–9. Original government documents are found at the National Archives of the United States in College Park, Maryland, and the presidential libraries, which are located from Massachusetts to California. British government documents are found at the National Archives (formerly the Public Records Office) at Kew Gardens in London.

Almost without exception, Scarecrow Press's historical dictionaries on individual African countries are outstanding, with Samuel Decalo's volume on Chad, though dated, a source so remarkable in its depth and research that it is the best available English source on that country. *American Foreign Relations since 1600: A Guide to the Literature*, edited by Robert L. Beisner for the Society for Historians of American Foreign Relations, provides annotated entries on the key books and journal articles of U.S. foreign policy.

The best overview of the entirety of U.S.–Africa relations, though dated, is Peter Duignan and Lewis H. Gann, *The U.S. and Africa: A History*. Piero Gleijeses, *Conflicting Missions: Havana, Washington, and Africa, 1959–1976*, uses sources in six different languages, is evenhanded, and writes beautifully in one of the best examples of multi-archival research in the writing of cold war history. Peter J. Schraeder, *United States Foreign Policy toward Africa: Incrementalism, Crisis and Change*, takes the story into the early 1990s. Works on the pre–cold war relationship focus primarily on the Barbary Wars and the founding and history of Liberia, with both subjects seeing a large number of excellent works in the past decade due to the rise of Islamist terror and Liberia's collapse. Among the best on Liberia are Claude A. Clegg III, *The Price of Liberty: African Americans and the Making of Liberia*, Richard L. Hall, *On Africa's Shore: A History of Maryland in Liberia, 1837–1857*, Ibrahim K. Sundiata, *Brothers and Strangers: Black Zion, Black Slavery, 1914–1940*, Marie Tyler-McGraw, *An African Republic: Black and White Virginians in the Making of Liberia*. Especially good on the Barbary Wars are Frederick C. Leiner, *The End of Barbary Terror: America's 1815 War against the Pirates of North Africa*, A.B.C. Whipple, *To the Shores of Tripoli: The Birth of the U.S. Navy and Marines*, and Joseph Wheelan's *Jefferson's War: America's First War on Terror, 1801–1805*.

African Americans and Africa is a relatively new field that has had some of the best and most creative work on the U.S.–Africa relationship. Important books include Thomas Borstelmann, *The Cold War and the Color Line: American Race Relations in the Global Arena*, James H. Meriwether, *Proudly We Can Be Africans: Black Americans and Africa, 1935–1961*, Brenda Gayle Plummer, *Rising Wind: Black Americans and U.S. Foreign Affairs, 1935–1960*, Carol Anderson, *Eyes Off the Prize: The United Nations and the African American Struggle for Human Rights, 1944–1955*, and Penny M. Von Eschen, *Against Empire: Black Americans and Anticolonialism, 1937–1957*.

The role of the Central Intelligence Agency (CIA) is well covered in John Prados, *Safe for Democracy: The Secret Wars of the CIA*, Douglas Little's "Mission Impossible: The CIA and the Cult of Covert Action in the Middle East," *Diplomatic History*, and Robert M. Gates gives the CIA's perspective in

From the Shadows: The Ultimate Insider's Story of Five Presidents and How They Won the Cold War.

Because Egypt is the only African country that has been important for U.S. foreign policy, works specifically dealing with presidents' Africa policy are limited in number. On Harry S. Truman, see Macharia Munene *The Truman Administration and the Decolonisation of Sub-Saharan Africa.* Scholarship on the foreign policy of Dwight D. Eisenhower, once negative, began to turn very positive beginning in the 1980s. This is not true about work on his Africa policy, which is very critical. The best work is James H. Meriwether, "'A Torrent Overrunning Everything': Africa and the Eisenhower Administration" in Kathryn C. Statler and Andrew Johns, eds., *The Eisenhower Administration, the Third World, and the Globalization of the Cold War,* and Ray Takeyh, *The Origins of the Eisenhower Doctrine: The US, Britain, and Nasser's Egypt, 1953–1957.* On Kennedy, Richard D. Mahoney, *JFK: Ordeal in Africa,* supplements his historical research with inside information, and Arthur M. Schlesinger Jr., *A Thousand Days: John F. Kennedy in the White House.*

For the Richard M. Nixon and Ford administrations, Roger Morris is devastating but willfully naïve in *Uncertain Greatness: Henry Kissinger and American Foreign Policy,* Jeremi Suri is impressed with his subject in *Henry Kissinger and the American Century,* Kissinger himself is excellent in *White House Years* and *Years of Upheaval,* but revisionist in the negative sense of the word in *Years of Renewal.* Nixon himself is good on his Middle East policy in *RN* but overplays his own role in the Arab–Israeli War of 1973. Fittingly, he barely mentions sub-Saharan Africa. Jimmy Carter's administration has generated several excellent books including his own *The Blood of Abraham,* and Zbigniew Brzezinski's *Power and Principle: Memoirs of the National Security Adviser,* which is surprisingly tough on Carter's policy in the Horn of Africa. Historian Andrew DeRoche likes Andrew Young but is fair in his criticisms in *Andrew Young: Civil Rights Ambassador.* For the Ronald W. Reagan administration, George P. Schultz, *Turmoil and Triumph: My Years as Secretary of State,* is encyclopedic, Chester A. Crocker thoroughly covers *High Noon in Southern Africa: Making Peace in a Rough Neighborhood,* and Michael Radu's collection, *The New Insurgencies: Anticommunist Guerillas in the Third World,* uses case studies to give the conservative argument for the Reagan Doctrine in Africa. On George H.W. Bush, Herman J. Cohen, *Intervening in Africa: Superpower Peacemaking in a Troubled Continent,* explains Bush's surprisingly active post–cold war Africa policy.

On Africa, excellent overviews of post–World War II African history include Martin Meredith, *The Fate of Africa: From the Hopes of Freedom to the Heart of Despair: A History of Fifty Years of Independence,* and Paul Nugent, *Africa since Independence: A Comparative History*, which takes an anthropological approach. Avoid Wikipedia, which is often a cyber battlefield for Africa's domestic political struggles. Journalists have also proven to be excellent and entertaining sources, especially when they leave the Africa beat and write books on their experiences. Howard W. French, *A Continent for the Taking: The Tragedy and Hope of Africa*, Blaine Harden, *Africa: Dispatches from a Fragile Continent*, and David Lamb, *The Africans*, are the best. Writing for *Newsweek* from the 1950s into the 1980s, Arnaud de Borchgrave had unparalleled access to policy makers in the United States, Africa, and Europe. Stanley Meisler's reportage for the *Los Angeles Times*, 1967–1973 and freelancing thereafter, available at www.stanleymeisler.com, is also excellent.

Economic development, or its lack, is the subject of numerous works. The classic statement, written when the future seemed bountiful, is Gunnar Myrdal, *Economic Theory and Underdeveloped Regions*. W.W. Rostow's *The Stages of Economic Growth*, vastly influential in the United States, provided the formula for economic takeoff. A few scholars correctly foresaw that these policies would not work as planned: from the Left, René Dumont, *False Start in Africa*, and from the Right, P.T. Bauer, *Economic Analysis and Policy in Underdeveloped Countries*. Following their path 45 years later, William Easterly, *The White Man's Burden*, and George Ayittey, *Africa Unchained*, explain how to reform failed developmental policies. Jeffrey Sachs, *The End of Poverty*, makes the case for reforming the development paradigm along with vast infusions of cash.

Robert Kaplan brilliantly presents the Afro-Pessimist vision of the future in his "The Coming Anarchy" in *The Atlantic Monthly*, which has come true in vast swaths of the continent. The AIDS epidemic in Africa is a part of Kaplan's dismal vision, and it has generated numerous excellent books. Helen Epstein, *The Invisible Cure*, provides a proven way to fight it based on the experience in Uganda. Perhaps even Kaplan would admit that continued movement toward democracy and economic freedom in many African countries, Western efforts to tie this progress to debt relief, and dramatic increases in funding by Western governments and non-governmental organizations to fight African diseases are offering much more hope than seemed possible in the 1990s. This latter story is yet to have a book dedicated to it, although Sachs comes closest.

On the former Soviet Bloc's cold war role in Africa, Odd Arne Westad won the Bancroft Prize for *The Global Cold War: Third World Interventions and the Making of Our Times*, Christopher Andrew and Vasili Mitrokhin, *The World Was Going Our Way: The KGB and the Battle for the Third World*, use documents that Mitrokhin copied from Soviet files before defecting to the West, and Robert Legvold, *Soviet Policy in West Africa*, is still valuable after almost 40 years because of the access he had to policy makers. Zbigniew Brzezinski's article in *Africa and the Communist World*, which he edited, gives insight into his Africa policy as national security adviser. Chris Alden, *China in Africa: Partner or Hegemon?*, and Joshua Eisenman, Kurt Campbell, and Eric Heginbotham, eds., *China and the Developing World: Beijing's Strategy for the Twenty-First Century*, discuss China's growing role as a power in Africa unconcerned about human rights, and the "new cold war" with the United States.

For North Africa, Michael B. Oren, *Power, Faith, and Fantasy: America in the Middle East, 1776 to the Present*, is encyclopedic and, as in the nature of first editions for such vast undertakings, rife with errors, mostly small. For the post–World War II period, Peter L. Hahn, *Crisis and Crossfire: The United States and the Middle East since 1945*, is a short but outstanding overview, William B. Quandt brings scholarly and policy-making knowledge to *Peace Process: American Diplomacy and the Arab–Israeli Conflict since 1967*, Douglas Little's *American Orientalism: The United States and the Middle East since 1945* is excellent and unharmed by his postmodern approach. Most of the works cited above on the Nixon, Ford, and Carter administrations also deal heavily with North Africa, primarily Egypt. Matthew Connelly's *A Diplomatic Revolution: Algeria's Fight for Independence and the Origin of the Post Cold War Era* is ground-breaking. Differing perspectives on the Suez Crisis of 1956 are found in Henry Kissinger, *Diplomacy*, Diane B. Kunz, *The Economic Diplomacy of the Suez Crisis*, Peter L. Hahn, *The United States, Great Britain, and Egypt, 1945–1956*, and David Tal, ed., *The 1956 War: Collusion and Rivalry in the Middle East*. Libya is well covered, with Ronald Bruce St. John, *Libya and the United States: Two Centuries of Strife*, Joseph T. Stanik, *El Dorado Canyon: Reagan's Undeclared War with Qaddafi*, and Brian L. Davis, *Qaddafi, Terrorism, and the Origins of the U.S. Attack on Libya* providing differing analyses.

For West Africa, see William Attwood, *The Reds and the Blacks*, which covers his experience as ambassador to Guinea and Kenya, Robert B. Shepard, *Nigeria, Africa, and the United States: From Kennedy to Reagan*, and W. Scott Thompson, *Ghana's Foreign Policy, 1957–1966: Diplomacy, Ideology, and the New State*. Despite researching the book while a graduate student, Thompson received excellent access to Ghanaian political and military leaders and U.S. policy makers, typical for scholars during the 1960s and a source of tremendous envy to those writing today.

Crawford Young's *Politics in the Congo: Decolonization and Independence*, remains the best book on the Congo 40 years after its publication and is one of the finest examples of the old political science, combining political analysis, history, economics, sociology, and reportage. The Congo Crisis was as close as the United States came to actual military involvement in sub-Saharan Africa, and is well covered in the scholarly literature. Lise Namikas uses the most recently declassified documents from the Western and Eastern Blocs in her dissertation, *Battleground Africa: The Cold War and the Congo Crisis, 1960–65*. Many of the leading Western and United Nations (UN) participants later told their stories, including Larry Devlin, *Chief of Station, Congo: A Memoir of 1960–67*, Michael P.E. Hoyt, *Captive in the Congo: A Consul's Return to the Heart of Darkness*, Dayal Rajeshwar, *Mission for Hammarskjöld*, Conor Cruise O'Brien, *To Katanga and Back: A U.N. Case History*, and Carl Van Horn, *Soldiering for Peace*. Ludo de Witte's *The Assassination of Lumumba*, translated by Ann Wright and Renée Fenby, forced the Belgian government to open its files, proving the Belgian role in his assassination and exonerating the United States. The book is marred by a crude economic determinism and conspiracy theories, well dissected by Brian Urquhart, "The Tragedy of Lumumba," in *The New York Review of Books*. Urquhart took part in the UN peacekeeping operation and his autobiography, *A Life in Peace and War*, his biography of Ralph Bunche, *Ralph Bunche: An American Odyssey*, and his biography of Dag Hammarskjöld, *Hammarskjold*, also cover the crisis. Journalist Smith Hempstone, *Rebels, Mercenaries, and Dividends: The Katanga Story*, provides a useful corrective to the scholarly consensus on Katanga and its leader, Moïse Tshombe.

The Rwandan genocide has generated an extensive library, with journalist Philip Gourevitch's *We Wish to Inform You That Tomorrow We Will be Killed with Our Families: Stories from Rwanda* especially important because his work was read by officials in the Clinton administration including the president himself. Samantha Power's *"A Problem from Hell": America and the Age of Genocide* is devastating about the U.S. role as is Jared Cohen's *One Hundred Days of Silence: America and the Rwanda Genocide*. Sudan's Darfur region has already generated a large body of work, notably Julie Flint et al., *War in Darfur and the Search for Peace* and M.W. Daly's *Darfur's Sorrow: A History of Destruction and Genocide*. Reporters Nat Hentoff of the *Village Voice* and Nicholas D. Kristoff of the *New York Times* have done excellent work on Sudan and Darfur, as has Smith College professor Eric Reeves on his website, www.sudanreeves.org.

For the wars on the Horn of Africa, Tom J. Farer's *War Clouds on the Horn of Africa: A Crisis for Détente* was published just as Ethiopia began to move toward Marxism–Leninism and was read by many officials in the Carter administration, as was the book's second edition, *War Clouds on the Horn of Africa: The Widening Storm*. Donna R. Jackson, *Jimmy Carter and the Horn of Africa*, uses the latest sources from the Western and Eastern Bloc archives. Michela Wrong's *I Didn't Do It for You: How the World Betrayed a Small African Nation*, is excellent on Eritrea. Mark Bowden's *Black Hawk Down: A Story of Modern War* dramatically tells the story of the U.S. intervention and withdrawal from Somalia, Richard Connaughton, *Military Intervention and*

Peacekeeping: The Reality, explains why the intervention failed, and Peter J. Schraeder, "From Ally to Orphan: Understanding U.S. Policy toward Somalia after the Cold War," in James M. Scott, ed., *After the End: Making U.S. Foreign Policy in the Post–Cold War World*, puts the intervention in long-term perspective. Smith Hempstone, *Rogue Ambassador: An African Memoir*, describes his efforts to push Kenya's President Daniel arap Moi to democratize.

For the U.S. role in southern Africa's struggle for black-majority rule, outstanding works include Robert K. Massie's comprehensive *Loosing the Bonds: The United States and South Africa in the Apartheid Years*, Thomas Borstelmann, *Apartheid's Reluctant Uncle: The United States and Southern Africa in the Early Cold War*, Thomas J. Noer, *Cold War and Black Liberation: The United States and White Rule in Africa, 1948–1968*, William Minter, *King Solomon's Mines Revisited: Western Interests and the Burdened History of Southern Africa*, Witney Schneidman, *Engaging Africa: Washington and the Fall of Portugal's Colonial Empire*, and Piero Gleijeses' *Conflicting Missions* is excellent on Southern Africa. Former CIA agent John Stockwell, *In Search of Enemies: A CIA Story*, gives a jarring account of U.S. intervention in Angola, and Elaine Windrich, *The Cold War Guerilla: Jonas Savimbi, the U.S. Media and the Angolan War*, is very critical of Western media coverage of Savimbi. The conservative perspective is covered by essays in Michael Radu's *The New Insurgencies* and Dennis L. Bark's collection, *The Red Orchestra: The Case of Africa*, and by Fred Bridgland, *The War for Africa: Twelve Months That Transformed a Continent* and *Jonas Savimbi: A Key to Africa*. Hilton Hamann, *Days of the Generals*, makes the South African case. *Ethnic Power Mobilized: Can South Africa Change?* by Heribert Adam and Hermann Giliomee is crucial for understanding the Afrikaaner mind-set.

The United States and the struggle for Zimbabwe is well covered by Andrew DeRoche, *Black, White, and Chrome: The United States and Zimbabwe, 1953 to 1998*, while Gerald Horne, *From the Barrel of a Gun: The United States and the War against Zimbabwe, 1965–1980*, is comprehensive but marred by economic determinism and an unproductive postmodern approach. Anthony Lake, *The Tar Baby Option: American Policy toward Southern Rhodesia*, is an excellent primer on bureaucratic politics and shows in sometimes excruciating detail the politics behind the Byrd Amendment and President Nixon's decision to engage rather than repel southern Africa's white governments as a more effective method for inducing liberalization.

The African role of the United Nations and its leaders is well argued in Stanley Meisler's *Kofi Annan: A Man of Peace in a World of War* and *United Nations: The First Fifty Years*. Works on peacekeeping cited above by Brian Urquhart look at its history, and Richard Connaughton makes the case for "peacemaking" instead of "peacekeeping."

Internet sources not discussed above include the CIA's *World Fact Book*, Public Broadcasting Service (PBS) sites that supplement programs from the "Frontline" television series dealing with the Rwanda and Darfur genocides, and Strategypage.com, which includes reportage and essays by specialists on the Global War on Terror and regional conflicts as well as summaries of the latest news reportage.

DOCUMENT COLLECTIONS

Beisner, Robert L., ed. *American Foreign Relations since 1600: A Guide to the Literature.* 2 vols. Santa Barbara, Calif.: ABC-CLIO, 2003.

Cold War International History Project Bulletin. *The Cold War in the Third World and the Collapse of Détente in the 1970s.* Washington, D.C.: Woodrow Wilson International Center for Scholars, Winter 1996/1997, Issues 8–9.

Legum, Colin, ed. *Africa Contemporary Record.* London: Holmes & Meier, vols. 1–28, 1968–2002.

National Commission on Terrorist Attacks upon the United States. *The 9/11 Commission Report: Final Report of the National Commission on Terrorist Attacks upon the United States.* New York: Norton, 2004.

National Security Archive. *South Africa and the United States: The Declassified History: A National Security Archive Documents Reader.* New York: New Press, 1993.

———. *South Africa: The Making of U.S. Policy, 1962–1989.* Microfiche. Alexandria, Va.: Chadwyck-Healey, 1991.

U.S. Department of State. *Foreign Relations of the United States (FRUS).* Washington, D.C.: U.S. Government Printing Office, 1948.

UNITED STATES

General

Bender, Gerald J., James S. Coleman, Richard Sklar, eds. *African Crisis Areas and U.S. Foreign Policy.* Berkeley: University of California Press, 1985.

Birdsall, Nancy, Milan Vaishnave, and Robert L. Ayres, eds. *Short of the Goal: U.S. Policy and Poorly Performing States.* Washington, D.C.: Center for Global Development, 2001.

Bodry-Sanders, Penelope. *African Obsession: The Life and Legacy of Carl Akeley.* Jacksonville, Fla.: Batax Museum Publishing, 1998.

Brands, H.W. *The Specter of Neutralism: The United States and the Emergence of the Third World, 1947–1960*. New York: Columbia University Press, 1989.

Chester, Edward W. *Clash of Titans: Africa and U.S. Foreign Policy*. Philadelphia, Pa.: Orbis Books, 1974.

Clough, Michael. *Free at Last? U.S. Policy toward Africa and the End of the Cold War*. New York: Council on Foreign Relations Press, 1992.

Crabb Jr., Cecil V. *The Doctrines of American Foreign Policy: Their Meaning, Role, and Future*. Baton Rouge: Louisiana State University Press, 1982.

Dickson, David. *United States Foreign Policy towards Sub-Saharan Africa*. Lanham, Md.: University Press of America, 1985.

Duignan, Peter, and Lewis H. Gann. *The United States and Africa: A History*. New York: Cambridge University Press, 1987.

Engerman, David C., et al. *Staging Growth: Modernization, Development, and the Global Cold War*. Amherst: University of Massachusetts Press, 2003.

Garthoff, Raymond L. *Détente and Confrontation: American–Soviet Relations from Nixon to Reagan*. Rev. ed. Washington, D.C.: Brookings Institution, 1994.

Gilman, Nils. *Mandarins of the Future: Modernization Theory in Cold War America*. Baltimore, Md.: Johns Hopkins University Press, 2003.

Gleijeses, Piero. *Conflicting Missions: Havana, Washington, and Africa, 1959–1976*. Chapel Hill: University of North Carolina Press, 2003.

Goldschmidt, Walter, ed. *The United States and Africa*. Westport, Conn.: Praeger, 1963.

Gordon, David F., et al. *The United States and Africa: A Post–Cold War Perspective*. New York: W.W. Norton, 1998.

Haass, Richard N, ed. *Transatlantic Tensions: The United States, Europe, and Problem Countries*. Washington, D.C.: Brookings Institution Press, 1999.

Hahn, Peter L., and Mary Ann Heiss, eds. *Empire and Revolution, The United States and the Third World since 1945*. Columbus: Ohio State University Press, 2000.

Herbst, Jeffrey. *U.S. Economic Policy toward Africa*. New York: Council on Foreign Relations Press, 1992.

Hunt, Michael H. "Conclusions: The Decolonization Puzzle in US Policy: Promise versus Performance." In David Ryan and Victor Pungong, eds. *The United States and Decolonization: Power and Freedom*. New York: St. Martin's, 2000.

Jackson, Henry F. *From the Congo to Soweto: U.S. Foreign Policy toward Africa since 1960*. New York: Morrow, 1982.

Kansteiner, Walter H., and J. Stephen Morrison. *Rising U.S. Stakes in Africa: Seven Proposals to Strengthen U.S.–Africa Policy*. Washington, D.C.: Center for Strategic & International Studies, 2004.

Kent, John. "The United States and the Decolonization of Black Africa, 1945–63." In David Ryan and Victor Pungong, eds. *The United States and Decolonization: Power and Freedom.* New York: St. Martin's, 2000.

Lake, Anthony, and Christine Todd Whitman. *More Than Humanitarianism: A Strategic U.S. Approach to Africa.* New York: Council on Foreign Relations Press, 2007.

Lyman, Princeton, and Patricia Dorff, eds. *Beyond Humanitarianism: What You Need to Know about Africa and Why It Matters.* New York: Council on Foreign Relations Press, 2007.

Metz, Steven. "American Attitudes towards Decolonization in Africa." *Political Science Quarterly* 99, no. 3 (1984): 515–534.

Minter, William, Gail Hovey, and Charles Cobb Jr., eds. *No Easy Victories: African Liberation and American Activists over a Half Century, 1950–2000.* Trenton, N.J.: Africa World Press, 2008.

Moore, John Allphin, Jr., and Jerry Pubantz. *To Create a New World? American Presidents and the United Nations.* New York: Peter Lang, 1999.

Morgan, Ted. *A Covert Life: Jay Lovestone: Communist, Anti-Communist, and Spymaster.* New York: Random House, 1999.

Newsom, David D. *The Imperial Mantle: The United States, Decolonization, and the Third World.* Bloomington: Indiana University Press, 2001.

Ohaegbulam, Festus Ugboaja. *U.S. Policy in Postcolonial Africa: Four Case Studies in Conflict Resolution.* New York: Peter Lang, 2004.

Packenham, Robert A. *Liberal America and the Third World: Political Development Ideas in Foreign Aid and Social Science.* Princeton, N.J.: Princeton University Press, 1973.

Richards, Yevette. *Maida Springer: Pan-Africanist and International Labor Leader.* Pittsburgh, Pa.: University of Pittsburgh Press, 2000.

Richburg, Keith B. *Out of America: A Black Man Confronts Africa.* Updated ed. New York: Harcourt, 1998.

Rothchild, Donald, and Edmond J. Keller, eds. *Africa–US Relations: Strategic Encounters.* Boulder, Colo.: Lynne Rienner, 2006.

Schetter, Conrad, and Bernd Kuzmits. "United States and Africa: 'Uncle Sam' or 'Uncle Scrooge'?" In Jurgen Ruland, Theodor Hanf, and Eva Manske. *U.S. Foreign Policy toward the Third World: A Post–Cold War Assessment.* Armonk, N.Y.: M.E. Sharpe, 2005.

Schraeder, Peter J. *United States Foreign Policy toward Africa: Incrementalism, Crisis and Change.* New York: Cambridge University Press, 1994.

Scott, James M. *After the End: Making U.S. Foreign Policy in the Post–Cold War World.* Durham, N.C.: Duke University Press, 1998.

Skinner, Elliott P. *Beyond Constructive Engagement: United States Foreign Policy toward Africa.* St. Paul, Minn.: Paragon House, 1986.

Smith, R. Drew, ed. *Freedom's Distant Shores: American Protestants and Post-Colonial Alliances with Africa*. Waco, Texas: Baylor University Press, 2006.

Smock, David R., and Chester A. Crocker. *African Conflict Resolution: The U.S. Role in Peacemaking*. Washington, D.C.: United States Institute of Peace Press, 1995.

Staniland, Martin. *American Intellectuals and African Nationalists, 1955–1970*. New Haven, Conn.: Yale University Press, 1991.

Stoner, John Charles. *Anti-Communism and African Labor: The AFL-CIO in Africa, 1955–1975*. Doctoral diss. New York: Columbia University, 2001.

Von Eschen, Penny M. *Satchmo Blows Up the World: Jazz Ambassadors Play the Cold War*. Cambridge, Mass.: Harvard University Press, 2004.

Westad, Odd Arne. *The Global Cold War: Third World Interventions and the Making of Our Times*. New York: Cambridge University Press, 2007.

Wonkeryor, Edward Lama, et. al. *American Democracy in Africa in the Twenty-First Century?* Cherry Hill, N.J.: Africana Homestead Legacy, 2000.

African Americans and Africa

Anderson, Carol. *Eyes Off the Prize: The United Nations and the African American Struggle for Human Rights, 1944–1955*. New York: Cambridge University Press, 2003.

Arthur, John A. *Invisible Sojourners: African Immigrant Diaspora in the United States*. Westport, Conn.: Praeger, 2000.

Borstelmann, Thomas. *The Cold War and the Color Line: American Race Relations in the Global Arena*. Cambridge, Mass.: Harvard University Press, 2003.

Bozorgmehr, Mehdi, and Alison Feldman, eds. *Middle Eastern Diaspora Communities in America*. New York: Kevorkian Center for Near Eastern Studies, New York University, 1996.

Campbell, James T. *Middle Passages: African-American Journeys to Africa, 1787–2005*. New York: Penguin Press, 2007.

Davis, David Brion. *The Problem of Slavery in Western Culture*. Ithaca, N.Y.: Cornell University Press, 1966.

Dodson, Howard, and Sylviane Diouf, eds. *In Motion: The African American Migration Experience*. Washington, D.C.: Schomburg Center for Research in Black Culture and National Geographic Society, 2004.

Gaines, Kevin K. *American Africans in Ghana: Black Expatriates and the Civil Rights Era*. Chapel Hill: University of North Carolina Press, 2006.

Eltis, David. *The Rise of African Slavery in the Americas*. New York: Cambridge University Press, 2000.

Henry, Charles P. *Foreign Policy and the Black (Inter)National Interest*. Albany: State University of New York Press, 2002.

———, ed. *Ralph J. Bunche: Selected Speeches and Writings*. Ann Arbor: University of Michigan Press, 1996.

King, Kenneth. *Pan-Africanism and Education: A Study of Race Philanthropy and Education in the Southern States of America and East Africa*. New York: Oxford University Press, 1971.

Klein, Herbert S. *The Atlantic Slave Trade*. New York: Cambridge University Press, 1999.

Krenn, Michael L., ed. *The African-American Voice in U.S. Foreign Policy since World War II*. New York: Garland, 1998.

———. *The Color of Empire: Race and American Foreign Relations*. Dulles, Va.: Potomac Books, 2007.

Lovejoy, Paul E. *Africans in Bondage: Studies in Slavery and the Slave Trade*. Madison: University of Wisconsin Press, 1986.

Meriwether, James Hunter. *Proudly We Can Be Africans: Black Americans and Africa, 1935–1961*. Chapel Hill: University of North Carolina Press, 2002.

Plummer, Brenda Gayle. *Rising Wind: Black Americans and U.S. Foreign Affairs, 1935–1960*. Chapel Hill: University of North Carolina Press, 1996.

———, ed. *Window on Freedom: Race, Civil Rights, and Foreign Affairs, 1945–1988*. Chapel Hill: University of North Carolina Press, 2003.

Rawley, James A., and Stephen D. Behrendt. *The Transatlantic Slave Trade: A History*. Lincoln: University of Nebraska Press, 2005.

Robinson, Randall. *Defending the Spirit: A Black Life in America*. New York: Penguin, 1998.

Rosenberg, Jonathan. *How Far the Promised Land? World Affairs and the American Civil Rights Movement from the First World War to Vietnam*. Princeton, N.J.: Princeton University Press, 2005.

Scott, William R. *The Sons of Sheba's Race: African-Americans and the Italo-Ethiopian War, 1935–1941*. Bloomington: Indiana University Press, 1993.

Smallwood, Stephanie E. *Saltwater Slavery: A Middle Passage from Africa to American Diaspora*. Cambridge, Mass.: Harvard University Press, 2007.

Suleiman, Michael W., ed. *Arabs in America: Building a New Future*. Philadelphia, Pa.: Temple University Press, 1999.

Thomas, Hugh. *The Slave Trade: The Story of the Atlantic Slave Trade, 1440–1870*. New York: Simon & Schuster, 1999.

Thornton, John. *Africa and Africans in the Making of the Atlantic World, 1400–1800*. New York: Cambridge University Press, 1998.

Von Eschen, Penny M. *Race against Empire: Black Americans and Anticolonialism, 1937–1957*. Ithaca, N.Y.: Cornell University Press 1997.

Waters, Mary C., and Reed Ueda. *The New Americans: A Guide to Immigration since 1965*. Cambridge, Mass.: Harvard University Press, 2007.

Williams, Walter L. *Black Americans and the Evangelization of Africa, 1877–1900*. Madison: University of Wisconsin Press, 1982.

Pre-1945

Anderson, Robert Earle. *Liberia, America's African Friend*. Chapel Hill: University of North Carolina Press, 1952.

Burin, Eric. *Slavery and the Peculiar Solution: A History of the American Colonization Society*. Gainesville: University Press of Florida, 2005.

Canney, Donald. *Africa Squadron: The U.S. Navy and the Slave Trade, 1842–1861*. Lanham, Md.: Potomac Books, 2006.

Clegg III, Claude A. *The Price of Liberty: African Americans and the Making of Liberia*. Chapel Hill: University of North Carolina Press, 2004.

Diouf, Sylviane A. *Dreams of Africa in Alabama: The Slave Ship* Clotilda *and the Story of the Last Africans Brought to America*. New York: Oxford University Press, 2007.

Dugard, Martin. *Into Africa: The Epic Adventures of Stanley and Livingstone*. New York: Broadway Books, 2003.

Fox, Early Lee. *The American Colonization Society, 1817–1840*. Baltimore, Md.: Johns Hopkins Press, 1919.

Funk, Arthur Layton. *The Politics of Torch: The Allied Landings and the Algerian Putsch, 1942*. Lawrence, Kan.: University Press of Kansas, 1974.

Hall, Richard L. *On Africa's Shore: A History of Maryland in Liberia, 1834–1857*. Baltimore, Md.: Maryland Historical Society, 2005.

Harris, Brice, Jr. *The United States and the Italo-Ethiopian Crisis*. Palo Alto, Calif.: Stanford University Press, 1964.

Harris, Joseph E. *African-American Reactions to War in Ethiopia 1936–1941*. Baton Rouge: Louisiana State University Press, 1994.

Huffman, Alan. *Mississippi in Africa: The Saga of the Slaves of Prospect Hill Plantation and Their Legacy in Liberia Today*. New York: Gotham Books, 2005.

Jeal, Tim. *Stanley: The Impossible Life of Africa's Greatest Explorer.* New Haven, Conn.: Yale University Press, 2007.

Lambert, Frank. *The Barbary Wars: American Independence in the Atlantic World*. New York: Hill & Wang, 2005.

Lapsansky-Werner, Emma, and Margaret Hope Bacon, eds. *Back to Africa: Benjamin Coates and the Colonization Movement in America, 1848–1880*. University Park, Pa.: Pennsylvania State University Press, 2005.

Leiner, Frederick C. *The End of Barbary Terror: America's 1815 War against the Pirates of North Africa*. New York: Oxford University Press, 2006.

Manela, Erez. *The Wilsonian Moment: Self-Determination and the International Origins of Anticolonial Nationalism*. New York: Oxford University Press, 2007.

Newman, James L. *Imperial Footprints: Henry Morton Stanley's African Journeys*. Dulles, Va.: Potomac Books, 2006.

Parker, Richard B. *Uncle Sam in Barbary: A Diplomatic History*. Gainesville: University Press of Florida, 2004.

Scott, William. *The Sons of Sheba's Race: African-Americans and the Italo-Ethiopian War, 1935–1941*. Bloomington: Indiana University Press, 1993.

Staudenraus, P.J. *The African Colonization Movement, 1816–1865*. New York: Columbia University Press, 1961.

Sundiata, Ibrahim K. *Brothers and Strangers: Black Zion, Black Slavery, 1914–1940*. Durham, N.C.: Duke University Press, 2004.

———. *Black Scandal: America and the Liberian Labor Crisis, 1929–1936*. Philadelphia: Institute for the Study of International Issues, 1980.

Tyler-McGraw, Marie. *An African Republic: Black and White Virginians in the Making of Liberia*. Chapel Hill: University of North Carolina Press, 2007.

Wheelan, Joseph. *Jefferson's War: America's First War on Terror, 1801–1805*. New York: Carroll & Graf, 2003.

Whipple, A.B.C. *To the Shores of Tripoli: The Birth of the U.S. Navy and Marines*. Reprint ed. Novato, Calif.: Naval Institute Press, 2001.

Yarema, Allan. *The American Colonization Society: An Avenue to Freedom?* Lanham, Md.: University Press of America, 2006.

Central Intelligence Agency (CIA)

Copeland, Miles. *The Game of Nations: The Amorality of Power Politics*. New York: Simon & Schuster, 1969.

———. *The Game Player: Confessions of the CIA's Original Political Operative*. London: Aurum Press, 1989.

Doyle, David W. *True Men and Traitors: From the OSS to the CIA: My Life in the Shadows*. New York: John Wiley & Sons, 2001.

Eveland, Wilbur Crane. *Ropes of Sand: America's Failure in the Middle East*. New York: Norton, 1980.

Gates, Robert M. *From the Shadows: The Ultimate Insider's Story of Five Presidents and How They Won the Cold War*. New York: Simon & Schuster, 1996.

Little, Douglas. "Mission Impossible: The CIA and the Cult of Covert Action in the Middle East." *Diplomatic History* 28, no. 5 (November 2004): 663–701.

Prados, John. *Safe for Democracy: The Secret Wars of the CIA*. Chicago, Ill.: Ivan R. Dee, 2006.

Ranelagh, John. *The Agency: The Rise and Decline of the CIA*. New York: Simon & Schuster, 1986.

Ray, Ellen, et al. *Dirty Work 2: The CIA in Africa*. Secaucus, N.J.: Lyle Stuart, 1979.

Treverton, Gregory. *Covert Action: The Limits of Intervention in the Postwar World*. New York: Basic, 1987.

Weiner, Tim. *Legacy of Ashes: The History of the CIA*. New York: Doubleday, 2007.

Peace Corps

Cobbs-Hoffman, Elizabeth. *All You Need to Love: The Peace Corps and the Spirit of the 1960s*. Cambridge, Mass.: Harvard University Press, 1998.

Fischer, Fritz. *Making Them Like Us: Peace Corps Volunteers in the 1960s*. Washington, D.C.: Smithsonian Institution Press, 1998.

Franklin D. Roosevelt Administration

Donohugh, Agnes Crawford. *The Atlantic Charter and Africa from an American Standpoint: A Study by the Committee on Africa, the War, and Peace Aims*. New York: Phelps-Stokes Fund, 1942.

McPhee, Nancy, Douglas Brinkley, and David Richard Facey-Crowther, eds. *The Atlantic Charter*. New York: MacMillan, 1994.

Harry S. Truman Administration

Lacey, Michael J., ed. *The Truman Presidency*. New York: Cambridge University Press, 1989.

Munene, G. Macharia. *The Truman Administration and the Decolonization of Sub-Saharan Africa*. Nairobi, Kenya: Nairobi University Press, 1995.

Dwight D. Eisenhower Administration

Ambrose, Stephen. *Eisenhower: Soldier and President*. New York: Simon & Schuster, 1990.

Brands, H.W. *Cold Warriors: Eisenhower's Generation and American Foreign Policy*. New York: Columbia University Press, 1988.

Eisenhower, Dwight D. *Mandate for Change: Memoirs, 1953–1956*. Garden City, N.Y.: Doubleday, 1963.

——. *Waging Peace: Memoirs, 1956–1961*. Garden City, N.Y.: Doubleday, 1965.

Ferrell, Robert. *The Eisenhower Diaries*. New York: Norton, 1981.

Hughes, John Emmett. *The Ordeal of Power: A Political Memoir of the Eisenhower Years*. New York: Atheneum, 1963.

Immerman, Richard. *John Foster Dulles: Piety, Pragmatism, and Power in U.S. Foreign Policy*. Wilmington, Del.: Scholarly Resources, 1999.

——, ed. *John Foster Dulles and the Diplomacy of the Cold War*. Princeton, N.J.: Princeton University Press, 1990.

Immerman, Richard, and Robert Bowie. *Waging the Peace: How Eisenhower Shaped an Enduring Cold War Strategy*. New York: Oxford University Press, 1999.

Kaufman, Burton I. *Trade and Aid: Eisenhower's Foreign Economic Policy, 1953–1961*. Baltimore, Md.: Johns Hopkins University Press, 1982.

McMahon, Robert J. "Eisenhower and Third World Nationalism: A Critique of the Revisionists." *Political Science Quarterly* 101, no. 3 (1986): 453–475.

Meriwether, James H. "'A Torrent Overrunning Everything': Africa and the Eisenhower Administration." In Kathryn C. Statler and Andrew Johns, eds. *The Eisenhower Administration, the Third World, and the Globalization of the Cold War*. Lanham, Md.: Rowman & Littlefield, 2006.

Neff, Donald. *Warriors at Suez: Eisenhower Takes America into the Middle East*. Brattleboro, Vt.: Amana Books, 1988.

Rostow, W.W. *Eisenhower, Kennedy, and Foreign Aid*. Austin, Texas: University of Texas Press, 1985.

Sangmuah, Egya N. "Eisenhower and Containment in North Africa, 1956–1960." *Middle East Journal* 44, no. 1 (Winter 1990): 76–91.

Statler, Kathryn C., and Andrew L. Johns, eds. *The Eisenhower Administration, the Third World, and the Globalization of the Cold War*. Lanham, Md.: Rowman & Littlefield, 2006.

Takeyh, Ray. *The Origins of the Eisenhower Doctrine: The US, Britain and Nasser's Egypt, 1953–1957*. New York: Palgrave Macmillan, 2000.

White Jr., George, *Holding the Line: Race, Racism, and American Foreign Policy toward Africa, 1953–1961*. Lanham, Md.: Rowman & Littlefield, 2005.

Yaqub, Salim. *Containing Arab Nationalism: The Eisenhower Doctrine and the Middle East*. Chapel Hill: University of North Carolina Press, 2004.

John F. Kennedy Administration

Bass, Warren. *Support Any Friend: Kennedy's Middle East and the Making of the U.S.–Israel Alliance*. New York: Oxford University Press, 2003.

Kunz, Diane B., ed. *The Diplomacy of the Crucial Decade: American Foreign Relations during the 1960s*. New York: Columbia University Press, 1994.

Latham, Michael E. *Modernization as Ideology: American Social Science and "Nation Building" in the Kennedy Era.* Chapel Hill: University of North Carolina Press, 2000.

Mahoney, Richard D. *JFK: Ordeal in Africa.* New York: Oxford University Press, 1983.

Noer, Thomas J. *Soapy: A Biography of G. Mennen Williams.* Ann Arbor: University of Michigan Press, 2005.

Paterson, Thomas G., ed. *Kennedy's Quest for Victory: American Foreign Policy, 1961–1963.* New York: Oxford University Press, 1989.

Rusk, Dean, as told to Richard Rusk. *As I Saw It.* Daniel S. Papp, ed. New York: W.W. Norton, 1990.

Schlesinger Jr., Arthur M. *A Thousand Days: John F. Kennedy in the White House.* Boston, Mass.: Houghton Mifflin, 1965.

Schoenbaum, Thomas J. *Waging Peace and War: Dean Rusk in the Truman, Kennedy, and Johnson Years.* New York: Simon & Schuster, 1988.

Lyndon B. Johnson Administration

Cohen, Warren I. "Balancing American Interests in the Middle East: Lyndon Baines Johnson vs. Gamal Abdul Nasser." In Warren I. Cohen and Nancy Bernkopf Tucker, eds. *Lyndon Johnson Confronts the World: American Foreign Policy, 1963–1968.* New York: Cambridge University Press, 1994.

Johnson, Lyndon B. *The Vantage Point: Perspectives of the Presidency, 1963–1969.* New York: Holt, Rinehart and Winston, 1971.

Little, Douglas. "Nasser Delenda Est: Lyndon Johnson, the Arabs, and the 1967 Six-Day War." In H.W. Brands, ed. *The Foreign Policies of Lyndon Johnson: Beyond Vietnam.* College Station: Texas A&M University Press, 1999.

Lyons, Terrence. "Keeping Africa off the Agenda." In Warren I. Cohen and Nancy Bernkopf Tucker, eds. *Lyndon Johnson Confronts the World: American Foreign Policy, 1963–1968.* New York: Cambridge University Press, 1994.

Richard M. Nixon Administration

Ambrose, Stephen E. *Nixon.* 3 vols. New York: Simon & Schuster, 1987–1991.

Dallek, Robert. *Nixon and Kissinger: Partners in Power.* New York: Harper Perennial, 2007.

Hersh, Seymour M. *The Price of Power: Kissinger in the Nixon White House.* New York: Summit, 1983.

Isaacson, Walter. *Kissinger: A Biography.* New York: Simon & Schuster, 1992.

Kissinger, Henry. *Crisis: The Anatomy of Two Major Crises*. New York: Simon & Schuster, 2003.

——. *The White House Years*. Boston, Mass.: Little, Brown, 1979.

——. *Years of Upheaval*. Boston, Mass.: Little, Brown, 1982.

Morris, Roger. *Uncertain Greatness: Henry Kissinger and American Foreign Policy*. New York: Harper & Row, 1977.

Nixon, Richard M. *RN: The Memoirs of Richard Nixon*. New York: Simon & Schuster, 1990.

Schulzinger, Robert D. *Henry Kissinger: Doctor of Diplomacy*. New York: Columbia University Press, 1989.

Suri, Jeremi. *Henry Kissinger and the American Century*. Cambridge, Mass.: Belknap, 2007.

Gerald R. Ford Administration

Ford, Gerald R. *A Time to Heal: The Autobiography of Gerald R. Ford*. New York: Harper & Row, 1979.

Kissinger, Henry. *Years of Renewal*. New York: Simon & Schuster, 1999.

Moynihan, Daniel Patrick, with Suzanne Weaver. *A Dangerous Place*. Boston, Mass.: Little, Brown, 1978.

James E. "Jimmy" Carter Administration

Brinkley, Douglas G. *The Unfinished Presidency: Jimmy Carter's Journey beyond the White House*. New York: Viking, 1998.

Brzezinski, Zbigniew. *Power and Principle: Memoirs of the National Security Adviser, 1977–1981*. New York: Farrar, Straus, and Giroux, 1983.

Carter, Jimmy. *Beyond the White House: Waging Peace, Fighting Disease, Building Hope*. New York: Simon & Schuster, 2007.

——. *The Blood of Abraham*. Boston, Mass.: Houghton Mifflin, 1985.

——. *Keeping Faith: Memoirs of a President*. New York: Bantam, 1982.

DeRoche, Andrew J. *Andrew Young: Civil Rights Ambassador*. Wilmington, Del.: Scholarly Resources, 2003.

Jackson, Donna R. *Jimmy Carter and the Horn of Africa: Cold War Policy in Ethiopia and Somalia*. Jefferson, N.C.: McFarland, 2007.

Jones, Bartlett C. *Flawed Triumphs: Andy Young at the United Nations*. Lanham, Md.: University Press of America, 1996.

Quandt, William B. *Camp David: Peace Making and Politics*. Washington, D.C.: Brookings Institution, 1986.

Rosenbaum, Herbert D., and Alexej Ugrinsky, eds. *Jimmy Carter: Foreign Policy and Post-Presidential Years*. Westport, Conn.: Greenwood, 1994.

Sneh, Itai Natzizenfield. *The Future Almost Arrived: How Jimmy Carter Failed to Change U.S. Foreign Policy*. New York: Peter Lang Publisher, 2008.

Thornton, Richard C., ed. *The Carter Years: Toward a New Global Order*. New York: Paragon House, 1991.

Vance, Cyrus R. *Hard Choices: Critical Years in America's Foreign Policy*. New York: Simon & Schuster, 1983.

Wenn, Stephen R., and Jeffrey P. Wenn. "Muhammad Ali and the Convergence of Olympic Sport and U.S. Diplomacy in 1980: A Reassessment from Behind the Scenes at the U.S. State Department." *Olympika: The International Journal of Olympic Studies* 2, no. 1 (1993): 45–66.

Young, Andrew. "The United States and Africa: Victory for Diplomacy." *Foreign Affairs* 59, no. 4 (America and the World 1980).

Ronald W. Reagan Administration

Baker, Pauline. *The United States and South Africa: The Reagan Years*. New York: Foreign Policy Association, 1984.

Bangura, Abdul Karim. *United States–African Relations: The Reagan–Bush Era*. New York: Peter Lang, 2001.

Crocker, Chester A. *High Noon in Southern Africa: Making Peace in a Rough Neighborhood*. New York: W.W. Norton, 1993.

Davies, J.E. *Constructive Engagement? Chester Crocker & American Policy in South Africa, Namibia & Angola*. Athens: Ohio University Press, 2007.

Lagon, Mark P. *The Reagan Doctrine: Sources of American Conduct in the Cold War's Last Chapter*. Westport, Conn.: Praeger, 1994.

Scott, James M. *Deciding to Intervene: The Reagan Doctrine and American Foreign Policy*. Durham, N.C.: Duke University Press, 1996.

Shultz, George P. *Turmoil and Triumph: My Years as Secretary of State*. New York: Scribner's, 1993.

Westad, Odd Arne. "Reagan's Anti-Revolutionary Offensive in the Third World." In Olav Njølstad, ed. *The Last Decade of the Cold War: From Conflict Escalation to Conflict Transformation*. New York: Frank Cass, 2004.

Woodward, Bob. *Veil: The Secret Wars of the CIA, 1981–1987*. New York: Simon & Schuster, 1987.

George H.W. Bush Administration

Baker III, James A. *The Politics of Diplomacy: Revolution, War, and Peace, 1989–1992*. New York: Putnam, 1995.

Bush, George, and Brent Scowcroft. *A World Transformed*. New York: Knopf, 1998.

Cohen, Herman J. *Intervening in Africa: Superpower Peacemaking in a Troubled Continent.* New York: Macmillan, 2000.

William J. "Bill" Clinton Administration

Albright, Madeleine. *Madam Secretary: A Memoir.* New York: Miramax, 2003.
Christopher, Warren. *Chances of a Lifetime.* New York: Scribner, 2001.
Morrison, J. Stephen, and Jennifer G. Cooke, eds. *Africa Policy in the Clinton Years: Critical Choices for the Bush Administration.* Washington, D.C.: CSIS Press, 2001.
Timmerman, Ken. *Shakedown: Exposing the Real Jesse Jackson.* Washington, D.C.: Regnery Publishing, 2002.

George W. Bush Administration

Copson, Raymond W. *The United States in Africa: Bush Policy and Beyond.* New York: Palgrave Macmillan, 2007.
Le Sage, Andre, ed. *African Counterterrorism Cooperation: Assessing Regional and Subregional Initiatives.* Dulles, Va.: Potomac Books, 2007.
Lusane, Clarence. *Colin Powell and Condoleezza Rice: Foreign Policy, Race, and the New American Century.* Westport, Conn.: Praeger, 2006.

AFRICA

General

Agyeman, Opoku. *The Failure of Grassroots Pan-Africanism: The Case of the All-African Trade Union Federation.* Lanham, Md.: Lexington Books, 2003.
Campbell, Craig. *Blood Diamonds: Tracing the Deadly Path of the World's Most Precious Stones.* Boulder, Colo.: Westview, 2004.
Chan, Stephen. *Grasping Africa: A Tale of Achievement and Tragedy.* New York: Palgrave Macmillan, 2007.
Cutter, Charles H. *Africa: The World Today Series.* 42nd ed. Harpers Ferry, W.V.: Stryker-Post, 2007.
Dixon, Wheeler Winston, and Gwendolyn Audrey Foster. *A Short History of Film.* New Brunswick, N.J.: Rutgers University Press, 2008.
Duignan, Peter, and Lewis H. Gann. *Africa and the World.* Lanham, Md.: Rowman & Littlefield, 1972.
French, Howard W. *A Continent for the Taking: The Tragedy and Hope of Africa.* New York: Alfred A. Knopf, 2004.

Harden, Blaine. *Africa: Dispatches from a Fragile Continent*. New York: Norton, 1990.

Hargreaves, John D. *Decolonization in Africa*. London: Harlow, 1996.

Hawk, Beverly G. *Africa's Media Image*. Westport, Conn.: Greenwood, 1992.

Hubbard, Mark. *The Skull Beneath the Skin: Africa after the Cold War*. Boulder, Colo.: Westview, 2001.

Hugon, Phillipe. *African Geopolitics*. Trans. by Steven Rendall. Princeton, N.J.: Markus Wiener, 2008.

Kaplan, Robert. "The Coming Anarchy." *Atlantic Monthly* 273 no. 2 (Feb. 1994).

Laidi, Zaki. *The Superpowers and Africa: The Constraints of a Rivalry, 1960–1990*. Trans. by Patricia Baudoin. Chicago, Ill.: University of Chicago Press, 1990.

Lamb, David. *The Africans*. Updated ed. New York: Vintage, 1987.

Louis, William Roger, and Prosser Gifford, eds. *Decolonization and African Independence: The Transfer of Power, 1960–1980*. New Haven, Conn.: Yale University Press, 1988.

Marte, Fred. *Political Cycles in International Relations: The Cold War and Africa, 1945–1990*. Amsterdam, the Netherlands: VU University Press, 1994.

Mazrui, Ali. *Africa's International Relations: The Diplomacy of Dependency and Change*. Boulder, Colo.: Westview, 1977.

McCann, James C. *Maize and Grace: Africa's Encounter with a New World Crop, 1500–2000*. Cambridge, Mass.: Harvard University Press, 2005.

Meredith, Martin. *The Fate of Africa: From the Hopes of Freedom to the Heart of Despair: A History of Fifty Years of Independence*. New York: PublicAffairs, 2005.

Nugent, Paul. *Africa since Independence: A Comparative History*. New York: Palgrave Macmillan, 2004.

Peterson, Scott. *Me against My Brother: At War in Somalia, Sudan, and Rwanda*. New York: Routledge, 2001.

Schwab, Peter. *Africa: A Continent Self-Destructs*. New York: Palgrave Macmillan, 2002.

Wright, Stephen. *African Foreign Policies*. Boulder, Colo.: Westview, 1998.

Development, Business, and Foreign Aid

Amin, Samir. *Unequal Development: Social Formations at the Periphery of the Capitalist System*. Hassocks, England: Harvester Press, 1978.

Ayittey, George B.N. *Africa Unchained: The Blueprint for Africa's Future*. New York: Palgrave Macmillan, 2006.

Bauer, P.T. *Dissent on Development: Studies and Debates in Development Economics*. Cambridge, Mass.: Harvard University Press, 1972.

———. *Economic Analysis and Policy in Underdeveloped Countries*. London: Routledge, & Kegan Paul, 1965.

Berkman, Steve. *The World Bank and the Gods of Lending*. Sterling, Va.: Kumarian Press, 2008.

Calderisi, Robert. *The Trouble with Africa: Why Foreign Aid Isn't Working*. New York: Palgrave Macmillan, 2006.

Collier, Paul. *The Bottom Billion: Why the Poorest Countries Are Failing and What Can Be Done about It*. New York: Oxford University Press, 2008.

De Waal, Alex. *Famine Crimes: Politics and the Disaster Relief Industry in Africa*. Bloomington: University of Indiana Press, 1998.

Dichter, Thomas W. *Despite Good Intentions: Why Development Assistance to the Third World Has Failed*. Amherst: University of Massachusetts Press, 2003.

Dumont, René. *False Start in Africa*. Westport, Conn.: Praeger, 1962.

Easterly, William. *The White Man's Burden: Why the West's Efforts to Aid the Rest Have Done So Much Ill and So Little Good*. New York: Penguin, 2006.

Eberstadt, Nicholas. *Foreign Aid and American Purpose*. Washington, D.C.: American Enterprise Institute for Public Policy Research, 1988.

Engerman, David C. et al., eds. *Staging Growth: Modernization, Development, and the Global Cold War*. Amherst: University of Massachusetts Press, 2003.

Ghazvinian, John. *Untapped: The Scramble for Africa's Oil*. New York: Harcourt, 2007.

Hook, Steve, ed. *Foreign Aid toward the Millennium*. Boulder, Colo.: Lynne Rienner, 1996.

Humphreys, Macartan, Jeffery D. Sachs, and Joseph E. Stiglitz, eds. *Escaping the Resource Curse*. New York: Columbia University Press, 2007.

Keen, David. *The Benefits of Famine: A Political Economy of Famine and Relief in Southwestern Sudan, 1983–1989*. Athens: Ohio University Press, 2008.

Lancaster, Carol. *Aid to Africa: So Much to Do, So Little Done*. Chicago, Ill.: University of Chicago Press, 1999.

Myrdal, Gunnar. *Economic Theory and Underdeveloped Regions*. London: Duckworth, 1957.

Rodney, Walter. *How Europe Underdeveloped Africa*. Washington, D.C.: Howard University Press, 1981.

Rostow, W.W. *The Stages of Economic Growth: A Non-Communist Manifesto*. New York: Cambridge University Press, 1960.

Sachs, Jeffrey. *The End of Poverty: Economic Possibilities for Our Time*. New York: Penguin, 2005.

Schraeder, Peter. *Intervention into the 1990s: U.S. Foreign Policy in the Third World*. Boulder, Colo.: Lynne Rienner, 1992.

Shaxson, Nicholas. *Poisoned Wells: The Dirty Politics of African Oil*. New York: Palgrave Macmillan, 2007.

Stiglitz, Joseph. *Globalization and Its Discontents*. New York: W.W. Norton, 2003.

Stoddard, Abby. *Humanitarian Alert: NGO Information and Its Impact on U.S. Foreign Policy*. Sterling, Va.: Kumarian Press, 2006.

Uvin, Peter. *Human Rights and Development*. Sterling, Va.: Kumarian Press, 2004.

Zimmerman, Robert. *Dollars, Diplomacy, and Dependency: Dilemmas of U.S. Economic Aid*. Boulder, Colo.: Lynne Rienner, 1993.

HIV/AIDS/Disease

Engel, Jonathan. *The Epidemic: A Global History of AIDS*. Washington, D.C. Smithsonian Books, 2006.

Epstein, Helen. *The Invisible Cure: Why We Are Losing the Fight Against AIDS in Africa*. New York: Picador, 2008.

Hunter, Susan. *Black Death: AIDS in Africa*. New York: Palgrave Macmillan, 2004.

Iliffe, John. *The African AIDS Epidemic: A History*. Athens: Ohio University Press, 2006.

Kalipeni, Ezekiel, et al., eds. *HIV and AIDS in Africa: Beyond Epidemiology*. Hoboken, N.J.: Wiley-Blackwell, 2003.

Terrorism

Davis, John, ed. *Africa and the War on Terrorism*. Boulder, Colo.: Ashgate, 2007.

Farah, Douglas. *Blood from Stones: The Secret Financial Network of Terror*. New York: Broadway Books, 2004.

Gould, Jennifer. "Thanks, But No Thanks: How the U.S. Missed a Chance to Get Bin Laden." *The Village Voice*. (31 October–6 November 2001). www.infowars.com/saved%20pages/Prior_Knowledge/village_voice.htm

Keenan, Jeremy. *The Dark Sahara: America's War on Terror in Africa*. London: Pluto Press, 2008.

Le Sage, Andre, ed. *African Counterterrorism Cooperation: Assessing Regional and Subregional Iniatives*. Dulles, Va.: Potomac Books, 2007.

Rotberg, Robert I. *Battling Terrorism in the Horn of Africa*. Washington, D.C.: Brookings Institution Press, 2005.

Shay, Shaul. *The Red Sea Terror Triangle: Sudan, Somalia, Yemen, and Islamic Terror*. Piscataway, NJ: Transaction, 2006.

Wright, Lawrence. *The Looming Tower: Al Qaeda and the Road to 9/11*. New York: Knopf, 2006.

North Africa

General

Badeau, John S. *The American Approach to the Arab World*. New York: Harper & Row, 1968.

Damis, John. "The United States and North Africa." In I. William Zartman and William Mark Habeeb. *Polity and Society in Contemporary North Africa*. Boulder, Colo.: Westview, 1993.

Dawisha, Adeed. *Arab Nationalism in the Twentieth Century: From Triumph to Despair*. Princeton, N.J.: Princeton University Press, 2002.

Eveland, Wilbur. *Ropes of Sand: America's Failure in the Middle East*. New York: W.W. Norton, 1980.

Freedman, Lawrence. *A Choice of Enemies: America Confronts the Middle East*. New York: PublicAffairs, 2008.

Gallagher, Charles. *The United States and North Africa: Morocco, Algeria, and Tunisia*. Cambridge, Mass.: Harvard University Press, 1963.

Hahn, Peter L. *Caught in the Middle East: U.S. Policy toward the Arab–Israeli Conflict, 1945–1961*. Chapel Hill: University of North Carolina Press, 2004.

———. *Crisis and Crossfire: The United States and the Middle East since 1945*. Annapolis, Md.: Potomac Books, 2005.

Kaufman, Burton I. The *Arab Middle East and the United States: Inter-Arab Rivalry and Super Power Diplomacy*. New York: Twayne, 1996.

Lesch, David W., ed. *The Middle East and the United States: A Historical and Political Reassessment*. Boulder, Colo.: Westview, 2007.

Little, Douglas. *American Orientalism: The United States and the Middle East since 1945*. Chapel Hill: University of North Carolina Press, 2004.

Louis, William Roger. *The British Empire in the Middle East, 1945–1951: Arab Nationalism, the United States, and Postwar Imperialism*. New York: Oxford University Press, 1984.

Lucas, Scott. "The Limits of Ideology: US Foreign Policy and Arab Nationalism in the Early Cold War." In David Ryan and Victor Pungong, eds. *The United States and Decolonization: Power and Freedom*. New York: St. Martin's, 2000.

McGhee, George. *Envoy to the Middle East: Adventures in Diplomacy*. New York: Harper & Row, 1983.

Oren, Michael B. *Power, Faith, and Fantasy: America in the Middle East, 1776 to the Present.* New York: W.W. Norton, 2007.

Ovendale, Ritchie. *Britain, the United States, and the Transfer of Power in the Middle East, 1945–1962.* New York: Leicester University Press, 1996.

Quandt, William B. *Decade of Decisions: American Policy toward the Arab–Israeli Conflict, 1967–1976.* Berkeley: University of California Press, 1977.

———. *Peace Process: American Diplomacy and the Arab–Israeli Conflict since 1967.* 3rd ed. Washington, D.C.: Brookings Institution, 2005.

Silverburg, Sanford R., and Bernard Reich. *United States Foreign Relations with the Middle East and North Africa.* Lanham, Md.: Rowman & Littlefield, 1994.

Stivers, William. *American's Confrontation with Revolutionary Change in the Middle East, 1948–1983.* New York: St. Martin's, 1986.

Yaqub, Salim. "Imperious Doctrines: U.S.–Arab Relations from Dwight D. Eisenhower to George W. Bush." *Diplomatic History* 26, no. 4 (Fall 2002): 571–591.

Zingg, Paul J. "The Cold War in North Africa: American Foreign Policy and Postwar Muslim Nationalism, 1945–1962." *The Historian* 39, no. 1 (1976): 40–61.

———. "The U.S. and North Africa: An Historiographical Wasteland." *African Studies Review* 16, no. 1 (1973): 107–117.

Zoubir, Yahia H. "The United States, the Soviet Union and the Decolonization of the Maghreb, 1944–1962." *Middle Eastern Studies* 31, no. 1 (1995): 58–84.

Algeria

Connelly, Matthew. *A Diplomatic Revolution: Algeria's Fight for Independence and the Origins of the Post–Cold War Era.* New York: Oxford University Press, 2002.

Gallagher, Charles F. *The United States and North Africa: Morocco, Algeria, and Tunisia.* Cambridge, Mass.: Harvard University Press, 1963.

Cherki, Alice. *Frantz Fanon: A Portrait.* Trans. by Nadia Benabid. Ithaca, N.Y.: Cornell University Press, 2006.

Hume, Cameron G. *Mission to Algiers: Diplomacy by Engagement.* Lanham, Md.: Lexington Books, 2006.

Quandt, William B. "Algeria." In Robert Chase, Emily Hill, and Paul Kennedy, eds. *The Pivotal States: A New Framework for U.S. Policy in the Developing World.* New York: W.W. Norton, 1999.

Wall, Irwin M. *France, the United States, and the Algerian War.* Berkeley: University of California Press, 2001.

Egypt

Alterman, Jon B. *Egypt and American Foreign Assistance 1952–1956: Hopes Dashed*. New York: Palgrave Macmillan, 2002.

Ashton, Nigel J. *Eisenhower, Macmillan and the Problem of Nasser: Anglo-American Relations and Arab Nationalism, 1955–59*. New York: St. Martin's, 1997.

Burns, William J. *Economic Aid and American Policy toward Egypt, 1955–1981*. Albany: State University of New York Press, 1985.

Finer, Herman. *Dulles over Suez: The Theory and Practice of His Diplomacy*. Chicago, Ill.: Quadrangle, 1964.

Freiberger, Steven Z. *Dawn over Suez: The Rise of American Power in the Middle East, 1953–1957*. Chicago, Ill.: Ivan R. Dee, 1992.

Hahn, Peter L. *The United States, Great Britain, and Egypt, 1945–1956: Strategy and Diplomacy in the Cold War*. Chapel Hill: University of North Carolina Press, 1991.

Holland, Matthew F. *America and Egypt: From Roosevelt to Eisenhower*. Westport, Conn.: Praeger, 1996.

Kingseed, Cole C. *Eisenhower and the Suez Crisis of 1956*. Baton Rouge: Louisiana State University Press, 1995.

Kissinger, Henry. *Diplomacy*. New York: Simon & Schuster, 1994.

Kunz, Diane B. *The Economic Diplomacy of the Suez Crisis*. Chapel Hill: University of North Carolina Press, 1991.

Kyle, Keith. *Suez*. New York: St. Martin's, 1991.

Louis, William Roger, and Roger Owens, eds. *Suez 1956: The Crisis and Its Consequences*. New York: Oxford University Press, 1989.

Lucas, W. Scott. *Divided We Stand: Britain, the US, and the Suez Crisis*. London: Hodder and Stoughton, 1991.

Owen, Roger. "Egypt." In Robert Chase, Emily Hill, and Paul Kennedy, eds. *The Pivotal States: A New Framework for U.S. Policy in the Developing World*. New York: W.W. Norton, 1999.

Sayed-Ahmed, Muhammad Abd el-Wahab. *Nasser and American Foreign Policy, 1952–1956*. London: LAAM, 1989.

Tal, David, ed. *The 1956 War: Collusion and Rivalry in the Middle East*. Portland, Ore.: Frank Cass, 2001.

Tripp, Charles, and Roger Owen, eds. *Egypt under Mubarak*. New York: Routledge, 1989.

Libya

Bills, Scott. *The Libyan Arena: The United States, Britain, and the Council of Foreign Ministers, 1945–1948*. Kent, Ohio: Kent State University Press, 1995.

Cooley, John K. *Libyan Sandstorm*. New York: Holt, Rinehart, and Winston, 1982.

Davis, Brian L. *Qaddafi, Terrorism, and the Origins of the U.S. Attack on Libya.* Westport, Conn.: Praeger, 1990.

El Warfally, Mahmoud G. *Imagery and Ideology in U.S. Policy toward Libya, 1969–1982.* Pittsburgh, Pa.: University of Pittsburgh Press, 1988.

Haley, Edward P. *Qaddafi and the United States since 1969.* Westport, Conn.: Praeger, 1984.

Matar, Khalil I., and Robert W. Thabit. *Lockerbie and Libya: A Study in International Relations.* Jefferson, N.C.: McFarland, 2004.

Ronen, Yehudit. *Qaddafi's Libya in World Politics.* Boulder, Colo.: Lynne Rienner, 2008.

St. John, Ronald Bruce. *Libya and the United States: Two Centuries of Strife.* Philadelphia: University of Pennsylvania Press, 2002.

Simons, Geoff. *Libya and the West: From Independence to Lockerbie.* London: Centre for Libyan Studies, 2003.

Stanik, Joseph T. *El Dorado Canyon: Reagan's Undeclared War with Qaddafi.* Annapolis, Md.: Naval Institute Press, 2002.

Morocco

Bookin-Weiner, Jerome B., and Mohammed El Mansour. *The Atlantic Connection: 200 Years of Moroccan–American Relations, 1786–1986.* Rabat, Morocco: Edino Press, 1990.

Damis, John. *U.S.–Arab Relations: The Moroccan Dimension.* Washington, D.C.: National Council on U.S.–Arab Relations, 1986.

Hall, Luella J. *The United States and Morocco, 1776–1956.* Metuchen, N.J.: Scarecrow, 1971.

Tuchman, Barbara. "Perdicaris Alive or Raisuli Dead!" In Tuchman, *Practicing History: Selected Essays.* New York: Knopf, 1981.

West Africa

General

Adebajo, Adekeye, and Ismail Rashid. *West Africa's Security Challenges: Building Peace in a Troubled Region.* Boulder, Colo.: Lynne Rienner, 2004.

Nwaubani, Ebere. *The United States and Decolonization in West Africa, 1950–1960.* Rochester, N.Y.: University of Rochester Press, 2001

Equatorial Guinea

Kiltgaard, Robert. *Tropical Gangsters: One Man's Experience with Development and Decadence in Deepest Africa.* London: IB Tauris, 1997.

Ghana

Attwood, William. *The Reds and the Blacks*. New York: Harper & Row, 1967.

Austin, Dennis. *Politics in Ghana, 1946–1960*. New York: Oxford University Press, 1966.

Birmingham, David. *Kwame Nkrumah: The Father of African Nationalism*. Athens: Ohio University Press, 1998.

Noer, Thomas. "The New Frontier and African Neutralism: Kennedy, Nkrumah, and the Volta River Project." *Diplomatic History* 8, no. 1 (1984).

Rahman, Ahmad A. *The Regime Change of Kwame Nkrumah: Epic Heroism in Africa and the Diaspora*. New York: Palgrave Macmillan, 2007.

Sherwood, Marika. *Kwame Nkrumah, the Years Abroad, 1935–1947*. East Lansing: Michigan State University Press, 1997.

Thompson, W. Scott. *Ghana's Foreign Policy, 1957–1966: Diplomacy, Ideology, and the New State*. Princeton, N.J.: Princeton University Press, 1969.

Guinea

Morrow, John H. *First American Ambassador to Guinea*. New Brunswick, N.J.: Rutgers University Press, 1968.

Liberia

Curtis, Susan. *Colored Memories: A Biographer's Quest for the Elusive Lester A. Walton*. Columbia: University of Missouri Press, 2008.

Ellis, Stephen. *The Mask of Anarchy: The Destruction of Liberia and the Religious Dimension of an African Civil War*. Updated ed. New York: New York University Press, 2006.

Fahnbulleh, Boima H. *Voices of Protest: Liberia on the Edge, 1974–1980*. Boca Raton, Fla.: Universal, 2005.

Gifford, Paul. *Christianity and Politics in Doe's Liberia*. New York: Cambridge University Press, 1993.

Hyman, Lester S. *United States Policy towards Liberia, 1822 to 2003: Unintended Consequences*. Cherry Hill, N.J.: Africana Homestead Legacy, 2007.

Kieh Jr., George K. *Dependency and the Foreign Policy of a Small Power: The Liberian Case*. San Francisco, Calif.: Mellen Research University Press, 1992.

Kulah, Arthur F. *Liberia Will Rise Again: Reflections on the Liberian Civil Crisis*. Nashville, Tenn.: Abingdon Press, 1997.

Levitt, Jeremy. *The Evolution of Deadly Conflict in Liberia from 'Paternaltarianism' to State Collapse*. Durham, N.C.: Carolina Academic Press, 2005.

Moran, Mary H. *Liberia: The Violence of Democracy*. Philadelphia: University of Pennsylvania Press, 2006.

Pham, John Peter. *Liberia: Portrait of a Failed State*. New York: Reed Press, 2004.

Sawyer, Amos. *Beyond Plunder: Toward Democratic Governance in Liberia*. Boulder, Colo.: Lynne Rienner, 2005.

Williams, Gabriel I.H. *Liberia: The Heart of Darkness*. New Bern, N.C.: Trafford, 2006.

Nigeria

Abegunrin, Olayiwola. *Nigerian Foreign Policy under Military Rule, 1966–1999*. Westport, Conn.: Praeger, 2003.

Ate, Bassey E. *Decolonization and Dependence: The Development of Nigerian–U.S. Relations, 1960–1984*. Boulder, Colo.: Westview, 1987.

Shepard, Robert B. *Nigeria, Africa, and the United States: From Kennedy to Reagan*. Bloomington: Indiana University Press, 1991.

Stremlau, John J. *The International Politics of the Nigerian Civil War, 1967–1970*. Princeton, N.J.: Princeton University Press, 1977.

Thompson, Joseph E. *American Policy and African Famine: The Nigeria–Biafra War, 1966–1970*. Westport, Conn.: Greenwood, 1990.

Central Africa

General

Clark, John F. *The African Stakes of the Congo War*. New York: Palgrave Macmillan, 2004.

Chad

Buijtenhuijs, Robert. "Chad in the Age of Warlords." In David Birmingham and Phyllis M. Martin, eds. *History of Central Africa*. Vol. 2. New York: Longman, 1998.

Nolutshungu, Samuel. *Limits of Anarchy: Intervention and State Formation in Chad*. Charlottesville: University Press of Virginia, 1996.

Taylor, Jeffrey A. *United States Intervention: The Case of Chad*. Master's thesis. Athens: Ohio University, 1990.

Congo

Collins, Carole. "Fatally Flawed Mediation: Cordier and the Congo Crisis of 1960." *Africa Today* 39, no. 3 (1992): 5–22.

Dayal, Rajeshwar. *Mission for Hammarskjöld: The Congo Crisis.* Princeton, N.J.: Princeton University Press, 1976.

Devlin, Larry. *Chief of Station, Congo: A Memoir of 1960–67.* New York: PublicAffairs, 2007.

De Witte, Ludo. *The Assassination of Lumumba.* Trans. by Ann Wright and Renée Fenby. New York: Verso, 2003.

May, Ernest, and Philip Zelikow, eds. *Dealing with Dictators: Dilemmas of U.S. Diplomacy and Intelligence Analysis, 1945–1990.* Cambridge, Mass.: MIT Press, 2007.

Gibbs, David N. *The Political Economy of Third World Intervention: Mines, Money, and U.S. Policy in the Congo Crisis.* Chicago, Ill.: University of Chicago Press, 1991.

Grove, Brandon. *Behind Embassy Walls: The Life and Times of an American Diplomat.* Colombia: University of Missouri Press, 2005.

Helmreich, Jonathan E. *United States Relations with Belgium and the Congo, 1940–1960.* Newark: University of Delaware Press, 1998.

Hempstone, Smith. *Rebels, Mercenaries, and Dividends: The Katanga Story.* Westport, Conn.: Praeger, 1962.

Hoskyns, Catherine. *The Congo since Independence: January 1960–December 1961.* New York: Oxford University Press, 1965.

Hoyt, Michael P.E. *Captive in the Congo: A Consul's Return to the Heart of Darkness.* Annapolis, Md.: Naval Institute Press, 2000.

Kalb, Madeleine. *The Congo Cables: The Cold War in Africa, from Eisenhower to Kennedy.* New York: Macmillan, 1982.

Kelley, Sean. *America's Tyrant: The CIA and Mobutu of Zaire.* Washington, D.C.: American University Press, 1993.

Leslie, Winsome J. *The World Bank and Structural Transformation in Developing Countries: The Case of Zaïre.* Boulder, Colo.: Lynne Rienner, 1987.

Minter, William. "The Limits of Liberal Africa Policy: Lessons from the Congo Crisis." *Transafrica Forum* 2, no. 3 (1984): 27–47.

Namikas, Lise. *Battleground Africa: The Cold War and the Congo Crisis, 1960–65.* Doctoral diss. Los Angeles: University of Southern California, 2001.

O'Brien, Conor Cruise. *To Katanga and Back: A U.N. Case History.* New York: Simon & Schuster, 1962.

Odom, Thomas. *Dragon Operations: Hostage Rescues in the Congo, 1964–65.* Ft. Leavenworth, Kan.: Combat Studies Institute, 1988.

Schatzberg, Michael G. *Mobutu or Chaos? The United States and Zaïre, 1960–1990*. Lanham, Md.: University Press of America, 1991.

Turner, Thomas. *The Congo Wars: Conflict, Myth, and Reality*. New York: Palgrave Macmillan, 2007.

Urquhart, Brian. "The Tragedy of Lumumba." *The New York Review of Books* 48, no. 15 (2001).

Van Horn, Carl. *Soldiering for Peace*. New York: David Mackay, 1967.

Wagoner, Fred E. *Dragon Rouge: The Rescue of Hostages in the Congo*. Washington, D.C.: National Defense Institute, 1980.

Weiss, Herbert. *Political Protest in the Congo*. Princeton, N.J.: Princeton University Press, 1967.

Weissman, Stephen R. *American Foreign Policy in the Congo, 1960–1964*. Ithaca, N.Y.: Cornell University Press, 1974.

Wrong, Michela. *In the Footsteps of Mr. Kurtz: Living on the Brink of Disaster in Mobutu's Congo*. New York: HarperCollins, 2001.

Young, Crawford. *Politics in the Congo: Decolonization and Independence*. Princeton, N.J.: Princeton University Press, 1965.

Young, Crawford, and Thomas Turner. *The Rise and Decline of the Zaïrian State*. Madison: University of Wisconsin Press, 1985.

Rwanda

Barnett, Michael. *Eyewitness to a Genocide: The United Nations and Rwanda*. Ithaca, N.Y.: Cornell University, 2003.

Callahan, David. *Unwinnable Wars: American Power and Ethnic Conflict*. New York: Hill & Wang, 1998.

Cohen, Jared. *One Hundred Days of Silence: America and the Rwanda Genocide*. Lanham, Md.: Rowman & Littlefield, 2007.

Dallaire, Lt. Gen. Roméo. *Shake Hands with the Devil: The Failure of Humanity in Rwanda*. New York: Carroll & Graf, 2005.

Feil, Scott R. *How the Early Use of Force Might Have Succeeded in Rwanda*. Washington, D.C.: Carnegie Commission on Preventing Deadly Conflicts, 1998.

Gourevitch, Philip. *We Wish to Inform You That Tomorrow We Will Be Killed with Our Families: Stories from Rwanda*. New York: Picador, 1998.

Grünfeld, Fred, and Anke Huijboom. *The Failure to Prevent Genocide in Rwanda*. New York: Brill, 2007.

Klinghoffer, Arthur J. *The International Dimension of the Genocide in Rwanda*. New York: New York University Press, 1998.

Kuperman, Alan J. *Limits of Humanitarian Intervention*. Washington, D.C.: Brookings Institution, 2001.

Melvern, Linda. *A People Betrayed: The Role of the West in Rwanda's Genocide*. London: Verso, 2004.

Power, Samantha. *"A Problem From Hell": America and the Age of Genocide*. New York: Basic, 2002.

Prunier, Gérard. *The Rwanda Crisis: History of a Genocide*. Rev. ed. New York: Columbia University Press, 2007.

Uvin, Peter. *Aiding Violence: The Development Enterprise in Rwanda*. West Hartford, Conn.: Kumarian Press, 1998.

Sudan

Burr, J. Millard, and Robert O. Collins. *Darfur: The Long Road to Disaster*. Princeton, N.J.: Markus Wiener, 2006.

Cheadle, Don, and John Prendergast. *Not on Our Watch: The Mission to End Genocide in Darfur and Beyond*. New York: Hyperion, 2007.

Daly, M.W. *Darfur's Sorrow: A History of Destruction and Genocide*. New York: Cambridge University Press, 2007.

De Waal, Alex, ed. *War in Darfur and the Search for Peace*. Cambridge, Mass.: Global Equity Initiative, Harvard University Press, 2007.

Flint, Julie, and Alex De Waal. *Darfur: A Short History of a Long War*. London: Zed, 2006.

Hari, Daoud. *The Translator: A Tribesman's Memoir of Darfur*. New York: Viking, 2008.

Petterson, Donald. *Inside Sudan: Political Islam, Conflict and Catastrophe*. Boulder, Colo.: Westview, 1999.

Prunier, Gérard. *Darfur: The Ambiguous Genocide*. Rev. ed. Ithaca, N.Y.: Cornell University Press, 2007.

Reeves, Eric. *A Long Day's Dying: Critical Moments in the Darfur Genocide*. Toronto, Ontario, Canada: Key Publishing House, 2007.

Totten, Samuel. *Genocide in Darfur: Investigating the Atrocities in the Sudan*. New York: Routledge, 2006.

East Africa

General

Barkan, Joel D. *Beyond Capitalism vs. Socialism in Kenya and Tanzania*. Boulder, Colo.: Lynne Rienner, 1994.

De Waal, Alexander, ed. *Islamism and Its Enemies in the Horn of Africa*. Bloomington: Indiana University Press, 2004.

Farer, Tom J. *War Clouds on the Horn of Africa: A Crisis for Détente*. New York: Carnegie Endowment for International Peace, 1979.

——. *War Clouds on the Horn of Africa: The Widening Storm.* New York: Carnegie Endowment for International Peace, 1979.

Habte Selassie, Bereket. *Conflict and Intervention in the Horn of Africa.* New York: Monthly Review, 1980.

Henze, Paul. "Ethiopia and Eritrea: The Defeat of the Derg and the Establishment of New Governments." In David R. Smock, ed. *Making War and Waging Peace: Foreign Intervention in Africa.* Washington, D.C.: United States Institute of Peace Press, 1993.

Kaplan, Robert D. *Surrender or Starve: The Wars behind the Famine.* Boulder, Colo.: Westview, 1988.

Lefebvre, Jeffrey A. *Arms for the Horn: U.S. Security Policy in Ethiopia and Somalia, 1953–1991.* Pittsburgh, Pa.: University of Pittsburgh Press, 1991.

Ottaway, Marina. *Soviet and American Influence in the Horn of Africa.* Westport, Conn.: Praeger, 1982.

Patman, Robert G. *The Soviet Union in the Horn of Africa: The Diplomacy of Intervention and Disengagements.* New York: Cambridge University Press, 1990.

Woodward, Peter. *The Horn of Africa: Politics and International Relations.* London: I.B. Tauris, 2002.

——. *U.S. Foreign Policy and the Horn of Africa.* Burlington, Vt.: Ashgate, 2006.

Eritrea

Erlich, Haggai. *The Struggle over Eritrea, 1962–1978.* Stanford, Calif.: Hoover Institution Press, 1983.

Henze, Paul B. "Eritrea." In Michael Radu, ed. *The New Insurgencies: Anticommunist Guerillas in the Third World.* New Brunswick, N.J.: Transaction, 1990.

Okbazghi, Yohannes. *Eritrea, a Pawn in World Politics.* Gainesville: University Press of Florida, 1991.

Wrong, Michela. *I Didn't Do It for You: How the World Betrayed a Small African Country.* New York: HarperCollins, 2005.

Ethiopia

Agyeman-Duah, Baffour. *The United States and Ethiopia: Military Assistance and the Quest for Security, 1953–1993.* Lanham, Md.: University Press of America, 1994.

Clapham, Christopher. *Transformation and Continuity in Revolutionary Ethiopia*. New York: Cambridge University Press, 1988.

De Waal, Alex. *Evil Days: Thirty Years of War and Famine in Ethiopia*. New York: Human Rights Watch, 1991.

Korn, David A. *Ethiopia, the United States and the Soviet Union, 1974–1985*. London: Croom Helm, 1986.

Tiruneh, Andargachew. *The Ethiopian Revolution, 1974–1987: A Transformation from an Aristocratic to a Totalitarian Autocracy*. New York: Cambridge University Press, 1993.

Kenya

Hempstone, Smith. *Rogue Ambassador: An African Memoir*. Sewanee, Tenn.: University of the South Press, 1997.

Somalia

Bowden, Mark. *Black Hawk Down: A Story of Modern War*. New York: Penguin, 2000.

Le Sage, Andre. *Political Islam and the War on Terrorism in Somalia*. New York: Cambridge University Press, 2008.

Rutherford, Kenneth R. *Humanitarianism under Fire: The U.S. and U.N. Intervention in Somalia*. Sterling, Va.: Kumarian Press, 2008.

Schraeder, Peter J. "From Ally to Orphan: Understanding U.S. Policy toward Somalia after the Cold War." In James M. Scott, ed. *After the End: Making U.S. Foreign Policy in the Post–Cold War World*. Durham, N.C.: Duke University Press, 1998.

Simons, Anna. *Networks of Dissolution: Somalia Undone*. Boulder, Colo.: Westview, 1996.

Stevenson, Jonathan. *Losing Mogadishu: Testing U.S. Policy in Somalia*. Annapolis, Md.: Naval Institute Press, 1995.

Stewart, Richard W. *The United States Army in Somalia, 1992–1994*. Washington, D.C.: Center of Military History, 2002.

Tanzania

Nyerere, Julius. *Ujamaa: Essays on Socialism*. New York: Oxford University Press, 1968.

Wilson, Amrit. *U.S. Foreign Policy and Revolution: The Creation of Tanzania*. London: Pluto Press, 1989.

Uganda

Nurnberger, Ralph D. "The United States and Idi Amin: Congress to the Rescue." *African Studies Review* 25, no. 1 (March 1982), 49–65.

Southern Africa

General

Bloomfield, Richard J. *Regional Conflict and U.S. Policy: Angola and Mozambique*. Algonac, Mich.: Reference Publications, 1988.

Borstelmann, Thomas. *Apartheid's Reluctant Uncle: The United States and Southern Africa in the Early Cold War*. New York: Oxford University Press, 1993.

Bridgland, Fred. *The War for Africa: Twelve Months that Transformed a Continent*. Gibraltar: Ashanti, 1993.

Kempton, Daniel R. *Soviet Strategy toward Southern Africa: The Liberation Movement Connection*. New York: Praeger, 1989.

Kitchen, Helen, ed. *Angola, Mozambique, and the West*. Westport, Conn.: Praeger, 1987.

Lemarchand, Rene, ed. *American Policy in Southern Africa: The Stakes and the Stance*. 2nd ed. Washington, D.C.: University Press of America, 1981.

MacQueen, Norrie. *The Decolonization of Portuguese Africa: Metropolitan Revolution and the Dissolution of Empire*. New York: Longman, 1997.

Marishine, Jeffrey. "The Religious Right and Low-Intensity Conflict in Southern Africa." In Jan P. Nederveen Pietersee, ed. *Christianity and Hegemony: Religion and Politics on the Frontiers of Social Change*. New York: Berg, 1992.

Minter, William. *Apartheid's Contras: An Inquiry into the Roots of War in Angola and Mozambique*. London: Zed, 1994.

———. *King Solomon's Mines Revisited: Western Interests and the Burdened History of Southern Africa*. New York: Basic, 1986.

Noer, Thomas J. *Cold War and Black Liberation: The United States and White Rule in Africa, 1948–1968*. Columbia: University of Missouri Press, 1985.

Papp, Daniel S. "The Angolan Civil War and Namibia: The Role of External Intervention." In David R. Smock, ed. *Making War and Waging Peace: Foreign Intervention in Africa*. Washington, D.C.: United States Institute of Peace Press, 1993.

Schneidman, Witney. *Engaging Africa: Washington and the Fall of Portugal's Colonial Empire*. Lanham, Md.: University Press of America, 2004.

Angola

Birmingham, David. *Empire in Africa: Angola and Its Neighbors*. Athens: Ohio University Press, 2006.

Bridgland, Fred. *Jonas Savimbi: A Key to Africa*. New York: Paragon House, 1987.

Chabal, Patrick, et al. *A History of Postcolonial Lusophone Africa*. Bloomington: Indiana University Press, 2002.

Chabal, Patrick, and Nuno Vidal, eds. *Angola: The Weight of History*. New York: Columbia University Press, 2007.

George, Edward. *The Cuban Intervention in Angola, 1965–1991: From Che Guevara to Cuito Cuanavale*. New York: Routledge, 2006.

Guimarães, Fernando Andresen. *The Origins of the Angolan Civil War: Foreign Intervention and Domestic Political Conflict*. New York: St. Martin's, 1998.

Hare, Paul. *Angola's Last Best Chance for Peace: An Insider's Account of the Peace Process*. Washington, D.C.: United States Institute of Peace Press, 1998.

James III, W. Martin. *A Political History of the Civil War in Angola, 1974–1990*. New Brunswick, N.J.: Transaction, 1991.

Maier, Karl. *Angola: Promises and Lies*. London: Serif, 1996.

Marcum, John A. *The Angolan Revolution*. Vol. 2 of *Exile Politics and Guerilla Warfare (1962–1976)*. Cambridge, Mass.: MIT Press, 1978.

Martin, James W. *A Political History of the War in Angola, 1974–1990*. New Brunswick, N.J.: Transaction, 1992.

Radu, Michael. "Angola." In Michael Radu, ed. *The New Insurgencies: Anticommunist Guerillas in the Third World*. New Brunswick, N.J.: Transaction, 1990.

Stockwell, John. *In Search of Enemies: A CIA Story*. New York: Norton, 1978.

Vines, Alex. *Angola Unravels: The Rise and Fall of the Lusaka Peace Process*. New York: Human Rights Watch, September 1999.

Williams, Abiodun. "Negotiations and the End of the Angolan Civil War." In David R. Smock, ed. *Making War and Waging Peace: Foreign Intervention in Africa*. Washington, D.C.: United States Institute of Peace Press, 1993.

Windrich, Elaine. *The Cold War Guerrilla: Jonas Savimbi, the U.S. Media and the Angolan War*. Westport, Conn.: Greenwood, 1992.

Mozambique

Finnegan, William. *A Complicated War: The Harrowing of Mozambique*. New ed. Berkeley: University of California Press, 1993.

Hanlon, John. *Mozambique: The Revolution under Fire*. London: Zed, 1984.

Henriksen, Thomas. *Revolution and Counter-Revolution in Mozambique*. Westport, Conn.: Greenwood, 1983.

Hume, Cameron. *Ending Mozambique's War: The Role of Mediation and Good Offices*. Washington, D.C.: United States Institute of Peace Press, 1994.

Schneidman, Witney W. "Conflict Resolution in Mozambique." In David R. Smock, ed. *Making War and Waging Peace: Foreign Intervention in Africa*. Washington, D.C.: United States Institute of Peace Press, 1993.

Vines, Alex. *Renamo: Terrorism in Mozambique*. Bloomington: Indiana University Press, 1991.

Wheeler, Jack, "Mozambique." In Michael Radu, ed. *The New Insurgencies: Anticommunist Guerillas in the Third World*. New Brunswick, N.J.: Transaction, 1990.

Namibia

Karns, Margaret P. "Ad hoc Multilateral Diplomacy: The United States, the Contact Group, and Namibia." *International Organization* 41, no. 1 (Winter 1987): 93–123.

Leys, Colin, and John S. Saul, eds. *Namibia's Liberation Struggle: The Two-Edged Sword*. London: James Currey, 1995.

South Africa

Adam, Heribert, and Hermann Giliomee. *Ethnic Power Mobilized: Can South Africa Change?* New Haven, Conn.: Yale University Press, 1979.

Chan, Stephen. *Exporting Apartheid: Foreign Policies in Southern Africa, 1978–1988*. New York: Palgrave Macmillan, 1990.

Coker, Christopher. *The United States and South Africa, 1968–1985: Constructive Engagement and Its Critics*. Durham, N.C.: Duke University Press, 1986.

Culverson, Donald R. *Contesting Apartheid: U.S. Activism, 1960–1987*. Boulder, Colo.: Westview, 1999.

Edgar, Robert E., ed. *Sanctioning Apartheid*. Trenton, N.J.: Africa World, 1990.

Hamann, Hilton. *Days of the Generals*. Cape Town, South Africa: Zebra, 2001.

Herbst, Jeffrey. "South Africa." In Robert Chase, Emily Hill, and Paul Kennedy, eds. *The Pivotal States: A New Framework for U.S. Policy in the Developing World*. New York: W.W. Norton, 1999.

Hesse, Brian J. *The United States, South Africa and Africa: Of Grand Foreign Policy Aims and Modest Means*. Burlington, Vt.: Ashgate, 2001.

Hull, Richard W. *American Enterprise in South Africa: Historical Dimensions of Engagement and Dissent*. New York: New York University Press, 1990.

Lyman, Princeton N. *Partner to History: The U.S. Role in South Africa's Transition to Democracy.* Washington, D.C.: United States Institute of Peace Press, 2002.

Mandela, Nelson. *Long Walk to Freedom.* Boston, Mass.: Little, Brown, 1995.

Massie, Robert K. *Loosing the Bonds: The United States and South Africa in the Apartheid Years.* New York: Doubleday, 1997.

Mokoena, Kenneth. *South Africa and the United States: The Declassified History.* New York: New Press, 1994.

Nesbitt, Francis Njubi. *Race for Sanctions: African Americans against Apartheid, 1946–1994.* Bloomington: Indiana University Press, 2004.

Sampson, Anthony. *Mandela: The Authorized Biography.* New York: HarperCollins, 1999.

Thomas, A.M. *The American Predicament: Apartheid and United States Foreign Policy.* Brookfield, Vt.: Ashgate, 1997.

Zambia

Anglin, D.T., and Timothy Shaw. *Zambia's Foreign Policy: Studies in Diplomacy and Dependence.* Boulder, Colo.: Westview, 1979.

Chan, Stephen. *Kaunda and Southern Africa: Image and Reality in Foreign Policy.* New York: St. Martin's, 1992.

Zimbabwe

DeRoche, Andrew. *Black, White, and Chrome: The United States and Zimbabwe, 1953 to 1998.* Trenton, N.J.: Africa World, 2001.

Gifford, Paul. "American Evangelicalism in Zimbabwe." In Jan P. Nederveen Pietersee, ed. *Christianity and Hegemony: Religion and Politics on the Frontiers of Social Change.* New York: Berg, 1992.

Horne, Gerald. *From the Barrel of a Gun: The United States and the War Against Zimbabwe, 1965–1980.* Chapel Hill: University of North Carolina Press, 2001.

Lake, Anthony. *The Tar Baby Option: American Policy toward Southern Rhodesia.* New York: Columbia University Press, 1976.

Stedman, Stephen Jay. *Peacemaking in Civil War: International Mediation in Zimbabwe.* Boulder, Colo.: Lynne Rienner, 1991.

Thompson, Carol B. *Challenge to Imperialism: The Frontline States in the Liberation of Zimbabwe.* Boulder, Colo.: Westview, 1986.

FORMER SOVIET BLOC AND CHINA

Alden, Chris. *China in Africa: Partner or Hegemon?* New York: Palgrave Macmillan, 2007.

Andrew, Christopher, and Vasili Mitrokhin. *The World Was Going Our Way: The KGB and the Battle for the Third World.* New York: Basic, 2005.

Bark, Dennis L., ed. *The Red Orchestra: The Case of Africa.* Stanford, Calif.: Hoover Institution Press, 1988.

Brzezinski, Zbigniew, ed. *Africa and the Communist World.* Stanford, Calif.: Stanford University Press, 1963.

Dexter, Bruce D. *The USSR in Third World Conflicts: Soviet Arms & Diplomacy in Local Wars, 1945–1980.* New York: Cambridge University Press, 1984.

Eisenman, Joshua, Kurt Campbell, and Eric Heginbotham, eds. *China and the Developing World: Beijing's Strategy for the Twenty-First Century.* New York: M.E. Sharpe, 2007.

Jolicoeur, Suzanne. *The Arc of Socialist Revolutions: Angola to Afghanistan.* Rochester, Vt.: Schenkman Books, 1982.

Legvold, Robert. *Soviet Policy in West Africa.* Cambridge, Mass.: Harvard University Press, 1970.

Ottaway, David, and Marina Ottaway. *Afrocommunism.* New York: Africana Publishing House, 1981.

Porter, Bruce D. *The USSR in Third World Conflicts: Soviet Arms and Diplomacy in Local Wars, 1945–1980.* New York: Cambridge University Press, 1984.

UNITED NATIONS, REGIONAL ORGANIZATIONS, AND PEACEKEEPING

Barnett, Michael, and Thomas G. Weiss, eds. *Humanitarianism in Question: Politics, Power, Ethics.* Ithaca, N.Y.: Cornell University Press.

Bekoe, Dorina A. *Implementing Peace Agreements: Lessons from Mozambique, Angola, and Liberia.* New York: Palgrave Macmillan, 2007.

Bolton, John. *Surrender Is Not an Option: Defending America at the United Nations.* New York: Simon & Schuster, 2007.

Boutros-Ghali, Boutros. *Unvanquished: A U.S.–U.N. Saga.* New York: Random House, 1999.

Coicaud, Jean-Marc. *Beyond the National Interest: The Future of U.N. Peacekeeping and Multilateralism in an Era of U.S. Primacy.* Washington, D.C.: United States Institute of Peace Press, 2007.

Connaughton, Richard. *Military Intervention and Peacekeeping: The Reality.* Burlington, Vt.: Ashgate, 2001.

Doyle, Michael W., and Nicolas Sambanis. *Making War and Building Peace: United Nations Peace Operations.* Princeton, N.J.: Princeton University Press, 2006.

El-Ayouty, Yassin, ed. *The Organization of African Unity after Thirty Years.* Westport, Conn.: Praeger, 1993.

Goulding, Marrack. *Peacemonger.* Baltimore, Md.: Johns Hopkins University Press, 2003.

Kennedy, Paul. *The Parliament of Man: The Past, Present, and the Future of the United Nations.* New York: Random House, 2006.

Marchak, Patricia. *No Easy Fix: Global Responses to Internal Wars and Crimes against Humanity.* Montreal, Quebec, Canada: McGill-Queen's University Press, 2007.

Mays, Terry M. *Historical Dictionary of Multinational Peacekeeping.* 2nd ed. Lanham, Md.: Scarecrow Press, 2004.

Meisler, Stanley. *Kofi Annan: A Man of Peace in a World of War.* Hoboken, N.J.: Wiley, 2006.

———. *United Nations: The First Fifty Years.* New York: Atlantic Monthly Press, 1995.

Shawcross, William. *Deliver Us from Evil: Peacekeepers, Warlords, and a World of Endless Conflict.* New York: Simon & Schuster, 2000.

Traub, James. *The Best Intentions: Kofi Annan and the UN in the Era of American World Power.* New York: Picador, 2007.

Urquhart, Brian. *Hammarskjöld.* New York: W.W. Norton, (with new preface) 1994.

Woronoff, Jon. *Organizing African Unity.* Metuchen, N.J.: Scarecrow, 1970.

JOURNALS

African Affairs
Diplomatic History
Foreign Affairs
Journal of Modern African Studies

INTERNET SOURCES

Ferroggiaro, William, ed. "The U.S. and the Genocide in Rwanda, 1994: Evidence of Inaction." Washington, D.C.: National Security Archive, 20 Au-

gust 2001. http://www.gwu.edu/~nsarchiv/NSAEBB/NSAEBB53/press
.html

———, ed. "The U.S. and the Genocide in Rwanda, 1994: Information, Intelligence and the U.S. Response." Washington, D.C.: National Security Archive, 24 March 2004. http://www.gwu.edu/~nsarchiv/NSAEBB/NSAEBB117/index
.htm

———, ed. "The U.S. and the Genocide in Rwanda, 1994: The Assassination of the Presidents and the Beginning of the 'Apocalypse.'" Washington, D.C.: National Security Archive, 7 April 2004. http://www.gwu.edu/~nsarchiv/
NSAEBB/NSAEBB119/index.htm

Frontline (Public Broadcasting Service television program). "On Our Watch: After the Genocide in Rwanda and the Ethnic Cleansing in Srebinica, the World Said, 'Never Again.' Then Came Darfur." http://www.pbs.org/wgbh/
pages/frontline/darfur

Frontline (Public Broadcasting Service television program). "The Triumph of Evil: How the West Ignored Warnings of the 1994 Rwanda Genocide and Turned Its Back on the Victims." http://www.pbs.org/wgbh/pages/frontline/
shows/evil

Strategypage.com

U.S. Central Intelligence Agency (search engine). http://www.foia.cia.gov/

———. *World Fact Book.* www.cia.gov/cia/publications/factbook

U.S. Department of State. *Foreign Relations of the United States.* www.state
.gov/r/pa/ho/frus

About the Author

Robert Anthony Waters Jr. (Ph.D. and J.D., University of Mississippi; B.A., University of Pennsylvania) is visiting assistant professor of history at Ohio Northern University and on leave from Southern University at New Orleans, where he is associate professor. He previously taught at Southwest Minnesota State University, the University of South Dakota, and Mississippi Valley State University. His work on U.S. relations with Africa and the Caribbean has appeared in *Diplomatic History*, *Revue Belge de Philologie et D'Histoire* (Belgium), and the *Political Science Reviewer*. He is writing a book on U.S. relations with Guyana, *Striking for Freedom? Kennedy, Johnson, the CIA, U.S. Labor, and British Guiana*, with Gordon O. Daniels, a native Guyanese. Waters is a former civil rights lawyer. He lived in Botswana during 1999 and 2000 with his wife, Sarah, who was a Fulbright Scholar at the University of Botswana.